Penelope Farmer is the author of several novels for adults, including *Eve*, *Her Story* and *Snakes and Ladders*. Her many children's books include *Charlotte Sometimes*, the inspiration for the song by the rock group the Cure. Her most recent books were two anthologies also based round autobiographical themes and family history, *The Book of Twins and Doubles*, followed by *Sisters*. She lives in London.

Sisters

AN ANTHOLOGY

Edited by Penelope Farmer

PENGUIN BOOKS

PENGUIN BOOKS

Published by the Penguin Group
Penguin Books Ltd, 27 Wrights Lane, London w8 5TZ, England
Penguin Putnam Inc., 375 Hudson Street, New York, New York 10014, USA
Penguin Books Australia Ltd, Ringwood, Victoria, Australia
Penguin Books Canada Ltd, 10 Alcorn Avenue, Toronto, Ontario, Canada M4V 3B2
Penguin Books India (P) Ltd, 11, Community Centre,
Panchsheel Park, New Delhi – 110 017, India
Penguin Books (NZ) Ltd, Private Bag 102902, NSMC, Auckland, New Zealand
Penguin Books (South Africa) (Pty) Ltd, 5 Watkins Street,
Denver Ext 4, Johannesburg 2094, South Africa

Penguin Books Ltd, Registered Offices: Harmondsworth, Middlesex, England

First published by Allen Lane The Penguin Press 1999
Published in Penguin Books 2000
1

Printed in England by Clays Ltd, St Ives plc

Contents

To my sister Sally, with love

Acknowledgements

Putting together an anthology is a shameless activity. So first of all I must thank all those people whose brains I have shamelessly picked, and whose overheard conversations stolen. To be more particular: I'd like to thank, especially, in no particular order; Mira Hamermesh for letting me use extracts from her unpublished piece on her and her sister; Colin Tudge, as usual, for letting me badger him for information on animal sisterhoods – and for helping this non-scientific brain understand fully the extract from *The Selfish Gene*! Hermione Lee for sending me her piece on operatic sisters – so reminding me about Rebecca West, among others; Ruth Fainlight for one very useful insight, and, with Alan Sillitoe, for alerting me to Harriet Martineau's autobiography; Maggie Mills for passing on Stella Tillyard's *Aristocrats*, and the work of Judy Dunn; Dawn Fozard for 'The Bunner Sisters' by Edith Wharton; and thanks to Carol O'Brien for the material from Hugh Small's *Florence Nightingale: Avenging Angel*, Peter Milne for some useful editorial comments on my introductions; my agent, Deborah Owen, for everything, as usual, and my editor, Margaret Bluman, for putting the idea to me – and for her help and encouragement throughout.

Oh and thanks too, finally, to the new and previously much maligned British Library. Which has been, most of the time, a revelation and a delight to work in.

The editor and publishers wish to thank the following for permission to use copyright material:

Fleur Adcock for an extract from 'Bluebell Seasons' in *Cherries on a Plate*, ed. M. Duckworth, Random House, New Zealand (1996), pp. 225–6; American Museum of Natural History for material from Margaret Mead, 'Manus Kinship', *Anthropological Papers of the American Museum of Natural History*, 34:2 (1934), pp. 282–6, 303; Associated Press for 'Twins' Bad Habits'; The Jane Austen Society for material from *My Aunt Jane Austen: A Memoir* (1952); Blackwell Publishers for material from Judy Dunn, *The Beginnings of Social Understanding* (1988), pp. 118–19; and *The Brontes: Interviews and Recollections* (1933); Blackwell Science Ltd for material from Phyllis Lee, 'Influence of Sibling on Infant's Relationship with Mother and Others' in *Primate Social Relationships*, ed. R. A. Hinde (1983); Bloomsbury Publishing Plc for material from Caroline Paul, *Fighting Fire* (1998); and *Selected Letters of Vanessa Bell*, ed. R. Miller (1993); Mark Bostridge and Rebecca Williams as literary executors of the Estate of the author for an extract from Vera Brittain, *Testament of Youth* (1933), pp. 311–12; Cambridge University Press for an extract from D. E. A. Mills, trs., *A Collection of Tales from Uji* (1970), pp. 385–6; Copyright Clearance Center, Inc, on behalf of Columbia University Press for material from Lynne Bennett, *Dangerous Wives and Sacred Sisters* (1983), pp. 246, 249–50; Cornell University Press for material from Karl von Frisch, *Bees: Their Vision, Chemical Senses, and Language*, revised edition (1950), pp. 55–6, 67, 69–71 and 74–5. Copyright © 1950, 1971 by Cornell University; Curtis Brown, Australia, on behalf of the author for an extract from Majorie Barnard, 'Habit' from *The Persimmon Tree* by Majorie Barnard (1945); Curtis Brown Ltd, London, on behalf of the estate of the author for material from Gerald Durrell, *My Family and Other Animals* (1959), Penguin Books, p. 171. Copyright © Gerald Durrell; and on behalf of the author for an extract from Elizabeth Bowen, 'A Queer Heart' from *The Collected Stories of Elizabeth Bowen*, Cape (1980), pp. 560–62. Copyright © Elizabeth Bowen, 1941; Curtis Brown Ltd, New York, on behalf of the author for an extract from

Marilynne Robinson, *Housekeeping*, Farrar Straus and Giroux, Inc. pp. 125–8. Copyright © 1981, Marilynne Robinson; Faber & Faber Ltd for material from Jayne Anne Phillips, *Shelter* (1996), pp. 250–51; and Banana Yoshimoto, *Amrita*, trs. Russell Wasden (1997), pp. 10–11; The Friends of Covent Garden for an extract from *Das Rheingold* trs. William Mann (1989); Victor Gollancz Ltd for material from Jessica Mitford, *Hons and Rebels* (1960), pp. 58–63; and Virginia Axline, *Dibs in Search of Self* (1966), pp. 152–3; Jane Goodall for an extract from her book, *In the Shadow of Man*, Collins (1971); Gregory & Radice Authors' Agent on behalf of the author for material from Diana Holman Hunt, *My Grandfather: His Life and Loves* (1969), Hamish Hamilton, pp. 282, 284–5; The *Guardian* for material from Laura Thompson, 'Isn't that You Know Who? Not Quite!', the *Guardian*, 11.4.98; Yasmin Kureishi, 'Intimacies: A Sister's Tale', the *Guardian*, 7.5.98; Geoffrey Gibbs, 'Sisters Reunited after Leaving Cruel Irish Orphanage', the *Guardian*, 12.2.98; and Luisa Dillner, 'Whose Life is It Anyway?', the *Guardian*, 29.4.97; Mira Hamermesh for an extract from her unpublished autobiography; HarperCollins Publishers Ltd for material from Amy Tan, *The Hundred Secret Senses* (1996), pp. 8–11; Jane Smiley, *A Thousand Acres* (1992), pp. 18–21; and Fay Weldon, *Big Women* (1997), pp. 338, 342–3; HarperCollins Publishers, Australia, for material from Anne Henderson, 'Sister Aileen Survives the Novitiate', from *Mrs McKillop's Sisters* by Anne Henderson (1997), Angus & Robertson; Margaret Mead, *Blackberry Winter* (1973), Angus & Robertson; and Beth Yapp, 'Houses, Sisters, Cities', Elizabeth Jolley, 'My Sister Dancing' and Dorothy Hewitt, 'The Darkling Sisters', from *Sisters*, ed. Drusilla Modjeska (1993), Angus & Robertson; Harvard University Press for material from Clyde Kluckhorn and Dorothy Leighton, *Children of the People*, pp. 99, 101. Copyright © 1947 by the President and Fellows of Harvard College; The Harvill Press for an extract from Jean Cocteau, *Les Enfants Terribles*, trs. Rosamund Lehmann (1955). Copyright © 1929 by Jean Cocteau. Copyright © English translation Harvill, 1955; A. M. Heath on behalf of the Mary McCarthy Literary Trust for material from Mary McCarthy, *A Nineteenth-Century Childhood*, Heinemann, pp. 92–103.

Cherries on a Plate, M. Duckworth (1996), Random House, New Zealand, pp. 174–7; The National Magazine Company Ltd for an extract from Amanda Craig, 'Sisters: Margaret Drabble and A S Byatt', *Good Housekeeping*, August (1998). Copyright © National Magazine Company; The *Observer* for material from Nicci Gerrard, 'The Soul of My Sister', The *Observer*, 8.12.96. Copyright © The *Observer* 1996; and an extract from the Review (Max Ernst), the *Observer*, 16.5.99, p. 14. Copyright © The *Observer* 1999; The Orion Publishing Group Ltd for material from Judith Thurman, *Isak Dinesen* (1982), Weidenfeld & Nicolson, pp.44–5, 60–61; Rena Kornreich Gellison and Heather Dune MacAdam, *Sisters in Auschwitz* (1997), Weidenfeld & Nicolson, pp. 124–6; Jane Goodall, *Through a Window* (1990), Weidenfeld & Nicolson, p. 168; and Elizabeth Thomas Marshall, *The Tribe of Tiger* (1994), Weidenfeld & Nicolson, pp. 61, 139; Peter Owen Publishers for extracts from William Goyen, *Savata, My Fair Sister* (1963), pp. 86–9; and Jane Bowels, 'Camp Cataract', in *Collected Works* by Jane Bowles (1984), pp. 392–6; Oxford University Press for material from Anne Lefroy, 'Original Memories of Jane Austen', *The Review of English Studies*, 29:155 (1988), pp. 418–20; and Richard Dawkins, *The Selfish Gene* (1978), pp. 173–5; and A. Murray, *No Money, No Honey: Prostitutes in Jakarta* (1991), OUP, East Asia, pp. 115–16; Oxford University Press, Eastern Africa, for material from J. A. Lijembe, 'The Little Boy Nurse', in *East African Childhood*, ed. Fox (1967), pp. 4–7; Penguin Books for slightly adapted material from Brian Clark, *The Sibling Constellation: The Astrology and Psychology of Sisters and Brothers*, Penguin Books, pp. 66–7. Copyright © Brian Clark, 1999; and material from Simone de Beauvoir, *Memoirs of a Dutiful Daughter*, trs. James Kirkup, Penguin Books (1963), pp. 42–5, 99, first published in France as *Mémoires d'une jeune fille rangée* by Editions Gallimard. Copyright © 1958 Librairie Gallimard; Anton Chekhov, *The Bear* in *Plays*, trs. Elisaveta Fen, Penguin Classics, 1954, pp. 42–5. Copyright © Edward O'Wilson, 1992; Helen Dunmore, *Talking to the Dead*, Viking, pp. 30–32. Copyright © Helen Dunmore,1996; Guy de Maupassant, *Boule de Suif and Other Stories*, trs. H. N. P. Sloman, Penguin Classics. Copyright © H. N. P.

Sloman, 1946; and Douglas H. Chadwick, *The Fate of the Elephant*, Viking, pp. 328–30. Copyright © Douglas H. Chadwick, 1992; and Aristophanes, *The Archarnians*, *The Clouds*, *Lysistrata*, trs. Alan H. Sommerstein, Penguin Classics, pp. 187–9. Copyright © Alan H. Sommerstein, 1973; Peters Fraser & Dunlop Group Ltd on behalf of the authors for extracts from Margaret Drabble, *A Summer Birdcage* (1962), Weidenfeld & Nicolson, pp. 170–71; Rebecca West, *The Fountain Overflows* (1957), Macmillan, pp. 154–5; and Helen Simpson, *Four Bare Legs in Bed* (1990), pp. 97–9; Justine Picardie for an extract from the *Observer*, Life Section, 28.3.97 included in *Before I Say Goodbye* by Ruth Picardie with Matt Seaton and Justine Picardie (1998) Penguin Books; Planet Syndication on behalf of the author for material from Sarah Litvinoff, 'An Accident of Birth', the *Independent on Sunday*, 2.11.97; Laurence Pollinger Ltd on behalf of the Estate of Frieda Lawrence Ravagli for material from D. H. Lawrence, *Women in Love* (1921), p. 171; Random House UK for material from L. P. Hartley, 'The Shrimp and the Anemone' in *Eustace and Hilda* (1958), Bodley Head, pp. 17–21; Virginia Woolf, *The Letters of Virginia Woolf* (1975), Hogarth Press; Virginia Woolf, *Moments of Being*, ed. Jeanne Schulkind (1978), Hogarth Press; Leonard Woolf, *The Wise Virgins/Beginning Again* (1914), Hogarth Press; Barbara Pym, *Some Tame Gazelle* (1950), Jonathan Cape, pp. 140–43; Jane Dunn, 'Introduction' to *A Very Close Conspiracy* (1990), Jonathan Cape, pp. 3–4; Katherine Anne Porter, 'The Fig Tree', in *Collected Stories* by Katherine Anne Porter (1969), Jonathan Cape, pp. 374–5; Hermione Lee, *Virginia Woolf* (1996), Chatto & Windus; Ruth Padel, 'Sisters' from *Rembrandt Would Have Loved You* (1996), Chatto & Windus; A. S. Byatt, *The Game* (1968), Chatto & Windus, pp. 276–7; V. S. Pritchett, 'Cage Birds', in *Collected Stories* by V. S. Pritchett, Chatto & Windus, pp. 280–83; Stella Tillyard, *Aristocrats* (1982), Chatto & Windus, pp. 96–7; Hilary and Piers du Pré, *A Genius in the Family* (1997), Chatto & Windus, pp. 49–52; Clare Longrigg, *Mafia Women* (1997), Chatto & Windus, pp. 12–5; Susanna Moore, *The Whiteness of Bones* (1989), Chatto & Windus, pp. 100–105; Thomas Mann, *Buddenbrooks*, trs. H. T. Lowe-Porter (1924), Martin Secker & Warburg, pp.235–5; Alberto

Moravia, 'Home is a Sacred Place', in *The Wayward Wife* by Thomas Mann (1960), Martin Secker & Warburg, p. 161–2; Angus Wilson, 'Raspberry Jam' in *The Wrong Set* (1949), Martin Secker & Warburg, pp. 155–60; Junichiro Tanizaki, *The Makioka Sisters*, trs. Edward G. Seidenstricker (1957), Martin Secker & Warburg, pp. 28–30; and Caroline Blackwood, *On the Perimeter* (1984), Heinemann, pp. 26–9; Radio Times for an extract by Deborah Moggach included in the *Radio Times*, 13–19 June 1998; Routledge for Sir Raymond Firth, 'Sisters', in *We the Tikopia* (1936); and material from Peter Townsend, *Family Life of Old People* (1957), pp. 106–7; Sage Publications, Inc, for an extract from Ronald Gallimore et al., *Culture Behavior and Education*, Vol. II (1974), pp. 148–51; Claire Seeber for an extract included in the *Independent*, 26.4.98; Sheil Land Associates Ltd for material from Kate Millett, *The Prostitute Papers*, Paladin, p. 75–6. Copyright © Kate Millett, 1975; Cynthia Moss, *Elephant Memories*, Elm Tree Books, pp. 127–8. Copyright © Cynthia Moss, 1988; and Robert Fagles, *The Oresteia*, Penguin Books, p. 189. Copyright © Robert Fagles, 1979; Yacinthy Stathopoulos-Calogeropoulos(Callas) for material from Jackie Callas, *Sisters* (1989), Macmillan, pp. 3–5, 162–4; The Society of Authors as literary representatives of the Estate of the author and The Provost and Scholars of King's College, Cambridge, for material from E. M. Forster, *Howards End* (1910), pp. 40–41, 308–15; and as literary representative of the Estate of the author for an extract from Virginia Woolf, *Professions for Women* (1942); Abner Stein on behalf of the author for an extract from Alice Munro, *The Peace of Utrecht* (1984), Penguin Books, pp. 202–3; Times Newspapers Ltd for material from Milton Lumky, 'Korean Sisters', *Times Magazine*, 28.1.98. Copyright © 1998, Times Newspapers Ltd; and Anna Blundy, 'Muslim Sister on Run from Vengeful Brother', *Times Magazine*, 14.1.98. Copyright © 1998, Times Newspapers Ltd; Transworld Publishers Ltd for material from Kate Atkinson, *Behind the Scenes at the Museum*, Doubleday, a division of Transworld Publishers Ltd, pp. 334–7. Copyright © 1995, Kate Atkinson; University Press of America Inc for an extract from C. Goodale, 'Siblings as Spouses: the Reproduction and Replacement of Kaulong Society', *Siblingship in Oceania*, ed. Mac Marshall,

Vikas Publishing House PVT Ltd for material from Saroj Pathak, 'The Trump Card', from *Gujarti Short Stories*, ed. S. J. Mohan (1982), pp. 54–5; Virago Press Ltd for material from Leonora Carrington, 'The Seventh Horse', in *The Sisters* by Leonora Carrington (1989), pp. 44–5; Willa Cather, *The Professor's House* (1925), Virago, 1981, pp. 81–6; Michelle Roberts, *During Mother's Absence* (1994), pp. 126–9; Elizabeth Taylor, 'Sisters', from *The Devastating Boys* by Elizabeth Taylor (1975), pp. 130–35; and Marilyn Duckworth, 'A Game of Pretend' from *Such Devoted Sisters*, ed. Shena Mackay (1994), pp. 58–9; A. P. Watt Ltd on behalf of Mme. V. M. Eldin for material from Arnold Bennett, *The Old Wives' Tale* (1908), pp. 26–9, 397–9; The Women's Press Ltd for an extract from Janet Frame, *To The Is-land* (1983), pp. 106–9.

Introduction

What is a sister? The short answer, of course, genetically speaking, is a female with whom you or I – anyone – shares one parent at least, and more usually two. At the same time the terms 'sister' and 'sisterhood' have so developed their own mythology that they have also come to stand as paradigm for other loving groups of women, not necessarily genetically related: nuns, nurses, feminists, whatever. All very simple and obvious so far; but of course it gets more complicated than that.

Take my family – my sisters – me. I have – or rather had – two sisters; and now, alas, just one. It means, I suppose, that I should understand perfectly well what a sister is, that I should therefore comprehend the mythology. But I don't entirely. I'll describe the who and what of my sisters in a moment; this may explain some of the uncertainty. But most likely the uncertainty, far from being unique to me, is common. Indeed I sense that for almost all of us, most of the time, sisterhood is always something out there, something other people have. And that even when we do, briefly, feel its reality here and now, it's always a messy, fragmentary, ambiguous, ambivalent thing, an indiscriminate jumble of love, hate, amity, enmity, only to be teased out bit by bit. It's the chief justification for this book, maybe; an anthology is bitty by name and nature. And certainly I don't feel any need to apologize for beginning it somewhat contentiously with the question posed by a letter in the *Independent* only the other day. What is a sister, asks the writer bemusedly. By implication, is a sister born, not made? Is sisterhood genetic or environmental, created by nature or nurture? From the wealth of material that follows, it may be possible to construct some reasonably truthful account. But the question, I'm certain, remains.

Back to my sisters and me. We, of course, made up between us the mythical number, three – three sisters. But I did not see us as such until we were well grown-up. For one thing, the elder of the two was my twin, and I never thought of her as my sister, simply, or even called her that; she was always just my twin. For another, the third sister arrived seven and a half years after we did. By the time she'd ceased to be a small child and basically, for us, a nuisance, we'd gone away to school. By the time she emerged from school I was married and bogged down by the exigencies of my own small children and a crumbling marriage. And within a few years of her finishing training – as a nurse – she disappeared to Australia. Not till 1978 when, only a year short of forty, I stayed with her in Sydney, did I begin to get to know her. And not till one night in September 1985 when we stayed up late one night together drinking, did I begin to understand that aspect of sisterhood which is involved in sharing and re-exploring a shared past. September of course is spring in Sydney. Its remaining irredeemably autumn in my northern-hemisphere head is not a bad metaphor for the dislocation that I felt at finding my memory of our childhood, through hers, turned topsy-turvy.

There was, strangely, no resentment, no anger between us. Just need and difference and loss and rediscovery. Twelve thousand miles away from where we'd started, we hugged and cried and wore each other out, sitting on, or when the embraces got too desperate, falling off, her orange-brown velvet sofa; with, all the time, the portrait of our grandmother, our mother's mother, staring benignly down at us. Despite the bottle of wine, we were neither of us drunk. And it was in retrospect one of the most painful and extraordinary nights of my life. Sisterhood? I think so. Certainly it's almost the first time I realized just how good, how important, sisterhood could be, whatever sisterhood is exactly. In our case, though we have never since quite recreated that closeness, it remains good – the more so, I suspect, because we remain, too, most of the time, 12,000 miles apart. But, still, the only questions it answers are those solely related to itself.

So what about the previous generations of sisters? My father's sisters, for instance, were inimical for much of their lives. Whereas my mother and her elder sister, who brought each other up, effectively, after their mother, the one in the portrait, fell downstairs and died when my mother was three and my Aunt Janet six, remained devoted throughout their lives, despite having little in common. To go back yet another generation, my maternal grandmother had no sisters, only a much younger half-brother. Given her early demise, I can't comment on the relationship between that brother and her, if there was one. His existence had, however, a profound effect on my family fortunes; being male, he inherited the greater part of my grandfather's considerable fortune. The economic weight of brothers, as against sisters, we will look at later. All I need say here is that but for him my mother might have been rich.

My paternal grandmother, by contrast, was the eighth of thirteen children. She had six sisters and seven brothers, none of whom I ever met. Since she gave birth to my father at the advanced age of fifty I barely knew her either, except as a very old woman when I was a very small child. But I have read the diary she kept when she was nineteen; I know that her siblings constituted the greater part of her social life. This was inevitable, I suppose, given the number of them. But it also appears to have been the norm in middle-class life before this century; in so many novels, Jane Austen's being the prime examples, most women's sisters are shown as their best if not their only friends, and brothers their only male friends.

Of my still older paternal grandfather's sisters I know nothing. Of my maternal grandfather's I know more – how could I not, given that the truly dreadful aspect of sisterhood in my family first made itself clear in them: we are a family with a damaging mutation on one of the two identified breast-cancer genes, BRCA1. But this knowledge was still a long way off when the two maiden aunts who took on my motherless mother and her sister both developed breast cancer. One, my Great-aunt May, outlived her surgically removed breast by more than twenty years before the bugger got her. The other great-aunt, Dolly, died in her early fifties, just like my mother and my twin sister after her. Since my younger sister and I have also had our brushes with the disease, it has swept clean through the three generations that I know of, even though some of us are lucky enough to have outwitted it for a good deal longer than others. You may call this shared doom sisterhood, but it's a kind we could happily do without. Sisterhood may be heaven; but it can equally, and sometimes simultaneously, be hell, and in many more ways than this; not just medically but socially, not just psychologically but emotionally speaking. And don't all we sisters know it.

All we sisters, I say. And, for now, let's put aside the still-vexed question of whether genes or shared upbringing, nature or nurture, make two women sisters. Let's ask instead – what if we had no sisters – siblings? This is not just a rhetorical question. For one thing becomes clear as soon as you manage – if you can – to clear away your own good or bad experience of siblinghood, and look less particularly and less irritably at such relationships in a wider context. Family relationships are our primary social relationships. Society starts right here, within the family. And the kinds of families we have tend to be reflected in the kinds of societies that evolve around them. Some sociologists suggest that the shift from families with large numbers of children to those with very few, two or three at most, is reflected in the shift to less hierarchical and more individualistic social structures.

In large families, for instance, like my grandmother's, parents have less time to devote to any particular child and older children have to be drafted in to help look after the younger. The eldest then develop almost the status of parent; they have to be looked up to, obeyed, respected, almost as parents. One of my granny's brothers had been ordained – she reported favourably on his sermons. Mavericks can and do surface in such circumstances – look at Elizabeth Bennett's silly sisters in Jane Austen's *Pride and Prejudice*; look at George Eliot in her less large but notably stuffy, hierarchical family – but mavericks have a rough time of it. In a small family, on the other hand, parents don't have such need to reinforce rank and obedience. A society full of small families cannot but be less hierarchical in outlook, more individualistic altogether.

But even so, sibling relationships, sibling tensions still exist. Children have to learn to share parents, to get along with their older or younger sisters or brothers from an early age. So what happens if families get still smaller; if we become a society of doted-on only children? What would a world without siblings, without uncles or aunts, without nephews and nieces, with only the vertical relationships between offspring, parents and grand-parents be like? A friend of mine, very short of aunts, uncles, cousins, nephews, nieces, her one brother dying childless, her son an only child, wonders if she's impoverished thereby. Would we all feel impoverished, if, as some commentators are foreseeing already, such families become the norm, given the reluctance of many women to interrupt their careers for any children, let alone several? In France, Italy, Russia, increasingly, families limit them-selves to one child by choice. The Chinese, in an attempt to cut down their ever-growing population, enforced such a limit by law on urban couples. One woman, worried by the over-indulged, overweight children she observed around her, set up sibling clubs to help them learn to share, to give way, to pick up social signals of all kinds in a rough-and-tumble setting that those of us brought up with siblings might see as mere mimicry of family life.

But if more and more societies go the same way, if sibling clubs, nurseries and play groups rather than their homes are going to be the places where most children learn to live alongside other children, then a book like this will evoke no recognition in its readers. Rather, it will describe something extinct, that has to be reinvented. In which case all the more reason for it, I think. And all the more reason for it to be as wide-ranging as possible. Forget any notion of neat little literary fragments. If I include more work by novelists and creative writers than anyone else, it's because imagination often understands these things better than intellect, let alone research, and certainly expresses it better. But I am aiming way beyond literature. I'd like to construct a thesis on sisters, if you like; at the very least to observe sisters in the widest possible context, from the popular conceptions of sisterhood that surface in the press to descriptions from all the relevant disciplines: anthropology, psy-chology, sociology, whatever. Since the family is an important unit in some animal species, and may have an evolutionary function that goes beyond the simple rearing of infants, I even look at animal behaviour; the way we human animals operate from within tight family groups could have been one element of our success as a species. And if so, why, how, what are the precise advantages and disadvantages of having sisters, in evolutionary as well as psychological terms, I wonder.

To judge from much of the material here, any answers are immensely devious, intensely subtle and immeasurably complicated. Nothing is as it seems. Love and hate may be interchangeable. Even where, for instance, dislike or love between a pair of sisters appears immutable, things aren't always so simple. The death of a loathed one can be equally if not more traumatic than the death of a loved one; hatred can be missed as much as love. (And not just in humans. I've experienced recently the pining of a cat for her dead sister, yet in life the pair showed no affection; on the contrary, they spat at each other jealously throughout their lives together.) Yet only by observing such relationships, by attempting to describe what we observe, can we begin to ask what society would be like without them. We could reinvent them in many different versions, that's for sure. For though some aspects of sisterhood do not seem to change through history, between societies, a close reading of the material here must make it clear that as family life shifts sociologically, geographically, historically, so do sibling relationships.

Two more practical points: first, I ignore the convention that sees sisterhood as relating only to the relationship between women, actual sisters or symbolic ones (and seems to think that only women have anything useful to say about such relationships). Men, too, have sisters and what sisters are is often reflected off those brothers, for men can also be transformed or warped by the existence of sisters. Still more interesting – to me – is the fundamental way in which social transitions affect the nature of brother/sister relationships, far more than they do the less formal, more day-to-day relationships between sisters. This I will look at closely in the relevant section.

And second, leaving aside the autobiographical interpolations, I go right against some other conventions of anthologizing. For instance, anthologies tend not to include more than one extract from the same writer, let alone from the same book. Here, though, the same names recur often, and for good reason. Sisterhood is not stasis, it's an ongoing dynamic, a relationship that usually lasts a lifetime, and where there is material – fictional, historical, biographical or autobiographical – that plots the changes over the short and long term, I think it would be short-sighted not to make use of it. I find, for instance, that the relationship between those extraordinary sisters, Vanessa Bell and Virginia Woolf, and what has been written about it by themselves and by others, articulates identifiable, if much less articulated, shifts, ambiguities and agonies in the rest of us. Rarefied they may seem; but their sisterhood at gut level was common.

I'm approaching sixty now myself. Having seen my own sisterhoods, both genetic and symbolic, progress through all kinds of loves, hates, separations and reunions, until death itself, I'm moved by encountering the same thing in others. I've been moved and often enlightened throughout the time spent gathering material for this book. So I hope its readers, wherever they come from – different places from mine certainly – from within sisterhoods or without, will also be moved, enlightened and even sometimes delighted by what they find.

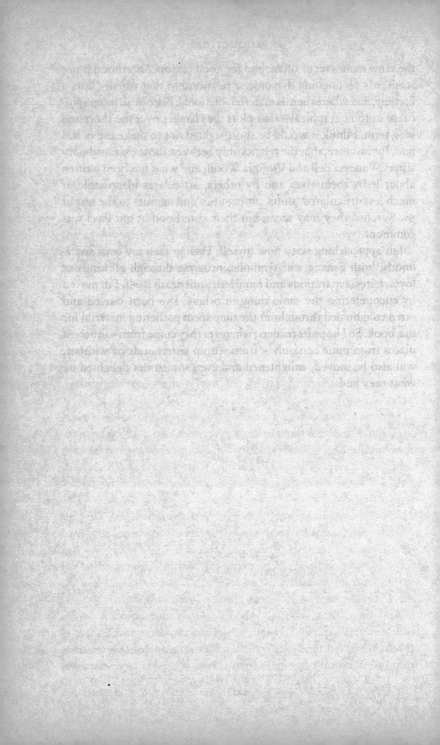

What is a Sister?

Sir: I read your article 'I'd never, ever, forgotten her. A family affair', which described how Joseph and Joyce were reunited as brother and sister, with great interest, because I, too, at the age of fifty-nine, have recently met my natural sister.

When I was a few weeks old I was given away by our parents for adoption. My sister was born eleven years later and only found out about me two years ago. For me, then, the story of Joseph and Joyce was compelling reading. But, like all these tales of lost and found, it was frustrating because these stories never go past the 'how we lost each other and the joy now that we have found each other' scenario.

But it is after the finding and meeting that the difficult bit kicks in. What, after all, is the relationship between two sisters who, until their middle age, had never known each other? We searched each other for likenesses and found many. We agreed that we could be the kind of person we'd have had as a friend. But we are not by any means sisters.

I have been brought up with two sisters, sandwiched between my adopted parents' two natural daughters. I know what it is to be a sister and to have sisters. But with this new-found sister we meet as two middle-aged equal adults. Am I her elder sister? Do I want that role? And does she want suddenly to be a younger sister, she who up until now has been a much-loved only child?

And then there is family history. Surely that is what forges brothers and sisters? All that my new-found sister and I share is DNA. We have found each other but how do we move this relationship on? We don't live near each other. We both have our own families, daughters and grandchildren, and they don't feel a part of the relationship.

So are we sisters or did we meet only to find that we are not? What does a shared set of blood and genes mean? We look fondly upon each other but we do not know what to do next.

What would your readers do?

Margaret Gosley
Letter in *Independent*, 21 September 1998

I

Childhood

Little can have quite the force, the poignancy, of the experience and memory we share as children within the family. In childhood the patterns of lifelong sibling relationships are established; in childhood, you could say, brothers and sisters are created by each other.

My former mother-in-law, for instance, used to meet her twin brother and their elder brother for dinner every year on the twins' birthday. Only the sister had married – and she only for long enough to produce three sons; her husband died when the eldest was thirteen. Thus the relationships between the three siblings remained not just primary, but secondary; the closest, as well as the longest-lasting relationship of their lives. And there they sat in their seventies, still enacting the pantomimes of sixty-odd years ago; the elder brother a posturing teenager, a bit camp, pleased with himself, the younger a beleaguered, Just Williamish twelve-year-old with a bullish Roman head, rubbing each other up, taunting each other politely on mostly aesthetic subjects, while the sister sat between them for ever silent, irritated, indulgent. As a child she had run away from the loud intellectual and aesthetic interests of her brothers so effectively that she'd become a champion swimmer, and elected to go to physical training college rather than to university. Only then, fascinated by the subject of anatomy on exactly the levels she'd rejected because of them, had she acknowledged her own potential and opted for medical school.

My younger sister was born when my twin sister and I were seven and a half. Unlike me, my twin did not wheel dolls round the garden in a doll's pram pretending they were real babies; presumably her self-chosen task of picking up after me absorbed all her maternal instincts. She was not, to my memory, particularly interested in the new arrival. (Or maybe she dared not be interested: having taken against the birth of my mother's previous baby she felt herself personally responsible for his death at the age of one week.) But I, like Harriet Martineau in the first extract here, was enchanted by it. I have a touching photograph of my pigtailed – already untidy – self sitting holding her, gazing down on her with a look of tender and bemused wonder. Even then, we'd been told that she was a double miracle. And as the story subsequently became part of our sibling mythology, the kind from which families and memory and life history are made, I think I had better tell it here.

My mother's blood was rhesus negative – a condition that never used to be checked. Had it been, our little brother would not have died; his condition was mild enough to be treated. The same would not be true of any subsequent baby; my mother was strongly advised against one. She ignored this advice, irresponsibly my sister thinks – she's a trained nurse. Nevertheless, born by Caesarean section in St Mary's Hospital in London, she became one of the first rhesus babies whose lives were saved by having their blood entirely changed at birth. A heroic procedure, now wholly superseded, the transfusion took hours; she still has scars on her legs to show for it. That was one miracle. The second occurred when her transfusion scars went septic. Alexander Fleming was then testing streptomycin in St Mary's. On the grounds that she was going to die anyway, he allowed this still untried substance to be used on her. It worked, obviously. Otherwise I would not have been able to hug her, weeping, on a sofa in Australia in 1985.

As I've said, we did not see enough of each other in childhood to develop a sisterly relationship. (The fact we lack that particular kind of baggage is, it occurs to me, another reason we get on so well now.) I ceased my baby-worship as soon as my little sister turned into an obstreperous toddler. Doted on by everyone for her curly fair hair and huge blue eyes, she looked just like the picture on the Toddylox packet, quite the reverse of us two dark-eyed, lank-haired, runtish scowlers. And yet we shared parents and an environment, and it was her wholly different view of them that made us both weep. My childhood, I thought, was happy (if my twin thought otherwise, we never got round to comparing things) and hers, it turned out, in many ways was not. Our mother, source of all comfort and safety, had stood at the centre of the world shared by my twin and me. Whereas my sister was barely sixteen when she died. Not only that, our mother had virtually ceased to mother her from the time the cancer had first manifested itself three years before. She hadn't felt able to cry for our mother at her death; she did not know who our mother was.

But even before then she'd been lonely; brought up as an only child, effectively, suffering from our parents' belief in the benefits of boarding-school, which took us away from family life and her. Our parents, too, seemed more occupied by their own lives during her childhood than during ours. She was often left to the mercies of my mother's portly former governess, whom we both saw as a dear old thing, but to my sister was a loathed, cantankerous old bully.

When my mother died, my father sold up and moved fifty miles away. Though I understand why he needed to, even to me, married and pregnant by then, it felt like losing childhood at a stroke. But it took much less from me than it took from my little sister. In a less extreme way, she relived the fate of my mother and her sister after their mother died; their father was so devastated by the loss of his wife that in order not to be reminded of her he sold everything. He did not let his children keep their toys, not so much as a teddy bear. All they had left of her and their infancy was each other – and the portrait under which we were weeping; fortunately it belonged to their grandfather, not to him. Since these things and the pain they generate filter down through the generations, to other siblings, I guess that this, too, was part of what my sister and I were weeping for that evening, years later and so far away. That our so-mourned grandmother looked down on us throughout was apt.

It makes me think, now, that it is such pain, pain encountered or shared in childhood, that connects siblings most irrevocably. Didn't I observe, unhappily, the way my own son and daughter were bound together by the collapse of my marriage when they were eight and ten? Haven't I always known how tightly my mother

3

and her sister were held by their mutual need and loss? And is this perhaps where the only child suffers most, in having no one with whom to share their childhood grief? (No one to inflict it, come to that!)

The photographs of child sisters in previous generations can be as telling as the stories. Here are my father's two inimical sisters, for instance, around 1910, side by side yet miles away from each other, the older one plump, the younger angular, wearing identical shirts and ankle-length skirts, nipped in at the waist by elastic belts, and staring out unsmiling. And here are my mother and her sister in albums labelled with their names, the pages empty from the date that their mother died. Both wear, for the most part, those child-unfriendly garments, those frilly hats, inflicted on Edwardian infants. In one photo, though, they are more casually dressed, posed against a painted sky, dotted with stars, in a photographer's studio. My aunt, very solemn in a tam-o'-shanter, is perched on the bottom of a cardboard moon alongside my eighteen-month-old mother, who is looking suspiciously moronic; a hyperactive child, she'd been drugged to keep her quiet by the pert-looking nanny who stands behind the fake moon, holding her perfunctorily and unmistakably making eyes at the photographer.

I have one photograph from after their mother's death. It shows the two sisters, aged seven and ten or so, sitting side by side on board their father's ship, each dressed up in his – on them – outsize naval caps and uniform jackets. Both scowling at the camera, they look far from happy. This is strange because the only good things they reported later of their wretched childhood were the visits to the ship, where they spent their time in such mischievous delights as making apple-pie beds for my grandfather's fellow officers. One made up a rhyme which my mother used to recite – 'There were two naughty little girls/ Their names were Jan and Peggy/ The one was very short and stout/ The other long and leggy.' It puzzled me, because, throughout our childhood at least, the short sister, our aunt Janet, was painfully thin, and my mother never struck me as particularly long, and certainly not as leggy.

And so to the material included here. As I've already said, I hardly knew what sisters were before I started gathering it. But seeing

4

other sisters as children has not only made me remember my little sister, but also discover, surprise, surprise, that the childhood of twin sisters has much in common with theirs; and I'm grateful for that. Aside from which, I've observed all over again the cruelties that children inflict on their siblings. Such charm and savagery, such innocent – sometimes, but more often far from innocent – insouciance remind me of fairy tales. Even the exquisite humour of what Fleur Adcock told her little sister Marilyn, for instance, cannot conceal the pain. Children *vis-à-vis* each other have enormous power. And childhood is a Kafkaesque world of arbitrary judgements and penalties, of enigmatic pronouncements and doom-filled confusion which sisters have the power to add to and invoke – as does Eustace's Hilda, for instance; and which, equally, they have the power to explain, to ease.

For siblings, as I've also found, can be touchingly kind to each other. Psychologists show infants of less than sixteen months concerned for sick or unhappy older sisters; and, less unexpectedly, not much older sisters concerned for them. They set up alliances amazingly early. Virginia Stephen was barely eighteen months old when she and Vanessa met under a table in their nursery and laid the foundations of their mutual appreciation and respect. There are other examples of sisters cooperating in play very early on – in Judy Dunn's dialogues for instance – from all around the world and from all ages. And, as they grow up, how children play and what they play with alters surprisingly little. The depiction of Bessie Head's doomed little sisters scolding their home-made dolls makes their mythic fate all the more terrible. I'm fond, too, of the small girls in the excerpt from that moral tale, *The Fairchild Family*, which I've known ever since I can remember, as I have the vividly alive and rather older sisters from *Little Women*. Re-exploring well-loved books is as much part of the pleasure in anthologizing as the delights of finding new ones.

Finally, let me be perverse and contradict myself for a moment. Despite everything I've said, a child – a sister – is not just the mother of the woman. The loves and hates and jealousies of children, the interactions between sisters and brothers exist absolutely in their own right; then and there, here and now. As all these pieces do.

They need to be seen like that, too, not merely as clues to the past, the present and the future.

From Autobiography

In November came the news which I had been told to expect. My sister Rachel had been with us in the country for a fortnight; and we knew that there was to be a baby at home before we went back; and I remember pressing so earnestly, by letter, to know the baby's name as to get a rebuff. I was told to wait till there was a baby. At last, the carrier brought us a letter one evening which told us that we had a little sister. I still longed to know the name, but dared not ask again. Our host saw what was in my mind. He went over to Norwich a day or two after, and on his return told me that he hoped I should like the baby's name now she had got one – 'Beersheba'. I did not know whether to believe him or not; and I had set my mind on 'Rose'. 'Ellen', however, satisfied me very well. Homesick before, I now grew downright ill with longing. I was sure that all old troubles were wholly my fault, and fully resolved that there should be no more. Now, as so often afterwards (as often as I left home), I was destined to disappoint. I scarcely felt myself at home before the well-remembered bickerings began; not with me, but from the boys being troublesome, James being naughty, and our eldest sister angry and scolding. I then and there resolved that I would look for my happiness to the new little sister, and that she should never want for the tenderness which I had never found. This resolution turned out more of a prophecy than such decisions, born of a momentary emotion, usually do. That child was henceforth a new life to me. I did lavish love and tenderness on her; and I could almost say that she has never caused me a moment's pain but by her own sorrows. There has been much suffering in her life; and in it I have suffered with her: but such sympathetic pain is bliss in comparison with such feelings as she has *not* excited in me during our close friendship of above forty years. When I first saw her it was as she was lifted out of her crib, at a fortnight old, asleep, to be shown to my late hostess, who had brought Rachel and me home. The passionate fondness I felt for her from that moment has been unlike any thing else I have felt in life, though I have made idols of not a few nephews and nieces. But she was a pursuit to me, no less than an attachment. I remember telling a young lady at the Gate-House Concert (a weekly undress concert) the next night, that I should now see the growth of a human mind from the very beginning. I told her this because I was very communicative to all who showed me sympathy in any degree. Years after, I found that she was so struck by such a speech from a child of nine that she had repeated it till it had spread all over the city, and people said somebody had put it into my head; but it was perfectly genuine. My curiosity *was* intense; and all my spare minutes were spent in the nursery, watching – literally watching – the baby. This was a great stimulus to me in my lessons, to which I gave my whole power, in order to get leisure the sooner. That was the time when I took it into my head to cut up the Bible into a rule of life, as I have already told; and it was in the nursery chiefly that I did it, – sitting on a stool opposite the nursemaid and baby, and getting up from my notes to devour the child with kisses. There were bitter moments and hours – as when she was vaccinated or had her little illnesses. My heart then felt bursting, and I went to my room, and locked the door, and prayed long and desperately. I knew then what the Puritans meant by 'wrestling in prayer'. One abiding anxiety which pressed upon me for two years or more was lest this child should be dumb: and if not, what an awful amount of labour was before the little creature! I had no other idea than that she must learn to speak at all as I had now to learn French, each word by an express effort; and if I, at ten and eleven, found my vocabulary so hard, how could this infant learn the whole English language? The dread went off in amazement when I found that she sported new words every day, without much teaching at first, and then without any. I was as happy to see her spared the labour as amused at her use of words in her pretty prattle.

Harriet Martineau, 1877

On the eve of her brother's birth, Jung asked his daughter, Agathli, what she would feel if a brother arrived tonight. The daughter responded 'I would kill him.'

Quoted in *The Sibling Constellation*,
Brian Clark 1999

From Shelter

Lenny's first memories of Alma are indistinct shadows and textures, yet she remembers the buggy, a huge contraption that rocked on its springs like a boat, whose spoked wheels were as big as a bicycle's. She tried to think if she'd seen the buggy recently, some piece of it, entangled with other cast-off relics in the basement. The hood had folded down like an accordion in the hot evenings, when the family ate supper outside on the picnic table. Audrey would cover the boat with sheer mosquito netting before she wheeled it over to the side of the yard and knelt down in the garden to weed. Lenny and Wes were supposed to stay occupied, 'Give me half an hour of quiet, I've had the two of them all day, and the house like a bake oven.' Her father Lenny remembers, so intensely, as though it were just the two of them and Audrey were lost to them both, huge with her pregnancy and then numb, gaunt, giggling with fatigue, or crying while the baby cried, or yelling about some mess Lenny had made. She drank pitchers of sun tea in the long afternoons to keep her milk up while Lenny sat on the steps of the front porch in a daze, worn out, refusing to nap, watching the two-lane down in the curve for a sign of Daddy's car.

Jayne Anne Phillips, 1995

From Reminiscences

Your mother [Vanessa Bell] was born in 1879, and as some six years at least must have passed before I knew that she was my sister, I can say nothing of that time. [. . .]

Our life was ordered with great simplicity and regularity. It seems to divide itself into two large spaces, not crowded with events, but in some way more exquisitely natural than any that follow; for our duties were very plain and our pleasures absolutely appropriate. Earth gave all the satisfaction we asked. One space was spent indoors, in the drawing-room and nursery, and the other in Kensington Gardens. [. . .] I remember too the great extent and mystery of the dark land under the nursery table, where a continuous romance seemed to go forward, though the time spent there was really so short. Here I met your mother, in a gloom happily encircled by the firelight, and peopled with legs and skirts. We drifted together like ships in an immense ocean and she asked me whether black cats had tails. And I answered that they had not, after a pause in which her question seemed to drop echoing down vast abysses, hitherto silent. In future I suppose there was some consciousness between us that the other held possibilities.

Virginia Woolf, published 1978

From Beginnings of Social Understanding

In considering the development of social understanding and of cooperation in particular, pretend play highlights some especially interesting changes in a child's abilities. In the context of a warm and affectionate sibling relationship, some children manage extremely early to take part in joint pretend play. [. . .]

The beginnings of these developments are seen as early as eighteen months. Take this example from an observation of eighteen-month-old Mary, whose older sister Polly has set up a pretend birthday party with a cake, in the sandpit in the garden. Both children are singing 'Happy Birthday'; in Mary's case the tune and the first two words are quite recognizable.

Family B (Study 1): Child of eighteen months

SIBLING. Dear Mary! You're three now.
CHILD (*nods*). Mmm.
SIB. You can go to school now.
CHILD (*nods*). Mmm.
SIB. Do you want to go to school now?
CHILD. Mmm.
SIB. All right then. (*Play voice*) Hello Mary, I'm Mrs Hunt. Do you want to help me do some of this birthday cake, do you? (*Ordinary voice*) We'd better do our birthday cake, hadn't we?
CHILD (*sings appropriately*). 'Happy birthday . . .' (*Both children walk around garden, singing.*)
SIB. We're at church now. We have to walk along. I'm like Mummy and you're like Baby. I'm Mummy. (*Play voice*) What, little one? We'd better go back to our birthday then.
CHILD (*sings*). 'Happy birthday . . .' (*Child holds hands up to sib to be carried.*)
SIB. That's all right, little girl. Are you going to sleep?

Judy Dunn, 1988

Siblings in India

Laksmamma (sister, six) told Mariamma (sister, three) to bring some small stones to her so they could cook. She brought her some stones, and Laksmamma made a cooking stove out of them. Then she told Mariamma to bring some water. Mariamma pretended to bring water and Laksmamma pretended to light the stove and cook.

The girls continued to play, and their sister, Hanumavva (thirteen) joined them. Mariamma brought sticks to Hanumavva and told her to put the pounding bundle inside the house or somebody would take it.

Susan Seymour, 'Sociocultural Contexts:
Examining Sibling Roles in South Asia', 1993

From My Sister Dancing

I like best to think of them, the two of them, as children, as brother and sister, playing a game my father described once when he was making cocoa one evening for my sister and me. The game he said was called horses and carts. They played the game at the kitchen table. They had a preserving jar, with a lid, full of nuts and bolts and nails and screws. They said the kitchen table was the road and they arranged the screws and the nuts and bolts all dotted up and down the table – dot-dot-dotty-dot along the table, they were the horses and carts going along the road, passing each other, turning in the road, stopping and starting – this game, my father explained, he played with his sister.

Elizabeth Jolley, 1996

From Women in Love

When they were together, doing the things they enjoyed, the two sisters were quite complete in a perfect world of their own. And this was one of the perfect moments of freedom and delight, such as children alone know, when all seems a perfect and blissful adventure.

D. H. Lawrence, 1921

From Looking for the Rain God

The family of the old man, Mokgobja, were among those who left early for the lands. They had a donkey cart and piled everything on to it, Mokgobja – who was over seventy years old; two little girls, Neo and Boseyong; their mother Tiro and an unmarried sister, Nesta; and the father and supporter of the family, Ramadi, who drove the donkey cart. In the rush of the first hope of rain, the man, Ramadi, and the two women, cleared the land of thorn-bush and then hedged their vast ploughing area with this same thorn-bush to protect the future crop from the goats they had brought along for milk. They cleared out and deepened the old well with its pool of muddy water and still in this light, misty rain, Ramadi inspanned two oxen and turned the earth over with a hand plough.

The land was ready and ploughed, waiting for the crops. At night, the earth was alive with insects singing and rustling about in search of food. But suddenly, by mid-November, the rain fled away; the rain-clouds fled away and left the sky bare. The sun danced dizzily in the sky, with a strange cruelty. Each day the land was covered in a haze of mist as the sun sucked up the last drop of moisture out of the earth. The family sat down in despair, waiting and waiting. Their hopes had run so high; the goats had started producing milk, which they had eagerly poured on their porridge; now they ate plain porridge with no milk. It was impossible to plant the corn, maize, pumpkin and water-melon seeds in the dry earth. They sat the whole day in the shadow of the huts and even stopped thinking, for the rain had fled away. Only the children, Neo and Boseyong, were quite happy in their little girl world. They carried on with their game of making house like their mother and chattered to each other in light, soft tones. They made children from sticks around which they tied rags, and scolded them severely in an exact imitation of their own mother. Their voices could be heard scolding the day long: 'You stupid thing, when I send you to draw water, why do you spill half of it out of the bucket!' 'You stupid thing! Can't you mind the porridge pot without letting the porridge burn!' And then they would beat the rag dolls on their bottoms with severe expressions.

The adults paid no attention to this; they did not even hear the funny chatter; they sat waiting for rain; their nerves were stretched to breaking-point willing the rain to fall out of the sky. Nothing was important, beyond that. All their animals had been sold during the bad years to purchase food, and of all their herd only two goats were left. It was the women of the family who finally broke down under the strain of waiting for rain. It was really the two women who caused the death of the little girls. Each night they started a weird, high-pitched wailing that began on a low, mournful note and whipped up to a frenzy. Then they would stamp their feet and shout as though they had lost their heads. The men sat quiet and self-controlled; it was important for men to maintain their self-control at all times but their nerve was breaking too. They knew the women were haunted by the starvation of the coming year.

Finally, an ancient memory stirred in the old man, Mokgobja. When he was very young and the customs of the ancestors still ruled the land, he had been witness to a rain-making ceremony. And he came alive a little, struggling to recall the details which had been buried by years and years of prayer in a Christian church. As soon as the mists cleared a little, he began consulting in whispers with his youngest son, Ramadi. There was, he said, a certain rain god who accepted only the sacrifice of the bodies of children. Then the rain would fall; then the crops would grow, he said. He explained the ritual and, as he talked, his memory became a conviction and he began to talk with unshakeable authority. Ramadi's nerves were smashed by the nightly wailing of the women and soon the two men began whispering with the two women. The children continued their game: 'You stupid thing! How could you have lost the money on the way to the shop! You must have been playing again!'

After it was all over and the bodies of the two little girls had been spread across the land, the rain did not fall. Instead, there was a deathly silence at night and the devouring heat of the sun by day.

A terror, extreme and deep, overwhelmed the whole family. They packed, rolling up their skin blankets and pots, and fled back to the village.

Bessie Head, 1977

From The Brontës: Interviews and Recollections

Monday 24 November 1834

I fed Rainbow, Diamond, Snowflake, Jasper Pheasant. This morning Branwell went down to Mr Driver's and brought news that Sir Robert Peel was going to be invited to stand for Leeds. Anne and I have been peeling apples for Charlotte to make an apple pudding and for Aunt's . . . Charlotte said she made puddings perfectly and she . . . of a quick but lim[i]ted intellect. Taby said just now Come Anne pilloputate [i.e. peel a potato] Aunt has come into the kitchin just now and said Where are your feet Anne Anne answered On the floor Aunt. Papa opened the parlour door and gave Branwell a letter saying Here Branwell read this and show it to your Aunt and Charlotte. The Gondals are discovering the interior of Gaaldine. Sally Mosley is washing in the back kitchin.

It is past twelve o'clock Anne and I have not tid[i]ed ourselves, done our bed work, or done our lessons and we want to go out to play We are going to have for dinner Boiled Beef, Turnips, potatoes and apple pudding The kitchin is in a very untidy state Anne and I have not done our music exercise which consists of *b major* Taby said on my putting a pen in her face Ya pitter pottering there instead of pilling a potate. I answered O Dear, O Dear, O Dear I will derectly With that I get up, take a knife and begin pilling. Finished pilling the potatoes Papa going to walk Mr Sunderland expected.

Anne and I say I wonder what we shall be like and what we shall be and where we shall be, if all goes on well, in the year 1874 – in which year I shall be in my 57th year. Anne will be in her 55th year Branwell will be going in his 58th year and Charlotte in her 59th year Hoping we shall all be well at that time We close our paper

Emily and Anne Brontë, 1834

From Memoirs of a Dutiful Daughter

We called her Poupette; she was two and a half years younger than me. People said she took after Papa. She was fair-haired, and in the photographs taken during our childhood her blue eyes always appear to be filled with tears. Her birth had been a disappointment, because the whole family had been hoping for a boy; certainly no one ever held it against her for being a girl, but it is perhaps not altogether without significance that her cradle was the centre of regretful comment. Great pains were taken to treat us both with scrupulous fairness; we wore identical clothes, we nearly always went out together; we shared a single existence, though as the elder sister I did in fact enjoy certain advantages. I had my own room, which I shared with Louise, and I slept in a big bed, an imitation antique in carved wood over which hung a reproduction of Murillo's *Assumption of the Blessed Virgin*. A cot was set up for my sister in a narrow corridor. While Papa was undergoing his army training, it was I who accompanied Mama when she went to see him. Relegated to a secondary position, the 'little one' felt almost superfluous. I had been a new experience for my parents: my sister found it much more difficult to surprise and astonish them; I had never been compared with anyone: she was always being compared with me. At the Cours Désir the ladies in charge made a habit of holding up the older children as examples to the younger ones; whatever Poupette might do, and however well she might do it, the passing of time and the sublimation of a legend all contributed to the idea that I had done everything much better. No amount of

15

effort and success was sufficient to break through that impenetrable barrier. The victim of some obscure malediction, she was hurt and perplexed by her situation, and often in the evening she would sit crying on her little chair. She was accused of having a sulky disposition; one more inferiority she had to put up with. She might have taken a thorough dislike to me, but paradoxically she only felt sure of herself when she was with me. Comfortably settled in my part of elder sister, I plumed myself only on the superiority accorded to my greater age; I thought Poupette was remarkably bright for her years; I accepted her for what she was – someone like myself, only a little younger; she was grateful for my approval, and responded to it with an absolute devotion. She was my liegeman, my *alter ego*, my double; we could not do without one another.

I was sorry for children who had no brother or sister; solitary amusements seemed insipid to me; no better than a means of killing time. But when there were two, hopscotch or a ball game were adventurous undertakings, and bowling hoops an exciting competition. Even when I was just doing transfers or daubing a catalogue with water-colours I felt the need of an associate. Collaborating and vying with one another, we each found a purpose in our work that saved it from all gratuitousness. The games I was fondest of were those in which I assumed another character; and in these I had to have an accomplice. We hadn't many toys; our parents used to lock away the nicest ones – the leaping tiger and the elephant that could stand on his hind legs; they would occasionally bring them out to show to admiring guests. I didn't mind. I was flattered to possess objects which could amuse grown-ups; and I loved them because they were precious: familiarity would have bred contempt. In any case the rest of our playthings – grocer's shop, kitchen utensils, nurse's outfit – gave very little encouragement to the imagination. A partner was absolutely essential to me if I was to bring my imaginary stories to life.

A great number of the anecdotes and situations which we dramatized were, we realized, rather banal; the presence of the grown-ups did not disturb us when we were selling hats or defying the Boche's artillery fire. But other scenarios, the ones we liked best, required to be performed in secret. They were, on the surface, perfectly innocent, but, in sublimating the adventure of our childhood, or anticipating the future, they drew upon something secret and intimate within us which would not bear the searching light of adult gazes. I shall speak further on of those games which, from my point of view, were the most significant. In fact, I was always the one who expressed myself through them; I imposed them upon my sister, assigning her the minor roles which she accepted with complete docility. At that evening hour when the stillness, the dark weight and the tedium of our middle-class domesticity began to invade the hall, I would unleash my fantasms; we would make them materialize with great gestures and copious speeches, and sometimes, spellbound by our play, we succeeded in taking off from the earth and leaving it far behind until an imperious voice suddenly brought us back to reality. Next day we would start all over again. 'We'll play *you know what*,' we would whisper to each other as we prepared for bed. The day would come when a certain theme, worked over too long, would no longer have the power to inspire us; then we would choose another, to which we would remain faithful for a few hours or even for weeks.

I owe a great debt to my sister for helping me to externalize many of my dreams in play: she also helped me to save my daily life from silence; through her I got into the habit of wanting to communicate with people. When she was not there I hovered between two extremes: words were either insignificant noises which I made with my mouth, or, whenever I addressed my parents, they became deeds of the utmost gravity; but when Poupette and I talked together, words had a meaning yet did not weigh too heavily upon us. I never knew with her the pleasure of sharing or exchanging things, because we always held everything in common; but as we recounted to one another the day's incidents and emotions, they took on an added interest and importance. There was nothing wrong in what we told one another; nevertheless, because of the importance we both attached to our conversations, they created a bond between us which isolated us from the grown-ups; when we were together, we had our own secret garden.

Simone de Beauvoir, 1959

From At the Bay

'Wait for me, Isa-bel! Kezia, wait for me!'

There was poor little Lottie, left behind again, because she found it so fearfully hard to get over the stile by herself. When she stood on the first step her knees began to wobble; she grasped the post. Then you had to put one leg over. But which leg? She never could decide. And when she did finally put one leg over with a sort of stamp of despair – then the feeling was awful. She was half in the paddock still and half in the tussock grass. She clutched the post desperately and lifted up her voice. 'Wait for me!'

'No, don't you wait for her, Kezia!' said Isabel. 'She's such a little silly. She's always making a fuss. Come on!' And she tugged Kezia's jersey. 'You can use my bucket if you come with me,' she said kindly. 'It's bigger than yours.' But Kezia couldn't leave Lottie all by herself. She ran back to her. By this time Lottie was very red in the face and breathing heavily.

'Here, put your other foot over,' said Kezia.

'Where?'

Lottie looked down at Kezia as if from a mountain height.

'Here where my hand is.' Kezia patted the place.

'Oh, *there* do you mean?' Lottie gave a deep sigh and put the second foot over.

'Now – sort of turn round and sit down and slide,' said Kezia.

'But there's nothing to sit down *on*, Kezia,' said Lottie.

She managed it at last, and once it was over she shook herself and began to beam.

'I'm getting better at climbing over stiles, aren't I, Kezia?'

Lottie's was a very hopeful nature.

The pink and the blue sunbonnet followed Isabel's bright red sunbonnet up that sliding, slipping hill. At the top they paused to decide where to go and to have a good stare at who was there already. Seen from behind, standing against the skyline, gesticulating largely with their spades, they looked like minute puzzled explorers.

Katherine Mansfield, 1922

From Bluebell Seasons

The cruellest trick I ever played on her (which I later obliterated
from my memory, although it is seared on hers) was to tell her that
her doll Pixie Ann had not always been a doll – 'She was a little
girl once but her father shot her and had her stuffed.' This struck
at her trust in both dolls and fathers. I cringe to think of it.

Fleur Adcock, 1996

From No Bed of Roses

Olivia had learned to read before she was six. For some reason, de
Belville had left us alone the evening my sister chose to flaunt her
erudition. Listening to her read aloud the Crucifixion from the Bible
in mounting gusto, I not only experienced man's inhumanity to
man, but that of sister to sister.

When she read of the crown of thorns and the soldier's stab in
the side of Jesus, my screams were heard down the entire row of
cottages. Gleefully persisting, Olivia continued reading of Christ's
journey up the Via Dolorosa, and only when she had reached the
part where the nails were being driven into his flesh was I rescued
by a neighbour from the last cottage on the row. Years later, when
I walked the same route that Christ had traversed, the incident
returned in all its horror. To this day I cannot look at a statue of
Christ on the crucifix or pass the Stations of the Cross without that
same anguish recurring.

Joan Fontaine, 1978

From History of the
Fairchild Family

Whilst they were looking at the ring they heard the sound of a carriage; it was Sir Charles Noble's, and Lady Noble was in it.

'Oh, Mr Fairchild!' she called out of the window of the carriage, 'I am in great trouble; I have lost my diamond ring, and it is of very great value. I went to the village this morning in the carriage, and as I came back, pulled off my glove to get sixpence out of my purse to give to a poor man somewhere in this lane, and I suppose that my ring dropped off at the time. I don't know what I shall do; Sir Charles will be sadly vexed.'

'Make yourself quite happy, madam,' said Mr Fairchild, 'here is your ring; Emily just this moment picked it up.'

Lady Noble was exceedingly glad when she received back her ring. She thanked Emily twenty times, and said, 'I think I have something in the carriage which you will like very much, Miss Emily; it is just come from London, and was intended for my daughter Augusta, but I will send for another for her.

So saying, she presented Emily with a new doll packed up in paper, and with it a little trunk, with a lock and key, full of clothes for the doll. Emily was so delighted that she almost forgot to thank Lady Noble; but Mr Fairchild, who was not quite so much overjoyed as his daughter, remembered to return thanks for this pretty present.

So Lady Noble put the ring on her finger, and ordered the coachman to drive home.

'Oh, papa, papa!' said Emily, 'how beautiful this doll is! I have just torn the paper a bit, and I can see its face; it has blue eyes and red lips, and hair like Henry's. Oh, how beautiful! Please, papa, to carry the box for me; I cannot carry both the box and the doll. Oh, this beautiful doll! this lovely doll!' So she went on talking till they reached home; then she ran before her papa to her mamma and sister and brother, and, taking the paper off the doll, cried out, 'How beautiful! Oh, what pretty hands! What nice feet! What blue eyes! How lovely! how beautiful!'

Her mother asked her several times where she had got this pretty doll; but Emily was too busy to answer her. When Mr Fairchild came in with the trunk of clothes, he told all the story; how that Lady Noble had given Emily the doll for finding her diamond ring.

When Emily had unpacked the doll, she opened the box, which was full of as pretty doll's things as ever you saw.

Whilst Emily was examining all these things, Henry stood by admiring them and turning them about; but Lucy, after having once looked at the doll without touching it, went to a corner of the room, and sat down in her little chair without speaking a word.

'Come, Lucy,' said Emily, 'help me to dress my doll.'

'Can't you dress it yourself?' answered Lucy, taking up a little book, and pretending to read.

'Come, Lucy,' said Henry, 'you never saw so beautiful a doll before.'

'Don't tease me, Henry,' said Lucy; 'don't you see I am reading?'

'Put up your book now, Lucy,' said Emily, 'and come and help me to dress this sweet little doll. I will be its mamma, and you shall be its nurse, and it shall sleep between us in our bed.'

'I don't want dolls in my bed,' said Lucy; 'don't tease me, Emily.'

'Then Henry shall be its nurse,' said Emily. 'Come, Henry, we will go into our playroom, and put this pretty doll to sleep. Will not you come, Lucy? Pray do come; we want you very much.'

'Do let me alone,' answered Lucy; 'I want to read.'

So Henry and Emily went to play, and Lucy sat still in the corner of the parlour. After a few minutes her mamma, who was at work by the fire, looked at her, and saw that she was crying; the tears ran down her cheeks, and fell upon her book. Then Mrs Fairchild called Lucy to her, and said:

'My dear child, you are crying; can you tell me what makes you unhappy?'

'Nothing, mamma,' answered Lucy; 'I am not unhappy.'

'People do not cry when they are pleased and happy, my dear,' said Mrs Fairchild.

Lucy stood silent.

'I am your mother, my dear,' said Mrs Fairchild, 'and I love you very much; if anything vexes you, whom should you tell it to but to your own mother?' Then Mrs Fairchild kissed her, and put her arms round her.

Lucy began to cry more.

'Oh, mamma, mamma! dear mamma!' she said, 'I don't know what vexes me, or why I have been crying.'

'Are you speaking the truth?' said Mrs Fairchild. 'Do not hide anything from me. Is there anything in your heart, my dear child, do you think, which makes you unhappy?'

'Indeed, mamma,' said Lucy, 'I think there is. I am sorry that Emily has got that pretty doll. Pray do not hate me for it, mamma; I know it is wicked in me to be sorry that Emily is happy, but I feel that I cannot help it.'

'My dear child,' said Mrs Fairchild, 'I am glad you have confessed the truth to me. Now I will tell you why you feel so unhappy, and I will tell you where to seek a cure. The naughty passion you now feel, my dear, is what is called Envy.'

Mrs Sherwood, 1807

Monkeys

Josie (two-year-old sister) takes Viv's nipple out of Celeste's (infant) mouth. Viv yanks Celeste away from Josie. Celeste squeaks. Josie has a tantrum. Viv displays, Josie grooms Viv.

Faye (three-year-old sister) pulls CT's tail *very hard*. CT (infant) squeaks.

Phyllis Lee, 'Influence of Sibling on Infant's Relationship with Mother and Others', 1983

From The Children of Sánchez

I did not think I could ever be pretty. I felt inferior because I was small and thin. My skin was too dark, my eyes slightly slanted, my mouth too large, my teeth too crowded. I searched for some good feature. My nose was straight but big, my hair very thick and dark but would not take a curl. I wished I were lighter-skinned and plump like Marta, with dimples like hers. I dreamed of being blond. Staring at myself in the water I thought, 'Consuelo, Consuelo, what a strange name. It doesn't even sound like the name of a person. It sounds very thin, as though it were breaking.'

The caretaker usually brought me out of my dreams, taking me by the shoulder and saying, 'What are you doing here? Don't you know you can't come up to the roof? Go play or I'll take you to the principal.' Blushing with shame, I would go down and sit in the sun in the little garden. When the first bell rang for us to go back to our classrooms, I would wait for the others to get lined up, because otherwise they almost always pushed me. I let them push without protesting; I was afraid of them.

My sister Marta wasn't afraid, of either girls *or* boys. She played with both. It made me furious to see her surrounded by boys, squatting with her legs apart, leaning on the ground with one hand, holding a marble in the other, calculating the distance. I used to embarrass her by making scenes when she was with her friends. Also, I didn't like her wandering around with Roberto. They would both play hooky and come home with their clothes dirty and torn. Sometimes when I went out looking for her I would see her hanging on the rear bumper of a bus, taking a free ride.

There always was trouble between Marta and me, especially when I wanted to delouse her, or have her wash the dishes, or make her clean her face with a damp rag. And I could never, never get her to sew. Trying to do this was the cause of big quarrels in which she would throw the iron at me or scratch my hands all over. Later, she would accuse me of having hit her and pulled her hair, and in a way she was right, though I don't remember having dragged her 'across the whole room and the courtyard', as she told my father.

As soon as she felt the first blow from me, Marta would answer with kicks, bites, pinches, scratches, and whatever else she could. When I saw her like that, I laughed so much I lost my strength. I would feel my stomach stretch like a rubber band, and then all I could do was hold her hands so she couldn't scratch me. When she didn't succeed in hurting me or if I had locked her in, she would throw herself on the floor and bang her head on the boards or against the wall. She would cry so much her face would get red and if one of my brothers saw her he would take it out on me without asking any questions.

[. . .]

As a matter of fact, I really didn't know how to treat Marta. I saw her as a candy doll, dressed in blue, on a white cake, but in reality there was no sugar in her. Instead of being sweet, she was spoiled and selfish. I looked upon her tantrums as the caprices of a five-year-old, which she would get over when she grew up. I would think, 'She doesn't want to lend her doll, but she will when she is a little older . . . She doesn't want to share her candy now, but later on she will.'

Oscar Lewis, 1962

From The Sisters

We were six years old that day – 9 November 1926. There was always a great deal of fuss made on birthdays, and one of mother's eccentricities was to send to Harrods for all our party frocks. The dresses were identical for both of us, fluffy confections with flounces of lace all down the skirt and more little frills edging the sleeves and neck. The dresses were worn over stiffly starched petticoats and tied with broad satin sashes. Nina's was pink, mine blue. [. . .]

We had finished breakfast, a birthday breakfast of a delicious sort of pudding made from semolina, milk and butter and sprinkled with raisins and fried almonds, which was always made on special occasions. We then went up to Sophie's room and stood there in the starched petticoats, waiting for the dresses to be slipped over our heads. It was my moment of revelation – until then I had never considered whether I was pretty, plain or ugly. We were bathed, powdered and brushed, standing side by side in front of the long heavy mirror. The dresses were taken carefully off the hangers and slipped over our heads and the satin bows tied securely behind. My mother looked at Nina and my eyes turned with hers. Nina seemed a spun-sugar fairy poised for flight. Her cheeks were tinged faintly with pink and her hair flowed down to her waist, polished and shining like strands of metallic silk. Mother said, 'Oh darling, you look beautiful!' Her eyes, and mine too (as though our eyes were controlled somehow by the same set of muscles), turned to my reflection in the mirror. A faint frown appeared between her high arched eyebrows. It was the time for thin, plucked and pencilled eyebrows. She bent over and tugged a frill here, pulled a flounce there and then stood back and bit her lip. 'Honestly, if you don't look pretty in this, I don't see how you ever can.'

I fought back the tears that sprang into my eyes and put on my stubborn face. I would not show that I was hurt. All the foolish pleasure I had taken in my appearance vanished. The dress was absurd on me. I was fat, and the frills and flounces made me look like a small, stuffed pig. The bow in my hair had been pulled so tight that my eyes slanted upwards in a weird Mongolian way, and my thick frizzy hair was already untidy and tangled. Taking our hands and sighing as though defeated, mother led us down the terrace where the photographer waited. Grandma had come down from her room for the occasion, and Father was there too and a few of the servants. By this time I was hanging back and doing my best to hide behind Sophie, so that as we came in, everyone first saw Nina and there were cries and murmurs and delight and admiration. I was then dragged out into the light. The silence that greeted my appearance was slight, before grandma came forward and kissed me. 'How nice both of you look,' she said.

Two delicate leather-back chairs with black velvet cushions had been placed against the trellised rose-covered wall. On these we were arranged, Nina of course sitting at once in a position that was at once erect and graceful, while the photographer and Sophie pulled and prodded me about, before he disappeared under his black cloth. Two photographs were taken and then the photographer said, pointing to Nina, 'Could I take a few more of this little lady?'

Nina smirked and preened herself, and unnoticed, I slunk away.

How to explain, after all these years, the feeling of blackness and hatred that enveloped me? I wandered in that radiant garden, shuddering under the blows to my pride and my, oh! so vulnerable heart. At that moment I knew – was convinced, that Nina was more loved because she was beautiful. I walked aimlessly till I came to one of the small enclosed gardens, hidden by tall trees and grassy around a shallow pool. Here I sat down in the dampness and began to pick at the hated dress. To my astonishment the frills came off easily when tugged; and absorbed in my new task, I began slowly and deliberately to rip off the flounces which were held with only the lightest, most delicate of stitches. Soon I had a pile of creamy glimmering stuff near me and I turned my attention to the sleeves and neckline. These were awkward to tug off, but I pulled and wrenched and at last they too were added to my pile. I took off the sash and the ribbon from my hair and piling everything together waded out into the pool. My white shoes and socks were naturally submerged in green slime and several startled frogs leapt out in alarm. I pressed my small pile of frills into the water but they kept drifting up and floating and it took a long time before they were completely saturated and sank to the bottom. For many years I would wake screaming in the night with the same nightmare. It was not the frills, but I who lay there at the bottom of the green and slimy pond, the dark water closing over my head.

[. . .]

This one memory was to remain my most important recollection of an unhappy childhood. I knew now as an incontrovertible fact, that I was ugly and Nina pretty.

Nergis Dalal, 1973

From My Sister Eileen

My sister and I had a lot of trouble in our youth trying to get cultured. Every time we made a small attempt to explore science, religion, or the fine arts, public opinion was against us. [. . .]

Eileen and I got mixed up in a scandal about Michael Arlen, not to mention the time Father actually called in the pastor of the East Cleveland Evangelical Church to remonstrate with Eileen because she buried her doll on Good Friday and expected it, or said she expected it (no one ever knew the real truth of the matter), to resurrect itself on Easter.

That doll business caused a terrible uproar in the family. Of course, I admit it with a little thoughtless of Eileen to let the neighbours in on the big experiment. Inquiring minds, ought, I suppose, to operate only in the bosom of the family.

At least that was Father's position. He was certainly furious when Mrs Griffin, a lady who was strongly *pro bono publico*, came rushing into the kitchen the night before Easter.

'Mr McKenney,' Mrs Griffin bleated, sidestepping great pools of Easter-egg dye, 'do you KNOW that your little girl Eileen has been COMMITTING SACRILEGE?'

'Uhmmm?' Father murmured. He was engrossed in dying a hard-boiled egg half blue and half red, an operation which he had boasted he could do blindfolded, it was that easy. Eileen and I were watching his pitiful attempts with the contempt they merited. He had already spoiled four eggs.

'Bobbie came home tonight and wanted to borrow Sue's doll. He said he wanted to crucify it and hurry up and bury it so that it could Rise tomorrow.' Mrs Griffin's outraged squeal echoed in our quiet kitchen. Eileen looked up from her work, and an expression of gentle modesty, of unassuming pride, flickered in her large blue eyes.

'He did, huh?' Father remarked pleasantly, and added as an afterthought, 'Tsk! Tsk!'

'Why, MR McKENNEY!' Mrs Griffin's howl rang out at the same instant that Father's egg slipped from his spoon and fell into the kettle of red dye.

'God damn it to hell!' Father said. Eileen and I turned our heads so that he should not see our complacent smiles. It does not pay, we early learned, to gloat over the misfortunes, however merited, of one's parents.

'Why, Mr McKenney,' Mrs Griffin repeated in a dying-swan voice. You could see she was pretty shaken.

Father wheeled, the spoon, still dripping red dye, in his hand. 'What do YOU want?' he screamed. Father had been trying to dye that egg two colours for more than an hour. He was a man who could never let a dare alone.

'Really! Mr McKenney!'

'Well,' said Father, gradually pulling himself together. He put down his spoon, very carefully, glanced murderously at his two daughters and led Mrs Griffin into the living-room.

'Bobbie Griffin,' Eileen murmured, as the lad's mother disappeared around the door, 'is a rat.'

She was right. Ten minutes later, Bobbie, armed with a flashlight and goaded by his mother, pointed out the very spot where Eileen's doll, Joe, renamed for the big experiment, had been carefully buried in our backyard. Father dug Joe up with a hand trowel at a little after ten o'clock that night, in spite of Eileen's tearful complaints. 'He'll Rise tomorrow and you won't have to trouble,' Eileen kept moaning.

Mrs Griffin and Father were of two minds about the whole situation. Mrs Griffin said Eileen really didn't believe Joe would Rise, she was just trying to ruin the faith of Mrs Griffin's angel-child Bobbie.

'Eileen!' Father intoned sternly, 'if you were really trying to prove to Bobbie that Joe couldn't and wouldn't Rise, you are a bad little girl and need punishing, but if you were only a little confused about Easter I will have Dr Ringing come to talk to you.'

Eileen chose Dr Ringing. She has been a realist from her tenderest years.

Ruth McKenney, 1938

From Little Women

'Christmas won't be Christmas without any presents,' grumbled Jo, lying on the rug.

'It's so dreadful to be poor!' sighed Meg, looking down at her old dress.

'I don't think it's fair for some girls to have plenty of pretty things, and other girls nothing at all,' added little Amy, with an injured sniff.

'We've got Father and Mother and each other,' said Beth contentedly from her corner.

The four young faces on which the firelight shone brightened at the cheerful words, but darkened again as Jo said sadly, 'We haven't got Father, and shall not have him for a long time.' She didn't say 'perhaps never', but each silently added it, thinking of Father far away, where the fighting was.

Nobody spoke for a minute; then Meg said in an altered tone, 'You know the reason Mother proposed not having any presents this Christmas was because it is going to be a hard winter for everyone; and she thinks we ought not to spend money for pleasure, when our men are suffering so in the army. We can't do much, but we can make our little sacrifices, and ought to do it gladly. But I am afraid I don't.' And Meg shook her head, as she thought regretfully of all the pretty things she wanted.

'But I don't think the little we should spend would do any good. We've each got a dollar, and the army wouldn't be much helped by our giving that. I agree not to expect anything from Mother or you, but I do want to buy *Undine and Sintram* for myself. I've wanted it *so* long,' said Jo, who was a bookworm.

'I planned to spend mine in new music,' said Beth, with a little sigh, which no one heard but the hearth brush and kettle holder.

'I shall get a nice box of Faber's drawing pencils. I really need them,' said Amy decidedly.

'Mother didn't say anything about our money, and she won't wish us to give up everything. Let's each buy what we want, and have a little fun. I'm sure we work hard enough to earn it,' cried Jo, examining the heels of her shoes in a gentlemanly manner.

'I know *I* do – teaching those tiresome children nearly all day, when I'm longing to enjoy myself at home,' began Meg, in the complaining tone again.

'You don't have half such a hard time as I do,' said Jo. 'How would you like to be shut up for hours with a nervous, fussy old lady, who keeps you trotting, is never satisfied, and worries you till you're ready to fly out of the window or cry?'

'It's naughty to fret, but I do think washing dishes and keeping things tidy is the worst work in the world. It makes me cross, and my hands get so stiff, I can't practice well at all.' And Beth looked at her rough hands with a sigh that any one could hear that time.

'I don't believe any of you suffer as I do,' cried Amy, 'for you don't have to go to school with impertinent girls, who plague you if you don't know your lessons, and laugh at your dresses, and label your father if he isn't rich, and insult you when your nose isn't nice.'

'If you mean *libel*, I'd say so, and not talk about *labels*, as if Papa was a pickle bottle,' advised Jo, laughing.

'I know what I mean, and you needn't be *statirical* about it. It's proper to use good words, and improve your *vocabilary*,' returned Amy, with dignity.

'Don't peck at one another, children. Don't you wish we had the money Papa lost when we were little, Jo? Dear me! how happy and good we'd be, if we had no worries!' said Meg, who could remember better times.

'You said the other day you thought we were a deal happier than the King children, for they were fighting and fretting all the time, in spite of their money.'

'So I did, Beth. Well, I think we are; for, though we do have to work, we make fun for ourselves, and are a pretty jolly set, as Jo would say.'

'Jo does use such slang words!' observed Amy, with a reproving look at the long figure stretched on the rug. Jo immediately sat up, put her hands in her pockets, and began to whistle.

'Don't Jo, it's so boyish!'

'That's why I do it.'

'I detest rude, unladylike girls!'

'I hate affected, niminy-piminy chits!'

'"Birds in their little nests agree,"' sang Beth, the peacemaker, with such a funny face that both sharp voices softened to a laugh, and the 'pecking' ended for that time.

Louisa M. Alcott, 1868–9

From The Sister's Gift

Kitty Somers and her brother George were the only children of Sir William Somers. She was of the most amiable disposition; her mien was most graceful, her manners gentle; and the beauty of her person was only to be outshone by the justness of her ideas, and the brilliancy of her wit. Master George, however, had not the happiness to be held so much in esteem by the young ladies and gentlemen with whom he associated, he was so ill-tempered, that he had always a pleasure in mortifying his schoolfellows, and had so little of the feelings of humanity, that he was frequently guilty of such acts of cruelty as shocked the rest of his companions; yet he did not want sense, for he could always construe his lesson or finish his theme before any other boy in the class, but never assisted any of them, in hopes of having the pleasure of seeing them whipped all round. Such are the faint outlines of the character of the brother and sister who are the subject of this volume. [. . .]

Unfortunately for this young pair they lost their papa and mama at a very early period [. . .] and Miss Kitty and Master George were each of them sent to different boarding-schools. [. . .]

At this time Miss Kitty was about twelve and Master George in the eighth year of his age. Upon their taking leave of each other [. . .] Miss Kitty said to him; 'Now, my dear brother, we must for the first time be parted; we are but young, but we have already witnessed the greatest misfortune that could have befallen us, in the death of our dear papa and mama; and though I cannot mention their names without shedding tears, yet I hope I shall never forget that he, who in his divine pleasure gave us our being, has an absolute right [. . .] to take it back again. [. . .] I am confident that an all-wise God would create us for no other purpose but to be happy, and we have nothing else to do to make ourselves completely so but to be virtuous.'

George burst out a-crying and could only say: 'Farewell my dear sister, I shall see you again in the Whitsuntide vacation.' But he no sooner saw his little galloway waiting for him in the courtyard, than he dried up his tears, mounted, clapped to his spurs, and set off a-galloping as merry as a Greek.

Miss Kitty went off a few days after to another school [. . .] where she soon became the admiration and delight of everyone that knew her. But Master George, as we have observed before, was of quite another cast; there was not a boy in the school for whom he had not a nickname; and he took a pleasure in setting his schoolfellows together by the ears. [. . .]

It was customary on a play day when the young gentlemen went a-birds-nesting to change their coats. And once Master George and Dicky Rooksby having made an exchange for the afternoon they went to amuse themselves in the fields as usual. But upon their return home [. . .] coming by an honest farmer's garden, George clambered over the hedge and pulled up about two hundred cabbage plants that the poor farmer had industriously put in the ground. [. . .] as he was getting over the hedge again one of the farmer's men [. . .] observed him. [. . .] The next morning the farmer made complaint to the Master of the Academy, [. . .] and declared that the culprit was dressed in a sky-blue coat. [. . .] as no other boy had a sky-blue coat except Master Rooksby the unfortunate youth was horsed and severely whipped, though innocent of the crime. [. . .]

If Master George had had either spirit or generosity, he would never have first injured the poor farmer, and then see an innocent person suffer for it [. . .] But so far from this, he absolutely exulted in seeing the distress of Master Rooksby, and was one of the first to assist in horsing him and to render his punishment as severe as possible. [. . .]

When Whitsuntide arrived [. . .] Master George spent the holidays with his sister. [. . .] Now it was that Miss Kitty had the opportunity of observing the ill-tendency of her brother's mind and disposition, and to apply those useful remedies, which were afterwards of so much service to him.

She would frequently observe him catching poor innocent flies, through the bodies of which he would stick pins and fasten them to a coach made of a card. [. . .]

Sometimes he would amuse himself with tying an old tin kettle or canister to the tail of any dog that was so unhappy as to fall his way; and then with a whip set them a-running and howling through the town [. . .]

The farmers all round the neighbourhood complained [. . .] that he abused their cattle, by sticking a sharp nail at the end of a long stick, with which he used to goad them [. . .] or laming them by terrible and repeated blows upon the feet.

But what provoked the young ladies most of all, was his taking Miss Scar's favourite cat, and carrying her to the top of the church towers, from whence, after tying two bladders about her neck he cruelly threw her over the battlements, imagining that she would fly down without being quite killed. [. . .]

Miss Kitty immediately imagined who had been the author of this cruelty; and taking her brother aside, she remonstrated with him to the following effect:

'My dear brother,' said she, 'it is with great uneasiness of mind that I have observed your vicious disposition, which if not checked in time, by a too frequent repetition of your naughty tricks they may become habitual; I am determined to let you see them in such a light as will chill you with horror.

'Can you imagine that those insects you torment have no feeling? [. . .] Suppose some great giant was to run a sword through your body? [. . .] Believe me, my dear, the smaller an animal is, the more acute its sensibility. [. . .]

'All your other frolics are equally cruel and unsupportable. Do you love to be frightened? If you do not, what pleasure can you take in frightening so many faithful dogs as you do? Suppose I was to prick your sides full of holes with my needles, would you not think me very hard-hearted? And are you not equally cruel, who, for wanton amusement, can gore all the cattle in the common fields! And lastly, [. . .] you have destroyed the favourite kitten of Miss Polly Scar; wantonly sported away the life of a little playful innocent animal. [. . .] Fie, fie!'

Master George blushed and seemed confounded, when Miss Kitty thus continued her discourse:

'It is universally allowed that you do not want sense. [. . .] You cannot suppose that the divine Being created these poor creatures merely to please the whim and caprice of mankind. [. . .] It is not in our power to create anything, and therefore what right have we to destroy an existence which we cannot restore? The man who, without remorse, can wantonly do these things, ought to be banished to the deserts of Arabia, there to live among lions, wolves and tigers, for he is not fit for society. [. . .] He who is not endowed with the delicate touch of compassion sinks even below the brutes themselves, for they are sometimes known to help and assist each other. [. . .]

Master George wept bitterly and declared to his sister, that she had painted the enormity of his vice in such striking colours that they shocked him in the greatest degree, and promised ever after to be as remarkable for generosity, compassion, and every other virtue, as he had hitherto been for cruelty, frowardness, and ill-nature. It is with pleasure, we can add, that he faithfully kept his word, and is now one of the best little masters in the whole universe.

The Sister's Gift, or The Bad Boy Reformed, 1826 (anon.)

From The Shrimp and the Anemone

'Eustace! Eustace!' Hilda's tones were always urgent; it might not be anything very serious. Eustace bent over the pool. His feet sank in its soggy edge, so he drew back, for he must not get them wet. But he could still see the anemone. Its base was fastened to a boulder, just above the water-line. From the middle of the other end, which was below, something stuck out, quivering. It was a shrimp, Eustace decided, and the anemone was eating it, sucking it in. A tumult arose in Eustace's breast. His heart bled for the shrimp, he longed to rescue it; but, on the other hand, how could he bear to rob the anemone of its dinner? The anemone was more beautiful than the shrimp, more interesting and much rarer. It was a 'plumose' anemone; he recognized it from the picture in his Natural History, and the lovely feathery epithet stroked the fringes of his mind like a caress. If he took the shrimp away, the anemone might never catch another, and die of hunger. But while he debated, the un-swallowed part of the shrimp grew perceptibly smaller.

Once more, mingled with the cries of the sea-mews and pitched even higher than theirs, came Hilda's voice.

'Eustace! Eustace! Come here! The bank's breaking! It's your fault! You never minded your side!'

Here was another complication. Ought he not perhaps to go to Hilda and help her build up the bank? It was true he had scamped his side, partly because he was piqued with her for always taking more than her fair share. But then she was a girl and older than he and she did it for his good, as she had often told him, and in order that he might not overstrain himself. He leaned on his wooden spade and, looking doubtfully round, saw Hilda signalling with her iron one. An ancient jealousy invaded his heart. Why should *she* have an iron spade? He tried to fix his mind on the anemone. The shrimp's tail was still visible but wriggling more feebly. Horror at its plight began to swamp all other considerations. He made up his mind to release it. But how? If he waded into the water he would get his socks wet, which would be bad enough; if he climbed on to the rock he might fall in and get wet all over, which would be worse. There was only one thing to do.

'Hilda,' he cried, 'come here.'

His low soft voice was whirled away by the wind; it could not compete with the elements, as Hilda's could.

He called again. It was an effort for him to call: he screwed his face up: the cry was unmelodious now that he forced it, more like a squeak than a summons.

But directly she heard him Hilda came, as he knew she would. Eustace put the situation before her, weighing the pros and cons. Which was to be sacrificed, the anemone or the shrimp? Eustace stated the case for each with unflinching impartiality and began to enlarge on the felicity that would attend their afterlives, once this situation was straightened out – forgetting, in his enthusiasm, that the well-being of the one depended on the misfortune of the other. But Hilda cut him short.

'Here, catch hold of my feet,' she said.

She climbed on to the boulder, and flung herself face down on the seaweedy slope. Eustace followed more slowly, showing respect for the inequalities of the rocks. Then he lowered himself, sprawling uncertainly and rather timidly, and grasped his sister's thin ankles with hands that in spite of his nine years still retained some of the chubbiness of infancy. Once assumed, the position was not uncomfortable. Eustace's thoughts wandered, while his body automatically accommodated itself to the movements of Hilda, who was wriggling ever nearer to the edge.

'I've got it,' said Hilda at last in a stifled voice. There was no elation, only satisfaction in her tone, and Eustace knew that something had gone wrong.

'Let me look!' he cried, and they struggled up from the rock.

The shrimp lay in the palm of Hilda's hand, a sad, disappointing sight. Its reprieve had come too late; its head was mangled and there was no vibration in its tail. The horrible appearance fascinated Eustace for a moment, then upset him so much that he turned away with trembling lips. But there was worse to come. As a result of Hilda's forcible interference with its meal the anemone had been partially disembowelled; it could not give up its prey without letting its digestive apparatus go too. Part of its base had come unstuck and was seeking feebly to attach itself to the rock again. Eustace took Hilda's other hand and together they surveyed the unfortunate issue of their kind offices.

'Hadn't we better kill them both?' asked Eustace with a quaver in his voice, 'since they're both wounded?'

He spoke euphemistically, for the shrimp was already dead.

But Hilda did not despair so easily.

'Let's put it in the water,' she suggested. 'Perhaps that'll make it come to.'

A passing ripple lent the shrimp a delusive appearance of life; when the ripple subsided it floated to the surface, sideways up, and lay still.

'Never mind,' said Hilda, 'we'll see if the anemone will eat it now.'

Again they disposed themselves on the rock, and Hilda, with her head downwards and her face growing redder every minute, tried her hardest to induce the anemone to resume its meal. For the sake of achieving this end she did not shrink from the distasteful task of replacing the anemone's insides where they belonged, but her amateur surgery failed to restore its appetite and it took no interest in the proffered shrimp.

'I wish we'd let them alone,' sobbed Eustace.

'What would have been the good of that?' demanded Hilda, wiping her brother's eyes. He stood quiescent, his hands hanging down and his face turned upwards, showing no shame at being comforted and offering no resistance, as though he was familiar with the performance and expected it. 'We had to do something,' Hilda continued. 'We couldn't let them go on like that.'

'Why couldn't we?' asked Eustace. All at once, as the thought struck him, he ceased crying. It seemed to cost him as little effort to stop as it costs a dog to wake out of sleep. 'They didn't mean to hurt each other.'

The disaster that had overtaken their remedial measures was so present to him that he forgot the almost equally painful situation those measures had been meant to relieve, and thought of the previous relationship of the shrimp and the anemone as satisfactory to both.

'But they *were* hurting each other,' remarked Hilda. 'Anyhow the anemone was eating the shrimp, if you call that hurting.'

Eustace could see no way out of this. His mind had no power to consider an unmixed evil, it was set upon happiness. With Hilda's ruthless recognition of an evil principle at the back of the anemone affair his tears started afresh.

'Now don't be a cry-baby,' Hilda not at all unkindly admonished him. 'There's Gerald and Nancy Steptoe coming, nasty things! If you stand still a minute,' she went on, preparing with the hem of her blue frock to renew the assault upon his face, 'they'll think it's only the wind.'

The appeal to Eustace's pride was one Hilda tried only for form's sake; she thought it ought to weigh with him, but generally, as she knew, it made him irritable.

'I want to go and talk to Nancy,' he announced. His attitude to other children was tinged with a fearful joy, altogether unlike his sister's intolerant and hostile demeanour. 'Gerald's left her by herself again: he's climbing up the cliffs, look, and she daren't go.'

'What do you want to talk to her for?' asked Hilda, a trifle crossly. 'It's her fault, she shouldn't have let him.'

'She can't stop him,' said Eustace. His voice had a triumphant ring, due partly to his knowledge of the Steptoes' private concerns and partly, as Hilda realized, to a feeling of elation at the spectacle of Gerald's independence. This spirit of rebellion she resolved to quench.

'Come along,' she said authoritatively, snatching his hand and whirling him away. 'You know,' she continued, with an exaggeration of her grown-up manner, 'you don't really want to talk to Nancy. She's stuck-up, like they all are. Now we'll see what's happened to the pond. Perhaps we shall be in time to save it.'

They scampered across the sands, Eustace hanging back a little and trying to wave to the lonely Nancy, who, deserted by her daring and lawless brother, had begun to dig herself a castle. Now that they seemed to be out of harm's way Hilda stopped and looked back. They could just see the ground plan of Nancy's fortress, which she had marked out on the sand with a spade and which was of an extravagant extent.

'She'll never get that done,' Hilda remarked. 'They're always the same. They try to make everything bigger than anybody else, and then they leave it half done and look silly.'

'Should we go and help her?' suggested Eustace. Nancy looked very forlorn, labouring away at the outer moat of her castle.

'No,' Hilda replied. 'She can do it quite well herself, or she could if Gerald would have come away from those cliffs where he's no business to be, and may very likely cause an avalanche.'

'I want to go,' cried Eustace, suddenly obstinate.

'I say you can't,' said Hilda half teasingly.

'I will, I want to!' Eustace almost screamed, struggling to get free. Bent like a bow with the effort, his feet slipping from under him, his hat off, and his straight fair hair unpicturesquely rumpled, he looked very childish and angry. Hilda kept him prisoner without much difficulty.

Some three and a half years older than Eustace, she was a good deal taller and the passion and tenacity of her character had already left its mark on her heart-shaped, beautiful face. Her immobility made a folly of Eustace's struggles; her dark eyes looked scornfully down.

'Diddums-wazzums,' she at last permitted herself to remark. The phrase, as she knew it would, drove her brother into a frenzy. The blood left his face; he stiffened and stopped struggling, while he searched his mind for the most wounding thing to say.

'I want to play with Nancy,' he said at last, averting his eyes from his sister and looking small and spiteful. 'I don't want to play with you. I don't ever want to play with you again. I don't love you. You killed the shrimp and you killed the anemone' (he brought this out with a rush; it had occurred to him earlier to taunt Hilda with her failure, but a generous scruple had restrained him), 'and you're a murderer.'

Hilda listened to the beginning of the speech with equanimity; her features continued to reflect disdain. Then she saw that Nancy Steptoe had stopped digging and could both see and hear what was passing. This unnerved her; and the violence and venom of Eustace's attack touched her to the quick. The words were awful to her. An overwhelming conviction came to her that he did not love her, and that she was a murderer. She turned away, with great ugly sobs that sounded like whooping-cough.

'Then *go*,' she said.

L. P. Hartley, 1958

From Behind the Scenes at the Museum

Auntie Mabel might as well have said, 'Mind you go straight to the duck pond,' because as soon as we're in the field we make a beeline for the big pond where Auntie Mabel's ducks and geese congregate. We [. . .] have never seen the duck pond in winter before and for a second we all pause and look in astonishment because it is a magical place, a frozen icescape of sparkling white and all the snow-covered trees on the island in the middle look as if they would chime if you shook them like trees in a fairy story. [. . .]

A few geese waddle at the edges of the pond while one or two ducks are swimming in lazy circles moving a slurry of ice crystals around on the surface of the water to stop it from freezing, but most of the birds are ice-bound on the little island in the middle and set up a flurry of quacking and honking when they see us approaching. 'Oh, we should have brought some bread!' Patricia wails. Gillian yelps with delight when she finds a solid sheet of ice at the far side of the pond, banging her foot on it like a demented Disney rabbit. 'Be careful, Gillian,' Patricia warns and wanders off, walking a pair of ducks around the pond. Pearl rushes after Gillian, jumping up and down as she watches our sister perform the miracle of walking on water. Gillian has nearly reached the island when the ice gives a frightening *Crack!* and moves a little so that you can see the edges of it where it dwindles away and becomes liquid again, thanks to the ducks' marathon swimming efforts. Pearl has already got both feet on the ice and Gillian is laughing and shouting at her, 'Come on! Come on, don't be a coward! Cowardy-custard Pearl!' because she knows that's the one way to goad Pearl into doing things. I shout at Pearl to come back and Gillian is furious with me, yelling, 'Shut up, Ruby! You're just a big baby!' and I look round wildly for Patricia, but she's disappeared behind a clump of frosted trees and I can't see her. Pearl has walked nearly halfway out on to the ice and I can actually see it moving, with a slight see-saw motion, and I begin to cry. All the time Gillian continues to shout, 'Come on, come on, Pearl!' when all of a sudden the ice that Pearl is standing on tilts and I watch in horror as she simply slides off as if she'd been tipped on a chute and slips into the water, quite slowly and feet first, and as she drops into the water her body twists round so that she's facing me and the last thing I see is her face, stretched in horror, and the last words she ever says, before the black water claims her, hang on the freezing air, forming ice crystals of sound long after the little white pompon on her hat has disappeared.

All I can do is stand there with my mouth open wide, one long, unwavering scream of hysteria coming out of it, and although I'm aware of the dreadful ululating noise that's coming from inside me, and aware of Gillian on the island screaming at Patricia to hurry up and Patricia herself sprinting round the pond towards us, despite this cacophony – joined now by all the geese – all I can really hear are Pearl's words which have found a home inside my skull, creating dreadful ricocheting echoes – '*Ruby, help me! Ruby, help me!*'

Patricia dives into the water and comes up again almost immediately, retching with the cold, her stringy hair plastered to her head, but she blinks like a strange amphibian and forces herself under the water again. By this time the commotion has reached not only Uncle Tom's cottage but the neighbouring farm as well and people seem to come running from everywhere churning up the smooth white snow. Someone drags a shivering, blue Patricia out of the water and wraps her in a rough, dirty jacket and carries her away and one of the farm labourers wades confidently into the water but has to start swimming almost straight away, gasping with shock, because the duck pond is unexpectedly full.

But Pearl has floated away under the ice somewhere and refuses to be found. It is only several hours later when the men have brought hooks and long-sticks to fish for Pearl, that she agrees to come out of hiding. One of the men, big, with pocked skin and a heavy jaw, carries her in his arms, holding her away from his body as if she was something immensely fragile and important, which she is, of course, and all the way across the trodden snow of the field his body judders with the sobs he's trying to suppress.

And my heart is breaking, breaking into great jagged icy splinters.

I breathe in big noisy gulps because I'm drowning on air, and if I could cast a spell to stop time – suspend it for ever and ever, so that the cobwebs grew over my hair and the ducks stopped in the middle of their circles and the feathers lay still on the air, drifting through time for ever – then I would do it.

Pearl's limp little body is laid on the kitchen table but Auntie Mabel shoos us out of the room and across the passage to the front parlour. Patricia has already been dispatched to hospital. Gillian sits in an armchair and stares at her feet. The parlour smells of camphor and old wood. The only sound is the ticking of a carriage clock which chimes the quarter-hours with a tinkling carillon. I don't feel up to sitting in a chair and curl up instead in a little ball behind the sofa and I lie there, quite numb, hearing – not Pearl's dreadful words – but Gillian's.

As Patricia was dragged out of the pound, screaming and kicking, desperate to get back into the water and find Pearl, Gillian remained stranded on the island (they fetched a little rowing-boat eventually to get her off). As the men began their search for Pearl, Gillian jumped up and down like a savage in a story-book, executing her own personal tribal dance. Terrified that she'd be blamed for what had happened, she pointed at me and screamed until her lungs gave out, 'It was her, it was her, it was her. Ruby pushed her in, she pushed Pearl in the water. I saw her! I saw her!' and I just stood there, dumbstruck, staring at the frozen grass under the ice, where a long white feather from one of Auntie Mabel's geese had found a cold nest.

Kate Atkinson, 1995

2

The Nature of Sisters

INTRODUCTION

This section, the heart of the book, comes in three parts: first the two myths of sisterhood, unqualified love and unqualified hate, and thereafter the altogether messier, more ambiguous reality, sisterhood itself.

Altruism, then: purely sisterly love. 'Little birds in their nests agree,' says Beth in *Little Women*, to stop her sisters quarrelling. If sisterly quarrels are the reality, the birds which agree with each other are the myth of sisterhood, just like Beth herself. (Her sisters, fortunately, are not so perfect, to the relief of the rest of us.) Belonging to the same myth is the unconditional, selfless love of all those sweet sisters glorified in the second-rate Victorian children's books I once devoured, thereby filling myself with guilt feelings. Such altruism always puts the welfare of the sister or brother first, makes the sister willing to surrender her own freedom and opportunities for those of her siblings, and even, in extreme circumstances to die for one of them, Sophocles' Antigone, for instance (not that she's in the least sweet), risks death to give her brother honourable burial; the wild swans' sister stands at the stake for her brother's sake; in Auschwitz, Rena Gelissen promises to die with her sister, rather than let her die alone. (Most of us, fortunately, do not have to face such situations, and have no idea how we'd behave if we did.)

Altruism can, of course, be forced by genetics – compatible bone marrow may confront a not necessarily willing sister with the duty of surrendering some of hers to save her sister, as in one piece here. It may impose itself as a result of gender – look at Caroline Herschell or Dorothy Wordsworth; or of birth order, where, for instance, an elder sister has to help look after younger siblings in large or motherless families, as in the case of my mother's elder sister, or of Charlotte Brontë, come to that. In my generation, the half-hour between me and my twin sister was enough to make her take on the role of responsible elder sister, finding things I'd lost, getting me to school on time – 'Why don't you leave her to get on with it, and go off to school by yourself?' our mother would ask. 'But I can't just leave her,' protested my sister. In the course of this, naturally, she built up some of the resentments which are the underside of the much-vaunted sweetness, the myth of the perfect sister.

The evolutionary psychologists have suggested that sibling willingness to care for one another or even to surrender their own chance of reproducing has an evolutionary origin. Sisters and brothers, after all, have at least half their genes in common, so that a sister who forgoes her own marriage chances on behalf of her siblings or their children is helping some of her genes to survive in further generations. Stories of sisterly altruism among humans, such as the Bunner sisters or Saroj Pathak's 'The Trump Card', and, still more, stories of one sister acting as a surrogate womb for an infertile sister's child, might usefully be looked at in this way. Even where no progeny are involved there could be some echo of this behaviour.

Naturally, among humans reality is never so simple – and often ironic. (The elder Bunner sister's altruism in passing on her lover to her younger sister lands her in a bad marriage, and the sickly offspring does not survive.) The evolutionary case is more straightforward among animals, and still more so among some insects. Richard Dawkins describes ant and bee sisters as being three quarters genetically identical; for them it makes more sense to help raise siblings than to produce offspring sharing fewer of their genes. In many animal species, particularly those who live in matriarchal groups like lions and elephants, females are observed minding younger siblings or their sisters' young. Among many breeds of birds, offspring from earlier broods in a breeding season may be roped in to help feed nestlings from subsequent ones, while the young of some sea birds, and those of some animals – foxes, for instance – may delay their own breeding on behalf of younger sisters and brothers. Your sisters' offspring are, of course, less genetically close to you than your full sisters; but as they still carry some of your genes they are worth protecting, though not so much as your own young. Ostriches show precisely the evolutionary mathematics. If her sister is absent when some predator appears, a female ostrich will gather up her sister's chicks with her own. But she will place her own young at the centre of the group, the safest place, leaving her less genetically close nephews and nieces to face the danger on the outside.

So we come to the other myth: inimical sisters. Among female wild dogs, it seems, though sisters occasionally cohabit while breeding, their relations 'tend to be tense and hostile'. This sounds exactly like my father's two sisters, whose hostility, however, was both understandable and inevitable. My grandmother never much liked the elder one, my Aunt Olive. Even without her ill-luck in being born too soon after the death of my grandmother's beloved third son, she was very like her father and the opposite of her mother in everything. She had no sense of humour, and was also extremely stupid. Her beauty and her fine singing voice hardly helped – given her middle-class background, she would never have been allowed to make use of the latter professionally. And though her beauty attracted men, their admiration, reacting with her being under-valued at home, so went to her head that my grandmother never trusted her alone with them. One summer just after the First World War she even sent my ten-year-old father along as chaperone when Aunt Olive cycled to see boyfriends on a local air station. In the end she married a charming but naughty man whom my grand-mother could not stand. They not only failed to produce children – her miscarriages were blamed by her mother and her sister on her flightiness – but both were rumoured to have had affairs. A strong air of disapproval accompanied their visits to the family home. Her younger sister, Aunt Ruth, on the other hand, less beautiful, but much more intelligent, was loved by her mother, and was like her besides. She was very domestic, could sew and knit, and hated what they both called Abroad, spoken in tones of horror, as fervently as her mother. She married a far more solid and worthy man, and gave my grandparents three grandsons. She could hardly bring herself to cross the English Channel.

How the loved and the unloved sisters got on as children I don't know. Later, when I knew them, I lumped them together mainly because of the way both clung, sartorially, to the days of their youth. Aunt Olive, preferring the lean lines of thirties' clothes, turned thirties' ghost in widowhood; powdering her face with what looked like flour, she sat at the table still wearing her grey droop-brimmed hat, her fitted grey coat, whenever she came to lunch. Aunt Ruth wore her hair in a bun on the nape of her neck, with side puffs beside her ears; she wore long cardigans, long beads, very pointed shoes. I understood where she came from when the twenties' episodes of the *Forsyte Saga* first went out on television; my Aunt Ruth was Irene to the life. The circumstances of the sisters' final falling out, though, could stand for everything that predisposed them to dislike each other. Shortly after my grandmother's death, they were discussing how to divide her jewels when Aunt Olive said: 'There's only one thing I really want – Mummy's pearl necklace.' Aunt Ruth's hand flew at once, guiltily, to her neck; to the same pearl necklace given to her by her mother a month or two before – or so she claimed. Olive chose not to believe her, and after the bitter exchange that followed they never spoke to each other again. I don't think you can count some stilted small talk when they were both in their eighties and their dutiful younger brother, my father, perhaps unwisely, took them out together for the odd, excruciating pub lunch. The feud appalled my mother, whose only close relationship as a child had been with her sister. Before she died, she made all of us promise never to fight over property of any kind, nor have we, so far as I know.

That the myths of sisterly hatred – and love, too – are true is, of course, why the Cinderella stories remain so potent, both among those who identify with the beautiful and good younger sister, and among those who identify with the mocked, inimical and ugly older ones (though they might be less willing to admit it). But – and this is where we reach sisterhood itself – in actual relationships, the myths of love and of hate are rarely mutually exclusive. Some sisterhoods lurk nearer the hate end of the spectrum, others nearer the other end; most lie somewhere in between. Mixed feelings exist in relationships with symbolic sisters, too, our friends for instance, but at least we can choose those sisters; we can't choose our genetic ones. Having always been there, they have none of the allure of the stranger, offer no possibility of jumping over the family fence to the greener grass on the far side. Their very existence, let alone their presence, keeps us physically tethered to more prosaic pastures, to old ways of going on; that's one reason for resenting even well-loved siblings. But it is also the reason we love them – for, equally perversely, the very familiarity of sisters is part of their attraction. With sisters you can let down your guard. With them you have both a past and languages in common – the description inserted here of how bee sisters communicate is absolutely to the point and also apposite to the correspondence between sisters which follows. Siblings and long-term partners, too, are the only people who can finish your sentences for you. (Over-close sibling partnerships – as between twins – can lead to you never finishing your sentences, thereby driving friends or partners mad. I know.)

In the end, it is precisely the ambiguity of the feelings sisters have for each other that makes them interesting. Good writers about sisters all have in common a capacity to pin it down – it's no accident that some of the best writing comes in this section. Jane Austen (who had a notably loving relationship with her sister Cassandra) caught this ambiguity, at a time when much conventional fiction opted for the myths; she shows the mutually devoted Marianne and Elinor exasperating each other. Twentieth-century stories, of course, can be much more open about the tragic, comic, messy reality. For me, Jane Bowles catches better than any the pain and complexity of a bond that can only be escaped through death, and not even then, entirely. I wonder if she had a sister? I'm not sure I want to know.

A. ALTRUISTIC SISTERS

From Goblin Market

One may lead a horse to water,
Twenty cannot make him drink.
Though the goblins cuffed and caught her,
Coaxed and fought her,
Bullied and besought her,
Scratched her, pinched her black as ink,
Kicked and knocked her,
Mauled and mocked her,
Lizzie uttered not a word;
Would not open lip from lip
Lest they should cram a mouthful in:
But laughed in heart to feel the drip
Of juice that syruped all her face,
And lodged in dimples of her chin,
And streaked her neck which quaked like curd.
At last the evil people
Worn out by her resistance
Flung back her penny, kicked their fruit
Along whichever road they took,
Not leaving root or stone or shoot;
Some writhed into the ground,
Some dived into the brook
With ring and ripple,
Some scudded on the gale without a sound,
Some vanished in the distance.

In a smart, ache, tingle,
Lizzie went her way;
Knew not was it night or day;
Sprang up the bank, tore thro' the furze,
Threaded copse and dingle,

And heard her penny jingle
Bouncing in her purse, –
Its bounce was music to her ear.
She ran and ran
As if she feared some goblin man
Dogged her with gibe or curse
Or something worse:
But not one goblin skurried after,
Nor was she pricked by fear;
The kind heart made her windy-paced
That urged her home quite out of breath with haste
And inward laughter.

   She cried 'Laura', up the garden,
'Did you miss me?
Come and kiss me.
Never mind my bruises,
Hug me, kiss me, suck my juices
Squeezed from goblin fruits for you,
Goblin pulp and goblin dew.
Eat me, drink me, love me;
Laura, make much of me:
For your sake I have braved the glen
And had to do with goblin merchant men.'

   Laura started from her chair,
Flung her arms up in the air,
Clutched her hair:
'Lizzie, Lizzie, have you tasted
For my sake the fruit forbidden?
Must your light like mine be hidden,
Your young life like mine be wasted,
Undone in mine undoing
And ruined in my ruin,
Thirsty, cankered, goblin-ridden?' –
She clung about her sister,
Kissed and kissed and kissed her:
Tears once again

Refreshed her shrunken eyes,
Dropping like rain
After long sultry drouth;
Shaking with anguish fear, and pain,
She kissed and kissed her with a hungry mouth.

[. . .]

   Swift fire spread through her veins, knocked at
      her heart,
Met the fire smouldering there
And overbore its lesser flame;
She gorged on bitterness without a name:
Ah! fool, to choose such part
Of soul-consuming care!
Sense failed in the mortal strife:
Like the watch-tower of a town
Which an earthquake shatters down,
Like a lightning-stricken mast,
Like a wind-uprooted tree
Spun about,
Like a foam-topped waterspout
Cast down headlong in the sea,
She fell at last;
Pleasure past and anguish past,
Is it death or is it life?

   Life out of death.
That night long Lizzie watched by her,
Counted her pulse's flagging stir,
Felt for her breath,
Held water to her lips, and cooled her face
With tears and fanning leaves;
But when the first birds chirped about their eaves,
And early reapers plodded to the place
Of golden sheaves,
And dew-wet grass
Bowed in the morning winds so brisk to pass,

And new buds with new day
Opened of cup-like lilies on the stream,
Laura awoke as from a dream,
Laughed in the innocent old way,
Hugged Lizzie but not twice or thrice;
Her gleaming locks showed not one thread of grey,
Her breath was sweet as May
And light danced in her eyes.

Christina Rossetti, 1862

Twins' bad habits

A Russian woman who doesn't drink alcohol was tired of getting drunk, and her sister was tired of feeling sick from cigarettes when she doesn't smoke. The sisters are forty-eight-year-old Siamese twins who are joined at the trunk and share a circulatory system. When Dasha Krivoshlyapov drank, Masha Krivoshlyapov suffered. And when Masha smoked, Dasha suffered. They stopped their habits earlier this month, the Itar-Tass news agency reported yesterday. The sisters share two legs, but each has two arms.

– AP, Moscow

Independent, 1998

Whose Life is it Anyway?

The *News of the World* is heartily congratulating itself for persuading Susan Squires to reconsider donating her bone marrow to her sister Angela, who has leukaemia. Susan, who apparently has a phobia about hospitals, was unable even to ring her sister's consultant to discuss the procedure. No worries. The newspaper did it for her. Dr Paul Kelsey, a consultant haematologist, is reported to have popped over to Susan's house and offered a less invasive procedure in which immature blood cells are taken from her blood-stream. [. . .]

Pressurized is putting it mildly. In first reporting the story, the *News of the World* published a letter to Susan from her mother saying: 'Just writing to tell you Angela won't be here much longer.' The letter suggested that to save her sister she should be able to put up with some discomfort.

The newspaper reported how Angela's son pleaded with Susan to help and then shouted 'bitch' at her when this failed. In the newspaper's considered editorial view, 'She says she's scared of hospitals. If she sticks to her decision, she'll have a lot more to be frightened of: the utter contempt of every man, woman, and child in the country.'

The *News of the World* was not the only sophisticated media adviser. Other newspapers offered moving accounts of people who had donated various pieces of themselves to siblings (all apparently without any side-effects). GMTV had a sweet interview with a brother and sister which concluded with the sister saying something along the lines of, 'Well let's hope she does change her mind, otherwise she'll have a death on her hands.' And in case threats didn't work, that nice Dr Hilary offered to be on hand to assist Susan personally.

Luisa Dillner, *Guardian*, 29 April 1997

From Antigone

Scene, before the Royal Palace at Thebes. Time, early morning.
Enter ANTIGONE *and* ISMENE

ANTIGONE. Ismene, dear in very sisterhood,
    Do you perceive how Heaven upon us two
    Means to fulfil, before we come to die,
    Out of all ills that grow from Oedipus –

What not, indeed? for there's no sorrow or harm,
No circumstance of scandal or of shame
I have not seen, among your griefs, and mine.
And now again, what is this word they say
Our Captain-general proclaimed but now
To the whole city? Did you hear and heed?
Or are you blind, while pains of enemies
Are passing on your friends?

ISMENE.   Antigone,
To me no tidings about friends are come,
Pleasant or grievous, ever since we two
Of our two brothers were bereft, who died
Both in one day, each by the other's hand.
And since the Argive host in this same night
Took itself hence, I have heard nothing else,
To make me happier, or more miserable.

ANTIGONE. I knew as much; and for that reason made you
Go out of doors – to tell you privately.

ISMENE. What is it? I see you have some mystery.

ANTIGONE. What! has not Creon to the tomb preferred
One of our brothers, and with contumely
Withheld it from the other? Eteocles
Duly, they say, even as by law was due,
He hid beneath the earth, rendering him honour
Among the dead below; but the dead body
Of Polynices, miserably slain,
They say it has been given out publicly
None may bewail, none bury, all must leave
Unwept, unsepulchred, a dainty prize
For fowl that watch, gloating upon their prey!
This is the matter he has had proclaimed –
Excellent Creon! for your heed, they say,
And mine, I tell you – mine! and he moves hither,
Meaning to announce it plainly in the ears
Of such as do not know it, and to declare
It is no matter of small moment; he

Who does any of these things shall surely die;
The citizens shall stone him in the streets.
So stands the case. Now you will quickly show
If you are worthy of your birth or no.

ISMENE. But O rash heart, what good, if it be thus,
Could I effect, helping or hindering?

ANTIGONE. Look, will you join me? will you work with me?

ISMENE. In what attempt? What mean you?

ANTIGONE.   Help me lift
The body up –

ISMENE.   What, would you bury him?
Against the proclamation?

ANTIGONE.   My own brother
And yours I will! If you will not, I will;
I shall not prove disloyal.

ISMENE.   You are mad!
When Creon has forbidden it?

ANTIGONE.   From mine own
He has no right to stay me.

ISMENE.   Alas, O sister,
Think how our father perished! self-convict –
Abhorred – dishonoured – blind – his eyes put out
By his own hand! How she who was at once
His wife and mother with a knotted noose
Laid violent hands on her own life! And how
Our two unhappy brothers on one day
Each on his own head by the other's hand
Wrought common ruin! We now left alone –
Do but consider how most miserably
We too shall perish, if despite of law
We traverse the behest or power of kings.
We must remember we are women born,
Unapt to cope with men; and, being ruled
By mightier than ourselves, we have to hear
These things – and worse. For my part, I will ask
Pardon of those beneath, for what perforce
I needs must do, but yield obedience

> To them that walk in power; to exceed
> Is madness, and not wisdom.

ANTIGONE.   Then in future
> I will not bid you help me; nor henceforth,
> Though you desire, shall you, with my goodwill,
> Share what I do. Be what seems right to you;
> Him will I bury. Death, so met, were honour;
> And for that capital crime of piety,
> Loving and loved, I will lie by his side.
> Far longer is there need I satisfy
> Those nether Powers, than powers on earth; for there
> For ever must I lie. You, if you will,
> Hold up to scorn what is approved of Heaven!

ISMENE. I am not one to cover things with scorn;
> But I was born too feeble to contend
> Against the state.

ANTIGONE.   Yes, you can put that forward;
> But I will go and heap a burial mound
> Over my most dear brother.

ISMENE.   My poor sister,
> How beyond measure do I fear for you!

Sophocles, *c.*440 BC, translated by Sir George Young, 1906

The Johnson Sisters

'Would I have a baby for a best friend? I'm not sure,' Julie says, patting her belly. 'But I had no reservations about doing it for my sister and her husband.

'Some people who have heard what I'm doing have said to me, "There is no way I could do something like this for my sister." I can't understand that. To me it seems, gosh, well why wouldn't you, if that's what your sister and her husband need? I knew how badly they wanted a child and they couldn't have one. If it took me to do it, that's fine. I don't know what kind of relationship other sisters have but this seems normal to us. It's just not a big deal.'

'We were in the kitchen of Julie's apartment just after swimming at her pool,' Janet recollects. 'The whole family knew we'd been trying to have a baby for several years, and Julie just asked, "Would you want me to have a baby for you?"'

Two years would pass before Janet, who has a doctorate in maths education, was ready to consider her sister's proposal. By then, she'd been through the fertility clinic routine and thousands of dollars' worth of low- and high-tech procedures, including in-vitro fertilization.

[. . .]

They had every intention of using a doctor for the artificial insemination, but ran into difficulty finding a physician willing to assist them. That's when Janet remembered the turkey baster.

'I was watching one of those horrible Geraldo shows about an older husband and younger wife. They couldn't have children because his sperm count was low. So they used the sperm of his teenage son. It was casually reported they'd done the fertilization with a turkey baster. [. . .]'

It's okay to laugh. At the time they thought it was pretty hilarious, too. Nevertheless, Janet and her husband went baster shopping at a kitchen-supply store. Mark preferred a metal model, thinking it would be more sterile; Janet, concerned about her sister's comfort, thought it would be too cold, so they settled for a plastic bulb baster which they sterilized in their dishwasher. With the help of an ovulation kit, they figured out the right time of the month, and on the appointed day Julie came to their house.

'Mark did his thing,' Janet says with a big grin on her face, 'and he handed me the baster. I'd never used one and we hadn't practised how it worked, so when I took hold of the bulb I accidentally squeezed it and half the sperm came out. I thought, "Well, so much for this idea." But I gave it to Julie anyway and told her to keep her finger over the tip. We were all laughing.'

Julie went into the bedroom by herself. 'I didn't need any help. It was easier than putting in a tampon. Then I stood on my head up against the wall, and I played little mind games with myself not to get bored. After twenty minutes Janet came in and then we ate dinner.'

'We were all making jokes about what a fiasco it was, such a comedy of errors,' Janet says. 'We called it premature basting.' But they repeated the whole thing the next day, just in case it might work after all.

One month later, Julie's period was late. Despite two positive results with home pregnancy test kits, Janet couldn't believe they'd actually been successful.

'I was sure she'd read the instructions wrong. After eight years and a turkey baster, it couldn't be this easy.' A visit to the doctor's office confirmed that yes, it could. Janet remembers, 'When Julie called me, I kept saying, "You'll never have to buy us another present as long as you live. Not a birthday. Not an anniversary. Never."'

One thing these sisters are very clear about is who the baby belongs to. 'I've always thought of the baby as Janet and Mark's,' Julie says firmly. 'It will be my little niece or nephew.'

'I feel Julie isn't just giving us a baby, she's giving a person a life,' Janet says. 'We're all very lucky.'

[. . .]

John Franklin Wittley was born weighing in at seven pounds, twelve ounces. Both mothers and child are doing fine.

Carol Saline, 1994

From Bunner Sisters

Ann Eliza had become suddenly aware that Mr Ramy was looking at her with unusual intentness. Involuntarily her hand strayed to the thin streaks of hair on her temples, and thence descended to straighten the brooch beneath her collar.

'You're looking very well today, Miss Bunner,' said Mr Ramy, following her gesture with a smile.

'Oh,' said Ann Eliza nervously. 'I'm always well in health,' she added.

'I guess you're healthier than your sister, even if you are less sizeable.'

'Oh, I don't know. Evelina's a mite nervous sometimes, but she ain't a bit sickly.'

'She eats heartier than you do; but that don't mean nothing,' said Mr Ramy.

Ann Eliza was silent. She could not follow the trend of his thought, and she did not care to commit herself further about Evelina before she had ascertained if Mr Ramy considered nervousness interesting or the reverse.

But Mr Ramy spared her all further indecision.

'Well, Miss Bunner,' he said, drawing his stool closer to the counter, 'I guess I might as well tell you fust as last what I come here for today. I want to get married.'

Ann Eliza, in many a prayerful midnight hour, had sought to strengthen herself for the hearing of this avowal, but now that it had come she felt pitifully frightened and unprepared. Mr Ramy was leaning with both elbows on the counter, and she noticed that his nails were clean and that he had brushed his hat; yet even these signs had not prepared her!

At last she heard herself say, with a dry throat in which her heart was hammering: 'Mercy me, Mr Ramy!'

'I want to get married,' he repeated. 'I'm too lonesome. It ain't good for a man to live all alone, and eat noding but cold meat every day.'

'No,' said Ann Eliza softly.

'And the dust fairly beats me.'

'Oh, the dust – I know!'

Mr Ramy stretched one of his blunt-fingered hands toward her. 'I wisht you'd take me.'

Still Ann Eliza did not understand. She rose hesitatingly from her seat, pushing aside the basket of buttons which lay between them; then she perceived that Mr Ramy was trying to take her hand, and as their fingers met a flood of joy swept over her. Never afterwards, though every other word of their interview was stamped on her memory beyond all possible forgetting, could she recall what he said while their hands touched; she only knew that she seemed to be floating on a summer sea, and that all its waves were in her ears.

'Me – me?' she gasped.

'I guess so,' said her suitor placidly. 'You suit me right down to the ground, Miss Bunner. Dat's the truth.'

A woman passing along the street paused to look at the shop-window, and Ann Eliza half hoped she would come in; but after a desultory inspection she went on.

'Maybe you don't fancy me?' Mr Ramy suggested, discountenanced by Ann Eliza's silence.

A word of assent was on her tongue, but her lips refused it. She must find some other way of telling him.

'I don't say that.'

'Well, I always kinder thought we was suited to one another,' Mr Ramy continued, eased of his momentary doubt. 'I always liked de quiet style – no fuss and airs, and not afraid of work.' He spoke as though dispassionately cataloguing her charms.

Ann Eliza felt that she must make an end. 'But, Mr Ramy, you don't understand. I've never thought of marrying.'

Mr Ramy looked at her in surprise. 'Why not?'

'Well, I don't know, har'ly.' She moistened her twitching lips. 'The fact is, I ain't as active as I look. Maybe I couldn't stand the care. I ain't as spry as Evelina – nor as young,' she added, with a last great effort.

'But you do most of de work here, anyways,' said her suitor doubtfully.

'Oh, well, that's because Evelina's busy outside; and where there's only two women the work don't amount to much. Besides, I'm the oldest; I have to look after things,' she hastened on, half pained that her simple ruse should so readily deceive him.

'Well, I guess you're active enough for me,' he persisted. His calm determination began to frighten her; she trembled lest her own should be less staunch.

'No, no,' she repeated, feeling the tears on her lashes. 'I couldn't, Mr Ramy, I couldn't marry. I'm so surprised. I always thought it was Evelina – always. And so did everybody else. She's so bright and pretty – it seemed so natural.'

'Well, you was all mistaken,' said Mr Ramy obstinately.

'I'm so sorry.'

He rose, pushing back his chair.

'You'd better think it over,' he said, in the large tone of a man who feels he may safely wait.

'Oh no, no. It ain't any sorter use, Mr Ramy. I don't never mean to marry. I get tired so easily – I'd be afraid of the work. And I have such awful headaches.' She paused, racking her brain for more convincing infirmities.

'Headaches, do you?' said Mr Ramy, turning back.

'My, yes, awful ones, that I have to give right up to. Evelina has to do everything when I have one of them headaches. She has to bring me my tea in the mornings.'

'Well, I'm sorry to hear it,' said Mr Ramy.

'Thank you kindly all the same,' Ann Eliza murmured. 'And please don't – don't –' She stopped suddenly, looking at him through her tears.

'Oh, that's all right,' he answered. 'Don't you fret, Miss Bunner. Folks have got to suit themselves.' She thought his tone had grown more resigned since she had spoken of her headaches.

For some moments he stood looking at her with a hesitating eye, as though uncertain how to end their conversation; and at length she found courage to say (in the words of a novel she had once read): 'I don't want this should make any difference between us.'

'Oh, my, no,' said Mr Ramy, absently picking up his hat.

'You'll come in just the same?' she continued, nerving herself to the effort. 'We'd miss you awfully if you didn't. Evelina, she –' She paused, torn between her desire to turn his thoughts to Evelina, and the dread of prematurely disclosing her sister's secret.

'Don't Miss Evelina have no headaches?' Mr Ramy suddenly asked.

'My, no, never – well, not to speak of, anyway. She ain't had one for ages, and when Evelina *is* sick she won't never give in to it,' Ann Eliza declared, making some hurried adjustments with her conscience.

'I wouldn't have thought that,' said Mr Ramy.

'I guess you don't know us as well as you thought you did.'

'Well, no, that's so; maybe I don't. I'll wish you good day, Miss Bunner;' and Mr Ramy moved toward the door.

'Good day, Mr Ramy,' Ann Eliza answered.

She felt unutterably thankful to be alone. She knew the crucial moment of her life had passed, and she was glad that she had not fallen below her own ideals. It had been a wonderful experience, full of undreamed-of fear and fascination; and in spite of the tears on her cheeks she was not sorry to have known it. Two facts, however, took the edge from its perfection: that it had happened in the shop, and that she had not had on her black silk.

Edith Wharton, 1892/1916

From The Selfish Gene

Social insect individuals are divided into two main classes, bearers and carers. The bearers are the reproductive males and females. The carers are the workers – infertile males and females in the termites, infertile females in all other social insects. Both types do their job more efficiently because they do not have to cope with the other. But from whose point of view is it efficient? The question which will be hurled at the Darwinian theory is the familiar cry: 'What's in it for the workers?'

Some people have answered, 'Nothing.' They feel that the queen is having it all her own way, manipulating the workers by chemical means to her own selfish ends, making them care for her own teeming brood. [. . .] The opposite idea is that the workers 'farm' the reproductives, manipulating them to increase their productivity in propagating replicas of the workers' genes. To be sure, the survival machines that the queen makes are not offspring to the workers, but they are close relatives nevertheless. It was Hamilton who brilliantly realized that, at least in the ants, bees, and wasps, the workers may actually be more closely related to the brood than the queen herself is! This led him, and later Trivers and Hare, on to one of the most spectacular triumphs of the selfish gene theory. The reasoning goes like this.

Insects of the group known as the Hymenoptera, including ants, bees, and wasps, have a very odd system of sex determination. Termites do not belong to this group and they do not share the same peculiarity. A hymenopteran nest typically has only one mature queen. She made one mating flight when young and stored up the sperms for the rest of her long life – ten years or even longer. She rations the sperms out to her eggs over the years, allowing the eggs to be fertilized as they pass out through her tubes. But not all the eggs are fertilized. The unfertilized ones develop into males. A male therefore has no father, and all the cells of his body contain just a single set of chromosomes (all obtained from his mother) instead of a double set (one from the father and one from the mother) as in ourselves. [. . .]

A female hymenopteran, on the other hand, is normal in that she does have a father, and she has the usual double set of chromosomes in each of her body cells. Whether a female develops into a worker or a queen depends not on her genes but on how she is brought up. That is to say, each female has a complete set of queen-making genes, and a complete set of worker-making genes (or, rather, sets of genes for making each specialized caste of worker, soldier, etc.). Which set of genes is 'turned on' depends on how the female is reared, in particular on the food she receives.

Although there are many complications, this is essentially how things are. We do not know why this extraordinary system of sexual reproduction evolved. No doubt there were good reasons, but for the moment we must just treat it as a curious fact about the Hymenoptera. [. . .] It means that the sperms of a single male, instead of all being different as they are in ourselves, are all exactly the same. A male has only a single set of genes in each of his body cells, not a double set. Every sperm must therefore receive the full set of genes rather than a 50 per cent sample, and all sperms from a given male are therefore identical. [. . .]

Things start to get intriguing when we come to sisters. Full sisters not only share the same father: the two sperms that conceived them were identical in every gene. The sisters are therefore equivalent to identical twins as far as their paternal genes are concerned. If one female has a gene *A*, she must have got it from either her father or her mother. If she got it from her mother then there is a 50 per cent chance that her sister shares it. But if she got it from her father, the chances are 100 per cent that her sister shares it. Therefore the relatedness between hymenopteran full sisters is not ½ as it would be for normal sexual animals, but ¾.

It follows that a hymenopteran female is more closely related to her full sisters than she is to her offspring of either sex. As Hamilton realized (though he did not put it in quite the same way) this might well predispose a female to farm her own mother as an efficient sister-making machine. A gene for vicariously making sisters replicates itself more rapidly than a gene for making offspring directly. Hence worker sterility evolved. It is presumably no accident that true sociality, with worker sterility, seems to have evolved no fewer than eleven times *independently* in the Hymenoptera and only once in the whole of the rest of the animal kingdom, namely in the termites.

Richard Dawkins, 1978

From The Trump Card

But why should I bother? Let the husband and wife acquire the capacity to build their life on their own strength. Why should I be concerned?

But let there be some caution. Let not Pappu's meals become irregular. He may not have his afternoon snacks, but at least his two meals . . . and his joy of going to school with the satchel should not be shattered.

When I leave this house, I shall take a roundabout route to my office by bus number 27, so that if Pappu turns that way, I can occasionally jump off the bus and remanage into his satchel to ensure that he is studying well. Even while returning from office at six, I would be able to hear in Pappu's mischievous voice how the affairs of that household have gone to pieces.

'Aunty's charge!' This woman, unmarried and unowned, has great affection for Pappu. But now, how long and for whose sake to strive frantically to collect the provident fund? For Pappu, of course! Is that so? Really? That was their idea, wasn't it?

The unmarried sister going on supporting her brother and his wife . . . How long? Till the moment of death? Discussions about sarees, fashions, jewellery, material things of life, desire to maintain the standard of living . . . and altercations day in and day out . . . all for the sake of keeping the house intact!

I have spent forty-two years of my life wondering where something had snapped, where it needed to be joined, who had to be supported in what manner – maintaining my chastity and keeping my spinsterhood pure.

If I had been in a position to live a life of my desire, I would have gone a long way, spending my time with the in-laws. But this? I am here to protect the brick of my father's house. In that house, I sacrificed, for the sake of the generation that followed my father, my youth, my aspiration, my longing for a married life. And now, in the new generation, Romi and Pappu have grown.

Already twelve years . . . Pappu is twelve years old. He, too, would grow into a young man . . . 'Aunty, you understand nothing at all! I have got to have the guide. And I must have eight annas as my pocket money. And because my parents beat me, I must have Aunty's protection!'

Whatever his Aunty says would always assure him that he would be a great prince after studying a lot. And bhabhi would sleep in peace. 'Well, let Aunty bother her head. She has brought up Pappu. She would bring up Romi now. Why should we worry?' After Romi, some other baby-cry, and then some illness, delivery trouble, operation – in every situation, Aunty is coming handy, is she?

Saroj Pathak, 1982

From The Wild Swans

An innumerable concourse of people crowded together to witness the burning of the witch. A miserable horse, a walking skeleton, dragged the cart in which she sat. A loose smock of sackcloth had been thrown over her, and her beautiful long hair hung down upon her shoulders, surrounding her noble face, childishly pious, like that of an angel. She was as pale as death, and there was a scarcely perceptible movement of her lips, whilst her fingers with strained velocity strove to finish the almost-accomplished task, which she would not give up, even on her way to death. At her feet lay the ten finished shirts.

'Look at the witch!' the rabble cried, 'how she presses her lips together. There is no hymn-book in her hands – no, she is going on with her horrid sorcery. Let us tear the satanic work into a thousand shreds.'

They began to press upon her, intending to deprive her of the fruits of the noblest sisterly sacrifice and love, when eleven white swans surrounded her, and the crowd fell back in terror.

'That is a sign from heaven of her innocence,' many whispered, but they dared not say it out loud.

The executioner now laid hold of the unfortunate Princess's hand, when hastily she threw the eleven shirts over the swans, and in their places there suddenly stood eleven handsome Princes; but the youngest of them had a swan's wing instead of one of his arms, for one sleeve was wanting to his shirt, though his good sister Eliza had striven with unexampled industry to finish it.

'Now I may speak,' she said. 'I am innocent.'

And the people, who saw what had happened, bowed down before her, as before a saint, whilst she sank lifeless into her brothers' arms, so violently had anxiety, fear, and pain affected her.

'Yes, she is innocent!' her eldest brother exclaimed.

Hans Andersen, 1835

From Caroline Lucretia Herschel, Memoir

During this summer I lost the only female acquaintances (not friends) I ever had an opportunity of being very intimate with by Bulmer's family returning again to Leeds. For my time was so much taken up with copying music and practising, besides attendance on my brother when polishing, since by way of keeping him alive I was constantly obliged to feed him by putting the victuals by bits into his mouth. This was once the case when, in order to finish a seven-foot mirror, he had not taken his hands from it for sixteen hours together. In general he was never unemployed at meals, but was always at those times contriving or making drawings of whatever came in his mind. Generally I was obliged to read to him whilst he was at the turning lathe or polishing mirrors, *Don Quixote*, *Arabian Nights' Entertainment*, the novels of Sterne, Fielding, &c.; serving tea and supper without interrupting the work with which he was engaged . . . and sometimes lending a hand. I became in time as useful a member of the workshop as a boy might be to his master in the first year of his apprenticeship. [. . .]

My brother began his series of sweeps when the instrument was yet in a very unfinished state, and my feelings were not very comfortable when every moment I was alarmed by a crack or fall, knowing him to be elevated fifteen feet or more on a temporary cross-beam instead of a safe gallery. [. . .]

That my fears of danger and accidents were not wholly imaginary, I had an unlucky proof on the night of the 31 December. The evening had been cloudy, but about ten o'clock a few stars became visible, and in the greatest hurry all was got ready for observing. My brother, at the front of the telescope, directed me to make some alteration in the lateral motion, which was done by machinery, on which the point of support of the tube and mirror rested. At each end of the machine or trough was an iron hook, such as butchers use for hanging their joints upon, and having to run in the dark on ground covered a foot deep with melting snow, I fell on one of these hooks, which entered my right leg above the knee. My brother's call, 'Make haste!' I could only answer by a pitiful cry, 'I am hooked!' He and the workmen were instantly with me, but they could not lift me without leaving nearly two ounces of my flesh behind. The workman's wife was called, but was afraid to do anything, and I was obliged to be my own surgeon by applying aquabusade and tying a kerchief about it for some days, till Dr Lind, hearing of my accident, brought me ointment and lint, and told me how to use them. At the end of six weeks I began to have some fears about my poor limb, and asked again for Dr Lind's opinion: he said if a soldier had met with such a hurt he would have been entitled to six weeks' nursing in a hospital. I had, however, the comfort to know that my brother was no loser through this accident, for the remainder of the night was cloudy, and several nights afterwards afforded only a few short intervals favourable for sweeping, and until 16 January there was no necessity for my exposing myself for a whole night to the severity of the season.

Caroline Herschel, published 1876

William and Dorothy Wordsworth

William Wordsworth on his sister Dorothy

She is my eyes and ears . . .

*

She in the midst of all, preserved me still
A poet, made me seek beneath that name
My office upon earth and nowhere else.

From *The Prelude*

Dorothy Wordsworth on William

I am very sure that love will never bind me closer to any human being than Friendship binds me to William, my earliest, my dearest Male Friend.

*

When I think of Winter I hasten to furnish our little Parlour. I close the Shutters, set out the Tea-table, brighten the Fire. When our Refreshment is ended I produce our work, and William brings his book to our Table and contributes at once to our Instruction and amusement, and at Intervals we lay aside the Book and each hazard our observations upon what has been read without fear of ridicule or Censure. We talk over past days, we do not sigh for Pleasures beyond our humble Habitation, 'The central point of all our joys.'

Dorothy Wordsworth to Jane Pollard, 16 February 1793

*

Wednesday, 14th [April 1802]. William did not rise till dinner time. I walked with Mrs C. I was ill out of spirits – disheartened. Wm and I took a long walk in the Rain.

Thursday, 15th. It was a threatening misty morning – but mild. We set off after dinner from Eusemere. Mrs Clarkson went a short way with us but turned back. The wind was furious and we thought we must have returned. [. . .] When we were in the woods beyond Gowbarrow park we saw a few daffodils close to the water side. We fancied that the lake had floated the seeds ashore and that the little colony had so sprung up. But as we went along there were more and yet more and at last under the boughs of the trees, we saw that there was a long belt of them along the shore, about the breadth of a country turnpike road. I never saw daffodils so beautiful they grew among the mossy stones about and about them, some rested their heads upon these stones as on a pillow for weariness and the rest tossed and reeled and danced and seemed as if they verily laughed with the wind that blew upon them over the lake, they looked so gay ever glancing ever changing. The wind blew directly over the lake to them. There was here and there a little knot and a few stragglers a few yards higher up but they were so few as not to disturb the simplicity and unity and life of that one busy highway. We rested again and again. The bays were stormy, and we heard the waves at different distances and in the middle of the water like the sea. [. . .]

Dorothy Wordsworth, *The Grasmere Journals*

Jung

Jung's sister Gertrude was also very helpful, mostly, I believe, in typing his manuscripts.

Barbara Hannah, *Jung, His Life and His Works*, 1977

From The Sisters

She went up to the attic. The top of the house was engulfed in a deep silence, rats and bats peopled the spiral staircases. Drusille arrived finally before a door which she opened with a large key attached to a chain around her neck.

'Juniper?' she said. 'Are you there?'

'As usual,' answered a voice out of the gloom. 'I don't move.'

'I've brought you something to eat. Are you better today?'

'My health is always excellent, sister.'

'You're ill,' replied Drusille in an irritated voice. 'Poor little thing.'

'It's Thursday, isn't it?'

'Yes, as a matter of fact, it is Thursday.'

'Then I'm allowed a candle. Have you brought me one?'

Drusille hesitated a moment, then she spoke with an effort. 'Yes, I've brought you a candle. I am good to you.'

Silence.

Drusille lit the candle, illuminating a dirty little attic without windows. Perched on a rod near the ceiling, an extraordinary creature looked at the light with blinded eyes. Her body was white and naked; feathers grew from her shoulders and round her breasts. Her white arms were neither wings nor arms. A mass of white hair fell around her face, whose flesh was like marble.

'What have you brought me to eat?' she asked, jumping on her perch.

The moment she saw the creature moving, Drusille slammed the door behind her. But Juniper had eyes for nothing but the honey.

'You've got to make it last at least six days,' Drusille said.

Juniper ate for some time in silence.

'Drink,' she said finally. Drusille held out a glass of water, but Juniper shook her head.

'Not that, not today. I need red . . .'

Drusille laughed. 'No you don't . . . Last time you drank red, you bit me. It excites you too much. Water's good for thirst.'

'Red,' insisted Juniper in a monotonous voice. 'Else I'll scream.'

With a quick gesture, Drusille brought a knife from between her breasts. She held it to her sister's throat, who jumped on her perch with raucous cries, like a peacock.

A little later Juniper spoke in a tear-choked voice. 'I don't mean you harm, I only want a small glass, no more. I'm so thirsty, so thirsty. Dear Drusille, I want only a single drop . . . and afterwards a look at the beautiful new moon for five minutes . . . Nobody will see me, nobody, I promise you, I swear it. I'll lie on the roof and look at the moon. I won't go away, I'll come back once I've seen the moon.'

Drusille laughed silently. 'And then what? Perhaps you'd like me to catch the moon to light up your attic? Listen, Juniper. You're ill, very ill. I only want what's best for you, and if you go out on the roof you'll catch cold, you'll die . . .'

'If I don't see the moon tonight, I'll be dead tomorrow.'

Drusille screamed with rage. 'Will you please shut up? Isn't what I do for you enough?'

Suddenly the two sisters head the noise of a car approaching below. The servants began to shout orders and insult one another.

'I have to go now,' announced Drusille, trembling. 'Go to sleep.'

'Who is it?' Juniper hopped on her perch.

'Mind your own business,' replied Drusille.

'Rats, bats, and spiders are my business.'

'I've given you socks to knit. Go knit.'

Juniper lifted her strange arms as if wanting to fly away. 'My hands aren't made for knitting.'

'Then knit with your feet.' And Drusille left so hastily she forgot to lock the door behind her.

Leonora Carrington, 1989

From The Fate of the Elephant

A related study by Phyllis Lee, who worked with the Amboseli team, concerned allomothers – the immature females who help take care of older females' babies within the family. As early as age three, females begin looking after their little brothers, sisters, or cousins, keeping the infants out of trouble and alerting the mother if serious danger develops.

Douglas Chadwick, 1992

From unpublished autobiography

When she left home in April 1938, I missed her. How badly, I only discovered, by the urge to write to her daily. The letters were often written in the classroom, during lessons, rendering me inattentive to the teachers.

When the war broke out, the longing to be reunited with her become a magnet which was responsible for my *idée fixe*, of 'going' to Palestine.

Mother wrung her hands. 'Day dreaming again! Going to Palestine in the middle of the war? It's crazy!'

Father, the incurable optimist, tried to reassure her. 'Let her go and find out for herself that leaving home is no picnic! She'll soon come running back home. Just wait and see.'

For safety, he ordered my older brother to be my chaperon until our speedy return. This, in turn, saved my brother's life. One could say that the combined unreasonableness – first my sister's ideological zeal, followed by my *idée fixe* – produced incalculable survival consequences for my brother. [. . .]

[My sister] was determined to get me out of Vilno. If there was any chance to get Jews out of Europe, her 'little' sister had to be amongst them. Much later in life I learned what it involved. In spite of her limited resources and social connections, she never gave up the hope of finding a way to get me to Palestine. She wrote letters to the High Commissioner, pleading for special consideration. The 'White Paper' restrictions on Jewish immigration to Palestine, instigated before the outbreak of the war, was still binding. But minors were outside this rule, which gave my sister hope. She besieged the Youth Aliyah organization, whose task it was to try to scoop up from war-torn Europe as many children as possible, bring them to safety and eventually to Palestine. But even for minors, the number of certificates and financial resources were restricted. Henrietta Szold, the distinguished director of the Youth Aliya organization, had the final say in the selection. In despair, failing to get an interview with her deputy, my sister decided to seek out Henrietta Szold herself at her Jerusalem residence. She kept up her vigil on Henrietta Szold's doorstep until, late one evening, she had a chance to pounce on her. My sister pleaded for her intervention. Touched by the eighteen-year-old girl's devotion to her sister, she invited her in. Once inside, my sister produced a bundle of my letters. She read aloud one of them which described my loneliness and despair. That did it, I was put on the list! Sadly, the process of 'selection' meant that for each new name placed on the list, somebody else's had to be crossed off. Being 'selected', or chosen to stay alive (a tragic term rooted in the Nazi practice in the death camps), is a blessing and a curse. It sits oppressively on my consciousness. Although, at the time, neither my sister nor I could have known that her fight to get me to Palestine was a life saver.

Mira Hamermesh, 1997

From Rena's Promise

I am concerned about Danka's depression. She doesn't seem to care about getting her own bowl of soup. This is something beyond her fear of the kapos serving the food. She seems so downtrodden, as if she's giving up on any hope of survival and this depression is eating away at her soul. She is absent; her eyes are glazed over most of our waking hours. I don't think that she's too far away, but I know I must try to do something before she goes beyond my grasp. Struggling with what to do about my sister's failing faith, I finally decide that there is no other course but to confront her.

It is late. The rest of the block is sleeping fitfully. 'Danka,' I whisper into the dark, 'are you asleep yet?'

'No.'

'What's bothering you? Something's wrong, I know it. Why're you so sad?'

'I don't know.'

'Please talk to me. How can I help you if I don't know what's going on in your head? I feel you shrinking away from me. You have to tell me what's wrong.'

'What sense is there to this?'

'To Auschwitz-Birkenau?' I'm puzzled.

'To everything.' She pauses. 'What if there's a selection and I'm selected to die?'

'What makes you say that?'

'You look better than me. You aren't losing so much weight and you're still strong. What if I can't make it?' Slowly it dawns on me.

'Remember those two sisters?' I take her hand. 'And how the one begged to go with the other one?' She nods in the shadows. 'I will do the same, if it comes to that.'

'They don't allow it all the time, though. That was the first selection. They were soft. Now if someone begs to go with their mama, or sister, or daughter, they laugh and push them away.'

'I will do whatever it takes, even if I must strike the SS.'

'Then they will kill you immediately – that's no good.'

There is something else lurking behind her eyes. It isn't dying alone she's afraid of, but I'm not sure which fear is possessing her. 'What is it you're really afraid of?'

'Being thrown in the truck,' she confesses. 'They treat us like rotten meat . . . I don't want to be discarded like that, thrown on to the flatbeds . . . I'm afraid of what Erna said. Maybe there won't be enough gas, and I'll go into the crematorium still alive . . . What if they're trying to conserve the gas?'

I cannot answer that question. I cannot give her any promises or assurances that there will be enough gas to kill us when we arrive at the ultimate destination of all prisoners in Auschwitz-Birkenau. I cannot promise her that because I cannot lie to my sister, but I can promise one thing.

Everyone is sleeping around us, but with everyone talking out of their heads all the time anyway, no one pays us any attention – it's too commonplace to hear voices and screams in the night.

'Sit up, Danka. Come on, sit up.' I hold out my hand. 'You see my hand here.' I put her hand on mine and look into her eyes. 'Our parents are standing here in front of us and my hand is the Holy Book and on this book and before our parents I make this oath to you: that from this day on, if you are selected I will join you no matter what. I swear that you will not go on to the trucks alone.'

It is pitch-black in the blocks, but I can almost see the light flicker back on in my sister's eyes as I make this promise. Exhausted, I release her hand and we fall back against the cold wood, pulling our blanket close around our bodies. Sleep comes swiftly, carrying us away to a land where there are no shadows.

At lunch the next day, Danka stands in line and receives her first full helping of soup in months.

Rena Gellisen, 1997

From Goblin Market

For there is no friend like a sister
In calm or stormy weather:
To cheer one on the tedious way,
To fetch one if one goes astray,
To lift one if one totters down
To strengthen while one stands.

Christina Rossetti, 1862

B. INIMICAL SISTERS

The Mitfords

NANCY MITFORD. Sisters are a defence against life's cruel circumstances.

JESSICA MITFORD. Sisters *are* life's cruel circumstances.

From The Sisters

Nina said, 'Do you remember that ghastly school? It was the only part of our childhood that I would change. That awful grim building and those bloody nuns.' I stared in astonishment. 'Grim? It was a lovely building and the nuns were so kind.' We stared at each other blankly, our memories lying between us like a bridge, the same bridge but seen from different sides.

Nergis Dalal, 1973

From Savata, My Fair Sister

Until one day I was told by the Lord to go visit Savata and to reason out with her, to try to help her. I went to the Bishop's Lodgings, and what did I find but good Persian rugs on the floor, new satin slip covers on the furniture and I don't know what else. 'Savata,' I said, 'I hear you have a cluster of diamonds shape of the Star of David and a Persian lamb coat, added to all the rest of this display.' Where Savata had before a deep voice for preaching and for singing, she now had a little pussy voice that made me sick at my stomach. She was put-on from head to toe, and it was the working of Mr Canaan Johnson, believe you me.

'Savata, my fair sister,' I said, 'your voice has done changed, your hair has changed in colour toward the red side, I cannot believe you are my same sister. Let your sister look you over.'

Savata would not look me in the eye.

'You will not look your sister in the eye,' I said, 'but you will scan *her* over to a T to see how stout she is because of her diabetes and to see the varicose veins in her legs from carrying too much weight. I am still in the service of the Lord, despite my personal appearance.'

'You eat too much cream things,' said Savata.

To this I said right out, 'Savata let your sister see your diamonds and your Persian lamb.'

Savata was standoffish about it and said she did not display her private possessions openly. She said she wore them only around the house.

'This is around the house,' I said, 'so let me see you in them. I hear tell you blind your congregation with the diamond cluster on Sundays – let it shed a little of its light on your poor sister.'

She purred and said Canaan Johnson would not like her to display her things openly.

'How close can you get?' I queried her, 'in a room with your own flesh and blood kin?'

Savata prissed and said we had different fathers and I knew it. Now how uncharitable can you get?

Then I had to let go and tell Savata my true feelings, as the Lord had instructed me to if pressed, and for her good. I said, 'Savata you are a Daughter of Babylon and you know what that is. That man Canaan Johnson is laying up all day studying up while you're out working. He's bound to get the best of you in the end, if he hasn't already. You're paying him to. He is the Devil Incarnit. Will you please listen to your sister that you used to look for creesy-greens with in the marshes to make poke salad, that you walked barefooted with in the meadows, singing to Jesus. Remember your mother who raised you up under the apple trees. If you do not remember the days of your youth then may your tongue cleave to the roof of your mouth. We will discard the fact that you ran off to St Louis and danced in the Sepia Revue of 1952 and remember only that I rescued you up to Philadelphia and saved your soul and put you on the right track. Do not backslide!'

Oh I told her. 'You are the fair one,' I said, 'and you are marked off to do a special service by Jesus, and you are just having the wool pulled over your eyes by this studying man. He is smart, I grant you that, and knows Hebrew and studies up all day in his room; but he is studying up, at your expense, to leave you in the end; and pocket all your earnings in his pocket.'

Savata only whined back '*uh-huh*' in that ungodly Lana Turner voice. But I went on.

'You must withdraw him as business manager of the Light of the World Holiness Church and reinstate me before all is lost to the Devil. I have had to go back to house-cleaning because I have withdrawn myself from the Church. My preaching papers are laying dormant in my bureau drawer, but they are up to date. You know I am overweight and have sugar-poisoning to boot. Savata, my sister that the Lord blessed,' I intoned, '*will you listen to me?*'

But Savata stood calm and cold before me with her arms in a prissy position as if she was embracing herself . . . what that man Canaan Johnson had put into her, among other things, though he was very bright, granted.

William Goyen, 1963

Sisters

Why should the iron scrollwork
   Over windows
In this Islington-Byzantine church

Where we're listening to Mary Black
   And downing St Patrick's wine from plastic cups,
So sing to me of you?

I'm here in my life. You're elsewhere
   In yours. The whole thing's clear.
I'm fine. But all this overwrought

Victorian iron
   (That writhing flow and curl
Rock-hard against the night)

Won't let me be. It goes on shouting so
   Embarrassingly, vividly
Of you, I'm frightened. Women will get to know.

The ones all round me, all these *Guardian*
   Journalists: why don't they rise
In a body, bellowing *j'accuse*?

Ruth Padel, 1998

From Women in Love

Then there started a revulsion from Gudrun. She finished life off so thoroughly, she made things so ugly and so final. [. . .] And it was such a lie. This finality of Gudrun's, this dispatching of people and things in a sentence, it was all such a lie. Ursula began to revolt from her sister.

D. H. Lawrence, 1921

From Howards End

'Do you agree?' asked Margaret. 'Do you think music is so different to pictures?'

'I – I should have thought so, kind of,' he said.

'So should I. Now, my sister declares they're just the same. We have great arguments over it. She says I'm dense; I say she's sloppy.' Getting under way, she cried: 'Now, doesn't it seem absurd to you? What *is* the good of the Arts if they're interchangeable? What is the good of the ear if it tells you the same as the eye? Helen's one aim is to translate tunes into the language of painting, and pictures into the language of music. It's very ingenious, and she says several pretty things in the process, but what's gained, I'd like to know? Oh, it's all rubbish, radically false. If Monet's really Debussy, and

Debussy's really Monet, neither gentleman is worth his salt – that's my opinion.'

Evidently these sisters quarrelled.

E. M. Forster, 1910

From The Children of Sánchez

Consuelo's version

One morning, on Ash Wednesday, I arrived before the children left for school. Conchita, Manuel's youngest girl, came over to tell me that Marta had bathed them in cold water. It was very cold that day and naturally it made me angry, although I said nothing for fear of a quarrel. I told Concha not to worry but to put on her sweater. Marta was in the kitchen and without further ado she began to scream at me. 'And what business is it of yours, you daughter-of-a-whore!' She called me a rotting slut, a public whore, and things I cannot repeat. Then she wanted to hit me and, not being a saint I defended myself. I didn't want to fight but she was out of her mind, kicking and scratching and yelling insults. I still cannot explain why my sister always hated me.

Marta's version

Conchita complained to my sister that I had bathed her in cold water. That made Consuelo angry. She turned to me and said, 'If you had any shame you wouldn't even show your face.'

'Shame? What have I got to be ashamed about?'

'Sure. Even though my *papá* is supporting you, even though Manuel buys you your clothes and puts food in your mouth, you aren't able to take care of his children properly. It is obvious they are not your children. Manuel is supporting you and you do this to his kids!'

'Supporting me? He is not that good-hearted. If he barely gives enough for his children, he won't be giving to others.' Would you believe it? She said that to me, and it wasn't only Conchita who was bathed that way, but all of them. My sister kept it up, too.

'Your children are being supported, and you still have the nerve to be touchy.'

'Yes,' I said, 'but you are not the one who is supporting me. When did I ever ask you for anything?'

'Oh,' she says, 'then give me back all the clothes I gave you.'

'What clothes?' I had a few clothes then, but they were made out of dress lengths my *papá* brought me, or were ones I bought myself on payments. Consuelo had given me a little jumper and robe that didn't fit her. Her boss's wife had given her a bunch of clothes, but that was all she had passed on to me, because they were of no use to her. She kept telling me that she was the one who had been clothing me and it was a lie. If she ever gave me anything, it was old stuff that didn't fit her any more.

So I up and open the wardrobe. 'Go ahead, take out your dresses. If you think I have clothes of yours here, take them out.' It made me mad because she said that all I did was whore around, opening my legs so that they could give me kids. 'If it comes to whores, who knows who is a bigger one! All my children are from the same father. So far you haven't been a procuress for me, have you?'

It made me mad to hear her talk that way, especially because she went to live with Jaime after breaking up with Mario. Yes, she was stupid enough to go back to Jaime after losing her piece, as we say here, and of course it didn't work because all he did was take revenge on her for the times she had humiliated him. I don't know how it was that she didn't become pregnant . . . she says she didn't let him use her once, but I don't see how that is possible since they slept in the same bed. She got sick with anger and finally left Jaime. But later she began to paint herself up again and have nice clothes and manicures and who knows how she got them. She worked but spent all her money on rent and food and things for her new apartment. Naturally, what she earned wouldn't cover those expenses.

I reminded her of all that. 'Just because you have no children, doesn't prove a thing! Who knows how you get rid of them.'

I pulled out the jumper and ripped it. It had been too big for me and I had paid to remodel it, so I had the right to tear it.

'Here is your dress!'

'Miserable one!' That was her favourite word. 'Miserable fool! Don't tear my dress. Don't tear it!' When she saw it torn apart, she started for the wardrobe, to rip my clothes. 'Now, you'll see,' she yelled.

So I stepped in and tangled with her. We really fought, scratching and tearing each other's clothes. I didn't realize it until later. For the moment, I was so mad I couldn't see anything. Marí, who was pregnant then, came in and separated us. The children saw the whole thing and didn't make it to school that day. I didn't even notice when Consuelo left.

Oscar Lewis, 1962

From Les Enfants Terribles

Next day at table they were still kicking one another. Above the tablecloth their host saw smiling faces; a silent war went on below.

Jean Cocteau, 1929

From The Luong Sisters

In 1979, Saan was a skinny ten-year-old living in Vietnam, the youngest in a desperately poor family of five older sisters and one brother. At that time, the Communist rulers decreed that upon reaching fifteen, a child could be taken away to work for the country. Some children were never seen by their families again. [. . .] Saan's parents decided to try to save their littlest girl by pirating her out of Vietnam before the government came to look for her.

'My mother told me we were going to visit my grandmother in the country,' Saan begins. 'But the way we went was different, and she said we were going to stop at another place first.

'Just before we leave, everybody is unusually nice to me. My sisters buy me things, get me clothes, and I'm thinking, "Wow, this is a big change." Usually they're too busy to pay any attention to me. They even take me out to a restaurant, and we were so poor we could never afford to go out to eat. They know I'm going away. I don't.

'We got to this place and my mother left me with her friend and said she'd be back soon. But the boat had to take off before she came, or else the Communists would catch us. My uncle was supposed to be with me, but he got arrested. He yelled at me to run to the boat. I didn't know what was happening or where I was going. I just did what he told me. There were a hundred and fifty of us on a seventeen-foot boat. All I can see are strange people and I don't understand anything.'

[. . .]

The refugee camp on the Malaysian border where Saan was eventually interned housed seven thousand people. She was squeezed into a tiny hut with twenty-four others – including her mother's friend, whom she finally found.

[. . .]

After a year and a half in the refugee centre, Saan was relocated to Hawaii, where the daughter of her mother's friend lived. [. . .]

'Every day I go to school until two and I go to work until 9 p.m. And I think how different my life would be if I had my sisters with me. [. . .]

'I pray for my sisters to come here so they could help me and do the things older sisters are supposed to do for younger ones. I write them how I wish they were here so we can do things together and talk like American sisters do. They write back and say the same. So all the years go by, and I have these hopes and dreams that one day they'll come and we'll be so happy.'

[. . .] 'One year passed. Another year. Another year. Finally I just start writing to everybody.' Saan wrote to the embassy in Thailand, to her senator, to the US State Department, to one congressman after the other. Finally, in the fluorescent glare of an airport lounge, she was reunited with her parents and three of her five sisters – fourteen years after their separation. When she'd left them, she was a frail, sheltered Vietnamese child. Now she was a twenty-four-year-old American woman with a son and a daughter of her own.

'I was so happy and excited. I had my children draw the welcome signs in Chinese and Vietnamese. But once I see them in the airport, it's like they just see me yesterday. I cry, but there are no hugs or kisses. Not like a normal family. I think deep down inside they must be happy, too. But they don't show it. My dad and mom look glad to see me, but not my sisters. They don't seem to want to know anything about my life without them all these years.

'Then the next day, they tell me they want to go home. [. . .] It costs five thousand dollars to bring them here. I don't have money to send them back.

'They're always complaining. In Vietnam, they were spoiled. They never work a day. My mother took care of them. Here they have to work in a sewing factory. They say it's tough and boring and cold. Oh my god, this is not what I expected! I think my sisters will listen to what I have to say. They'll help me take care of my children so I can go back and get my high school degree. But nobody even wants to stay with me. [. . .]

'Every time we see each other, we can laugh and talk, but once we go down to something personal or deep, the party's over. Its doesn't matter how much older they are – one is thirty-five, one is thirty-four, and one is thirty-eight – or how young I am. We're supposed to talk to each other and take care of each other. But my connection with them has a line. We go so far and that's it.

'Part of me is in pain; they don't know anything I'm feeling. It hurts to see the three of them very close and good friends. They know everything about what the other wants and likes, but they say I can never be a part of them because I'm too American.

'Maybe it would be better if they hadn't come at all, and I just had my dream of what it would be like if we are all here, sisters together. Inside of me I love them. I try to think they love me too, even though they don't act like they do. I do have to accept that I can't change them. I can't force them to be what I want. I can't make them love me. That was just a dream.'

Carol Saline, 1994

From Women in Love

The two sisters were like a pair of scissors snipping off everything that came athwart them; or like a knife and a whetstone, the one sharpened against the other.

D. H. Lawrence, 1921

Florence and Parthenope Nightingale

I believe [Florence] has little or none of what is called charity or philanthropy. She is ambitious – very – and would like to regenerate the world with a grand *coup de main* or some fine institution, which is a very different thing. Here she has a circle of admirers who cry up everything she says or does as gospel. It is the intellectual part which interests her, not the manual. When she nursed me everything which intellect or kind intention could do was done but she was a shocking nurse. Whereas her influence on people's minds and her curiosity in getting into a variety of minds is insatiable, after she has got inside they generally cease to have any interest for her.

Parthenope Nightingale, 1855

'What have my mother and my sister ever done for me? They like my glory, they like my pretty things. Is there anything else they like in me?' Above all [Parthenope's] ungrateful and spiteful behaviour [. . .] [has] caused 'the disease which is now bringing me to my grave'.

Florence Nightingale, 1857, quoted Hugh Small, 1998

From Père Goriot

'Thank you, Delphine! In my present dreadful troubles I expected better of you: but then you never did care for me.'

'Oh, yes, she cares for you, Nasie,' cried Goriot, 'she was telling me so not long ago. We were talking about you, and she maintained that you were beautiful while she was only pretty.'

'Pretty!' repeated the Countess. 'She's as pretty as a cold hard iceberg!'

'Even if I were what you think me,' said Delphine, reddening, 'how have you behaved towards me? You cast me off, you closed the door of every house I wanted to visit against me, you have never missed an opportunity of making me suffer. And when did I ever come as you did to screw our poor father's fortune out of him, a thousand francs at a time, and reduce him to the plight he's in now? That's your work, my dear sister. I have come to see my father as often as I could. I did not turn him out of the house and then come and lick his hand when I needed him. I did not even know that he had spent that twelve thousand francs for me. I am careful and economical and you know it! Moreover I never asked Papa for the presents he has sometimes given me, I'm not a beggar.'

'You were better off than I was: Monsieur de Marsay was rich, as you have some reason to know. You were always as sordid and mean as people who care for money are. Goodbye, I have neither sister nor –'

'Hush, Nasie!' cried Goriot.

'Only a sister like you could repeat what no one believes any more, you're a horrid unnatural creature!' said Delphine.

'Children, children, hush! or I will kill myself before your eyes.'

'There, Nasie, I forgive you,' Madame de Nucingen said. 'You are unhappy. But I am kinder than you are. How could you say that to me just when I felt ready to do anything to help you, even to making it up with my husband, which I wouldn't do for my own sake, nor for –? But after all it's just like all the other cruel things you have done to me in the last nine years.'

'Children, children, kiss and be friends!' said their father. 'You are both angels.'

'No, let me alone!' screamed the Countess, shaking off the hand Goriot had laid on her arm. 'She has far less pity for me than my husband. Anyone would imagine she was the pattern of all the virtues!'

'I would rather people thought I owed money to Monsieur de Marsay, than confess that Monsieur de Trailles costs me more than two hundred thousand francs,' retorted Madame de Nucingen.

'Delphine!' cried the Countess, taking a step towards her.

'I only tell you the truth in return for your lies about me,' the Baroness said coldly.

'Delphine! you're a –'

She had no chance of finishing her sentence, for Goriot threw himself between the two sisters, laid one hand restrainingly on her arm and covered her mouth with the other.

'Goodness, Father! what on earth have you been handling this morning?' she said.

Honoré de Balzac, 1834

Gertrude Stein on Her Sister Berta

It is natural not to care about a sister, certainly when she is four years older and grinds her teeth at night.

From The Professor's House

Early in November there was a picturesque snowstorm, and that day Kathleen telephoned her father at the university, asking him to stop on his way home in the afternoon and help her to decide upon some new furs. As he approached McGregor's spick-and-span bungalow at four o'clock, he saw Louie's Pierce-Arrow standing in front, with Ned, the chauffeur and gardener, in the driver's seat. Just then Rosamond came out of the bungalow alone, and down the path to the sidewalk, without seeing her father. He noticed a singularly haughty expression on her face; her brows drawn together over her nose. The curl of her lips was handsome, but terrifying. He observed also something he had not seen before – a coat of soft, purple-grey fur, that quite disguised the wide, slightly stooping shoulders he regretted in his truly beautiful daughter. He called to her, very much interested. 'Wait a minute, Rosie. I've not seen that before. It's extraordinarily becoming.' He stroked his daughter's sleeve with evident pleasure. 'You know, these things with a kind of lurking purple and lavender in them are splendid for you. They make your colour prettier than ever. It's only lately you've begun to wear them. Louie's taste, I suppose?'

'Of course. He selects all my things for me,' said Rosamond proudly.

'Well, he does a good job. He knows what's right for you.' St Peter continued to look her up and down with satisfaction. 'And Kathleen is getting new furs. You were advising her?'

'She didn't mention it to me,' Rosamond replied in a guarded voice.

'No? And what do you call this, what beast?' he asked ingenuously, again stroking the fur with his bare hand.

'It's *taupe.*'

'Oh, moleskin!' He drew back a little. 'Couldn't be better for your complexion. And is it warm?'

'Very warm – and so light.'

'I see, I see!' He took Rosamond's arm and escorted her to her car. 'Give Louie my compliments on his choice.' The motor glided away – he wished he could escape as quickly and noiselessly, for he was a coward. But he had a feeling that Kathleen was watching him from behind the sash curtains. He went up to the door and made a long and thorough use of the foot-scraper before he tapped on the glass. Kathleen let him in. She was very pale; even her lips, which were always pink, like the inside of a white shell, were without colour. Neither of them mentioned the just-departed guest.

'Have you been out in the park, Kitty? This is a pretty little storm. Perhaps you'll walk over to the old house with me presently.' He talked soothingly while he took off his coat and rubbers. 'And now for the furs!'

Kathleen went slowly into her bedroom. She was gone a great while – perhaps ten actual minutes. When she came back, the rims of her eyes were red. She carried four large pasteboard boxes, tied together with twine. St Peter sprang up, took the parcel, and began untying the string. He opened the first and pulled out a brown stole. 'What is it, mink?'

'No, it's Hudson Bay sable.'

'Very pretty.' He put the collar round her neck and drew back to look at it. But after a sharp struggle Kathleen broke down. She threw off the fur and buried her face in a fresh handkerchief.

'I'm so sorry, Daddy, but it's no use today. I don't want any furs, really. She spoils everything for me.'

'Oh, my dear, my dear, you hurt me terribly!' St Peter put his hands tenderly on her soft hazel-coloured hair. 'Face it squarely, Kitty; you must not, you cannot, be envious. It's self-destruction.'

'I can't help it, Father. I *am* envious. I don't think I would be if she let me alone, but she comes here with her magnificence and takes the life out of all our poor little things. Everybody knows she's rich, why does she have to keep rubbing it in?'

'But, Kitty dear, you wouldn't have her go home and change her coat before coming to see you?'

'Oh, it's not that, Father, it's everything! You know we were never jealous of each other at home. I was always proud of her good looks and good taste. It's not her clothes, it's a feeling she has inside her. When she comes towards me, I feel hate coming towards me, like a snake's hate!'

St Peter wiped his moist forehead. He was suffering with her, as if she had been in physical anguish. 'We can't, dear, we can't, in this world, let ourselves think of things – of comparisons – like that. We are all too susceptible to ugly suggestions. If Rosamond has a grievance, it's because you've been untactful about Louie.'

'Even if I have, why should she be so revengeful? Does she think nobody else calls him a Jew? Does she think it's a secret? I don't mind being called a Gentile.'

'It's all in the way it's done, you know, Kitty. And you've shown that you were a little bored with all their new things, now haven't you?'

'I've shown that I don't like the way she overdresses, I suppose. I would never have believed that Rosie could do anything in such bad taste. While she is here among her old friends, she ought to dress like the rest of us.'

'But doesn't she? It seems to me her things look about like yours.'

'Oh, Father, you're so simple! And Mother is very careful not to enlighten you. We go to the Guild to sew for the Mission fund, and Rosie comes in in a handmade French frock that cost more than all our dresses put together.'

'But if hers are no prettier, what does it matter how much they cost?' He was watching Kathleen fearfully. Her pale skin had taken on a greenish tinge – there was no doubt about it. He had never happened to see that change occur in a face before, and he had never realized to what an ugly, painful transformation the common phrase 'green with envy' referred.

Willa Cather, 1925

From Rushen Coatie

There was once a king and a queen, as many a one has been; few have we seen, and as few may we see. But the queen died, leaving only one bonny girl, and she told her on her deathbed: 'My dear, after I am gone, there will come to you a little red calf, and whenever you want anything, speak to it, and it will give it you.'

Now, after a while, the king married again an ill-natured wife, with three ugly daughters of her own. And they hated the king's daughter because she was so bonny. So they took all her fine clothes away from her, and gave her only a coat made of rushes. So they called her Rushen Coatie, and made her sit in the kitchen nook, amid the ashes.

[. . .]

Then the young prince put out a proclamation that whoever could put on the glass slipper should be his bride. All the ladies of his court went and tried to put on the slipper. And they tried and tried and tried, but it was too small for them all. Then he ordered one of his ambassadors to mount a fleet horse and ride through the kingdom and find an owner for the glass shoe. He rode and he rode to town and castle, and made all the ladies try to put on the shoe. Many a one tried to get it on that she might be the prince's bride. But no, it wouldn't do, and many a one wept, I warrant, because she couldn't get on the bonny glass shoe. The ambassador rode on and on till he came at the very last to the house where there were the three ugly sisters. The first two tried it and it wouldn't do, and the queen, mad with spite, hacked off the toes and heels of the third sister, and she could then put the slipper on, and the prince was brought to marry her, for he had to keep his promise. The ugly sister was dressed all in her best and was put up behind the prince on horseback, and off they rode in great gallantry. But ye all know, pride must have a fall, for as they rode along a raven sang out of a bush –

> 'Hackèd Heels and Pinchèd Toes
> Behind the young prince rides,
> But Pretty Feet and Little Feet
> Behind the cauldron bides.'

'What's that the birdie sings?' said the young prince.

'Nasty lying thing,' said the stepsister, 'never mind what it says.'

But the prince looked down and saw the slipper dripping with blood, so he rode back and put her down. Then he said 'There must be some one that the slipper has not been tried on.'

'Oh, no,' said they, 'there's none but a dirty thing that sits in the kitchen nook and wears a rushen coatie.'

But the prince was determined to try it on Rushen Coatie, but she ran away to the grey stone, where the red calf dressed her in her bravest dress, and she went to the prince and the slipper jumped out of his pocket on to her foot, fitting her without any chipping or paring. So the prince married her that very day, and they lived happy ever after.

Retold by Joseph Jacobs, 1898

Korean Sisters

Lieutenant Tom Hume of the Irvine Police Department in California laid out the charges: Jeen Han, a twenty-two-year-old Korean woman, had plotted to kill Sunny, her identical twin sister, so that she could assume her identity. This was, said Hume, in a sound bite that was pounced upon with glee by the media, a classic case of 'the evil twin and the good twin'.

'It's almost like a movie plot,' added Sergeant Al Murray, helping to ensure that it soon might be. The details of the case were simple, if bizarre, explained the police in Irvine, an hour south of Los Angeles. Jeen and Sunny Han – Sunny is the elder twin by five minutes – had not been getting along for some time. Jeen, the 'evil twin', had escaped from prison and had hired two teenage boys to help her to kill Sunny, the 'good twin'.

Jeen believed that, with Sunny dead, she would be able to take her credit cards, her car, her whole life, said the police; no longer would she be dogged by her own criminal past and her poor credit history. 'Jeen Han wanted to eliminate Sunny, take over her residence and go on to lead a more beneficial life,' Murray told reporters.

It seemed that the Irvine police had everything worked out. But in November 1996, within days of conspiracy to murder and other charges being brought against Jeen Han and her two accomplices, Archie Bryant, sixteen, and John Sayarath, fifteen, events began to take a peculiarly American twist.

In a jailhouse interview, Jeen insisted that Sunny was making up the whole thing because she was angry with Jeen for having told Sunny's boyfriend secrets about her. These secrets were never revealed, but Sunny's boyfriend did subsequently dump her. 'I called my sister after I was arrested,' said Jeen. 'She said, "I wish you were dead." She told me that I should go to prison for twenty years. She's getting a kick out of me being in jail. She was really mad. She told me that I needed psychiatric help.'

What had actually happened that day, said Jeen, was that she had gone to Sunny's flat to retrieve her driver's licence and some clothes. She had only brought the boys along because she was scared of her sister. 'What my sister is saying is not true,' Jeen insisted. 'I'm fighting those charges.'

This defiance appeared to alarm Sunny. 'The good twin has moved out of her place,' Hume told reporters. 'She fears for her safety. She's got every reason to be scared – this scheme was pretty close to completion.'

By hyping the Han sisters as 'good and evil twins', the Irvine police, perhaps unconsciously, were tapping into an ancient myth that has often been used to explain man's dual nature.

The Times magazine, 28 January 1998

Sister Maude

Who told my mother of my shame,
  Who told my father of my dear?
Oh who but Maude, my sister Maude,
  Who lurked to spy and peer.

Cold he lies, as cold as stone,
   With his clotted curls about his face:
The comeliest corpse in all the world
   And worthy of a queen's embrace.

You might have spared his soul, sister,
   Have spared my soul, your own soul too:
Though I had not been born at all,
   He'd never have looked at you.

My father may sleep in Paradise,
   My mother at Heaven-gate:
But sister Maude shall get no sleep
   Either early or late.

My father may wear a golden gown,
   My mother a crown may win;
If my dear and I knocked at Heaven-gate
   Perhaps they'd let us in:
But sister Maude, oh sister Maude,
   Bide *you* with death and sin.

Christina Rossetti

From Goodbye Mother

Fascinated, we all gather round to watch the spectacle that is Mother. Her intestines bubble and splutter in a series of explosions; the excrement dribbles down her legs – which have also started to bubble and splutter – mingling with the vapours given off by the murky orange and green liquid oozing from every pore. Her feet, which have also turned into shiny balloons, burst open, inundating our lips as we avidly devour them with kisses. Mother, Mother, we chant as we circle round and round, intoxicated by the exhalations from her heaving body. In the midst of this apotheosis Ofelia suddenly pauses, gazes radiantly at Mother for a few seconds, goes out of the room and

10

here she is back again, brandishing the huge kitchen knife only Mother could (and did) use. 'Now I know what to do!' she cries, interrupting our ceremony. 'Now I know what to do. At last I've deciphered her message . . . Mother,' she goes on turning her back on us and drawing closer, 'here I am, here we are, steadfast and true, ready to obey your every command. Happy to have devoted ourselves and to continue to devote ourselves to you alone, now and for ever . . .' Odilia, Otilia and Onelia also draw near and fall on their knees by the bed, moaning gently. I stay standing by the window. Ofelia ends her speech and goes up to Mother's side. Clutching the huge kitchen knife with both hands she plunges it up to the hilt into her own stomach and, in a frantic flurry of twitching limbs, falls on the sprawling, teeming morass that is now Mother. Otilia's, Odilia's and Onelia's moans rise to a rhythmic crescendo that is intolerable

11

(for me, the only one listening).

12

The wondrous perfume of Mother's and Ofelia's rotting bodies transports us. Both of them are crawling with glistening maggots, and we are riveted to the spot by the spectacle of the transformation process. I look on as Ofelia's corpse, by now in an advanced stage of decomposition, merges with that of Mother to form a single festering, murky mass whose fragrance permeates the whole atmosphere. I also observe the covetous look in Odilia's and Otilia's eyes as they gaze at the heaving mound . . . The odd beetle scuttles in and out of the cavities in either corpse. Right now a rat, tugging at the wondrous heap with all its might, has made off with a piece of flesh (Mother's? Ofelia's?) . . . As if acting on the same impulse, obeying the same command, Otilia and Odilia fling themselves on the remains and – both at the same time – grab the kitchen knife. A brief but violent battle ensues over Mother and Ofelia, sending the magnificent rats scurrying for cover and making the beetles retreat into the mound's innermost recesses. With a deft forward lunge Odilia seizes control of the knife and, clasping it with both hands, makes ready to plunge it into her bosom. But Otilia, breaking free, snatches the weapon away from her. 'How dare you!' she screams at Odilia, stepping on to the heaving mound. 'So you thought you could join her before me, did you? I'll show her I'm the most devoted of the lot.' Before Odilia can stop her, she plunges the knife into her breast and falls on to the heap . . . Whereupon Odilia, in a frenzy, pulls the weapon out of Otilia's chest. 'You selfish bitch! You always were a selfish bitch!' she shrieks at her dying sister. And plunges the knife into her heart, dying (or pretending to die) before Otilia, whose body is still twitching. Both of them eventually expire on top of the mound, locked in a final, furious embrace.

Reinaldo Arenus, translated by Jo Labanyi, 1995

From Camp Cataract

'To hell with sisters,' said Beryl. 'Give 'em all a good swift kick in the pants.'

Jane Bowles, 1984

C. SISTERHOOD

From My Sister Dancing

Once, years ago, my sister wanted to sell me her bicycle.

'Sisters do not buy and sell with each other,' my mother said, 'sisters share.'

Elizabeth Jolley, 1996

Ah, how good and perfect you have been to me, you – my own beloved sisters – heart and eyes overflow when I think of you!

Elizabeth Barrett Browning – letter, 1847

From The Tribe of Tiger

When new land is difficult to find, mother cats often share with their children, keeping their sons with them until they are full grown and keeping their daughters or some of their daughters even longer, sometimes even dividing the ranch with one or more daughters. Lions and house cats carry the practice to an extreme, so that the members of a pride – really a group of females who are related to each other, grandmothers, mothers, daughters, sisters, nieces, and grandchildren – own one enormous ranch together. The area owned by a pride of lionesses can be hundreds of square miles, particularly in southern Africa, where game is sparse, while the area owned by a group of house cats is usually someone's farm, particularly the barn and its surroundings, where most of the mice are. Female cats share nests with their sisters and help to birth, groom, feed, protect, and teach one another's children.

[. . .]

Like housecats, lionesses cooperate in child care. It is not unusual to see a lioness striding along with cubs of different ages stumbling behind her. Lionesses nurse one another's cubs as cats do and even teach one another's cubs. My brother once came upon a lioness holding a struggling warthog in her front paws while two large cubs and two small cubs looked on, very interested. From the bushes, a second lioness watched. In short, as long as food is available, there are few disadvantages to group life for lionesses and virtually none for lion cubs. Even if a mother is away for long periods, she can know that her infants are safe, held close between the warm thighs of their aunt or their grandmother, fed by her four black nipples, and protected by her brave lion heart.

Elizabeth Marshall Thomas, 1994

From Carson McCullers

Before her death, I would have said that I knew Carson better than anyone did – that I knew her very well indeed. This would have been the truth as I saw it at the time, and at times I am still tempted to think that I knew her the best. After all, I knew her for forty-five years and lived with her off and on for much of that time. We shared the same heritage, the same parents, the same brother, the same room that looked out on the same holly tree and Japanese magnolia, and for the first twelve years of my life, the same mahogany bed. But we were sisters – sometimes intimate friends, sometimes enemies and at times strangers.

Margarita G. Smith, 1975

From In the Shadow of Man

We have been able to detect similarities – either physical make-up or behavioural characteristics – or both – in all the pairs of male friends that we have known ... we suspect in fact that pairs of male friends may often be siblings.

The only two adult females we know who enjoyed this sort of friendship were almost certainly sisters; not only did they look alike facially, but they had the same massive build, and both were prone to perform charging displays stamping on the ground and swaggering in a manner more typical of males. They were the only two adult females I ever saw playing with each other, rolling about on the ground, tickling one another and panting with laughter, each with her infant cradled in one arm.

Jane Goodall, 1971

Jane and Cassandra Austen

My dear Edward

You have asked me to put on paper my recollections of Aunt Jane, & to do so would be both on your account & her's a labour of love if I had but a sufficiency of material.

I am sorry to say that my reminiscences are few; surprisingly so, considering how much I saw of her in childhood, & how much intercourse we had in later years. I look back to the first period but find little that I can grasp of any substance, or certainty: it seems now all so shadowy! I recollect the frequent visits of my two Aunts, & how they walked in wintry weather through the sloppy lane between Steventon & Dean in pattens, usually worn at that time even by Gentlewomen.

I remember too their bonnets: because though precisely alike in colour, shape & material, I made it a pleasure to guess, & I believe always guessed right, which bonnet & which Aunt belonged to each other – Children do not think of Aunts, or perhaps of any grown up people as young; yet at the time to which I now refer my Aunts must have been very young women – even a little later, when I might be nine or ten yrs. old I thought it so very odd, to hear Grandpapa speak of them as 'the Girls'. 'Where are the Girls?' 'Are the Girls gone out?'

[. . .]

Aunt Jane was the general favourite with children, her ways with them being so playful, & her long circumstantial stories so delightful! These were continued from time to time, & begged for of course at all possible or impossible occasions, woven, as she proceeded out of nothing, but her own happy talent for invention. Ah! if but one of them could be now recovered!

[. . .]

I am not sure but that Aunt Cassandra's disposition was the most equally cheerful of the two. Their affection for each other was extreme; it passed the common love of sisters, and it had been so from childhood. My Grandmother talking to me once [of] bygone times, & of that particular time when my Aunts were placed at the Reading Abbey School, said that Jane was too young to make her going to school at all necessary, but it was her own doing; she *would* go with Cassandra; 'if Cassandra's head had been going to be cut off Jane would have her's cut off too' –

Anna Lefroy, 1864

Virginia Woolf and Vanessa Bell

You cannot think how I depend on you, and when you're not there the colour goes out of my life as water from a sponge; and I merely exist, dry and dusty. This is the exact truth; but not a very beautiful illustration of my complete adoration of you; and longing to sit, even saying nothing, and look at you.

VW to VB, 1937

You do know how much you help me. I can't show it and feel so stupid and such a wet blanket often but I couldn't get on at all if it weren't for you.

VB to VW

How do you manage to see only one thing at a time? [. . .] I suppose you are, as Lytton once said, the complete human being of us all; and your simplicity is really that I take in much more than I do, who intensifies atoms . . .

VW to VB, 10 August 1909

From A Visit to the Cemetery

Alice looked at her. Liddy was slow sometimes. 'Are you coming or are you not?' she cried, pulling her sleeve free and going on a few steps.

'Alice?'

Alice didn't want to turn around, but there was something in Liddy's voice that made her turn back. Liddy was standing just where she left her, looking backward at their mother's grave.

'What?'

Alice knew her voice was grumpy, but she really wanted to get to the gate. She hated this place.

And Liddy looked as if she was prepared to stay there for ever.

'Do you ever think about it at all, Alice?'

What she meant Alice both knew and did not know, so she took her choice.

'I don't know what you're talking about,' she said.

Liddy turned around slowly and in her eyes there was an expression that could not be misread or misunderstood.

'It's so awful,' she said, 'isn't it?' and she shuddered.

Almost as quickly as Liddy herself had averted her eyes from the bone on the grave, Alice averted hers from her sister.

'Oh, Liddy!' she exclaimed impatiently, 'If I thought you were going to take on like this I'd never have come with you.' She paused, casting around in her mind for some way to smooth out the awkwardness of the moment. 'After all we must all die – we know that,' she said lamely.

But Liddy was incorrigible.

'That's what I mean,' she said quietly.

Alice was at a loss.

'Well, after all we can console ourselves that it's only the body that is buried, the soul . . .'

Not exactly rudely, however, and not exactly impatiently, Liddy shrugged her shoulders.

'I sometimes think that's the worst of it,' she said, in a voice so low Alice had to bend forward to hear it. 'I can never believe that I won't go on feeling: feeling the cold and the damp – you know, even after –'

'Liddy! Liddy!' Alice stumbled across the tufted grass to her. If she said a single other word of the sentence she would have clapped her hands over her mouth.

But Liddy didn't finish it. She had begun to sob softly.

'And to think,' she said after a minute, 'that in a few years, perhaps sooner, poor Father –' she sobbed, 'just think of it – poor Father will be put down here too.'

This was dreadful. Alice felt helpless. She always knew Liddy felt things differently from her, but she never knew her to carry on like this. She couldn't think what to do, and when at that moment near her foot she saw a white bone she gave it a kick. Hateful place: it was all bones. That one might have been brought in by some mongrel, but it could just as easily be a human bone: the place was disgusting. It was enough to give anyone the creeps. Oh, if only Mother had been buried in the new cemetery where everything was so neat and orderly Liddy would not have got into this state! Jem Flagg, the gravedigger up at the new cemetery, always boasted that he'd give five pounds to anyone that found a bone after him!

'Well, thanks be to goodness we won't be buried here, anyway!' she said impulsively.

'We won't?' Liddy looked up in such surprise that the tears that were slowly rolling down her cheeks were jerked abruptly into the air.

'Of course not,' Alice cried. 'Not unless we are old maids!' But that seemed so untoward a thing that she made a playful grimace. Then, seeing that Liddy had smiled, if wanly, she put on an arch expression. 'We'll be buried with our husbands,' she said.

'Oh, Alice!' Liddy knew that Alice used to talk about boys with her friends, but she had never said anything like that to her before. She felt herself blushing, and was furious about it until she saw that Alice was blushing a little too.

'It's true!' said Alice defensively. 'The first death in the family means that you have to buy a plot – surely you know that! That's why Mother was buried here, because of that baby she had before any of us, the one that died. Father bought a plot here then, and now even though it's years and years ago since then, and there is a new cemetery now, Mother had to be buried here, and so will Father. But there aren't any more plots to be got here now, thanks be to God, so our husbands will have to provide them – in the new cemetery - thanks be to God again!'

Our husbands: it was an intoxicating thought. Liddy looked across the graveyard to the gate; it was turning out to be a beautiful evening, although you wouldn't notice that in the graveyard, everything was so dark with the ivy, and the old stones with their shadows overlapping everywhere, made a sort of double gloom.

Although there was hardly room for two to walk together, she recklessly linked her arm in her sister's and began to move towards the gate. A great feeling of sisterly affection had come over her, and it seemed to her that it wasn't just a matter of chance that they had picked this evening to come out together. It was as if something for a long time suppressed in her at last had begun to force upwards towards the light.

Mary Lavin, 1964

From Manus Kinship

Sister to Sister – Piloan

As the problem of seniority in Manus is so heavily bound up with economics, it does not intrude itself upon relationships between female siblings to anything like the same extent as among men. Sisterhood as a status of near contemporaries is much stronger. It begins to function earlier in a woman's life and is also more subject to disruption from residence arrangements than that of brotherhood. Girls are withdrawn from the play groups at puberty or sometimes a little before puberty. By this time they are all betrothed. The exigencies of avoidance and the demand for surveillance both militate against the continuation of childhood comradeship between non-related female age mates. Adolescent girls are thrown back upon sisters and female parallel cousins for companionship. The girl at first menstruation has, as her closest group of companions, her sisters, real or classificatory. Elder–younger sister relationships are reinterpreted into the mother–daughter situation, without however the element of strain which arises from the rivalry for the father's allegiance which is encouraged in the young child. If sisters live near each other, they continue to see a good deal of each other, subject to the demands for avoidance between the elder sister and the younger sister's husband. These avoidances do, however, prevent full intimacy.

Margaret Mead, 1934

From Hons and Rebels

Although Boud and I had fought and quarrelled unremittingly throughout childhood, by the time she was eighteen and I was fifteen we had, surprisingly, become great friends. Boud had grown from a giant-sized schoolgirl into a huge and rather alarming debutante. Almost six feet tall, with a thick blond mane of hair, she towered over her fellows at the various debutante functions like a big Santa Claus among the Christmas dolls. [. . .]

Boud had always had a flair for a certain baroque style of decorative art. In a sort of original variation of collage, she had created huge canvases depicting historical scenes: Hannibal crossing the Alps, with a background of clay mountains, the silver trappings of Hannibal and his army picked out in tinfoil; Noah's Ark, with bits of real fur pasted on the animals. As a debutante, she began to apply this talent to her selection of clothes. She shone like an enormous peacock in flashing sham jewels, bought at a theatrical costumer's, and immense brocade evening dresses. To my mother's consternation, she bought a sham tiara, resplendent with rubies, emeralds and pearls, and insisted on wearing it to dances. She was generally out to shock – to '*épater les bourgeois*', as my mother disapprovingly put it – and in this she succeeded. Boud's dissatisfaction with life mirrored my own. I applauded her outrages, roared when she stole some writing paper from Buckingham Palace and wrote to all her friends on it, cheered when she took her pet rat to dances.

[. . .]

Boud [. . .] was a bored and restless participant in the ritual of 'coming out'. She was casting about for something more exciting, more intriguing than the London season offered – something proscribed by the parents, something amazing, shocking . . .

Diana's house seemed like a good beginning, for we had been forbidden to visit her when, after a few years of marriage, she and Bryan were divorced. [. . .]

Debo and I saw nothing of Diana for over a year, but for Boud it was a different matter. Freed from schoolroom, governess and daily walks, she could now come and go as she pleased, and unknown to the Revereds she made many a surreptitious visit to Diana's. There she met Sir Oswald Mosley, whom Diana later married. Mosley's political career had led him through the Conservative Party, the Labour Party and the New Party, an abortive venture that had lasted only about a year, in spite of heavy backing by Lord Rothermere and the *Daily Mail*. He was now busily engaged in organizing the British Union of Fascists, which Boud immediately joined.

'Don't you *long* to join too, Decca? It's *such* fun,' she begged, waving her brand new black shirt at me.

'Shouldn't think of it. I hate the beastly Fascists. If you're going to be one, I'm going to be a Communist, so there.'

In fact, this declaration was something more than a mere automatic taking of opposite sides to Boud: the little I knew about the Fascists repelled me – their racism, super-militarism, brutality. I took out a subscription to the *Daily Worker*, bought volumes of Communist literature and literature that I supposed to be Communist, rigged up some home-made hammer-and-sickle flags. [. . .]

Boud and I both avoided the company of the Grown-Ups at this time as much as we could. At Swinbrook, we lived in the DFD except for mealtimes. We divide it down the middle, and Boud decorated her side with Fascist insignia of all kinds – the Italian fasces, a bundle of sticks bound with rope; photographs of Mussolini framed in passe partout; photographs of Mosley trying to look like Mussolini; the new German swastika, a record collection of Nazi and Italian youth songs. My side was fixed up with my Communist library, a small bust of Lenin purchased for a shilling in a second-hand shop, a file of *Daily Workers*. Sometimes we would barricade with chairs and stage pitched battles, throwing books and records until Nanny came to tell us to stop the noise.

[. . .]

The endless schoolroom talk of 'What are we going to do when we grow up?' changed in tone. 'I'm going to Germany to meet Hitler,' Boud announced. 'I'm going to run away and be a Communist,' I countered. Debo stated confidently that she was going to marry a duke and become a duchess. 'One day he'll come along. The duke I love . . .' she murmured dreamily. Of course, none of us doubted for a minute that we should reach the objectives we had set for ourselves; but perhaps seldom have childhood predictions materialized with greater accuracy.

Although Boud's interest in Fascism had at first been kept a secret from the grown-ups, it soon leaked out. She begged to be allowed to go to Germany. 'But, darling, I thought you didn't like Abroad,' my mother said. (Boud had always refused to learn French because she thought it an affected language, and France was somehow synonymous with Abroad to us.)

It was the year of Hitler's accession to power. Boud's announced intention was to go to Germany, learn German, and meet the Führer. My parents put up much less opposition than might have been expected. Perhaps the thought of another London season of sham tiaras and tame rats let loose in ballrooms was a bit more than my mother could contemplate with any pleasure. Boud was allowed to go.

Within six months, she came home for a brief visit, having accomplished both her objectives. She already spoke fairly fluent German, and had met not only Hitler, but Himmler, Goering, Goebbels, and others of the Nazi leaders. 'How on earth did you actually manage to get to know them?' we asked in some amazement. Boud explained that it had been fairly simple; she had reserved a nightly table in the Osteria Bavaria restaurant, where they often went. Evening after evening she sat and stared at them, until finally a flunkey was sent over to find out who she was. On learning that she was an English Fräulein, an admirer of the Nazis, and a member of the British Union of Fascists, Hitler invited her to join them at their table. Thereafter she became one of their circle, saw them constantly in Munich, accompanied them to meetings, rallies, the Olympic Games.

'As I thought! Hitler's just another subhuman, like The Poor Old Male, and you subdued him with the power of the human eye,' I said bitterly.

But Boud wouldn't be teased about her devotion to the Nazis. She was completely and utterly sold on them. The Nazi salute – 'Heil Hitler!' with hand upraised – became her standard greeting to everyone, family, friends, the astonished postmistress in Swinbrook village. Her collection of Nazi trophies and paraphernalia now overflowed our little sitting-room – bundles of Streicher's anti-Semitic paper, *Der Stürmer*; an autographed copy of *Mein Kampf*; the works of Houston Stuart Chamberlain, a nineteenth-century forerunner of Fascist ideologists; albums of photographs of Nazi leaders.

About this time the ban on Diana was lifted, and she again became a visitor at Swinbrook. Family relationships took a sudden turn, and Boud and Diana, formerly far from friendly, became thick as thieves.

Diana accompanied Boud to Germany and was also admitted to the Nazi inner circle. Their activities soon reached the newspapers, and a columnist reported that Hitler had declared them to be 'perfect specimens of Aryan womanhood'. The press made much of the prophetic nature of Boud's Christian names – Unity Valkyrie.

[. . .]

I still loved Boud for her huge, glittering personality, for her rare brand of eccentricity, for a kind of loyalty to me which she preserved in spite of our now very real differences of outlook. When I thought about it, I had a sad and uneasy feeling that we were somehow being swept apart by a huge tidal wave over which we had no control; that from the distance a freezing shadow was approaching which would one day engulf us. Sometimes we even talked of what would happen in a revolutionary situation. We both agreed we'd simply have to be prepared to fight on opposite sides, and even tried to picture what it would be like if one day one of us had to give the order for the other's execution.

Jessica Mitford, 1960

Maria Callas

What could I say? All her complexes were there in that one situation: her desire to be loved and her desire to compete with me, her sister . . .

Jackie Callas

From The Sisters: A Domestic Tale

'We were speaking of Lady Tasteless; you must know her two girls are both handsome, but very different; Ellen takes after her father, is plump, round-faced, with funny eyes, and a mouth that gives animation to her whole countenance from its playful dimples. Her form is short and almost grievously *embonpoint*: on the other hand, Louisa is tall, slender, with fine languishing eyes, and a pale complexion, quite fit for a tragic muse; and yet, did their silly mother bring out these two girls precisely the reverse of what nature and common sense intended. The gay Ellen was armed with a fine cambric handkerchief, and a smelling-bottle, and performed the whole evening the character of "a pensive nun, devout and pure", under pretext of a distressing headache, in order to look interesting; while poor Louisa, who was really labouring under a trifling indisposition, was under orders to shake the "light fantastic toe" in every corner of the room, and to look smilingly "with all her might", by way of looking charming. The consequence of this was just what might have been expected; at the very moment when Sir Hugh Dashwell was condoling with Ellen, and she ought to have answered him with dying softness, she burst into a horse-laugh at the grimaces of old Lord Hobbledown; and when Louisa, with extreme fatigue, having got down the fourth dance, was assuring her partner that "she trod on air", she dropt on the floor in a fainting fit – and the thing being really a fit, you know, they were all obliged to go home together, and left everybody behind to laugh at them.'

Mrs Hofland, 1828

From Culture, Behavior and Education

Adolescents rely on interdependence and shared functioning among siblings to get their work done, organize responsibilities for personal convenience, and to avoid unpleasant confrontations with adults. Rather than negotiation with adults, which is rarely possible, young people often share the work and resolve problems among themselves, reducing the need for adult leadership and intervention in order to accommodate personal interests, needs, and plans.

One senior girl who was the eldest sister gave an explicit description [. . .] of these tactics:

She asked to be in an evening activity at school and her father refused her permission because the mother worked at night and he needed her at home. She surmised that he didn't want to be bothered by the younger children. The first evening she volunteered to do the dishes for her next oldest sister if she would babysit the kids. After cleaning up the kitchen she asked her father for a ride, and mentioned the sister would take care of the 'small kids'. He had just seen the girl doing dishes. She got to go. On later evenings she brought the siblings snacks and provided the helpful sister with a running account of events and tickets to the eventual performance. Apparently her father was content for the eldest to participate and even to provide her a ride as long as the tasks were taken care of, even though he had originally refused her request. The initiative in figuring out satisfactory conditions was up to her and the negotiation was with siblings rather than him. His input was not to care who did what in the solution. The younger sister had had some hopes to be in the activity, but relief from her disliked dishwashing and a chance to hear what was going on and see the performance was certainly better than the turndown her father would have given a request to go. Our informant concluded with the comment, 'We take turns that way,' indicating a chance to go out gained by cooperation would go to the sister another time.

Ronald Gallimore, Joan W. Boggs and Cathie Jordan, 1974

'You're my sister. Liking doesn't come into it.'

Beth Yapp

From The Early Diary of Fanny Burney

Saturday, 7 January 1769

O dear! O dear! how melancholy has been to us this last week, the first of this year! Never during my life have I suffer'd more severely in my mind, I do verily believe! – But God be praised! I hope it is now over! The poor Susette, who I told you was disappointed of her Lynn journey by a violent cold, was just put to Bed somewhat better when I wrote to you this day se'night – I soon after went to her, and found her considerably worse. She talk'd to me in a most affecting style, her voice and manner were peculiarly touching.

'My dear Fanny,' cried she, 'I love you dearly – my *dear* sister! – have I any *more* sisters?' – O how I was terrified – shock'd – surprised! – 'O yes!' continued she, 'I have sister Hetty – but I don't wish her to come to me now, because she'll want me to drink my barley water, and I can't – but I will if *you* want me – and where's papa?' For my life I could not speak a word, and almost choak'd myself to prevent my sobbing. 'O dear! I shall die!' 'My dear girl.' 'O but I must though! – But I can't help it – it is not my fault you know!' – Tho' I almost suffocated myself with smothering my grief, I believe she perceived it, for she kiss'd me, and again said, 'How I love you! my *dear* Fanny! – I love you dearly!' 'My sweet Girl!' cried I – 'you – you *can't* love me so much as I do you!' 'If I was Charly I should love you – indeed I should – Oh! – I shall die!' – 'But not *yet*, my dear love – not *yet*!' 'Oh yes – I shall! – I should like to see papa first tho'.'

In short, she talk'd in a manner *inconceivably* affecting – and how greatly I was shock'd, *no* words can express. My dear papa out of town too! – We sent immediately for Mr Heckford, an excellent apothecary, who has attended our family many years. He bled her immediately, and said it would not be safe to omit it – She continued much the same some hours. Between one and two I went to bed, as she was sleeping, and Hetty and the maid sat up all night, for Hetty was very urgent that I should. She had a shocking night. At seven o'clock Mr Heckford was again call'd. She had a blister put on her back; he beg'd that a physician might be directly applied to, as she was in a very dangerous way! – O my good God! what did poor Hetty and myself suffer! –

Dr Armstrong was sent for – and my good Aunt Nanny who is the best nurse in England, tender, careful, and affectionate, and but too well experienced in illness. We were much inclined to send an express after my dear papa to Lynn, but resolved to wait while we possibly could. Unfortunately Mr, Mrs and Miss Molly Young all came very early to spend the day here – I never went *to* them, or *from* Susy, till dinner, and then I could eat none, nor speak a word. Never, I believe, shall I forget the shock I received that night. The fever increased – she could not swallow her medicines, and was quite delirious – Mr Heckford said indeed she had a very poor chance of recovery! He endeavour'd himself to give her physick, which he said was *absolutely* necessary, but in vain – she rambled – breathed short, and was terribly suffering – her disorder he pronounced an inflammation of the breast – 'I am sorry to say it,' said he, 'but indeed at *best* she stands a *very* poor chance!' I felt my blood freeze – I ran out of the room in an anguish beyond *thought* – and all I could do was to almost rave – and *pray*, in such an agony! O what a night she had! We all sat up – She slept perpetually, without being at all refresh'd, and was *so* light-headed! I kept behind her pillow, and fed her with barley water in a teaspoon the whole night, without her knowing of it at all – indeed she was dreadfully bad! On Monday however, the Dr and apothecary thought her *somewhat* better, tho' in great danger. We all sat up again. We wrote to papa, not daring to conceal the news, while her life was thus uncertain – On Tuesday, they ventured to pronounce her out of danger – We made Hetty go to bed, and my aunt and I sat up again – and on Wednesday, we two went to bed, the dear girl continuing to mend, which she has, tho' very slowly, ever since. My beloved papa and mama have both wrote to us quite, kindly –

Tuesday

My sweet Susette is almost well. I think of nothing else but to thank God Almighty enough, which I am obliged to run out of the room to do twenty times a day, for else I cannot breathe – I feel as if I had an asthma except when I am doing that.

Wednesday

Papa's come back, and we are all happier than ever we were in our lives.

Thursday, 19 January

Well, my dear creature, we have great hopes and expectations of happiness tomorrow. Susette is *quite* recovered. We are going to a great party at Mrs Pringle's – When Susette is well enough, she is still to go to Lynn where mama and Charttie and Bessy and Miss Allen will pass the winter. Adieu – *pour le présent*.

Fanny Burney, 1769

From Pride and Prejudice

When Jane and Elizabeth were alone, the former, who had been cautious in her praise of Mr Bingley before, expressed to her sister how very much she admired him.

'He is just what a young man ought to be,' said she, 'sensible, good-humoured, lively; and I never saw such happy manners! – so much ease, with such perfect good breeding!'

'He is also handsome,' replied Elizabeth, 'which a young man ought likewise to be, if he possibly can. His character is thereby complete.'

'I was very much flattered by his asking me to dance a second time. I did not expect such a compliment.'

'Did not you? *I* did for you. But that is one great difference between us. Compliments always take *you* by surprise, and *me* never. What could be more natural than his asking you again? He could not help seeing that you were about five times as pretty as every other woman in the room. No thanks to his gallantry for that. Well, he certainly is very agreeable, and I give you leave to like him. You have liked many a stupider person.'

'Dear Lizzy!'

'Oh! you are a great deal too apt you know, to like people in general. You never see a fault in anybody. All the world are good and agreeable in your eyes. I never heard you speak ill of a human being in my life.'

'I would wish not to be hasty in censuring any one; but I always speak what I think.'

'I know you do; and it is *that* which makes the wonder. With *your* good sense, to be so honestly blind to the follies and nonsense of others! Affectation of candour is common enough; – one meets it everywhere. But to be candid without ostentation or design – to take the good of everybody's character and make it still better, and say nothing of the bad – belongs to you alone. And so, you like this man's sisters too, do you? Their manners are not equal to his.'

'Certainly not; at first. But they are very pleasing women when you converse with them. Miss Bingley is to live with her brother and keep his house; and I am much mistaken if we shall not find a very charming neighbour in her.'

Elizabeth listened in silence, but was not convinced; their behaviour at the assembly had not been calculated to please in general; and with more quickness of observation and less pliancy of temper than her sister, and with a judgement too unassailed by any attention to herself, she was very little disposed to approve them.

Jane Austen, 1813

From Women in Love

The sisters found a little place where a tiny stream flowed into the lake, with reeds and flowery marsh of pink willow-herb and a gravelly bank to the side. Here they ran delicately ashore, with their frail boat, the two girls took off their shoes and stockings and went through the water's edge to the grass. The tiny ripples of the lake were warm and clear, they lifted their boat on to the bank, and looked round with joy. They were quite alone in a forsaken little stream-mouth, and on the knoll just behind was the clump of trees.

'We will bathe just for a moment,' said Ursula, 'and then we'll have tea.'

They looked round. Nobody could notice them, or could come up in time to see them. In less than a minute Ursula had thrown off her clothes and had slipped naked into the water, and was swimming out. Quickly, Gudrun joined her. They swam silently and blissfully for a few minutes, circling round their little stream-mouth. Then they slipped ashore and ran into the grove again, like nymphs.

'How lovely it is to be free,' said Ursula, running swiftly here and there between the tree trunks, quite naked, her hair blowing loose. The grove was of beech trees, big and splendid, a steel-grey scaffolding of trunks and boughs, with level sprays of strong green here and there, whilst through the northern side the distance glimmered open as through a window.

When they had run and danced themselves dry, the girls quickly dressed and sat down to the fragrant tea. They sat on the northern side of the grove, in the yellow sunshine facing the slope of the grassy hill, alone in a little wild world of their own. The tea was hot and aromatic, there were delicious little sandwiches of cucumber and of caviare, and winy cakes.

'Are you happy, Prune?' cried Ursula in delight, looking at her sister.

'Ursula, I'm perfectly happy,' replied Gudrun gravely, looking at the westering sun.

'So am I.'

D. H. Lawrence, 1921

Virginia Woolf and Vanessa Bell

To Vanessa Bell

Manorbier, [*Pembrokeshire*]
Wednesday [26 August 1908]

Beloved,

I had a piteous disappointment yesterday. I kept your letter till teatime, and went for a long walk planning a surprise at the end. I lost my way, sat on a hedge and directed myself all wrong by the map, and had to tramp till 6. The one thing that quickened my step was the thought of your letter – and when I got home, rushed to my room looked on the table. There was nothing there!

Nor is there any letter this morning. Damn these posts! But lamentations are dull. Reginald Smith bandies compliments with me, wont entirely give up the idea, and says that if I had read more I shouldn't think and write with that originality which the Cornhill loves! Of course, I had been posing as an illiterate woman, who had twice as much difficulty in writing an article as other people.

[. . .]

O dear O dear! The second and last post has come, and there is no letter again. Are you ill, have you been shot, or is it merely some trick of the posts? I can't make out how it can take 3 days to get a letter here – I have tried to walk myself into a philosophic mood, in the churchyard, but I cant help feeling melancholy. It rains and blows – and here I must sit and wait till tomorrow morning – and perhaps even then –

However, I must take a book and read, and try to forget all about you. There are poisonous gnats (in north London) I read; perhaps you have been stung – or do you remember that young lady of title last year, whom Violet felt for so much, whose husband shot her by mistake for a rabbit.

A woman [Mrs Luard] – colonels wife – has been murdered in Kent – All the consolation I get is a card from the London Library to say that I can have Saxons book on astrology [recommended by him] if I want it.

I am inclined to stay here till Monday now; my tooth has stopped aching, and I see I shant have done my writing till Sunday, and I am much happier here than I should be in London. Much happier! – that is mere optimism. I dont see how I am to stagger to the end of this sheet when I dont know whether you are in a state to read it. I turn to your letter and try to make out that you have no post out on Sunday, and only one early in the morning on weekdays, so that, if you missed this, I should not get a letter till tomorrow morning. I sink to the lowest depths of acquiescence, and consider that after all we are mere lumps of flesh, propelled about the world for a reason, and our sufferings are shocks leading nowhere. I am myself a worm, with a spade cutting through it.

It is now thundering out at sea, and some silly women, out for a holiday, are bathing. It is too fantastic of them – but they wont drown. Monster that you are – I adore you.

Yr B. [VW]

To Virginia Stephen [Woolf]

Cleeve House, Melksham, Wilts.
20 April [1908]

My Billy,

I have been reading your MS and so has Clive. I believe he has many small criticisms to give you. I have marked two places only I think which I will show you. I cannot give you real criticism of course but I think it is extraordinarily interesting. I like the part about Mother best. It seems to me that you really get into your stride when you begin to write about her, and I think, as far as I can tell, that you have given a very good idea of her – much the best I have seen. I think you also give a very true idea of Stella, but she is more difficult to get hold of. Some of your phrases about her bring her back to me very vividly, but it is impossible for me to know quite what they would mean to anyone who didn't know her. But I should think you have made her a very real person and also have given the relationship between the two very well. Of course I can only talk as do laymen about a portrait and tell you whether I think it like or not. [. . .] I think you have got the whole thing remarkably well constructed, especially considering what a forest of people and events you had to clear out and put in order. You have got them all very well together and the whole story moves on in good order and is an artistic whole – so it seems to me. I shall tell you much more when I see you, but I leave all literary criticism to Clive.

I had your letter from St Ives this morning. *Don't* give up the best bedroom, for you will want it to sit in probably and Clive and I shall want separate rooms. He tried here sleeping in the dressing-room, but gave it up as he couldn't get to sleep again after once being waked by Julian, so will you get us another room? As we shan't want a large double room you had much better keep the one you are in, in case you want to write in it.

We shall get to St Ives at 7.10 on Friday. Will you order a short vehicle to bring me and the nurse and baby from the station with one box and perambulator, and unless they should arrive beforehand also another two boxes, Julian's cradle and bath? These last we shall send off in advance so they may come before we do, but if not we shall find them at St Ives and bring them up with us.

Poor Billy, I am giving you practical jobs which you hate, although you do dispatch them with great brilliance – but I don't think there is anything else.

I suppose your landlady will send up my nurse's meals to her room. Otherwise there is nothing unusual.

I shall look for your handsome red tie and soft nose at St Ives – Oh God, what a joyful sight.

Your
VB

From Vanessa Bell

. . . if their relationship was, from childhood, based on an exchange of natural affection and unforced admiration, it was also veined with antagonism and fortified by mutual need.

Frances Spalding, 1983

Elephant Greetings

[*Elephant groups are almost always made up of related females and their offspring; these may be genetic sisters, aunts, mothers and grandmothers, or, sometimes, more distantly related females. But in all cases the relationship is definitely of 'sisterhood' at its closest. This is a description of how such actual or nominal sisters greet each other.*]

. . . the best indicator of the strength of the bonds between elephants is the greeting ceremony. Almost all elephants will greet one another but the nature and intensity of the greeting depends on who the elephants are, what their relationship is and, if it is a close one, how long they have been separated. If Slit Ear's family joins Estella's while feeding in Longinye, some of the family members might greet with an exchange of trunks – that is, put the tips of their trunks in each other's mouths. Usually a subordinate animal will be the one to initiate the greeting. It almost always occurs among the younger members of the two families and there are no accompanying vocalizations. Slit Ear would not deign to greet anyone in this manner; nor would Estella for that matter, so they would basically ignore one another while the other members of their families quietly greeted each other.

A greeting within the family, however, is a very different thing. Once in a while Tia will break off from Slit Ear and feed on her own with her two calves. It may be an accidental separation or it may be deliberate on Tia's part. Slit Ear can be very competitive over food and Tia always gives way to her. But for whatever reason they separate, which is not often, their reunions always involve a special ceremony. If they have been separated for only a short while, say a few hours, then the greeting will be at low intensity. Tia might join Slit Ear by walking up to her and lifting her head, raising and flapping her ears, and rumbling the throaty 'greeting rumble'. Depending on her mood, Slit Ear will usually answer in the same way, overlapping with Tia's rumble. They might then reach trunks towards each other. If Tia has been separated for a few days then the greeting ceremony will inevitably be far more intense and carried out with great energy and excitement. The two subgroups of the family will run together, rumbling, trumpeting, and screaming, raise their heads, click their tusks together, entwine their trunks, flap their ears, spin around and back into each other, urinate and defecate, and generally show great excitement. A greeting such as this will sometimes last for as long as ten minutes. I believe that the greeting ceremony maintains and reinforces the bonds among the family members.

Cynthia Moss, 1988

From Antigone

ISMENE (to Antigone). 'How could I live alone without my sister?'

Sophocles, *c.* 440 BC

My sisters and I – we can talk to each other in ways we could never talk to anybody else, tell them things we'd never tell anybody else.

Woman met at a party

'It's such a pleasure to have a dear sister one's friend.'

Emily née Lennox to Caroline Lennox

From Aristocrats

Like Madame de Sévigné, the Lennox sisters often described their letters as conversational and sprawling, even while they aspired to a 'formed' style; so their writing was characterized by a deliberate sloppiness. 'Since you are so kind as to complain,' Sarah wrote to Emily in the mid-1770s, 'I am encouraged to begin one of my monthly magazines; for I think my letters very like them, a compound of unconnected stuff and a little sense *par-ci, par-là*.'

First and foremost, they believed, letters were conversations between writer and recipient in which both could construct and (paradoxically) display a private self. In letters they shared thoughts, troubles, jokes and gossip. Finishing off a long letter written to cheer Emily up during a troublesome pregnancy, Caroline wrote, 'Adieu, I'm tired of writing. I hate to be so much in areas, a constant regular correspondence is so much more comfortable. I don't expect you tho' to write much now, poor soul. Let me know just how you do and I'll write constantly to you, for believe me, conversing, sweet siss, with you is one of my greatest pleasures.' Emily agreed. 'When one receives a letter,' she wrote, 'sitting down immediately to answer it is like carrying on a conversation.' Once they started writing, Caroline and Emily were prolix. Often they felt they could not stop: Caroline wrote in 1759, 'Since you love a folio sheet of paper, dear siss, you shall have one. I'm sure I shall fill it, for when once I get into a talking or writing way there is no end of me.' Caroline called Emily 'the only person in the world I can freely open my mind to on all subjects, except Mr Fox'. All her life Caroline got up early in the morning, and before breakfast she would sit down in her dressing-room and write letters. Towards the end of the 1750s she started wearing spectacles for reading, writing and sewing. Peering through them at the thick creamy paper, she scribbled the story of her life, troubles and all, in what her husband and sons described as atrocious handwriting. 'I must wear you to death, sweet siss, with my complaints, but it is so comfortable to unburden one's mind.' 'Adieu, my dearest siss, I must always unburden my mind to you which is the only purport of this letter.' In happier times than these, Caroline and Emily swapped declarations of love. In 1762, Caroline wrote, 'believe me, except Mr Fox and my children, there is nothing I love in this world in the least to compare to you; nobody but Ste is so often in my thoughts; your happiness and peace of mind is one of the things I have most at heart.'

Stella Tillyard, 1982

From Howards End

By slight indications the sisters could convey much to each other.

E. M. Forster, 1910

From The Language of Bees

Bees in a Hive are Always Sisters

To study the behaviour of bees which have just discovered a rich source of food one may set out near the observation hive a glass dish filled with sugar-water. When a foraging worker comes to this feeding place she is marked with a coloured spot while she is sucking up the sugar, so that we can recognize her later in the hive. After she has returned to the hive our marked bee is first seen to deliver most of the sugar-water to other bees. Then she begins to perform what I have called a round dance. On the same spot she turns around, once to the right, once to the left, repeating these circles again and again with great vigour. Often the dance is continued for half a minute or longer at the same spot. Frequently the dancer then moves to another spot on the honeycomb and repeats the round dance and afterwards ordinarily returns to the feeding place to gather more sugar.

[. . .]

To learn whether the round dance imparts information about the direction in which food is to be found, I fed several numbered bees from my observation hive at a feeding place ten metres to the west. At each of four points in the meadow around the hive, to the north, south, east, and west, I placed on the ground a glass dish containing sugar-water scented by a little honey. A few minutes after the start of round dances in the hive new bees appeared simultaneously at all the dishes regardless of their direction. The message brought by a bee as she performed the round dance seemed to be a very simple one, one that carried the meaning 'Fly out and seek in the neighbourhood of the hive.'

[. . .]

For many years in performing experiments of this general kind I always placed the food in the immediate vicinity of the hive, partly for convenience and partly so that I could watch the bees at the same time both at the observation hive and at the feeding place. Occasional observations suggested that bees could also tell something about the distance from the hive to the feeding place. Since bees often gather food a mile or more from the hive, it would clearly be advantageous if a forager which had located a rich but distant source of food could convey to other bees some idea of its location as well as its odour. To study this interesting question I performed the following experiment in August 1944. Two feeding places were arranged, one ten metres and the other three hundred metres from the hive; both were visited by numbered bees from my observation hive. [. . .]

[. . .] When we now look into the observation hive we see a truly curious sight: all the bees marked at the ten-metre food source are performing round dances just like those described [. . .] But all the bees that have come from the more distant feeding place are dancing in quite a different manner. They perform what I have called a 'wagging dance'. They run a short distance in a straight line while wagging the abdomen very rapidly from side to side; then they make a complete 360° turn to the left, run straight ahead once more, turn to the right, and repeat this pattern over and over again. This wagging dance was one that I had observed many years before; but I had always taken it for the characteristic dance of bees bringing pollen to the hive, whereas now I saw that it was performed most vigorously by bees which were bringing in sugar solutions from the experimental feeding place at three hundred metres.

It soon became clear that my original interpretation had been incorrect. The error arose because I had always furnished sugar-water at feeding sites close to the hive, chiefly for convenience of observation. The pollen carriers, on the other hand, were arriving from their natural feeding places on flowers some distance away. [. . .] Hence I had seen round dances performed only by bees which were gathering nectar or sugar-water, and wagging dances only by pollen carriers. But once I realized that the two types of dances were related to the *distance* of the food source and not to the nature of the food, it was easy to show by suitable experiments that the dances of pollen gatherers are no different from those performed by nectar gatherers returning from the same distance.

[. . .]

When the feeding place is near the hive, bees which have been aroused by the round dances fly out in all directions and seek for food in the immediate vicinity. If the source is farther away, the bees learn from the wagging dance [. . .] the distance at which the newly discovered food lies. But in addition they learn the *direction* in which they must fly. [. . .] The language of bees is truly perfect, and their method of indicating the direction of food sources is one of the most remarkable mysteries of their complex social organization.

Karl von Frisch, 1950

From The Collectors: Dr Claribel and Miss Etta Cone

Although Claribel went to Europe each summer with Etta after the First World War, she no longer could organize herself for the rigours of travel on the Continent, so the procedure changed from that of their earlier trips together. Etta would now see Claribel settled into the Hotel Lutetia and then, after a month or so, would leave Paris with Nora Kaufman or with another nurse-companion from Baltimore, May Nice. Etta's travels were as ambitious as ever; she went to numerous cities in Italy, returning again and again to see her favourite paintings and buildings, which were old and loved friends by now. Members of her family in Baltimore or Greensboro would intermittently make the Grand Tour, and would be grateful for seeing the sights with Etta, feeling that they were 'getting more out of it'. They were, but Etta wasn't always, since it took a great deal of energy to act as a guide for novice travellers. She was a large woman and she continued to be visited with intestinal complaints such as she had known in her younger days in Munich. Even something like a toothache could ruin a trip for her.

With Claribel based in Paris and Etta travelling, the two resumed a daily correspondence. Claribel's letters were lengthy affairs, sometimes twenty or twenty-five pages; often she was unable to get one of her letters into an envelope – so she would divide the letter in two envelopes and mark them envelopes A and B, so they could be read in proper sequence. It was something of a problem for Claribel to keep Etta's itinerary firmly in her mind so that Etta would find a letter awaiting her when she arrived at a new hotel.

Etta wrote as faithfully, reporting on her travels, on the museums she had seen, on the objects she had purchased and how much they cost. How much everything cost was a matter freely discussed in the mail between the two sisters – Claribel thought nothing of mentioning how much her breakfast melon had cost her – and Etta returned the intimacy by reporting how much a favourite *pension* which they had stayed at since 1903 had dared to ask her in 1923!

Bargaining with dealers was fun too – and it was fully discussed down to the last sou in the sisters' letters.

Each provided a certainty of affection and intimacy for the other. By no means had their personality balance changed – Claribel still tended to be the talker she had always delighted in being. Etta was still shy with strangers. Claribel more than ever had to have life ordered to her comforts – though sleeping sitting in a chair, or fully clothed across her bed, which was a favourite habit of hers, might not seem a 'comfort' to others.

[. . .]

Nice little things were always happening to Claribel; often, though they seemed unimportant, they left Etta choked with envy. When the sisters bought theatre tickets in Paris they sometimes took Miss Kaufman and one of the Richards with them. Whichever Richard it was, he was also instructed to go to the theatre and purchase tickets. Two of the seats had to be in the first row on the aisle. One was for Claribel, the other for her packages and purses. The others always sat ten or twelve rows farther back. The party went in that fashion to see a ballet première. After they were seated, Etta saw Picasso sitting alone across the aisle from the majestic Claribel. At the two intermissions Claribel and Picasso sat and chatted. Etta would have given anything not to be sitting twelve rows behind her sister that night.

It was in 1926 that the art world finally acknowledged the Cone sisters as collectors. Dealers in Paris all knew the two fat, rich ladies from Baltimore, dressed meticulously in ankle-length black dresses. They were always treated with the exquisite courtesy reserved for those who combine breeding with money.

Barbara Pollack, 1962

From The Agüero Sisters

At the Miami airport, Reina was stunned to see a vision of her mother rushing towards her at the gate. Constancia looks so much like Mami now, down to the minutest details, that Reina couldn't help it – she studied her sister's face like a blind woman, tried to read with her hands the grace and terror that lay hidden there.

'What a strange way of being dead!' she finally exclaimed. It was her first direct utterance to Constancia in thirty years. Later, she stared at her sister for many more hours, considered her from every angle, until it made her frantic with grief.

Her first few nights in Miami, Reina slept in the same bed with Constancia, back to stomach, Reina on the outside protecting her slight, older sister, listening for messages from the dead. She and Constancia showered together, combed one another's hair, fed each other tidbits from their dinner plates. All the while, Reina kept watch over her sister's face as if it were a compelling tragedy.

Reina wonders whether Mami's face is only a superficial membrane, like her own patches of borrowed skin, or whether it penetrates further to the bone, to some basic molecular level. She can't help thinking how everything is fundamentally electric, how natural currents flow near the surface of the earth, telluric and magnetic, how she is pulled again and again into the charged fields of her sister's face.

If only Constancia would stop talking, stay mute sufficiently long enough for Mami to emerge. Reina finds intolerable the false expectations their mother's visage sets up. There is a part of Reina that wants to address Mami directly, to risk everything – even if it means eradicating her sister – in the hope of retrieving her past.

After their mother died, Papá sent Reina and Constancia to a boarding-school in Trinidad. That first rainy winter, a forest of politeness took root between them, starching the air they shared. Each time Reina tried to talk about Mami, Constancia covered her ears and hummed the national anthem. Although they spent years together at boarding-school, by habit or cowardice – Reina isn't sure which – she and Constancia never discussed their mother again.

*

Reina dives into the deep end of the condominium's pool with her eyes wide open. There's a dime and a gold hoop earring where the bottom slopes down. She plucks them from the concrete and leaves them on the rim of the pool. Then she swims with powerful strokes to the shallow end. One stroke, then two, and she's in the deep water. Two strokes more, and she's at the shallow end again.

This is a pool for pygmies, Reina thinks. Who else could be satisfied with these few drops of blue?

The sun is high in the sky. No interference from clouds. The ocean wrinkles with the slightest breeze. The city is in the distance, strangely flat and uninviting. Reina emerges from the water and shakes herself dry, a glorious titanic beast. Near her, sunglasses are lowered, shutters flung open. Her own pungent scent steams up from her mismatched skin.

At noon, Constancia calls down to Reina from the balcony, announcing lunch. It's delicious, as usual: *arroz con pollo*, fried plantains, a coconut flan for dessert, all served on fancy flowered plates.

'This is the century that Christianity has died out,' Constancia declares, picking the *petits pois* out of her rice. 'The metaphysical is taking over. People believe in miracles now instead of God.'

Reina reaches over and mashes her sister's peas with a fork, sucks them off the tines. She looks up at the past trapped in Constancia's face and doesn't know what to say.

The phone rings incessantly during their meal. One call after another from Constancia's clients, impatient for orders of lotions and creams. Her sister is nearly finished retro-fitting a bowling-ball factory into Cuerpo de Cuba's new manufacturing plant to meet the clamorous demand. Reina has volunteered to help Constancia with the remaining electrical work.

There's a stack of photographs on the kitchen table, taken before Constancia's affliction. Reina thumbs through the pictures, carefully examines them one by one. Her sister looks good, well groomed, younger than her fifty-two years, her body pliant and pampered, Reina notes, but lacking the tone of true succulence.

'Do you think this will pass?' Constancia is moody, restless. 'I'm not extinct yet, am I?'

Reina isn't certain she can stay with her sister if Mami's face disappears, isn't certain she can stay if it remains. She takes her sister's hand and pats it. It's a child's hand, lineless and smooth. What could there possibly be here still tempting the dead?

'I wish you'd stop that!' Constancia hisses all of a sudden. 'You've been doing it for days!'

Reina realizes with a start that she's been unconsciously whistling. She recognizes the melody, a traditional *changüi* from Oriente she once heard a *negrito* sing in Céspedes Park. *He nacido para ti, Nengón. Para ti, Nengón.* His singing had made Reina cry.

'I've been ingesting small amounts of sterling silver,' Constancia says, calmer now. She takes a denim pouch from her apron pocket, shows Reina the silver dust inside. 'I heard on the radio that it soothes hallucinations.'

Reina reaches for an apple from a bowl on the kitchen table. She doesn't want to say that the entire world should be eating silver dust, then, because everyone is hallucinating.

'Someone told me this might be an equatorial disease. I must have caught it here in Miami. There are lots of people from South America.' Constancia pinches a bit of silver dust and sprinkles it on the tip of her tongue. Then she washes it down with a glass of ice water. 'What I want to know is where *my* face went. Where has it disappeared to?'

Reina remembers a stray snatch of a poem, she doesn't know where from, maybe something her father read to her once. 'Life is in the mirror, and you are the original death.'

Of course, she doesn't tell Constancia this.

Cristina Garcia, 1997

From Howards End

Margaret bolted the door on the inside. Then she would have kissed her sister, but Helen, in a dignified voice, that came strangely from her, said:

'Convenient! You did not tell me that the books were unpacked. I have found nearly everything that I want.'

'I told you nothing that was true.'

'It has been a great surprise, certainly. Has Aunt Juley been ill?'

'Helen, you wouldn't think I'd invent that?'

'I suppose not,' said Helen, turning away, and crying a very little. 'But one loses faith in everything after this.'

'We thought it was illness, but even then – I haven't behaved worthily.'

Helen selected another book.

'I ought not to have consulted anyone. What would our father have thought of me?'

She did not think of questioning her sister, nor of rebuking her. Both might be necessary in the future, but she had first to purge a greater crime than any that Helen could have committed – that want of confidence that is the work of the devil.

'Yes, I am annoyed,' replied Helen. 'My wishes should have been respected. I would have gone through this meeting if it was necessary, but after Aunt Juley recovered, it was not necessary. Planning my life, as I now have to do –'

'Come away from those books,' called Margaret. 'Helen, do talk to me.'

'I was just saying that I have stopped living haphazard. One can't go through a great deal of –' she missed out the noun – 'without planning one's actions in advance. I am going to have a child in June, and in the first place conversations, discussions, excitement, are not good for me. I will go through them if necessary, but only then. In the second place I have no right to trouble people. I cannot fit in with England as I know it. I have done something that the English never pardon. It would not be right for them to pardon it. So I must live where I am not known.'

'But why didn't you tell me, dearest?'

'Yes,' replied Helen judicially. 'I might have, but decided to wait.'

'I believe you would never have told me.'

'Oh yes, I should. We have taken a flat in Munich.'

Margaret glanced out of the window.

'By "we" I mean myself and Monica. But for her, I am and have been and always wish to be alone.'

'I have not heard of Monica.'

'You wouldn't have. She's an Italian – by birth at least. She makes her living by journalism. I met her originally on Garda. Monica is much the best person to see me through.'

'You are very fond of her, then.'

'She has been extraordinarily sensible with me.'

Margaret guessed at Monica's type – 'Italiano Inglesiato' they had named it: the crude feminist of the South, whom one respects but avoids. And Helen had turned to it in her need!

'You must not think that we shall never meet,' said Helen, with a measured kindness. 'I shall always have a room for you when you can be spared, and the longer you can be with me the better. But you haven't understood yet, Meg, and of course it is very difficult for you. This is a shock to you. It isn't to me, who have been thinking over our futures for many months, and they won't be changed by a slight contretemps, such as this. I cannot live in England.'

'Helen, you've not forgiven me for my treachery. You *couldn't* talk like this to me if you had.'

'Oh, Meg dear, why do we talk at all?' She dropped a book and sighed wearily. Then, recovering herself, she said: 'Tell me, how is it that all the books are down here?'

'Series of mistakes.'

'And a great deal of the furniture has been unpacked.'

'All.'

'Who lives here, then?'

'No one.'

'I suppose you are letting it, though.'

'The house is dead,' said Margaret, with a frown. 'Why worry on about it?'

'But I am interested. You talk as if I had lost all my interest in life. I am still Helen, I hope. Now this hasn't the feel of a dead house. The hall seems more alive even than in the old days, when it held the Wilcoxes' own things.'

'Interested, are you? Very well, I must tell you, I suppose. My husband lent it on condition we – but by a mistake all our things were unpacked, and Miss Avery, instead of –' She stopped. 'Look here, I can't go on like this. I warn you I won't. Helen, why should you be so miserably unkind to me, simply because you hate Henry?'

'I don't hate him now,' said Helen. 'I have stopped being a schoolgirl, and, Meg, once again, I'm not being unkind. But as for fitting in with your English life – no, put it out of your head at once. Imagine a visit from me at Ducie Street! It's unthinkable.'

Margaret could not contradict her. It was appalling to see her quietly moving forward with her plans, not bitter or excitable, neither asserting innocence nor confessing guilt, merely desiring freedom and the company of those who would not blame her. She had been through – how much? Margaret did not know. But it was enough to part her from old habits as well as old friends.

'Tell me about yourself,' said Helen, who had chosen her books, and was lingering over the furniture.

'There's nothing to tell.'

'But your marriage has been happy, Meg?'

'Yes, but I don't feel inclined to talk.'

'You feel as I do.'

'Not that, but I can't.'

'No more can I. It is a nuisance, but no good trying.'

Something had come between them. Perhaps it was Society, which henceforward would exclude Helen. Perhaps it was a third life, already potent as a spirit. They could find no meeting place. Both suffered acutely, and were not comforted by the knowledge that affection survived.

'Look here, Meg, is the coast clear?'

'You mean that you want to go away from me?'

'I suppose so – dear old lady! it isn't any use. I knew we should have nothing to say. Give my love to Aunt Juley and Tibby, and take more yourself than I can say. Promise to come and see me in Munich later.'

'Certainly, dearest.'

'For that is all we can do.'

It seemed so. Most ghastly of all was Helen's common sense: Monica had been extraordinarily good for her.

'I am glad to have seen you and the things.' She looked at the bookcase lovingly, as if she was saying farewell to the past.

Margaret unbolted the door. She remarked: 'The car has gone, and here's your cab.'

She led the way to it, glancing at the leaves and the sky. The spring had never seemed more beautiful. The driver, who was leaning on the gate, called out, 'Please, lady, a message,' and handed her Henry's visiting-card through the bars.

'How did this come?' she asked.

Crane had returned with it almost at once.

[. . .]

Helen had not followed [Margaret] into the garden. The door once open, she lost her inclination to fly. She remained in the hall, going from bookcase to table. She grew more like the old Helen, irresponsible and charming.

'This *is* Mr Wilcox's house?' she inquired.

'Surely you remember Howards End!'

'Remember? I who remember everything! But it looks to be ours now.'

'Miss Avery was extraordinary,' said Margaret, her own spirits lightening a little. [. . .]

'Where's the piano, Meg?'

'I warehoused that in London. Why?'

'Nothing.'

'Curious, too, that the carpet fits.'

'The carpet's a mistake,' announced Helen. 'I know that we had it in London, but this floor ought to be bare. It is far too beautiful.'

'You still have a mania for under-furnishing. Would you care to come into the dining-room before you start? There's no carpet there.'

They went in, and each minute their talk because more natural.

'Oh, *what* a place for mother's chiffonier!' cried Helen.

'Look at the chairs, though.'

'Oh, look at them! Wickham Place faced north, didn't it?'

'North-west.'

[. . .]

'But the chairs show up wonderfully. Look where Tibby spilt the soup.'

'Coffee. It was coffee surely.'

Helen shook her head. 'Impossible. Tibby was far too young to be given coffee at that time.'

'Was father alive?'

'Yes.'

'Then you're right and it must have been soup. I was thinking of much later – that unsuccessful visit of Aunt Juley's, when she didn't realize that Tibby had grown up. It was coffee then, for he threw it down on purpose. There was some rhyme, "Tea, coffee – coffee, tea," that she said to him every morning at breakfast. Wait a minute – how did it go?'

'I know – no, I don't. What a detestable boy Tibby was!'

'But the rhyme was simply awful. No decent person could have put up with it.'

'Ah, that greengage tree,' cried Helen, as if the garden was also part of their childhood. 'Why do I connect it with dumb-bells? And there come the chickens. The grass wants cutting. I love yellowhammers –'

Margaret interrupted her. 'I have got it,' she announced. '"Tea, tea, coffee, tea,/ Or chocolaritee." That every morning for three weeks. No wonder Tibby was wild.'

'Tibby is moderately a dear now,' said Helen.

'There! I knew you'd say that in the end. Of course he's a dear.'

A bell rang.

'Listen! what's that?'

Helen said, 'Perhaps the Wilcoxes are beginning the siege.'

'What nonsense – listen!'

And the triviality faded from their faces, though it left something behind – the knowledge that they never could be parted because their love was rooted in common things. Explanations and appeals had failed; they had tried for a common meeting ground, and had only made each other unhappy. And all the time their salvation was lying round them – the past sanctifying the present; the present with wild heart-throb, declaring that there would after all be a future, with laughter and the voices of children. Helen, still smiling, came up to her sister. She said, 'It is always Meg.' They looked into each other's eyes. The inner life had paid.

E. M. Forster, 1910

From I Aim Carefully

I am extraordinarily self-sufficient while my sisters [. . .] need other people for happiness.

On the other hand, who am I kidding? Take away my family, [. . .] take away my sisters, and there is very little of *me* left . . .

And certainly no heart left for living.

Keri Hulme, 1996

From Camp Cataract

There were close to a hundred people dining on the terrace, and the water's roar so falsified the clamour of voices that one minute the guests seemed to be speaking from a great distance and the next right at her elbow. Every now and then she thought she heard someone pronounce her name in a dismal tone, and however much she told herself that this was merely the waterfall playing its tricks on her ears she shuddered each time at the sound of her name. Her very position next to the booth began to embarrass her. She tucked her hands into her coat sleeves so that they would not show, and tried to keep her eyes fixed on the foaming waters across the way, but she had noticed a disapproving look in the eyes of the diners nearest her, and she could not resist glancing back at the terrace every few minutes in the hope that she had been mistaken. Each time, however, she was more convinced that she had read their expressions correctly, and that these people believed, not only that she was standing there for no good reason, but that she was a genuine vagrant who could not afford the price of a dinner. She was therefore immensely relieved when she caught sight of Harriet advancing between the tables from the far end of the dining pavilion. As she drew nearer, Sadie noticed that she was wearing her black winter coat trimmed with red fur, and that her marceled hair remained neatly arranged in spite of the strong wind. Much to her relief Harriet had omitted to rouge her cheeks and her face therefore had regained its natural proportions. She saw Harriet wave at the sight of her and quicken her step. Sadie was pleased that the diners were to witness the impending meeting. 'When they see us together,' she thought, 'they'll realize that I'm no vagrant, but a decent woman visiting her sister. 'I thought you'd come out of the pine grove,' she called out, as soon as they were within a few feet of one another. 'I kept looking that way.'

'I would have ordinarily,' Harriet answered, reaching her side and kissing her lightly on the cheek, 'but I went to the other end of the terrace first, to reserve a table for us from the waiter in charge there. That end is quieter, so it will be more suitable for a long talk.'

'Good,' thought Sadie as they climbed up the knoll together. 'Her night's sleep has done her a world of good.' She studied Harriet's face anxiously as they paused next to the souvenir booth, and discovered a sweet light reflected in her eyes. All at once she remembered their childhood together and the great tenderness Harriet had often shown towards her then.

'They have Turkish pilaff on the menu,' said Harriet, 'so I told the waiter to save some for you. It's such a favourite that it usually runs out at the very beginning. I know how much you love it.'

Sadie, realizing that Harriet was actually eager for this dinner, the only one they would eat together at Camp Cataract, to be a success, felt the terrible leaden weight lifted from her heart; it disappeared so suddenly that for a moment or two she was like a balloon without its ballast; she could barely refrain from dancing about in delight. Harriet tugged on her arm.

'I think we'd better go now,' she urged Sadie, 'then after lunch we can come back here if you want to buy some souvenirs for Evy and Bert . . . and maybe for Flo and Carl and Bobby too . . .'

Sadie bent down to adjust her cotton stockings, which were

wrinkling badly at the ankles, and when she straightened up again her eyes lighted on three men dining very near the edge of the terrace; she had not noticed them before. They were all eating corn on the cob and big round hamburger sandwiches in absolute silence. To protect their clothing from spattering kernels, they had converted their napkins into bibs.

'Bert Hoffer's careful of his clothes too,' Sadie reflected, and then she turned to her sister. 'Don't you think men look different sitting all by themselves without women?' she asked her. She felt an extraordinary urge to chat – an urge which she could not remember ever having experienced before.

'I think,' Harriet replied, as though she had not heard Sadie's comment, 'that we'd better go to our table before the waiter gives it to someone else.'

'I don't like men,' Sadie announced without venom, and she was about to follow Harriet when her attention was arrested by the eyes of the man nearest her. Slowly lowering his corn cob to his plate, he stared across at her, his mouth twisted into a bitter smile. She stood as if rooted to the ground, and under his steady gaze all her newborn joy rapidly drained away. With desperation she realized that Harriet, darting in and out between the crowded tables, would soon be out of sight. After making what seemed to her a superhuman effort she tore herself away from the spot where she stood and lunged after Harriet shouting her name.

Harriet was at her side again almost instantly, looking up at her with a startled expression. Together they returned to the souvenir booth, where Sadie stopped and assumed a slightly bent position as if she were suffering from an abdominal pain.

'What's the trouble?' she heard Harriet asking with concern. 'Are you feeling ill?'

Instead of answering Sadie laid her hand heavily on her sister's arm and stared at her with a hunted expression in her eyes.

'Please try not to look so much like a gorilla,' said Harriet in a kind voice, but Sadie, although she recognized the accuracy of this observation (for she could feel very well that she was looking like a gorilla), was powerless to change her expression, at least for a moment or two. 'Come with me,' she said finally, grabbing Harriet's hand and pulling her along with almost brutal force. 'I've got something to tell you.'

She headed down a narrow path leading into a thickly planted section of the grove, where she thought they were less likely to be disturbed. Harriet followed with such a quick, light step that Sadie felt no pull behind her at all and her sister's hand, folded in her own thick palm, seemed as delicate as the body of a bird. Finally they entered a small clearing where they stopped. Harriet untied a handkerchief from around her neck and mopped her brow. 'Gracious!' she said. 'It's frightfully hot in here.' She offered the kerchief to Sadie. 'I suppose it's because we walked so fast and because the pine trees shut out all the wind . . . First I'll sit down and then you must tell me what's wrong.' She stepped over to a felled tree whose length blocked the clearing. Its torn roots were shockingly exposed, whereas the upper trunk and branches lay hidden in the surrounding grove. Harriet sat down; Sadie was about to sit next to her when she noticed a dense swarm of flies near the roots. Automatically she stepped toward them. 'Why are they here?' she asked herself – then immediately she spotted the cause, an open can of beans some careless person had deposited inside a small hollow at the base of the trunk. She turned away in disgust and looked at Harriet. Her sister was seated on the fallen tree, her back gracefully erect and her head tilted in a listening attitude. The filtered light imparted to her face an incredibly fragile and youthful look, and Sadie gazed at her with tenderness and wonder. No sound reached them in the clearing, and she realized with a pounding heart that she could no longer postpone telling Harriet why she had come. She could not have wished for a moment more favourable to the accomplishment of her purpose. The stillness in the air, their isolation, the expectant and gentle light in Harriet's eye, all these elements should have combined to give her back her faith – faith in her own powers to persuade Harriet to come home with her and live among them once again, winter and summer alike, as she had always done before. She opened her mouth to speak and doubled over, clutching at her stomach as though an animal were devouring her. Sweat beaded her forehead and she planted her feet wide apart on the ground as if this animal would be born. Though her vision was barred with pain, she saw Harriet's tear-filled eyes, searching hers.

'Let's not go back to the apartment,' Sadie said, hearing her own words as if they issued not from her mouth but from a pit in the ground. 'Let's not go back there . . . let's you and me go out in the world . . . just the two of us.' A second before covering her face to hide her shame Sadie glimpsed Harriet's eyes, impossibly close to her own, their pupils pointed with a hatred such as she had never seen before.

It seemed to Sadie that it was taking an eternity for her sister to leave. 'Go away . . . go away . . . or I'll suffocate.' She was moaning the words over and over again, her face buried deep in her hands. 'Go away . . . please go away . . . I'll suffocate . . .' She could not tell, however, whether she was thinking these words or speaking them aloud.

At last she heard Harriet's footstep on the dry branches, as she started out of the clearing. Sadie listened, but although one step followed another, the cracking sound of the dry branches did not grow any fainter as Harriet penetrated farther into the grove. Sadie knew then that this agony she was suffering was itself the dreaded voyage into the world – the very voyage she had always feared Harriet would make. That she herself was making it instead of Harriet did not affect her certainty that this was it.

Jane Bowles, 1984

From Blackberry Winter

Thinking about the contrasts between my sisters led me also to think about the other women in my mother's family and of the way in which, generation after generation, pairs of sisters have been close friends. In this they exemplify one of the basic characteristics of American kinship relations. Sisters, while they are growing up, tend to be very rivalrous and as young mothers they are given to continual rivalrous comparisons of their several children. But once the children grow older, sisters draw closer together and often, in old age, they become each other's chosen and most happy companions. In addition to their shared memories of childhood and of their relationships to each other's children, they share memories of the same home, the same home-making style, and the same small prejudices about housekeeping that carry the echoes of their mother's voice as she admonished them, 'Never fill the tea-kettle from the hot-water faucet,' and 'Wash the egg off the silver spoons at once,' and 'Dry the glasses first.' But above all, perhaps, sisters who have grown up close to one another know how their daydreams have been interwoven with their life experiences.

One of the happiest memories of my younger sisters' girlhood is of a Christmas when they drove home from Chicago in a blinding snowstorm and we celebrated together, enjoying all the food that was, for once, richly and generously on hand. I have a picture taken on that Christmas Day, the only occasion, after we had grown up, that all three of us were together.

My mother's next younger sister, Fanny, is now a very fragile old lady. She lives in a nursing home where she still entertains her friends and relatives at cocktails. Occasionally, she complains that some modern book she is reading – a book by Claude Lévi-Strauss, for example – is difficult. She is ninety-five, and seeing her so gay and so aware of the world around her gives an extraordinary pleasure to her nieces, her grandnieces, and her great-grandnieces. But she still laments that her sister Emily, my mother, is not with her to share her last years.

Margaret Mead, 1973

From The Wise Virgins

. . . that curiously strong love which often binds sister to sister . . . It outlives years and happiness and separation, violent quarrels, mutual knowledge and knowledge of faults, vices and meannesses. It may be doubted whether it does not rest upon the first and last feeling to flicker through the embryonic and dying body of everyone, love of oneself. [. . . if sisterly love] begins in and rests on selfishness, it manifests itself often in supreme unselfishness.

Leonard Woolf, 1914

3

Growing Up – Love and Marriage

INTRODUCTION

When my two children were fourteen and sixteen my son, on his own insistence, left their comprehensive and went away to school. The effect of it, on his sister and on him, was more than any of us could have imagined, and more than I or they understood at the time. 'This boy has a sibling problem,' commented my son's seemingly unimaginative yet percipient housemaster. His sister meanwhile became even more stroppy than usual, her desolation (and mine) eased only in part by the arrival of a seventeen-year-old lodger. My daughter thought him very square; in due course, unearthing some acceptable eccentricities, she made him a surrogate brother, and so we went on; but the loss, in particular her loss, remained. Along with my brush with cancer, it was one of the main factors, I suspect, that led to her near breakdown when she was just eighteen.

It makes me realize how much we underestimate the sense of loss, when, as is inevitable, sisters and brothers start growing up and begin to go their own ways. Or indeed when they are separated at any age. Seeing my former mother-in-law and her twin brother both burst into tears, in their seventies, reminded of the brother's departure to boarding-school at eight years old, I remembered at the effect on my twin of our six-month separation at the same age, after I contracted TB. In the case of my children, it was the younger sibling who left first; more usually, especially with two sisters, it's the younger child who suffers most from separation, which doesn't have to be geographical at all – it may simply be a shift from shared tastes and interests of childhood into a new, adolescent world. In that case, the empty bed in the shared room is figurative rather than actual. Sometimes, of course, the split can be a relief – genetic closeness between sisters doesn't necessarily come with compatible chemistry; some sisters (like my aunts, I suspect) are thankful to escape the intimacy forced on them by family life. But in our society, it's almost inevitable that sisters find themselves in due course embarking on worlds and experiences that their sisters or brothers do not share, and which may separate them for good.

Adolescence is commonly the dividing point; it brings such uncertainty of who and what you are – not to feel like a child any more, but not like an adult either – dividing teenagers from siblings on the one hand, and from parents on the other. It may be why adolescents like going around in gangs. In any event they retreat from the games they used to enjoy, from sisters still quite happy to play them; Marilynne Robinson catches very well the arbitrariness of it, the hurt bafflement of the younger sister. In due course the beginning of serious feelings for a boy (or girl come to that) makes for still more serious separations, beautifully described in Carson McCullers's story. In the nineteenth century, before the invention of adolescence, that stage took longer to arrive. Middle-class girls, in Anglo-Saxon cultures at least, remained children until, aged eighteen or so, they descended on London or New York or Boston to meet eligible young men at social functions. The process was called 'coming out' and 'doing the season' and could be held over till more than one sister was ready to 'come out' in families with sisters close in age and without unlimited funds. So it was for Mary McCarthy and her sister. So it was, too, for my grandmother, whose diary describes her adventures in London with an innocence and tedium both touching and alarming; the past as truly another country. When the season was over they went back home again and continued as before. For them the first real break with family and sisters came only on marriage.

Marriage still makes a difference, I suspect. I'm not sure quite how it works out when sisters have left home long before, in particular where one or both have been living with a partner. But the rituals of a wedding may still inflict a psychic break on as yet unmarried sisters. And where there is no marriage, the birth of a baby may do so; after that the new nuclear family takes precedence and sisters, like grandmothers, visit on sufferance rather than as of right.

I can't say I had much experience myself of the emotions felt by Marilyn Duckworth on the admittedly early marriage of her sister Fleur. I was the first sister to marry in my family, and far too overwhelmed by my own upheavals to be much aware of my twin's feelings. But I don't think she liked it much. Not least because yet again fortune seemed to be on my side. Our mother's falling ill almost at once, and dying only eight months later could not have helped; nor my pregnancy, shortly after. How involved my twin had felt, in fact, I realized when I woke up from my Caesarean to find her by my bed rather than in the north of Scotland, where she was supposed to be. Overwhelmed by a no means inaccurate conviction that something was wrong, she'd turned round in mid-journey and come running back. I was delighted to see her. All three of us, my little sister included, missed our mother badly when we gave birth; my twin didn't make up for this entirely, but she was – I was going to say better than nothing – but no, a good deal more than that.

What was in it for her exactly, I don't know. But certainly, my marriage, my baby, aroused her longings for both. Whether she would have tumbled into marriage with an alcoholic (or indeed with a psychopath twenty years later) but for me, I don't know either. I do know, however, that, for my youngest sister, finding herself sucked into my crumbling marriage, and those of my twin and our brother, was one factor in her decision to leave for Australia, as far away as she could get. Divorce is another thing that can force siblings together all over again. As I discovered myself, when my twin sister turned up on the doorstep clutching a large suitcase and her two small children, saying 'I've left him.' For six months thereafter we lived in the same house. Rediscovering our sisterhood was marvellous, surprisingly. It may even have delayed the collapse of my own marriage. Once, when my husband was complaining about me as usual, she said very sharply, 'You could try being nice to her.' A nice man at heart, he was as grateful for that warning as I was.

The most bitter of all sibling rivalries is competition over a man.

Jealousy can erupt among the closest of sisters; relations between Vanessa Bell and Virginia Woolf were never quite the same after Virginia's flirtation with Vanessa's husband Clive Bell. The problem was compounded by the very physical attachment of the sisters: Virginia seems to have felt usurped by Clive, in ways not simply emotional. Vanessa's weird outburst during Virginia's wedding several years later, reported by Virginia's husband, Leonard, indicates complicated feelings in her too. All this one might expect from that highly charged lot; yet even outside Bloomsbury, these things are never simple.

Much earlier, Vanessa had seemed to be getting involved with the husband of her dead half-sister, Stella. Though the religious and legal ban on marrying a deceased wife's sister, enjoined in the Book of Leviticus, had been lifted by then, it roused deep family disapproval. The issue, aired in a multitude of pamphlets and even novels, had exercised moralists throughout the nineteenth century; those who defied it, like Holman Hunt and his wife, Edith, the sister of his first wife Fanny, were ostracized in some quarters.

Outside Western and Christian traditions, on the other hand, no such taint of incest was seen; husbands were often expected to marry a dead wife's sister. This is a salutary reminder that much of what I've been saying about sisters relates, at least on institutional levels, only to Western experience. In traditional patrilineal societies, pre-teenage sisters could be removed from home to be brought up in their husband's families, and hardly saw their sisters again. In matriarchal societies, on the other hand, sisters might live in the same village or compound all their lives. (The same can happen, effectively, in our society, but out of choice; such outcomes are not dictated by social structures.) In either case, sibling relationships, with brothers in traditional patrilineal societies and sisters in matriarchal ones, were often much more significant emotionally and socially than those with spouses. A man from one such culture, asked which of his family he would rescue in the event of a flood, answered 'my sister', without hesitation. Wives and children could be replaced: sisters could not. Herodotus tells a similar story from ancient Persia, where a matron opts to save her brother from execution rather than her husband or sons. Such intimate feelings don't get written up by anthropologists. We need novelists to demonstrate the weight of them to us.

From Housekeeping

When Lucille came home she was carrying a bag in which there was a dress pattern with four yards of cream and brown checked wool. She explained that what seemed to me to be a dress was in fact a skirt and a small jacket. The jacket, she explained, could be worn open with a blouse or with a brown or cream skirt. The skirt could be worn with a blouse or sweater. When she had finished this outfit, she would make a brown skirt and get a sweater to match it. 'It will all be coordinated,' she said. 'It will go with my hair.' She was deeply serious. 'You have to help me. The instructions tell how to do it.' We cleared away the clutter on the kitchen table, which was considerable. Sylvie had taken lately to keeping tin cans. She washed the labels off with soap and hot water. There were now many of these cans on the counters and the window-sill, and they would have covered the table long since if Lucille and I had not removed them now and then. We did not object to them, despite the nuisance, because they looked very bright and sound and orderly, especially since Sylvie arranged them open end down, except for the ones she used to store peach pits and the keys from sardine and coffee cans. Frankly, we had come to the point where we could hardly object to order in any form, though we hoped that her interest in bottles was a temporary aberration.

We spread the big tan sheet of instructions out on the table. Lucille knelt on a chair and leaned across the table to read step 1. 'We'll need a dictionary,' she said, so I went to get one from the bookcase in the living-room. It was old, one of my grandfather's books. We had never used it before.

'The first thing to do,' Lucille said, 'is spread out the cloth. Then you pin on all the pieces of the pattern, and then you cut them out. Look up *pinking shears*.' I opened to *P*. At that place there were five dried pansies – one yellow, one blue-black, one mahogany, one violet, one parchment. They were flat and stiff and dry – as rigid as butterfly wings, but much more fragile. At *Q* I found a sprig of Queen Anne's lace, which was smashed flat and looked very like dill. At *R* I found a variety of roses – red roses, which had warped the page on each side a little to their shape, and pink wild roses.

'What are you doing?' Lucille asked.

'This dictionary is full of pressed flowers,' I said.

'Grandpa.'

'He put lady's slippers under *O*. Probably *orchids*.'

'Let me see that,' Lucille said. She took the book by each end of its spine and shook it. Scores of flowers and petals fell and drifted from between the pages. Lucille kept shaking until nothing more came, and then she handed the dictionary back to me. 'Pinking shears,' she said.

'What will we do with these flowers?'

'Put them in the stove.'

'Why do that?'

'What are they good for?' This was not a real question, of course. Lucille lowered her coppery brows and peered at me boldly, as if to say, It is no crime to harden my heart against pansies that have smothered in darkness for forty years. 'Why won't you help me with my dress? You just don't want to help.'

'I'll get another book to put them in.'

Lucille scooped up flowers and crushed them between her palms. I tried very hard to hit her with the dictionary, but she blocked it with her left elbow, and then slapped me very deftly on the left ear. I dropped the dictionary on the floor. I was furious, of course, and determined to land a blow, but somehow she fended off every one with her bony forearms, and still managed to punch me in the ribs. 'All right,' I said, 'I *won't* help.' And I walked out of the kitchen and up the stairs.

She yelled, 'You were *never* going to! *Never!*' I was amazed at her passion. I sat down on my bed with a book open, so that if she came up to rage at me more I could pretend to be reading. In a minute she stamped upstairs and stood outside the closed door. 'You were just *looking* for an excuse not to help, and you *found* it! Very *nice*! Thanks a *lot*!' she yelled, and went downstairs. A few minutes later she came up again and shouted, 'I can do it myself, you know! You're no help, anyway. All you ever do is just stand around like some stupid zombie!'

There was a good deal of truth in all this. I considered my uselessness exculpatory, in fact, though I wanted to make some more dignified defence, especially since I owed Lucille two blows. But that would come later. 'I can't hear you, Lucille,' I called sweetly. 'You'll have to speak louder.'

'Oh, right,' she said. 'Very funny. Really clever,' and these were the last words she spoke to me for several days. Even Sylvie noticed. 'What's gotten into you girls?' she would say.

Marilynne Robinson, 1981

From A Nineteenth-Century Childhood

'. . . your mother does so much enjoy London, and it is really useful to me to be at the British Museum every day just now, I must remember. You will enjoy your season.'

'Oh, no, father, we shall not for a single moment. We have no clothes – we are dowdy. Nothing could satisfy me but to be simply tremendously smart and dash round the Park, driving a barouche and pair with a tiger on the back seat,' says Mary fiercely, a swift vision of a totally unattainable elegance darting into her head.

Adela then grumbles too. 'Yes, and just look at our engagements. The Archbishop's Garden Party and the Bishop's Garden Party. Old Sir Theodore's jaunt, and then there's that hop at Lady A's. She only knows about twelve young men – all under life-size or with squints.'

'This is absurd,' says Mr Kestell. 'You want me to exclaim over and over again like Mrs Allen, when she took Catherine Morland to Bath: "If only we had some acquaintance here!" As a matter of fact you know perfectly well that lots of fun will crop up, and before you know where you are, you are in a whirl of most delightful parties, my dear children,' says Mr Kestell, thinking that the grumbling must really cease.

But Mary goes on querulously. 'Then the awful shopping. Everything lovely too expensive – dying of heat in shops, and coming out with nothing but a nervous breakdown!'

'My dear, my dear! Your father ought to have had ten thousand a year at least. You must be *good*!' says Mr Kestell.

'Mary, you adore shopping,' says Adela severely.

We have all been rather like babies waking up from sleep and wailing at absolutely nothing. But it is a thundery, stifling afternoon. After some fragrant tea out of Mrs Darcy's Crown Derby, we feel refreshed, and soon our mood completely changes. [. . .]

Adela and I in the late afternoon stroll through Hanover Square and Bond Street, tantalized as we flatten our noses abstemiously in the 'street of elegant shops'. We both adore shoes, hats, and gowns. Then we jingle down to Knightsbridge in a hansom, and here we flatten again, and then make a self-indulgent plunge inside. We buy green shoes, to wear with white muslin Sir Joshua dresses.

'Cleanliness *can't* be combined with poverty,' says Adela. [. . .]

'No, I know, it's impossible,' says Mary, and she pounces upon white silk stockings to wear with green shoes. In the end we spend a great deal, and everything is put down to Mrs Kestell's account. [. . .]

That evening, Mrs Kestell at her writing-table is writing to one of her friends:

'Adela and Mary are off, radiant, to their dance, looking like flowers in their calyxes, with their sweet young faces in their white and green.'

'Why *do* they say these things to each other?' says Adela in the hansom trotting across the Park to the dance at Mrs Tallboys' on Campden Hill. [. . .]

'Yes, and all the time mother knows quite well what a devil's heart lies under Mary's Burne-Jonesy sweetness,' says Adela.

'And that M. Anatole France isn't in it for Adela's cynicism, though she drifts about being thought a very sweet creature!' says Mary.

[. . .]

And now we are trip-clip-clopping, trip-clip-clopping up through the leafy bowers of Campden Hill, and stop at a tall Norman Shaw architected house – alight, and pass through marble, up marble [. . . on] and across the parquet floor to the fascinating, artistic, gracious hostess, and to the massive, comfortable chaperons in their rich waisted velvets and long trains, seated in formidable yet customary array.

We have dance programmes given us, on which is printed only one word, 'Valse', all the way down, interspersed twice with the word 'Lancers'. Soon, in our shimmering white or pink satins, with our long white kid gloves, elegant waists and sprays of flowers on the left side of our bodices, our hair coiled on the nape of our necks or on the top of our heads, our trains first swirling about our feet, then gracefully caught up and managed, we fall with our partners into the swinging rhythm of that old Blue Danube Valse.

Duennas and chaperons were fast going out even at that date; but at this house many lorgnons still bristled, and elderly heads nodded together over the young things whirling round the centre of the room; for Mrs Tallboys had a passion for young people, and invited her eminent contemporaries to come and watch them as though they were a lot of young sea lions plunging about, at whom it was a great pleasure to look. [. . .]

Over one partner's shoulder one would see, for instance, that Mr Henry James had come in. A few more whirls round, and one has a glimpse at his face, which betrays that nervous suffering which a sense of the shortcomings of words was apt to throw him into at any moment. [. . .]

Another round of the long Valse and one perceives that old Herr Joachim and his quartette have come in after a concert, and Mrs Tallboys takes him down to the dining-room to sup with the élite of his English musical circle of adorers.

[. . .]

And now, at this distance of time, I hear a faint popping of corks, and laughter at the 'flash' of talk that passes across the little supper tables in the tapestried room; I remember rapid exchanges of confidences with intimate cousins; a light tap with a fan on my shoulder draws my attention. I feel the absorption of happy lovers, or the hidden tragedies of men loving and not loved, or of young girls loving and not loved; sentimental Valse music tearing at their hearts.

The bright trivial animation of the ballroom I cannot reproduce. I feel it is muffled now, faded, and ghostly.

[. . .]

When her dance is over, 'Who were the blots?' Mrs Tallboys asks an intimate friend as she comes back into her emptied room, having said goodnight to most of her guests. Though gracious and romantic, Mrs Tallboys is also satirical.

Adela and I, animated and dishevelled, still a little out of breath after the last extra, get into our hansom and wave goodnight to Fitzgerald.

As the horse trots gently through the London dawn, we begin to yawn and feel a great fatigue; then we lie back in our corner silent; two puppets limp on their strings after the drama is ended.

Mary McCarthy, 1924

From Like That

It was hotter than ever. The lawn was beginning to grow dark and the locusts were droning out so shrill and steady that you couldn't notice them unless you thought to. The sky was bluish grey and the trees in the vacant lot across the street were dark. I kept on sitting on the front porch with Mama and Papa and hearing their low talk without listening to the words. I wanted to go in our room with Sis but I was afraid to. I wanted to ask her what was really the matter. Was hers and Tuck's fuss so bad as that or was it that she was so crazy about him that she was sad because he was leaving? For a minute I didn't think it was either one of those things, I wanted to know but I was scared to ask. I just sat there with the grown people. I have never been so lonesome as I was that night.

If I ever think about being sad I just remember how it was then – sitting there looking at the long bluish shadows across the lawn and feeling like I was the only child left in the family and that Sis and Dan were dead or gone for good.

It's October now and the sun shines bright and a little cool and the sky is the colour of my turquoise ring. Dan's gone to Tech. So has Tuck gone. It's not at all like it was last fall, though. I come in from High School (I go there now) and Sis maybe is just sitting by the window reading or writing to Tuck or just looking out. Sis is thinner and sometimes she looks to me in the face like a grown person. Or like, in a way, something has suddenly hurt her hard. We don't do any of the things we used to. It's good weather for fudge or doing so many things. But no, she just sits around or goes for long walks in the chilly late afternoons by herself. Sometimes she'll smile in a way that really gripes – like I was such a kid and all. Sometimes I want to cry or hit her.

But I'm as hard-boiled as the next person. I can get along by myself if Sis or anybody else wants to. I'm glad I'm thirteen and still wear socks and can do what I please. I don't want to be any older if I get like Sis has. But I wouldn't. I wouldn't like any boy in the world as much as she does Tuck. I'd never let a boy or anything make me act like she does. I get lonesome – sure – but I don't care. I know there's no way I can make myself stay thirteen all my life, but I know I'd never let anything really change me at all – no matter what it is.

I skate and ride my bike and go to the school football games every Friday. But when one afternoon the kids all got quiet in the gym basement and then started telling certain things – about being married and all – I got up quick so I wouldn't hear and went and played basketball. And when some of the kids said they were going to start wearing lipstick and stockings I said I wouldn't for a hundred dollars.

You see I'd never be like Sis is now. I wouldn't. Anybody could know that if they knew me. I just wouldn't, that's all. I don't want to grow up – if it's like that.

Carson McCullers, 1972

From The Old Wives' Tale

When Constance came to bed, half an hour later, Sophia was already in bed. The room was fairly spacious. It had been the girls' retreat and fortress since their earliest years. Its features seemed to them as natural and unalterable as the features of a cave to a cave-dweller. It had been repapered twice in their lives, and each papering stood out in their memories like an epoch; a third epoch was due to the replacing of a drugget by a resplendent old carpet degraded from the drawing-room. There was only one bed, the bedstead being of painted iron; they never interfered with each other in that bed, sleeping with a detachment as perfect as if they had slept on opposite sides of St Luke's Square; yet if Constance had one night lain down on the half near the window instead of on the half near the door, the secret nature of the universe would have seemed to be altered. The small fire-grate was filled with a mass of shavings of silver paper; now the rare illnesses which they had suffered were recalled chiefly as periods when that silver paper was crammed into a large slipper-case which hung by the mantel-piece, and a fire of coals unnaturally reigned in its place – the silver paper was part of the order of the world. The sash of the window would not work quite properly, owing to a slight subsidence in the wall, and even when the window was fastened there was always a narrow slit to the left hand between the window and its frame; through this slit came draughts and thus very keen frosts were remembered by the nights when Mrs Baines caused the sash to be forced and kept at its full height by means of wedges – the slit of exposure was part of the order of the world.

They possessed only one bed, one washstand, and one dressing-table; but in some other respects they were rather fortunate girls, for they had two mahogany wardrobes; this mutual independence as regards wardrobes was due partly to Mrs Baines's strong common sense, and partly to their father's tendency to spoil them a little. They had, moreover, a chest of drawers with a curved front, of which structure Constance occupied two short drawers and one long one, and Sophia two long drawers. On it stood two fancy workboxes, in which each sister kept jewellery, a savings-bank book, and other treasures, and these boxes were absolutely sacred to their respective owners. They were different, but one was not more magnificent than the other. Indeed, a rigid equality was the rule in the chamber, the single exception being that behind the door were three hooks, of which Constance commanded two.

'Well,' Sophia began, when Constance appeared, 'how's darling Mr Povey?' She was lying on her back, and smiling at her two hands, which she held up in front of her.

'Asleep,' said Constance. 'At least mother thinks so. She says sleep is the best thing for him.'

' "It will probably come on again," ' said Sophia.

'What's that you say?' Constance asked, undressing.

' "It will probably come on again." '

These words were a quotation from the utterances of darling Mr Povey on the stairs, and Sophia delivered them with an exact imitation of Mr Povey's vocal mannerism.

'Sophia,' said Constance, firmly, approaching the bed, 'I wish you wouldn't be so silly!' She had benevolently ignored the satirical note in Sophia's first remark, but a strong instinct in her rose up and objected to further derision. 'Surely you've done enough for one day!' she added.

For answer Sophia exploded into violent laughter, which she made no attempt to control. She laughed too long and too freely while Constance stared at her.

'*I* don't know what's come over you!' said Constance.

'It's only because I can't look at it without simply going off into fits!' Sophia gasped out. And she held up a tiny object in her left hand.

Constance started, flushing. 'You don't mean to say you've kept it!' she protested earnestly. 'How horrid you are, Sophia! Give it me at once and let me throw it away. I never heard of such doings. Now give it me!'

'No,' Sophia objected, still laughing. 'I wouldn't part with it for worlds. It's too lovely.'

She had laughed away all her secret resentment against Constance for having ignored her during the whole evening and for being on such intimate terms with their parents. And she was ready to be candidly jolly with Constance.

'Give it me,' said Constance, doggedly.

Sophia hid her hand under the clothes. 'You can have his old stump, when it comes out, if you like. But not this. What a pity it's the wrong one!'

'Sophia, I'm ashamed of you! Give it me.'

Then it was that Sophia first perceived Constance's extreme seriousness. She was surprised and a little intimidated by it. For the expression of Constance's face, usually so benign and calm, was harsh, almost fierce. However, Sophia had a great deal of what is called 'spirit', and not even ferocity on the face of mild Constance could intimidate her for more than a few seconds. Her gaiety expired and her teeth were hidden.

'I've said nothing to mother –' Constance proceeded.

'I should hope you haven't,' Sophia put in tersely.

'But I certainly shall if you don't throw that away,' Constance finished.

'You can say what you like,' Sophia retorted, adding contemptuously a term of opprobrium which has long since passed out of use: 'Cant!'

'Will you give it me or won't you?'

'No!'

It was a battle suddenly engaged in the bedroom. The atmosphere had altered completely with the swiftness of magic. The beauty of Sophia, the angelic tenderness of Constance, and the youthful, naïve, innocent charm of both of them, were transformed into something sinister and cruel. Sophia lay back on the pillow amid her dark-brown hair, and gazed with relentless defiance into the angry eyes of Constance, who stood threatening by the bed. They could hear the gas singing over the dressing-table, and their hearts beating the blood wildly in their veins. They ceased to be young without growing old; the eternal had leapt up in them from its sleep.

Constance walked away from the bed to the dressing-table and began to loose her hair and brush it, holding back her head, shaking it, and bending forward, in the changeless gesture of that rite. She was so disturbed that she had unconsciously reversed the customary order of the toilette. After a moment Sophia slipped out of bed and, stepping with her bare feet to the chest of drawers, opened her workbox and deposited the fragment of Mr Povey therein; she dropped the lid with an uncompromising bang, as if to say: 'We shall see if I am to be trod upon, miss!' Their eyes met again in the looking-glass. Then Sophia got back into bed.

Five minutes later, when her hair was quite finished, Constance knelt down and said her prayers. Having said her prayers, she went straight to Sophia's workbox, opened it, seized the fragment of Mr Povey, ran to the window, and frantically pushed the fragment through the slit into the Square.

'There!' she exclaimed nervously.

She had accomplished this inconceivable transgression of the code of honour, beyond all undoing, before Sophia could recover from the stupefaction of seeing her sacred workbox impudently violated. In a single moment one of Sophia's chief ideals had been smashed utterly, and that by the sweetest, gentlest creature she had ever known. It was a revealing experience for Sophia – and also for Constance. And it frightened them equally. Sophia, staring at the text, 'Thou God seest me,' framed in straw over the chest of drawers, did not stir. She was defeated, and so profoundly moved in her defeat that she did not even reflect upon the obvious inefficacy of illuminated texts as a deterrent from evil-doing. Not that she cared a fig for the fragment of Mr Povey! It was the moral aspect of the affair, and the astounding, inexplicable development in Constance's character, that staggered her into silent acceptance of the inevitable.

Constance, trembling, took pains to finish undressing with dignified deliberation. Sophia's behaviour under the blow seemed too good to be true; but it gave her courage. At length she turned out the gas and lay down by Sophia. And there was a little shuffling, and then stillness for a while.

'And if you want to know,' said Constance in a tone that mingled amicableness with righteousness, 'mother's decided with Aunt Harriet that we are *both* to leave school next term.'

Arnold Bennett, 1908

From The Sisters Rajevsky

. . . the understanding between Anyuta and [Dostoyevsky] became worse and worse. His friendship with the fourteen-year-old Tanja grew. She became each day more charmed with him and confided in him blindly. He naturally noticed her boundless worship and admiration, and was pleased with it. He was for ever holding Tanja up to her sister as an example.

When sometimes he uttered a deep thought, or made a paradoxical remark full of genius, or combated the whole accepted system of morals, Anyuta pretended not to understand him. While Tanja's eyes danced with delight, her sister answered him in order to irritate him with some stupid, trite truism.

'You have a dull and feeble mind,' exclaimed Dostoyevsky. 'Look at your sister. She is hardly more than a child. She understands me. It is she who has cleverness and insight.'

Tanja always blushed with pleasure, and if it had been necessary she would have let herself be cut in pieces for him.

And truly, however wonderful it may seem, the fourteen-year-old Tanja did understand him. [. . .]

In the depths of her heart Tanja was very glad that Dostoyevsky no longer cared as much for Anyuta as in the beginning of their acquaintance. She was ashamed of the feeling, and considered it a kind of treachery to her sister. Without being willing to admit it to herself, she sought to enter into a compromise with her conscience and to atone for her secret sin by special affectionateness and dutifulness, but her consciousness of sin did not prevent her involuntarily rejoicing when Anyuta and Dostoyevsky quarrelled.

Dostoyevsky called Tanja his little friend, and she thought in her innocence that she was dearer to him than her elder sister, and understood him better. He even praised her appearance to Anyuta.

'You fancy,' he said to the latter, 'that you are beautiful; but your little sister will in time be more beautiful than you. Her face is much more expressive, and she has regular gipsy eyes. You are only a rather pretty little German, that is all.'

Anyuta smiled disdainfully. Tanja, on the contrary, drank in with rapture this praise of her beauty, which she had never heard before.

'But is it really true?' she asked herself, anxiously; and she began to be full of grave fears lest her sister should be injured by the preference he showed her.

Tanja was very anxious to know what Anyuta herself thought of it, and if it was true that she would be beautiful when she grew up. This last question was of special interest to her. In St Petersburg both the sisters slept in the same room, and at night, when they were undressing, they had their most confidential chats. Anyuta stood as usual before her big looking-glass, and shook out her long fair hair, which at night she plaited in two long plaits. This occupation took time, for her hair was unusually long and silky, and she drew the comb gently and carefully through it. Tanja sat on her bed already undressed, with her hands clasped round her knees, thinking how she should begin the conversation which was so much in her mind.

'What silly things Dostoyevsky said today,' she began at last, trying to appear as indifferent as possible.

'Which things?' said Anyuta, for she had evidently quite forgotten what seemed to Tanja such an important conversation.

'Why, that I had gipsy eyes, and should be handsome some day,' said Tanja, and felt herself blushing red up to her ears.

Anyuta let her hands which held the comb sink, and turned her head with a graceful movement towards her sister.

'*You* fancy Dostoyevsky thinks *you* pretty, prettier than I am?' she asked, looking at Tanja with a sly, enigmatical look.

This crafty smile, those green, laughing eyes, and the fair, loose, flowing hair made her look like a regular water-nymph. In the big mirror on the wall close by the bed, Tanja saw her own little dark face, and compared it with her sister's. It would be wrong to say that the comparison pleased her, but her sister's self-satisfied tone irritated her, and she would not give in.

'Tastes differ!' she exclaimed, hotly.

'Yes, tastes differ strangely!' remarked Anyuta, calmly continuing to comb her hair.

Sonya Kovalevsky, 1885

From The Whiteness of Bones

Mamie had so far managed to learn little from Claire of the extraordinary circumstances that had brought her sister so happily and unexpectedly to Sixty-fifth Street and Park Avenue. Claire was not very forthcoming. It was more a matter of temperament than a need to conceal or a desire for privacy. She tended not to reconsider. She did not sift through the past for clues. Mamie had learned long ago that Claire saw things in a way altogether different from her own view, so Mamie was always very interested to hear Claire's version of things. She questioned Claire ceaselessly about the past, not because she required pure information, nor to reinforce her own cool, fastidious memory, but because the variations in the story thrilled her.

'You must have sneaked out to see Orval that time you said you were going to paddling practice.'

'I never made the crew and Orval was with his grandmother at McBryde Plantation.'

'I thought his grandmother drowned in that accident.'

'No.'

The constant surprise of this freshly created past confirmed Mamie's suspicion of her own individuality, and the individuality of others. It gave her, too, the beginning of an idea: memory, happily, was not the same thing as truth.

'Well, how did it happen then?'

'What?'

'With Orval. How did you get pregnant? It's awfully hard to get pregnant these days, isn't it?'

Mamie's own sexual life was limited. That is to say, the act of sexual intercourse had so far played only a small part in Mamie's life, while her sensuality was unexplored and unlimited. [. . .]

'It wasn't that hard,' Claire said. 'I'd been fucking him since I was thirteen.'

Mamie slowly rewrapped her cheeseburger and neatly repacked it in the bag. She rolled up the bag and set it down on the needlepoint rug between the beds. She was shocked.

'Why did you never tell me? I wanted to know.'

'Oh, Mamie.' Claire laughed. 'How could you have wanted to know if you didn't know?'

'I mean I would have helped you.'

'Helped me?'

'I would have been your friend and you could have told me things.'

'I tried to tell you once. Remember the time I had to go to the clinic because I said that I already had a Tampax in and I put in a second one? And when the nurse was cleaning up the room, she said, "Next time you have sex, girly, be sure to take it out." I told you what she said, as a way of telling you, and you said, "Oh, what a mean person."'

'I believed you.'

'Mamie, you believe everybody.'

'I don't really. But I believed you.'

Claire could no longer pretend that Mamie was not upset. She sighed loudly and moved over to Mamie's bed. They sat side by side.

'You didn't miss much,' Claire said gently. 'I used to sneak out to meet him during the summer. We did it the first time in the banyan tree.'

'The banyan?'

'It was pretty uncomfortable.'

'You used to say that Orval liked *me*.'

'I think he did. But then he gave up.'

'I do feel that I missed something. It might have been good for me if I had known.'

'You were always off fording a fucking river. Or reading.'

'You are this wonderful mutant, Claire,' said Mamie quietly. 'You have just what you need. You're not stupid and humourless like Aunt Alice and you're not dumb and serious like me. You're some genetic She-of-the-Future. You'll be all right. You'll be perfect.'

'And you won't be?'

'Oh. Me. I don't know about me. I wish I could be like you.'

'I always wanted to be like you. And care passionately about things. But I don't. I don't know why, but I don't. You've always had these strong feelings about things. I could feel strongly about your cheeseburger, however.'

Mamie eased herself back on to her pillow, leaving her legs hanging awkwardly over the side. She moved in the careful way of someone who has been slightly injured; someone who does not yet know the extent of the damage, but is moving cautiously none the less.

'No, I don't want it,' she said.

Susanna Moore, 1989

She is Going

For their elder sister's hair
Martha does a wreath prepare
Of bridal rose, ornate and gay:
Tomorrow is the wedding day:
        She is going.

Mary, youngest of the three,
Laughing idler, full of glee,
Arm in arm does fondly chain her,
Thinking, poor trifler, to detain her –
        But she's going.

Vex not, maidens, nor regret
Thus to part with Margaret.
Charms like yours can never stay
Long within doors; and one day
           You'll be going.

Charles Lamb

From A Game of Pretend

By the time the wedding happened there had been months – plenty of time for me to understand. But I didn't. I studied the surprising boxes of sherry and spirits as they were delivered to the house. I read the wedding invitations, and the lists of what Hester and her husband would need in their new home. But the future was well buried under all this paraphernalia and excitement. For the time being I was shut out of Hester's bedroom while she and her fiancé filled the room with smoke and other fuggy smells. I was shy about making noises in the next-door bathroom and learned how to spit toothpaste foam soundlessly.

On the day of the wedding the house was cluttered with visiting relations and I was transferred to a camp-bed in a small space. I didn't mind. It wasn't until all the relations were departed and the camp-bed folded up in the cupboard that I noticed what had happened. Hester had gone. Not just for a holiday. Gone. And I had forgotten to prepare myself for it. Her clothes had gone from her wardrobe. I could spit as noisily as I liked. I don't remember crying. It was worse than that. There is a phrase – 'My belly thinks my throat's been cut.' Yes – that describes the feeling well enough I think. Emptied out. Closed off.

Marilyn Duckworth, 1993

Virginia Woolf and Vanessa Bell

Kiss her most passionately in all my private places – neck –, and arm, and eyeball, and tell her – what new thing is there to tell her? – how fond I am of her husband.

VW to Clive Bell, 1907

Nessa is like a great child, more happy and serene than ever. [. . .] To be with her is to sit in autumn sunlight; but then there is Clive!

VW to Violet Dickinson, September 1907

Give my love to my sister, and if you like, kiss her left eye, with the eyelid smoothed over the curve, and just blue on the crest . . .

VW to Clive Bell, Friday, 22 March 1907

Nessa comes tomorrow – what one calls Nessa; but it means husband and baby; and of sister there is less than there used to be . . .

VW to Violet Dickinson, 25 August 1907

. . . to put it simply, Virginia was in love with her sister. And Vanessa depended on her more than she acknowledged.

Hermione Lee, *Virginia Woolf*, 1996

To Virginia Stephen

46, Gordon Square, Bloomsbury
Sunday

My Billy,

I think I *won't* lunch with you tomorrow. Perhaps you'll ask me another time to some lunch or dinner alone with you two, but I think I had better come back to lunch tomorrow.

[. . .]

Well, I'm afraid I was very inexpressive today, but although I had expected it, it was somehow so bewildering and upsetting when I did actually see you and Leonard together that I didn't know how to say what I felt. You do know, however, Billy, and Leonard too, that I do of course care for you. I won't say more than for anybody, but in a way that's quite special to you. Your happiness does matter frightfully to me and I do now feel quite happy about you, which really means that I think Leonard one of the most remarkable and charming people I know. I am looking forward very much to having him for a brother-in-law.

Goodnight, my dear couple, before I get too doddering.

Vanessa Bell, 2 June 1912

From Beginning Again

. . . our wedding ceremony was provided with an element of comic relief (quite unintended) characteristic of the Stephens. In the middle of the proceedings Vanessa interrupted the Registrar, saying: 'Excuse me interrupting; I have just remembered: we registered my son – he is two years old – in the name of Clement, and we now want to change his name to Quentin – can you tell me what I have to do?' There was a moment of astonished silence in the room as we all looked round sympathetically and saw the serious, slightly puzzled look on Vanessa's face. There was a pause while the Registrar stared at her with his mouth open. Then he said severely: 'One thing at a time, please, Madam.'

Leonard Woolf, 1964

'Hell hath no fury like a woman scorned . . . especially in favour of her sister.'

Joan Fontaine

From A Broadsheet Ballad

. . . This girl's name was Edith and she had a younger sister, Agnes. Their father was old Harry Mallerton, kept the British Oak at North Quainy; he stuttered. Well, this Edith had a love affair with a young chap, William, and having a very loving nature she behaved foolish. Then she couldn't bring the chap up to scratch nohow by herself, and of course she was afraid to tell her mother or father: you know how girls are after being so pesky natural, they fear, O they do fear! But soon it couldn't be hidden any longer as she was at home with them all, so she wrote a letter to her mother. [. . .]

By all accounts the mother was as angry as an old lion, but Harry took it calm like and sent for young William, who'd not come at first. He lived close by in the village so they went down at last and fetched him.

'Alright, yes,' he said, 'I'll do what's lawful to be done. There you are, I can't say no fairer, that I can't.'

'No,' they said, 'you can't.'

So he kissed the girl and off he went, promising to call in and settle affairs in a day or two. The next day Agnes, which was the younger girl, she also wrote a note to her mother telling her some more strange news.

'God above,' the mother cried out, 'can it be true, both of you girls, my own daughters, and by the same man! whatever were you thinking on, both of ye!' [. . .]

[She] was afraid to tell her husband at first, for old Harry was the devil born again when he was roused up, so she sent for young William herself, who'd not come again, of course, not likely. But they made him come, O yes, when they told the girls' father.

'Well may I go to my d-d-d-damnation at once!' roared old Harry – he stuttered, you know. [. . .] So he took off his coat, he took up a stick, he walked down the street to William and cut him off his legs. Then he beat him till he howled for mercy. [. . .] They do say as he beat him for a solid hour; I can't say as to that, but then Old Harry picked him up and carried him off [. . .] and threw him down in his kitchen between his own two girls like a dead dog. [. . .] Pretty girls both, girls you could get very fond of [. . .] like as two pinks they were. They had to decide which of them William was to marry. [. . .]

'I'll marry Agnes,' says he.

'You'll not' – says the old man – 'You'll marry Edie.'

'No I won't' – William says – 'it's Agnes I love and I'll be married to her or I won't be married to either e'er them.' All the time Edith sat quiet, dumb as a shovel, never a word, crying a bit; but they do say the young one went on like a . . . a young . . . Jew. [. . .]

'I'll marry Agnes,' [. . .] – William says – and they couldn't budge him. [. . .] at last Harry says: 'It's like this'. He pulled a half-crown out of his pocket and 'Heads it's Agnes,' he says, 'or tails it's Edith,' he says. [. . .] And it come down Agnes, yes, heads it was – Agnes – and so there they were. [. . .] and at that Agnes flung her arms round William's neck and was for going off with him then and there, ha! But this is how it happened about that. William [. . .] was a lodger in the village and his landlady wouldn't have him in her house one mortal hour when she heard of it; give him the rightabout there and then. He couldn't get lodgings anywhere else [. . .] so of course [. . .] Harry had to take him, and there they all lived together at the British Oak – all in one happy family. But they girls couldn't abide the sight of each other, so their father cleaned up an old outhouse in his yard [. . .] and put William and his Agnes out in it. And there they had to bide. They had a couple of chairs, a sofa and a bed [. . .] and made it quite snug.

[. . .] Edie was very sad and solemn then; a pretty girl, one you could like. [. . . She] never opened her lips to either of them again, and her father sided with her, too. What was worse, it came out after the marriage that Agnes was quite free of trouble – it was only a trumped-up game between her and William because he fancied her better than the other one. And they never had no child, them two, though when poor Edie's mischance came along, I'd be damned if Agnes wasn't fonder of it than its own mother, a jolly side more fonder, and William – he fair worshipped it. [. . .] William and Agnes worshipped it, and Edie – she just looked on it till the day of her death [. . .] 'Twas Agnes that died. She was found on the sofa one morning stone dead, dead as an adder. Poisoned! [. . .] Poisoned! [. . .]

This was the way of it. [. . .] One morning the mother went out in the yard to collect her eggs, and she began calling out, 'Edie, Edie, here a minute, come and look where that hen have laid her egg;' [. . .] And when Edie went out her mother led her round the back of the outhouse, and there on the top of a wall this hen had laid an egg. 'I would never have believed it, Edie,' she says [. . .] 'There now, Aggie, Aggie, here a minute, come and look where the hen have laid that egg.' And as Aggie didn't answer, the mother went in and found her on the sofa in the outhouse, stone dead. [. . .]

I don't know what would lie between two young women in a wrangle of that sort; some would get over it quick, but some would never sleep soundly any more, not for a minute of their mortal lives. Edie must have been one of that sort. There's people living there now as could tell a lot if they'd a mind to it. Some [. . .] could tell you the very shop where Edie managed to get hold of the poison, and could describe [. . .] just how she administered it in a glass of barley water. Old Harry knew all about it [. . .] but he favoured Edith and he never budged a word. Clever old chap was Harry and nothing came out against Edie at the inquest – nor the trial neither. [. . .]

A beautiful trial. The police came and fetched poor William.

They took him away and in due course he was hanged. [. . .] It was rough on him, but he hadn't played straight and nobody stuck up for him. They made out a case against him – there was some unlucky bit of evidence which I'll take my oath old Harry knew something about – and William was done for. [. . .] And Edith, she sat in court through it all, very white and trembling and sorrowful, but when the judge put his black cap on they do say she blushed and looked across at William and gave a bit of a smile. Well she had to suffer for his doings, so why shouldn't he suffer for hers. That's how I look at it. [. . .] Pretty girls they were both, as like as two pinks . . .

A. E. Coppard, 1921

From The Lute

A young man named Omar got on to his mare one day and rode over his father's land for many miles, looking for the right place to build a small house of his own. He came to a hill between the forest and the olive groves. This is the spot, he said. Here I can play my lute all day.

Little by little he built a cottage, bringing the materials from his father's house, and doing all the work himself. When it was done he furnished it with everything he needed for the pleasant life he intended to lead. His most important possession was his lute, which he had trained so that when anyone was coming it sounded its strings in warning. Then Omar would look into the opening under the strings and watch the person as he approached.

Outside the house he built an arbour of canes where he could lie back and drink his tea. And he would sit out there in the shade of the arbour with the green trees all around him, smoking kif and drinking tea. At length he would take down his lute and begin to play.

Farther down the valley lived two sisters whose father and mother had died, leaving them alone in a big house. The younger sister was still only a girl, and there was a handsome village lad with whom she was friendly. The older sister, who desired the boy for herself, caught sight of him talking to the girl under a tree. Later she questioned her.

'Who was that you were talking to?'

'The boy from the village.'

'What did he say to you?'

The girl smiled and looked very happy. 'He said beautiful words and wonderful things. Because I love him and he loves me.'

'What?' cried the woman. 'And you're not ashamed to say such a thing?'

'Why should I be? We're going to be married.'

The older sister jumped up and rushed out. She began to burn powders and to chant, and it was not long before she burst into the room with a scream and flung a handful of black powder over the girl. At that instant her sister no longer stood in front of her – only a camel, which she chained outside.

Mohammed Mrabat, translated by Paul Bowles, 1979

From Binnorie

Once upon a time there were two king's daughters lived in a bower near the bonny mill-dams of Binnorie. And Sir William came wooing the eldest and won her love, and plighted troth with glove and with ring. But after a time he looked upon the youngest, with her cherry cheeks and golden hair, and his love went out to her till he cared no longer for the eldest one. So she hated her sister for taking away Sir William's love, and day by day her hate grew and grew and she plotted and she planned how to get rid of her.

So one fine morning, fair and clear, she said to her sister, 'Let us go and see our father's boats come in at the bonny mill-stream of Binnorie.' So they went there hand in hand. And when they came to the river's bank the youngest got upon a stone to watch for the beaching of the boats. And her sister, coming behind her, caught her round the waist and dashed her into the rushing mill-stream of Binnorie.

'O sister, sister, reach me your hand!' she cried, as she floated away, 'and you shall have half of all I've got or shall get.'

'No, sister, I'll reach you no hand of mine, for I am the heir to all your land. Shame on me if I touch her hand that has come 'twixt me and my own heart's love.'

'O sister, O sister, then reach me your glove!' she cried, as she floated further away, 'and you shall have your William again.'

'Sink on,' cried the cruel princess, 'no hand or glove of mine you'll touch. Sweet William will be all mine when you are sunk beneath the bonny mill-stream of Binnorie.' And she turned and went home to the king's castle.

Retold by Joseph Jacobs, 1898

From The Sisters

Edith wrote:
'My mother bids me ask' (I did not tell you –
A widow with less guile than many a child.
God help the wrinkled children that are Christ's
As well as the plump cheek – she wrought us harm,
Poor soul, not knowing) 'are you ill?' (so ran
The letter) 'you have not been here of late.
You will not find me here. At last I go
On that long-promised visit to the North.
I told your wayside story to my mother
And Evelyn. She remembers you. Farewell.
Pray come and see my mother. Almost blind
With ever-growing cataract, yet she thinks
She sees you when she hears. Again farewell.'

Cold words from one I had hoped to warm so far
That I could stamp my image on her heart!
'Pray come and see my mother, and farewell.'
Cold, but as welcome as free airs of heaven
After a dungeon's closeness. Selfish, strange!
What dwarfs are men! my strangled vanity
Uttered a stifled cry – to have vext myself
And all in vain for her – cold heart or none –
No bride for me. Yet so my path was clear
To win the sister.

           Whom I wooed and won.
For Evelyn knew not of my former suit,
Because the simple mother worked upon
By Edith prayed me not to whisper of it.
And Edith would be bridesmaid on the day.

But on that day, not being all at ease,
I from the altar glancing back upon her,
Before the first 'I will' was uttered, saw
The bridesmaid pale, statuelike, passionless –
'No harm, no harm' I turned again, and placed
My ring upon the finger of my bride.

So, when we parted, Edith spoke no word,
She wept no tear, but round my Evelyn clung
In utter silence for so long, I thought
'What, will she never set her sister free?'

We left her, happy each in each, and then,
As though the happiness of each in each
Were not enough, must fain have torrents, lakes,
Hills, the great things of Nature and the fair,
To lift us as it were from commonplace,
And help us to our joy. Better have sent
Our Edith through the glories of the earth,
To change with her horizon, if true Love
Were not his own imperial all-in-all.

Far off we went. My God, I would not live
Save that I think this gross hard-seeming world
Is our misshaping vision of the Powers
Behind the world, that make our griefs our gains.

For on the dark night of our marriage-day
The great Tragedian, that had quenched herself
In that assumption of the bridesmaid – she
That loved me – our true Edith – her brain broke
With over-acting, till she rose and fled
Beneath a pitiless rush of Autumn rain
To the deaf church – to be let in – to pray
Before *that* altar – so I think; and there
They found her beating the hard Protestant doors.
She died and she was buried ere we knew.

I learnt it first. I had to speak. At once
The bright quick smile of Evelyn, that had sunned
The morning of our marriage, past away:
And on our home-return the daily want
Of Edith in the house, the garden, still
Haunted us like her ghost; and by and by,
Either from that necessity for talk
Which lives with blindness, or plain innocence
Of nature, or desire that her lost child
Should earn from both the praise of heroism,
The mother broke her promise to the dead,
And told the living daughter with what love
Edith had welcomed my brief wooing of her,
And all her sweet self-sacrifice and death.

Henceforth that mystic bond betwixt the twins –
Did I not tell you they were twins? – prevailed
So far that no caress could win my wife
Back to that passionate answer of full heart
I had from her at first. Not that her love,
Though scarce as great as Edith's power of love,
Had lessened, but the mother's garrulous wail

For ever woke the unhappy Past again,
Till that dead bridesmaid, meant to be my bride,
Put forth cold hands between us, and I feared
The very fountains of her life were chilled;
So took her thence, and brought her here, and here
She bore a child, whom reverently we called
Edith; and in the second year was born
A second – this I named from her own self,
Evelyn; then two weeks – no more – she joined,
In and beyond the grave, that one she loved.
    Now in this quiet of declining life,
Through dreams by night and trances of the day,
The sisters glide about me hand in hand,
Both beautiful alike, nor can I tell
One from the other, no, nor care to tell
One from the other, only know they come,
They smile upon me, till, remembering all
The love they both have borne me, and the love
I bore them both – divided as I am
From either by the stillness of the grave –
I know not which of these I love the best.

Alfred Lord Tennyson, 1890

From Lady Ann Foley

Lady Maria, eldest daughter of the Earl of C—y. was born in
December 1754; and married on 25 June 1775 to Andrew Bayntun,
Esquire, [. . .] by whom she has issue two daughters, and from
whom she was divorced in 1783. Of this lady, we shall hereafter
mention several very extraordinary circumstances, which will suf-
ficiently prove that she is composed of the same inflammable
material as her younger sister, and probably may have assisted her,
as well by precept as example, in conducting her amours.

So far, we think we have given authentic intelligence respecting

Lady Ann's amours; but as we promised to pay some attention to the proceedings of the elder sister, we shall not disappoint our readers, as it will evidently appear that such a pair of sisters are not generally to be found.

Lady Maria Coventry (afterwards Lady Maria Bayntun), sister to Lady Ann, has not indeed been detected in a shrubbery, in the open face of day, to gratify the eyes of a peeping Tom; but she has had peepers as well as her amiable sister, as will appear by the following evidence of Mary Nash. [. . .]

She says that shortly after Mr Cooper came to visit in Mr Bayntun's family, she observed the conduct of Mr Cooper and Lady Maria Bayntun to be very particular towards each other. [. . .] She further saith, that, on a night in the summer of 1781, Mr Bayntun being in London and Lady Maria and Mr Cooper in the dinner parlour [. . .] alone together, [. . .] she was called out into the yard by one of the menservants; that, on this occasion, she was told by one of [them] to look through a hole in the shutter of one of the windows of such parlour; [. . .] and saw Lady Maria Bayntun sitting on Mr Cooper's knee, with her arms around his neck, and kissing him. She further says that she was assisted by [. . .] Mr Bayntun's coachman to stand on a gate, opposite one of the said windows; and the witness [. . .] saw Lady Maria Bayntun standing with her face towards Mr Cooper, and her petticoats up; and then saw Mr Cooper kiss Lady Maria.

[. . .] Further particulars are mentioned by the Revd Mr Henry Bayntun, which show that the two sisters adopt nearly the same modes of conduct, in every particular. [. . .]

It is a melancholy reflection that infidelities are much more frequent among people of elevated rank. [. . .] A superintendence over domestic concerns engrosses much of the time and attention of those who act in a more humble sphere. [. . .] On the other hand, the lady of fashion abhors the idea of attending to domestic matters; she leads a life of dissipation, her hours hang heavy upon her hands, and she knows not how to kill time – An eternal round of sameness and insipidity disgusts them; and as a refuge from Ennui, they form a connection with one in nearly the same insipid line. [. . .]

Lady Ann, [. . .] it is said, intends to retire to a convent, there to bury herself from this wicked world, and to renounce all sensual thoughts and gratifications: and with the utmost contrition to look back on her past offences, and by the most rigid penance and austerity to expiate all her misdeeds.

Her sister, however, with some jocularity, advised her one day, to take Lord P— with her that he might act as a kind of father confessor; alleging that she did not doubt of his granting her many indulgences; that, upon most occasions, she would find very little difficulty in obtaining absolution, unless she should be guilty of downright imprudence, like that of sacrificing to the amorous deity in the open shrubbery, exposed to public view. Lady A did not relish this *jeu d'esprit* from Lady M—, and could not help recriminating in very severe, terms. She reminded her that they were sisters in iniquity as well as by consanguinity.

From The Life and Amours of Lady Ann Foley, developing the whole of her Intrigues from the time of her marriage [. . .] particularly with Lord M—, Col. F—zp—k, Capt. Ll—d, Mr St—r, the Earl of P—h, and others. [. . .] Together with some curious anecdotes of her sister, Lady Maria Bayntun, who, as her senior, had preceded her in the same spirited line, and probably encouraged her both by Precept and Example, 1782

A Ballad

An excellent new Ballad showing how Mr Mor—cai Ad—d—ms, Pothecary, was catch'd in bed with Miss — and Miss —, two Sisters by Mrs C— an honest Constable in St Andrew's Parish. [. . .] (To the tune of yon Commons and Peers, etc.)

I

An apothecary cloathed in black,
He had to his Patients two Sisters.
He laid them both flat on their Back,
And he gave them a couple of Glisters. Fal lal

II

While the one he was merrily slashing
In order to brisk up her Blood:
The other herself she was washing,
She knowing his glister was good. Fal lal

III

With speed into Bed she then went,
Having carefully laid by her Cloaths,
Saying here's a most charming a Scent,
And at each side of a Nettle a Rose. Fal lal

IV

My Dr, if with me you will marry,
I'll please you right well out of hand.
Cries well push't Pothecary,
You make the House shake when I stand. Fal lal

V

No wonder his Strength it is such,
No number of Whores can him Fright.
No mortal Man juggel'd as much
And so little of Credit got by't. Fal lal

VI

But I solemnly vow & protest
The poor will be left in the lurch,
If convicted he is of incest,
In a Sheet he must stand in the Church. Fal lal

VII

Besides a large Fine he must pay,
Which pleasing will be to most people,
For St Andrew's Church as they say,
Must needs have a very high Steeple. Fal lal

[. . .]

Dublin, 1726

From The Book of Genesis

And Laban said unto Jacob, 'Because thou art my brother, shouldest thou therefore serve me for nought? tell me, what shall thy wages be?'

And Laban had two daughters: the name of the elder was Leah, and the name of the younger was Rachel. Leah was tender-eyed; but Rachel was beautiful and well favoured. And Jacob loved Rachel; and said, 'I will serve thee seven years for Rachel thy younger daughter.'

And Laban said, 'It is better that I give her to thee than that I should give her to another man. Abide with me.'

And Jacob served seven years for Rachel; and they seemed unto him but a few days, for the love he had to her. And Jacob said unto Laban, 'Give me my wife, for my days are fulfilled, that I may go in unto her.'

And Laban gathered together all the men of the place, and made a feast. And it came to pass in the evening that he took Leah his daughter, and brought her to him; and he went in unto her. And Laban gave unto his daughter Leah Zilpah his maid for a hand-maid.

And it came to pass that in the morning, behold, it was Leah: and he said to Laban, 'What is this thou hast done unto me? did not I serve with thee for Rachel? wherefore then hast thou beguiled me?'

And Laban said, 'It must not be so done in our country, to give the younger before the firstborn. Fulfil her week, and we will give thee this also for the service which thou shalt serve with me yet seven other years.'

And Jacob did so, and fulfilled her week: and he gave him Rachel his daughter to wife also. And Laban gave to Rachel his daughter Bilhah his handmaid to be her maid. And he went in also unto Rachel, and he loved also Rachel more than Leah, and served with him yet seven other years.

And when the Lord saw that Leah was hated, he opened her womb: but Rachel was barren. And Leah conceived, and bore a son, and she called his name Reuben: for she said, 'Surely the Lord hath looked upon my affliction; now therefore my husband will love me.' And she conceived again, and bore a son; and said, 'Because the Lord hath heard that I was hated, he hath therefore given me this son also': and she called his name Simeon. And she conceived again, and bore a son; and said, 'Now this time will my husband be joined unto me, because I have borne him three sons': therefore was his name called Levi. And she conceived again, and bore a son: and she said, 'Now will I praise the Lord': therefore she called his name Judah; and left bearing.

And when Rachel saw that she bore Jacob no children, Rachel envied her sister, and said unto Jacob, 'Give me children, or else I die.'

And Jacob's anger was kindled against Rachel: and he said, 'Am I in God's stead, who hath withheld from thee the fruit of the womb?'

And she said, 'Behold my maid Bilhah, go in unto her; and she shall bear upon my knees, that I may also have children by her.'

And she gave him Bilhah her handmaid to wife: and Jacob went in unto her. And Bilhah conceived, and bore Jacob a son.

The Bible, 1610 translation

From A Tale of Two Sisters

'I know what you're about to ask me – have a little patience. Yes, I lived with them both. I married Dora officially in Germany – she wanted to stand under a canopy and she did – but, in actuality, I had two wives, two sisters, just like the patriarch Jacob. All I lacked was a Bilhah and a Zilpah. What would stop the likes of me? Not the Jewish and certainly not the Gentile laws. In the war, the whole human culture crumbled like a ruin. [. . .]

'I didn't want all this. It's one thing to have an adventure – it's quite another to make a permanent institution out of it. But it was out of my hands. From the moment the two sisters met, I was no longer a free man. They enslaved me with their love for me, their love towards each other, and their jealousy. One minute they would be kissing and crying from great devotion and suddenly they would begin to slug away, pull hair, and curse each other with words you wouldn't hear in the underworld. I had never before seen such hysteria or heard such screams. Every few days one of the sisters, or sometimes both, tried to commit suicide. One moment it would be quiet. The three of us might be sitting eating or discussing a book or picture – all of a sudden a horrible shriek and both sisters would be rolling on the floor, tearing pieces from each other. I'd run up, trying to separate them, but I'd catch a slam in the face or a bite and the blood would be dripping from me. Why they were fighting I would never know. Fortunately, we lived on the upper storey, a garret, and we had no neighbours on our floor. One of the sisters would run to the window and try to throw herself out, while the other seized a knife and went for her own throat. I'd grab one by the leg and take the knife away from the other. They'd howl at me and at each other. I'd try to find out what caused the outburst, but I learned in time that they didn't know the reason themselves. At the same time, I want you to know that both of them were intelligent in their own fashion. Dora had excellent taste in litera-ture. She'd offer an opinion about a book and it was accurate to the dot. Ytta was musically inclined. She could sing whole symphonies. When they had the energy, they displayed great capa-bility. They had picked up a sewing-machine somewhere and from scraps and pieces they sewed dresses of which the most elegant ladies would be proud. One thing both sisters shared, a complete lack of common sense. Actually, they shared many traits. At times it even seemed to me that they were two bodies with one soul. If there had been a tape recorder to take down the things they said, particularly at night, it would make Dostoyevsky seem trite. Com-plaints against God poured out of them, along with laments for the Holocaust that no pen could transcribe. What a person really is comes out only at night, in the dark. I know now that both of them were born crazy, not the victims of any circumstances. The circumstances, naturally, made everything worse. I myself became a psychopath living with them. Insanity is no less contagious than typhus.

Isaac Bashevis Singer, 1976

From Kinship and Marriage among the Tswana

The substitute (*seantlo*) for a dead or barren wife must also be one of her close relatives. The most favoured is her younger sister, especially the one linked to her. Failing a younger sister, an unmarried elder sister may be provided instead.

I. Schapera, 1950

. . . Another argument in favour of the marriage which I oppose, is that no person is so suitable to come into the place of a deceased wife or is likely to be kind to her motherless children, as her own sister . . . [But] . . . the whole question is not who is most likely to be kind to the motherless children, but what is the law of God? [. . .] Besides it is by no means a conceded point, that the sister of a deceased woman, married to her husband, is more likely than another woman to be kind to her children. It is said that orphans have been more frequently murdered by uncles and aunts than by any other person . . .

Anon, 1855

From Love versus Law: or Marriage with a Deceased Wife's Sister

'You speak, sir, in riddles,' replied I, my heart sinking within my bosom as I gazed on the cold, sarcastic face of the coarse, unfeeling being at my side.

'Of a truth, madam, I meant not to do so. Since, however, you have deigned to listen to me thus far, I will now speak more plainly, and in terms with which even the most ignorant and unlettered could not well misunderstand. If I mistake not, madam, the late Mr Belmont – your most respected husband – was twice married. His first marriage was childless?'

'Thus far, sir, you are correctly informed.'

'And for his second wife, Mr Belmont, I believe, married his deceased wife's sister?'

'That is so.'

'A marriage,' continued Bigsby, coldly, 'which the law of this country does not recognize. It is void, void, madam, as the law books say, *ab initio*; and as the church, which is also entitled to some weight in questions of this character, most clearly and indisputably confirms. So that, in fact, you see, in the eye of the law, you could no more be Mr Belmont's wife than a woman whom he had never seen – and your son, the offspring of that assumed marriage – whom you now seem to regard as the heir to Temple-Thorpe, would, in the eye of the law, also, be *nullus filius* – Or, in plain terms, a bas—'

'Hold, sir' shrieked I, suddenly recovering my self, 'you presume too far on the licence I have given you. Is it not enough that you have dared to cast an imputation upon me from which every honest woman must shrink with abhorrence and disgust; but you must also seek to brand my child with a name never breathed but coupled with infamy and disgust. Peace – peace, sir – I will bear no more' . . .

Joseph Middleton, 1855

From My Grandfather:
His Life and Loves

Fred has doubtless told you that Edith Waugh [sister of his dead wife, Fanny] is to be my wife spite of the Lords and the High Church parsons. I have seen her twice and I feel certain that she will adhere to her resolution now. There will however be a frightful explosion when she communicates her intention to her Mother. I must not however leave her at home with the family if they cannot recognize her right to do what she in her own conscience sees to be right and so I have told her that she must at once come to you if they make it uncomfortable at home. I know I can rely upon your goodness to befriend her. I only explain the need there may be for your hospitality because I can imagine that after she had exercised her courage enough to stop on knocking at the door for it to be opened she might not be able to unfold to you the need she was under to stay. This may or may not be before Sunday but in any case I have arranged to meet her at Hammersmith Station at 10½ on that morning to go to morning service and afterwards to come on to you to lunch at one or so. Should this be impracticable from any engagement you have please let me know.

Cyril stays at Margate another week.

Hunt's family all turned against him and Edith now. His own mother struck him out of her will – all she left him was his father's scrapbook. Uncle Holman threatened to disinherit him too. In September 1873 Hunt wrote to Stephens: 'I have done with Ewell.'

[. . .]

Mrs Waugh pointed out to Edith that under the terms of her father's will, she would not be eligible for a marriage settlement if her 'association' were illegal.

The more opposition they met and the more Edith depended on Hunt, the more protective he felt towards her. It was during the following months that they became so close and once more he fell in love with her.

[. . .]

Edith was married in church, 'a radiant bride in white', and at last (under Swiss law at least) she and Hunt were man and wife.

Cyril and a splendid English nurse whom they had recently engaged, joined them, probably in Venice.

Many problems lay ahead, not only in Syria.

Clare Stephens wrote 'a gently chiding letter' which welcomed them in Jerusalem. In the last confusion of their leaving they were 'a happy pair who seemed to have wandered off like Babes in the Wood', leaving behind 'boots, ice-machines, ground-glass bottle-stoppers, baby clothes, bolts of flannel from the Army and Navy and endless other essentials . . .'

None of this forgetfulness mattered very much. He loved her and she worshipped him for the rest of his life and after his death in 1910 for another twenty years.

I still own her carefully written instructions: 'The dedication of Holman's memoirs is to be copied and put in my hand when my body is burnt':

TO
MY WIFE

as one of my insufficient tributes to her whose constant virtues ever exalt my understanding of the nature and influence of womanhood.

She called this piece of paper 'my passport to *Heaven*' and often admitted to me how disturbing she found the idea that not only her beloved Holman, but Fanny too, would be waiting to greet her.

Diana Holman Hunt, 1969

From Some Tame Gazelle

While Mr Mold's proposal was being rejected in the drawing-room, Belinda was in the dining-room, writing a letter to Agatha. 'We have had remarkably mild weather lately,' she wrote, 'and I have been able to do a lot of gardening, in fact I have just been putting in the last of the bulbs. I have noticed your pink chrysanthemums showing buds, which is very early for them, isn't it?

'The Archdeacon preached a very fine sermon on Sunday

about the Judgement Day. We were all very much impressed by it. You will be glad to hear that he is looking well and has a good appetite.'

Here Belinda paused and laid down her pen. Was this last sentence perhaps a little presumptuous? Ought an archdeacon to be looking well and eating with a good appetite when his wife was away? And ought Belinda to write as if she knew about his appetite?

She turned to the letter again and added 'as far as I know' to the sentence about the appetite.

'It was so nice to see Nicholas Parnell again, and I think he enjoys coming here for a quiet holiday. He brought the deputy librarian, Mr Mold, with him. I don't know whether you have met him? Personally, his type does not appeal to me very much. He is supposed to be a great ladies' man, and is too fond of making jokes not always in the best of taste. Harriet saw him coming out of the Crownwheel and Pinion in the morning, which I thought a pity.'

Here Belinda laid down her pen again. Was she being quite fair to Mr Mold? She had allowed herself to get so carried away by her own feelings about him that she had rather forgotten she was writing to Agatha, in whom she did not normally confide.

'Still, I daresay he is a very nice man,' she went on, 'when one really knows him.'

This last sentence reminded Belinda that he had now been closeted in the drawing-room with Harriet for some considerable time. Belinda had not yet been able to decide why he had come, indeed, she had rather forgotten about the whole thing. Nothing was further from her mind than a proposal of marriage, and had she known what was going on, she would probably have rushed into the drawing-room, even if she had been wearing her old gardening mackintosh and galoshes, and tried her best to stop it, for one was never quite sure what Harriet would do. Especially after her apparent admiration of Mr Mold and her continual harping on the Prime of Life. Belinda went so far as to go into the hall, but could not bring herself to listen at the drawing-room door. From where she stood she could hear a low murmur of voices. It was no use being impatient, and the last thing she wanted was to see Mr Mold herself, so she went back to her letter. Writing to Agatha was not easy, more of a duty than a pleasure, but Belinda felt that she might like to hear some of the details of the parish life which the Archdeacon probably would not give her, so she wrote about the autumn leaves and berries they had used to decorate the church, the organist's illness and Miss Smiley's brave attempt to play at Evensong, the success of the Scouts' Jumble Sale and other homely matters.

At last she heard the sound of a door opening, then conversation and laughter. Harriet and Mr Mold had come out of the drawing-room. Belinda waited until she judged him safely out of the front door and then went eagerly into the hall to hear the result of his visit.

She found Harriet standing in front of the mirror, rubbing her hands together and looking pleased with herself. Her face was rather red and she looked more elegant than was usual at such an early hour of the day.

'Well,' she said, with a hint of triumph in her voice, 'that's that.'

'Yes,' said Belinda, 'but what? I hope you didn't promise him anything for the Library Extension Fund. There are far more deserving causes in the parish.'

'But, Belinda, surely you guessed why he had come?' said Harriet patiently, for really her sister was very stupid. 'He came to ask me to marry him,' she declared, smiling.

'Oh, *Harriet* . . .' Belinda was quite speechless. She might have known that something dreadful like this would happen. As if he would bother to come and ask for a subscription to the library funds! Her supposition seemed very vain and feeble now. Still, as Belinda would not have to live with them, perhaps she need not see very much of her over-jovial brother-in-law – that would be some consolation, though it would hardly make up for the loss of her sister. Of course, she supposed she could always have a companion to live with her, some deserving poor relation like Connie Aspinall, or she might advertise in the *Church Times*; somebody with literary interests and fond of gardening, a church-woman, of course. Belinda shuddered as she thought of the applications and the task of interviewing them; she was sure she would never have the strength to reject anyone, however unsuitable. Perhaps, after all, it would be better to live alone.

'Of course, I couldn't accept him,' said Harriet, rather loudly, for she had expected Belinda to show real interest, instead of just standing and staring at the floor.

The look of relief that brightened Belinda's face was pathetic in its intensity.

'Oh, *Harriet* . . .' again she was speechless. However could she have thought for a moment that her sister would do such a thing?

'Indeed I couldn't,' said Harriet calmly. 'Why I hardly know him, and you remember what Shakespeare said about when lovely woman stoops to folly . . .' she made a significant gesture with her hand.

Belinda frowned. 'I don't think it was *Shakespeare*, dear,' she said absently. 'I must ask Henry. I have an idea it may be Pope.' But what did it matter? Belinda was so overcome with joy and relief at Harriet's news that she kissed her impulsively and suggested that they should have some meringues for tea, as Harriet was so fond of them.

Together they went into the dining-room, where Harriet, with many ludicrous and exaggerated imitations, gave a demonstration of how Mr Mold had proposed to her.

'Oh, Harriet, you mustn't be so unkind!' protested Belinda, in the intervals of laughing, for her sister was really much funnier than Mr Mold could possibly have been. They laughed even more when the corsets were discovered under a cushion.

'Just imagine if Emily had brought him in here and he had discovered them while he was waiting. Or if the Archdeacon had when he came the other day,' chortled Harriet.

'Oh, Harriet,' said Belinda faintly. There was a vulgar, music-hall touch about it all that one could associate with Mr Mold but hardly with the Archdeacon.

'I expect he's consoling himself in the Crownwheel and Pinion,' said Harriet, 'so we needn't really pity him.'

She was perfectly right; so much so that, when he arrived at the vicarage rather late for lunch, Dr Parnell was constrained to whisper to his friend the Archdeacon, 'I fear poor Nathaniel is not entirely sober.'

Barbara Pym, 1950

From Habit

Jessie lit the porcelain lamp with the green shade and set it in the middle of the table among the litter of the sewing. She stood adjusting the wick, her face in shadow, and said:

'We'll have to have a serious talk about the silver and things, Cathy. We'd better settle it tonight before we get too busy.'

'What about them?' Catherine asked, biting off a thread.

'You must have your share. We'll have to divide them between us.' Jessie's voice was quite steady and her tone matter of fact.

'Oh, no,' cried Catherine, with a sharp note of passion in her voice. 'I don't want to take anything away.'

'They are as much yours as mine.'

'They belong here.'

'They belong to both of us, and I'm not going to have you go away empty-handed.'

'But, Jessie, I'll come back often. The house wouldn't seem the same without Mother's things. Don't talk as if I were going away for ever.'

'Of course you'll come back, but it won't be the same. You'll have a house of your own.'

'It won't be the same,' echoed Catherine very low.

'I specially want you to have Mother's rings. I've always wanted you to wear them. You've got such pretty hands and now you won't have to work so hard ... and the pendant. Father gave that to Mother for a wedding present so as you're the one getting married it is only fit you should wear it on your wedding day too. I'll have the cameos. I'm sort of used to them. And the cat's-eye brooch that I always thought we ought to have given Cousin Ella when Mother died.' Jessie drew a rather difficult breath.

'You're robbing yourself,' said Catherine, 'giving me all the best. You're the eldest daughter.'

'That has nothing to do with it. We must think of what is suitable. I think you ought to have the silver coffee things. They've seemed specially yours since that night – you remember – when Angus came. Perhaps they helped . . .'

Catherine made a funny little noise.

'I don't want the silver coffee set.'

'Yes, you do. They're heaps too fine for guests. They're good. What fair puzzles me is the work table. You ought to have it because after all I suppose I'll be keeping all the big furniture, but this room wouldn't be the same without it.'

'No,' cried Catherine. 'Oh, Jessie, no. Not the work table. I couldn't bear it.' And she put her head down among the white madapolam and began to cry, a wild, desperate weeping.

'Cathy, darling, what is it? Hush, Petie, hush. We'll do everything just as you want.'

'I won't strip our home. I won't.'

'No, darling, no, but you'll want some of your own friendly things with you.'

Jessie was crying a little too, but not wildly. 'You're overwrought and tired. I've let you do too much.' Her heart was painfully full of tenderness for her sister.

Catherine's sobs grew less at last, and she said in a little gasping, exhausted voice, 'I can't do it.'

'I won't make you. It can stay here in its old place and you can see it when you come on a visit.'

'I mean I can't get married and go away. It's harder than anything is worth.'

Jessie was aghast. They argued long and confusedly. Once Catherine said: 'I wish it had been you, Jessie.'

Jessie drew away. 'You don't think that I . . .'

'No, dear, only on general grounds. You'd have made such a

good wife and,' with a painful little smile, 'you were always the romantic one.'

'Not now,' said Jessie staunchly.

'I'll write to Angus now, tonight,' Catherine declared.

She wanted to be rid of this intolerable burden at once, although Jessie begged her to sleep on it. Neither of them had considered Angus, nor did they now. She got out the bottle of ink, and the pen with the cherry-wood handle, which they shared, and began the letter. She was stiff and inarticulate on paper, and couldn't hope to make him understand. It was a miserable, hopeless task but she had to go through with it.

While she bent over the letter, Jessie went out into the kitchen and relit the fire. She took the silver coffee pot, the sugar basin and the cream jug, and set them out on the tray with the best worked traycloth. From the cake tin she selected the fairest of the little cakes that had been made for the afternoon tea of guests arriving tomorrow. Stinting nothing, she prepared their supper. When she heard Catherine sealing the letter, thumping the flap down with her fist to make the cheap gum stick, she carried in the tray.

Although she felt sick with crying, Catherine drank her coffee and ate a cake. The sisters smiled at one another with shaking lips and stiff reddened eyelids.

'He won't come again now,' said Jessie regretfully, but each added in her heart, 'He was a stranger, after all.'

Marjorie Barnard, 1945

4

Older Sisters and Younger Sisters

INTRODUCTION

As a rule there is only one person an English girl hates more than she hates her mother; and that's her eldest sister!

> Freud, misquoting Bernard Shaw (who wrote 'As a rule
> there is only one person an English girl hates more than
> she hates her elder sister, and that's her mother!')

Freud's misquotation of Bernard Shaw, ironic or not, is a very Freudian slip. Despite his own problems with sisters, with a dead brother, his analysis of what forms adult personality did not touch on brothers or sisters. Maybe, an eldest child himself, he didn't rate them. The influence of parents was paramount, on the other hand. One consequence of the emphasis on such intergenerational problems as the Oedipus complex was that psychologists largely ignored the effect of siblings and the significance of birth order on psychic development, failing to observe till much later that elder, middle or youngest children have as many traits in common with each other as with their siblings. Elder children, for instance, conservative and anxious, are most likely to uphold parental tradition. Jane Austen's Elinor and George Eliot's Dorothea are typical in their different ways. In my own family, my brother is the only one of us to have remained politically conservative and to have opted for a lifestyle much like that in which we grew up. (His having married three times slightly skews the picture, but this is after all the late twentieth century; he's not the only Tory to have slipped that parental leash.)

As the eldest in our family, he did suffer particularly badly. It isn't easy being the elder brother of twins; his banishment to boarding-school at the age of eight hardly helped. We girls, spared this, had fewer difficulties in going our own ways. Our family came to span the English class system, more or less: while my twin was still alive, I could drink sherry and make polite conversation about golf in my brother's drawing-room one day, and on the next I'd be watching sport on television in my brother-in-law's tied agricultural cottage, my sister knitting, her husband tying ferret nets, both in turn leaping up to grab a twelve-bore and take pot-shots out of the window at passing pigeons. My Australian sister and I belong in places just as stereotypical, somewhere in between.

My twin sister suffered, I think, from being both middle child, in family terms, and elder sister in relation to me. As middle child she felt able to rebel, and did so more than any of us, though she was so quiet about it people assumed I was the wilder of the two. But the sternness, not to say rigidity of the elder sister manifested itself in the unbending way in which she rebelled, in which she reacted to most things, especially later in her life, and especially to me. Once she set her mind to something, nothing would move her. The curious thing was how tenuous her hold was on the title 'Miss Farmer' – for so she would have been in days when, outside the family, young women were called by their surnames. A mere half-hour did it, as that same half-hour left me fated to be 'Miss Penelope Farmer'. But had we been French, I as the second born would have been assumed to be the first conceived, and so the elder, entitled to be the unqualified 'Miss' or 'Mlle' Farmer; would I then, I wonder, have been more like her and she like me? Or was it just temperament made her the carer and me the cared-for, her the one with the continual frown and uneasy conscience, me the non-stop talker, irresponsible, insouciant. 'My elder daughter,' my father would say, 'my younger daughter,' leaving me with the indulgence that belongs to the youngest sibling – at least until our sister was born seven years later – and my twin with the cares of the world on her shoulders, and with, subsequently, in turn, two wrecked marriages and very far from ideal, needy husbands.

As a child, for instance, she'd blamed herself for our infant brother's death, because when we were told he'd been born she'd wished he'd die. I didn't know that till after she was dead. On the other hand I do remember how, when we were six or so, a quarrel over a pair of scissors led to her scratching my hand with them just hard enough to make it bleed. Overcome by guilt at that little thread of blood, she'd run away, and, crouching among the bushes in our garden, stayed hidden for almost four hours, an age for someone as young as that – and a reflection of her staying-power later. The terror and desperation of it still makes me sigh. It also makes me wonder, sadly, if there mightn't be one person in every family who functions as a kind of lightning conductor for family grief and trauma. The childhoods of both my parents were dreadful in different ways; was my twin, *my* elder sister, programmed to take the brunt of that pain?

I think of Charlotte Brontë. And this is where the matter gets complicated. Charlotte at school was the youngest of three sisters, very bright and lively. But her two elder sisters died when she was nine; suddenly, Mrs Gaskell reports, she changed completely. This seems to suggest that the gravity of an elder sister is not something you need learn from birth; you can also acquire it later by a stroke of fate. (And perhaps through grief, in such circumstances.) It might also reflect another curiosity of sibling order, that children unconsciously take on the roles available to them in a family; before her sisters' death the role of careful elder in the Brontë family had been filled. Where sisters remain close, the removal of one sibling almost always does effect such sea changes, I suspect – when my own twin died I found myself taking on roles that she'd annexed all our lives. And even where death is not the prime mover, it's true of many sisters, older and younger, that for one reason or another, their positions can reverse.

As a child, my naughty mother was virtually brought up by her older sister, my Aunt Janet. And Aunt Janet grew up still playing that role to other people – as a nurse, and also for a while as an Anglican nun. Since this meant her living in institutions most of her life, it was my much more worldly mother who had to look after her whenever she emerged. Indeed, but for my mother, my aunt would not have survived her convent. She contracted TB, but was told that she was malingering and was given no care. Only my horrified mother's lambasting of her Mother Superior got her out, despite her vows. On recovery my aunt became a Catholic convert – 'pervert' my mother called it, maybe not to my aunt's face, though I can't be sure.

There were times and still are places, of course, when no such teasing would have been permissible. Whatever the circumstances, elder sisters were respected as of right. Even in families with living mothers, they invariably did half the work of childcare and were looked up to as quasi adults, like the elder sisters Peter Townsend describes in fifties East London. In some societies and cultures, 'elder sister', 'elder brother' remain terms of respect to this day. This may or may not recompense those so honoured for childhoods largely spent caring for younger brothers and sisters. In many parts of the Third World this is still the case, judging by the number of small children carrying yet smaller children around on their backs. And though elder sisters are the main bearers of such burdens, in families without older girls, boys too may be expected to take their share (as in the account of the boy in section 7 of this book, left in daily charge of his baby sister). Such circumstances would, you might think, make a profound difference, between the elder sisters on whom these burdens were laid and the younger ones who would have got off much more lightly, besides being much more indulged by everyone from parents downwards; something equally true and equally resented by elder sisters in all parts of the globe.

Without doubt, the respect due to elder siblings – and the freedom of the younger – also created its resentments. Along with the responsibility went power, and inheritance of family goods. Out of such resentments, presumably – and not just from the observation of jealousy resulting from parental indulgence of younger sisters – came all those fairy tales about ugly and disagreeable older sisters and kind and beautiful younger ones. One elder sister, A. S. Byatt, wrote an alternative fairy tale for which, alas, I have no room here, in which the elder sister was the good and beautiful one for a change, and who could blame her – except possibly those younger sisters who spend their lives in the shadows of older sisters much more beautiful and more intelligent than themselves. For obviously, despite all I've said, many elder sisters do not fit the stereotypes exactly; my Aunt Olive was the giddy, pretty one, her sensible younger sister, Ruth, inherited her mother's pearl necklace. Many more try to assert their privileges in vain: 'It's not fair . . . I am the eldest . . .' And others whisper that at heart they are not the least like that, whatever is expected of them. But no one listens or cares. And in the end being the elder, privileged or not, willing or not, may lead later to watching a younger sister, not necessarily so beautiful or talented, get away with everything simply by virtue of having been the younger, like Elsie in V. S. Pritchett's 'Cage Birds'.

I don't know if my half-hour-older sister ever saw me in such a way. Maybe. Or maybe not. But had she survived longer, she would have been better off than most elder sisters, for their disadvantage in later life, in a world that hangs on to its youth, is simply that of being older, heading for decrepitude sooner than their younger sisters. Precisely the same age as *her* younger sister, my twin would not have suffered that.

From Life of Charlotte Brontë

Charlotte was considered the most talkative of the sisters – a 'bright, clever little child'. Her great friend was a certain 'Mellany Hane' (so Mr Brontë spells the name), whose brother paid for her schooling, and who had no remarkable talent except for music, which her brother's circumstances forbade her to cultivate. She was 'a hungry, good-natured, ordinary girl'; older than Charlotte, and ever ready to protect her from any petty tyranny or encroachments on the part of the elder girls. Charlotte always remembered her with affection and gratitude.

I have quoted the word 'bright' in the account of Charlotte. I suspect that this year of 1825 was the last time it could ever be applied to her. In the spring of it, Maria became so rapidly worse than Mr Brontë was sent for. He had not previously been aware of her illness, and the condition in which he found her was a terrible shock to him. He took her home by the Leeds coach, the girls crowding out into the road to follow her with their eyes over the bridge, past the cottages, and then out of sight for ever. She died a very few days after her arrival at home. Perhaps the news of her death falling suddenly into the life of which her patient existence had formed a part, only a little week or so before, made those who remained at Cowan Bridge look with more anxiety on Elizabeth's symptoms, which also turned out to be consumptive. She was sent home in charge of a confidential servant of the establishment; and she, too, died in the early summer of that year. Charlotte was thus suddenly called into the responsibilities of eldest sister in a motherless family. She remembered how anxiously her dear sister Maria had striven, in her grave, earnest way, to be a tender helper and a counsellor to them all; and the duties that now fell upon her seemed almost like a legacy from the gentle little sufferer so lately dead.

Mrs Gaskell, 1857

From Through a Window

When Winkle died, Wolfi was adopted by his elder sister, Wunda: the story of the nine-year-old female and her three-year-old brother is truly remarkable. Wolfi, despite his young age, showed fewer signs of depression than the other orphans and almost certainly this was because, long before Winkle died, the relationship between the siblings had been unusually close. Wunda had carried him frequently when the family travelled, not only because, like all elder sisters, she was fascinated with her small brother, but also because, from the time he was able to totter, Wolfi had wanted to follow her wherever she went. Again and again Wunda had set off about her own concerns, only to return when she heard the sad cries of her small brother as he tried, most desperately, to keep up. Then she would gather him up, and off they would go, together. It should not be thought that Wolfi's close relationship with his sister reflected adversely on Winkle's maternal abilities: she was a caring, affectionate and efficient mother from whom Wunda, undoubtedly, had learned much concerning child care. When Winkle died Wunda took over all her caretaking duties as a matter of course. Most amazing of all, this young female, not yet sexually mature, may have actually produced milk for her infant brother. Certainly he suckled, for several minutes every couple of hours or so, and he became very upset if Wunda tried to stop him. But even when we got very close to them we still couldn't be sure that he was actually getting milk from his sister. Perhaps he just found it reassuring to put his lips to her nipples.

Jane Goodall, 1990

From Stories, Songs and Sisters

I went through primary school in low classes but Helen always did well – often enormously well – at school. I don't remember resenting this in any way. On the whole I was proud of her success, though puzzled by my own failure, which persisted until I reached secondary school. I was a highly proficient reader, I wrote good compositions (as writing exercises were called in my days) and I gave lively morning talks. But in those days, neatness and accuracy were probably more highly prized than they are today. Helen was not only apt at self-expression, able to remember well, capable at mathematics and less likely to be distracted, but she was also neat and well controlled in the mechanics of writing and spelling. In infancy she shut the gate tidily after her, and at school she pressed lightly on the page with her sharpened pencil, just as we were supposed to do. None of the rest of us did as well at school, and Helen's success, which so delighted my parents, altered expectations for those who came after her. When I went through school there was no one ahead of me against whom I needed to be measured, but this was not the case for either Patricia or Cecil.

I tried to dominate Helen, but she refused to be dominated, though, in turn, she tried to dominate Patricia, at which stage I took Patricia's part in the family squabbles. Patricia seldom intruded on the territory I thought of as mine. Helen argued with Patricia, but took the side of our little brother Frank, who, several years later, apparently bossed Cecily around and tried out all kinds of tricks, holds and torments on her. But by that time I was away, a student at university, virtually a visitor in my childhood home.

In a way, I now think, I fell in love with my own childhood of songs, games and adventures, and I think I tried to stay with it for as long as possible. I felt none of the excitement and pride my own mother apparently felt when, totally unenlightened by her own mother, she finally understood the reproductive facts of life. What I felt, when the information was forced on me, was profound dismay. But, retaining childhood for myself involved the restriction of my sisters to childhood as well, and I became repressive and judgemental of their choices as they reached for adulthood.

Adolescence caused us to become strongly differentiated. My brother, a child as talkative as any of the rest of us, retreated to the sort of silence approved of in males of my family, and admired in New Zealand generally. My mother certainly approved of his new, mature, masculine silence. We sisters, though increasingly aware that our judgement never quite had the authority of our brother's where our mother was concerned, were at least allowed to talk – to gossip, argue, criticize and express feelings. My brother was expected to conceal his.

I tried organizing the family imagination wherever possible, even after I left home, and, with the willing complicity of my parents, I organized the idea of family and loyalty to tradition along fairly inflexible lines. I did not want our Christmas – the tree in the house, the presents under the tree, the shared opening of stockings in the morning – to change, for Christmas significantly encapsulated the general happiness of my childhood. I remember it as an ecstatic time, when I overflowed with feelings of love and with a flawless pleasure. I was furious when, in due course, I found Patricia was planning to spend Christmas Eve in town with her friends. I needed her presence in the house to be happy myself, so I lectured her on loyalty. I openly attacked her decision in a far more dictatorial way than either of my parents, though they were certainly taken aback by her sexual persona, which became individual and assertive when she was about thirteen or fourteen. I had refused to wear lipstick or put on make-up myself until I was about nineteen or twenty, and I needed the agreement of those around me, a resolution similar to mine, in order to stop the flow of time. Deviation seemed like treachery. But even in adolescence, even in early adulthood, 'Worraworra!' we would cry, turning out the lights and feeling for each other behind doors, under beds and through wardrobes.

'I have always been worried,' writes A. S. Byatt in the acknowledgements at the end of her book *The Djinn in the Nightingale's Eye* 'at being the eldest of three sisters.' But I am the eldest of four, the eldest of the fairy tale triumvirate plus one more, doomed by the determinism of fairy tales to make wrong choices. And my own worry, a curious worry since there is nothing that can be done about it now, is that I loomed over the three that came after me rather like a djinn, at times directing their lives by something rather sharper than example – by expecting them to act within the confinements of characters in my private story. But they have all turned out to be heroines in their own stories. And we are all still participants in a family game. 'Worraworra!' they cry to me from their various shadowy concealments, and I crawl through darkness, trying to find them, listening for their breathing and smothered laughter.

Margaret Mahy, 1996

From The Fountain Overflows

'Mamma,' I said, trying to be reasonable, 'we have to have Aunt Theodora in the house, though I don't want any of us to please her. Not to please her. [. . .] None of us but Cordelia would want to please her. Cordelia is . . .' I paused, choked by the intensity with which I wanted to murder her.

Now I recall my emotions at that moment, children seem to me a remarkable race. They want so much to murder so many people, and they so rarely murder anybody at all.

'Cordelia is such rubbish,' I concluded.

'Listen, Mamma,' exclaimed Cordelia, 'you see how it is, I am the eldest, but none of them treats me with the slightest respect. All the other girls at school who have younger sisters make them obey them and fetch things for them, and that is how it should be.'

'But perhaps,' suggested Mary, 'those other girls do not revolt their younger sisters by playing the violin and scooping all the high notes.'

'Aren't you glad, Mamma,' asked Richard Quin, 'that after having three little girls you had a little boy?'

Rebecca West, 1957

From Sense and Sensibility

'And how does dear, dear Norland look?' cried Marianne.

'Dear, dear Norland,' said Elinor, 'probably looks much as it always does at this time of year. The woods and walks thickly covered with dead leaves.'

'Oh,' cried Marianne, 'with what transporting sensations have I formerly seen them all. How have I delighted as I walked, to see them driven in showers about me by the wind! What feelings have they, the season, the air altogether inspired! Now there's no one to regard them. They are seen only as a nuisance, swept hastily off, and driven as much as possible from the sight.'

'It's not everyone,' said Elinor, 'who has your passion for dead leaves.'

Jane Austen, 1811

From My Aunt Jane Austen: A Memoir

I believe my two Aunts were not accounted very good dressers, and were thought to have taken to the garb of middle age unnecessarily soon – but they were particularly neat, and they held all untidy ways in great disesteem. Of the two, Aunt Jane was by far my favourite – I did not *dislike* Aunt Cassandra – but if my visit had at any time chanced to fall out during *her* absence, I don't think I should have missed her – whereas, *not* to have found Aunt Jane at Chawton, *would* have been a blank indeed. [. . .] I have spoken of the family union that prevailed amongst my Grandmother's children – Aunt Jane was a very affectionate sister to all her brothers – One of them in particular was her especial pride and delight: but of all her family, the nearest and dearest throughout her whole life was, undoubtedly her sister – her *only* sister. Aunt Cassandra was the older by three or four years, and the habit of looking up to her begun in childhood seemed always to continue – When I was a little girl, she would frequently say to me, if opportunity offered, that Aunt Cassandra could teach everything much better than *she* could – Aunt Cass *knew* more – Aunt Cass could tell me better whatever I wanted to know – all which, I ever received in respectful silence – Perhaps she thought *my* mind wanted a turn in *that* direction, but I truly believe she did always *really* think of her sister, as the superior to herself. The most perfect affection and confidence ever subsisted between them – and great and lasting was the sorrow of the survivor when the final separation was made –

Caroline Austen, published 1952

From Home is a Sacred Place

'Yes, I'm going . . . and you'll never see me again.' Red in the face, the girl went behind the wardrobe and pulled out from a recess a cloth suitcase with leather corners and finishings. Then she opened a drawer and started pulling things out and bundling them higgledy-piggledy into the suitcase.

'Now, come along!' interposed Giacomo, going up to her. 'Come along!'

But the girl thrust him away. 'Leave me alone, you!'

'You can go, as far as I'm concerned,' said her sister once again. She had remained standing beside the gramophone, a disconcerted look on her face.

'I'm going – don't worry – out of your filthy home.'

'Go, then,' said her sister sorrowfully, 'go as quick as you can.'

Lori this time made no reply. Resting the suitcase on her thigh and raising her knee, she closed it. She swept furiously across between Giacomo and her sister, went to the clothes-stand, took down a small, crumpled hat and left the room.

'Lori!' called her sister suddenly, as though giving way to a feeling that was too strong for her.

There was no answer. After a moment the whole flat shook as the front door was banged violently. Rina went and sat down on the edge of the bed and took her head between her hands.

Everything had happened so quickly that Giacomo had not had time to get over his first presumptuous conviction that his adventure was well under way and that there was nothing to do but follow the pleasant and easy path of events through to the end. He was still fully possessed by this intense and delightful feeling of certainty, even though the adventure had already evaporated.

Then there came over him an acute, grievous sense of boredom and disappointment and aimlessness. He looked at the woman sitting in her black, openwork undergarment on the edge of the bed which had been prepared to no purpose; her face was between her hands and he saw that she was weeping.

'When I think,' she said in an unsteady voice that trembled with

tears, 'of all I have done for her ... all the sacrifices I made ...
When she was a little girl and I was barely sixteen, it was I who
kept her alive, by my work. What would have become of her without
me? Holidays and clothes and everything I gave her. When she was
bigger I found her a job in a dressmaker's as a model ... For a long
time I went without bread myself so as to send her money. And
now you see how she treats me!'

She looked up at him between swollen and tearful eyelids that
no longer had anything vicious about them, and shook her head.

'Now, now, come along,' said Giacomo with an effort, sitting
down beside her and taking her hand; 'she'll come back.'

'No, she won't ... I know her. She won't come back so soon.
In fact she won't come back at all,' she stammered. She took a
handkerchief from under the pillow and blew her nose loudly.

Alberto Moravia, *The Wayward Wife*,
translated by Angus Davison, 1960

From Ripples in the Pool

' "You know how I treated my sisters when you were in detention!"
' "You have never told me," I said.

' "I feel I am to blame for their disappearance," she said. "After
all, I was their eldest sister and more privileged than they were. I had
received more education. I went to college and left them labouring at
Kabarikui's farm, trying to get school fees and pocket money for
me. At first we were all happy until they failed CPE. Then the
problems started. They began associating with men at that early
age. I advised them not to rush into unplanned marriages but they
wouldn't listen to me. They asked me to show them an alternative
as they had no hope of getting a job like mine in the government.
When I failed to find them a job, they roamed about in the town,
staying with this man and that. I was very angry with them, and I
started scolding them without mercy. I even told them never to call
me their sister. At the age of seventeen, these girls were drinking

cognacs and whiskies. They had become real street girls! Then one day something terrible happened. They came home very drunk. They started calling me names, and they were even rude to mother, an invalid at the time. Then do you know what I did? I'm ashamed to remember that day, and I'm only telling you this to show you how persecuted I feel. I, with all the pride of having never called in an outsider to help solve our family problems, asked Kefa Munene to come to our aid. He had just returned from detention and was a frequent visitor to our house. I shudder to remember what he did to Mumbi and Muthoni. It's one of those things that one can never forget. He tied them up like goats around two posts and beat them until their skin began to bleed. They cried and shouted for help, but he went on beating them like one possessed, telling them they needed to go to Manyani to experience a real beating. They remained tied the whole night, and when they were untied in the morning, they came to me and wished me goodbye. 'Farewell, sister,' they said, without malice or reproach. 'We shall no longer give you pain.' These are words that make me suffer whenever I remember them. I wish they had cursed me or sworn at me as they left. I wish they had even tried to hit me. Do you think I can ever be forgiven? It's eight years, eight solid years since they left home!"

'She stood up and leaned against the wall. Then all of a sudden she burst out crying. I tried to quieten her, but the more I tried to stop her, the more she went on weeping bitterly. In the end I left her to cry and when she had calmed down, she said faintly: "Do you think I am forgiven? How can I go on living with this burden of silence weighing heavily on my shoulders?"

'It was painful to see her like that. It was painful to see those big rings under her eyes. I begged her not to torment herself. She promised she would try to be happy. Three weeks later she decided to go to Gatugi and look for her husband whom she had not seen for a month. But she did not get there. The car she was travelling in was involved in an accident as you all know and she died on the spot' . . .

Rebeka Njau, 1975

In my family we always called my elder sister the sergeant-major . . .

Youngest brother in family of four, two brothers, two sisters

From Family Life of Old People

The Second Mother

After the death of the mother the eldest sister sometimes prevented or delayed the disintegration of the sibling group. She protected its unity. Her role was of particular importance if the mother died before all the children were married or when some of them were separated from their wives, or were widowed, crippled, infirm or mentally backward. She partly assumed her mother's role and looked after the interests of the family, taking responsibility for the family problems and continuing its traditions. One woman repeatedly mentioned her 'Samaritan sister', the eldest, who, in emergencies, had stood by each member of the family.

The elder sister's responsibility in adult life derived partly from her experience in childhood. A mother with several children in Bethnal Green expected her eldest daughter to look after some of the younger children in the day and help bath them and put them to bed. There were many references to the 'little mother' of from ten to fifteen who was almost as efficient as the mother in attending to the home and to young children. Indeed, some old people gave instances of the eldest daughter bringing up the children after the early death of the mother. Some, who *were* eldest sisters, talked of their siblings as if they were their children.

Talking about her brothers and sisters Mrs Duckworth said, 'When Mum died I sort of took her place. Me being the eldest I'd like to know how they all are. I'm the eldest, so I'm entitled to know. They all pop along to me.'

Mr Hawthorn said of his eldest sister, 'She was the only one who stayed single. She was like my second mother.'

Some married women had given a home to younger unmarried

brothers and sisters and a few still had them in their homes. Their role as second mother was strengthened because they were so much older. In many of the larger families of origin in Bethnal Green the eldest was often twenty and sometimes nearly thirty years older than the youngest. One woman had brought up and now lived near her youngest sister, eighteen years her junior. Such age differences reinforced the eldest sister's authority.

The part she played in caring for her siblings, if the mother died young, sometimes resulted in a close relationship between sibling and niece or nephew or cousin. The youngest in the family was sometimes of the same age as his eldest sister's children. A widow aged seventy-eight had almost a courtship relationship with a nephew of seventy, who lived on the other side of London. 'I meet Albert at 2.45 every Saturday at Marble Arch. We go in one of the parks or sit in Lyons Corner House and then go to a show.' They spent their holidays together and 'he gets me over a lot of my worries. He tells me not to go worrying and stops me being lonely.' The widow's mother died at an early age and she was brought up by her eldest sister, fifteen years older, along with this sister's children, the oldest of whom was Albert.

The eldest sister, like the mother, often refused to discriminate in her affections for different brothers and sisters. She said it was a rule not to have favourites (though like the mother, this ideal was not always practised). Her attitude differed from that of most old people, who expressed a particular affection for one brother or sister, usually one nearest them in age. One woman remarked that her siblings had always gone about in pairs of those nearest in age. Generally, with the exception of 'second mother' relationships, the greater the difference in age between siblings, the less they saw each other in old age.

Peter Townsend, 1957

Ruth Ellis

The last time Muriel Jakubait saw her baby sister Ruth Ellis was in Holloway prison, more than forty years ago. Even by the standards of an era that favoured execution as a form of justice, there was something particularly callous about Ruth's treatment in those final hours; she wasn't allowed to talk to Muriel or see her young son André alone. Jailers stood either side of Ruth while she tried to exchange a few last meaningful words with her sister through a small grille in her cell door.

'I felt like killing myself afterwards,' says Muriel, now seventy-seven and living in Woking. 'I last saw her a week before her death. I'd just had a baby and she would ask who it looked like. I kept asking, "Are you all right?", and she would say, "Don't worry, Muriel. I'm not worrying." I was so desperate to do something.'

Forty years later, Muriel is trying to clear her sister's name. She approached the Cardiff-based lawyers Bernard and Lynne de Maid several months ago to review Ruth's case. The de Maids are now preparing an application to the Criminal Cases Review Commission. Lynne de Maid says, 'We are looking for Ruth's murder conviction to be quashed and an alternative of manslaughter to be passed. We also hope for an apology for her execution.'

Ruth's story, minus the conclusion, seems sadly modern and familiar. She had a predilection for brutal men, from her first husband, George Ellis, to her tragic love affair with the feckless David Blakely.

Muriel's memories of their family life give some insight into Ruth's troubled personal life. 'We were never happy. My father was a professional musician, then lost his job when the talkies came. He would hit me, but I always used to shield Ruth by standing in front of her. I've always felt protective towards her, which is why I've always felt so full of guilt about what happened.'

Yet Muriel led a very different life to Ruth; settling down with her husband in south-east London and raising five children. She always tried to support her sister: 'She used to phone me a lot when she met Blakely. She said she felt life wasn't as great as she thought it would be. She told me she loved David, but he was such a two-timer.'

When Ruth was in Holloway, Muriel looked after André, who later committed suicide, aged thirty-six. 'He suffered the most. He and I went through it together.'

She remembers André's response the evening Ruth shot Blakely outside a pub in Hampstead. André, Desmond Cousen, who was Ruth's new boyfriend, and Ruth's mother arrived on her doorstep.

'My mother just said, "Ruth has shot Blakely – he's dead." I shouted at Desmond, "Who gave her the gun?" He never answered me. André told me later it was Desmond. "He cleaned it and gave it to her and then I never saw my mummy again."'

[. . . It] may be some forty years too late for Ruth Ellis, but for Muriel it's better than nothing. 'I can feel Ruth probing me. I can see her all the time, each time I look in the mirror, because we look so alike. Now I know I've got to fight for her, and set her free.'

Emma Cook, *Independent*, 15 August 1998

From Middlemarch

Early in the day Dorothea had returned from the infant school which she had set going in the village, and was taking her usual place in the pretty sitting-room which divided the bedrooms of the sisters, bent on finishing a plan for some buildings (a kind of work which she delighted in), when Celia, who had been watching her with a hesitating desire to propose something, said –

'Dorothea dear, if you don't mind – if you are not very busy – suppose we looked at mamma's jewels today, and divided them? It is exactly six months today since uncle gave them to you, and you have not looked at them yet.'

Celia's face had the shadow of a pouting expression in it, the full presence of the pout being kept back by an habitual awe of Dorothea and principle; two associated facts which might show a mysterious electricity if you touched them incautiously. To her relief, Dorothea's eyes were full of laughter as she looked up.

'What a wonderful little almanac you are, Celia! Is it six calendar or six lunar months?'

'It is the last day of September now, and it was the first of April when uncle gave them to you. You know, he said that he had forgotten them till then. I believe you have never thought of them since you locked them up in the cabinet here.'

'Well, dear, we should never wear them, you know.' Dorothea spoke in a full cordial tone, half caressing, half explanatory. She had her pencil in her hand, and was making tiny side plans on a margin.

Celia coloured, and looked very grave. 'I think, dear, we are wanting in respect to mamma's memory, to put them by and take no notice of them. And,' she added, after hesitating a little, with a rising sob of mortification, 'necklaces are quite usual now; and Madame Poinçon, who was stricter in some things even than you are, used to wear ornaments. And Christians generally – surely there are women in heaven now who wore jewels.' Celia was conscious of some mental strength when she really applied herself to argument.

'You would like to wear them?' exclaimed Dorothea, an air of astonished discovery animating her whole person with a dramatic action which she had caught from that very Madame Poinçon who wore the ornaments. 'Of course, then, let us have them out. Why did you not tell me before? But the keys, the keys!' She pressed her hands against the sides of her head and seemed to despair of her memory.

'They are here,' said Celia, with whom this explanation had been long meditated and prearranged.

'Pray open the large drawer of the cabinet and get out the jewel box.'

The casket was soon open before them, and the various jewels spread out, making a bright parterre on the table. It was no great collection, but a few of the ornaments were really of remarkable beauty, the finest that was obvious at first being a necklace of purple amethysts set in exquisite gold work, and a pearl cross with five brilliants in it. Dorothea immediately took up the necklace and fastened it round her sister's neck, where it fitted almost as closely as a bracelet; but the circle suited the Henrietta-Maria style of

Celia's head and neck, and she could see that it did, in the pier-glass opposite.

'There, Celia! you can wear that with your Indian muslin. But this cross you must wear with your dark dresses.'

Celia was trying not to smile with pleasure. 'O Dodo, you must keep the cross yourself.'

'No, no, dear, no,' said Dorothea, putting up her hand with careless deprecation.

'Yes, indeed you must; it would suit you – in your black dress now,' said Celia, insistingly. 'You *might* wear that.'

'Not for the world, not for the world. A cross is the last thing I would wear as a trinket.' Dorothea shuddered slightly.

'Then you will think it wicked in me to wear it,' said Celia, uneasily.

'No, dear, no,' said Dorothea, stroking her sister's cheek. 'Souls have complexions too: what will suit one will not suit another.'

'But you might like to keep it for mamma's sake.'

'No, I have other things of mamma's – her sandalwood box, which I am so fond of – plenty of things. In fact, they are all yours, dear. We need discuss them no longer. There – take away your property.'

Celia felt a little hurt. There was a strong assumption of superiority in this Puritanic toleration, hardly less trying to the blond flesh of an unenthusiastic sister than a Puritanic persecution.

'But how can I wear ornaments if you, who are the elder sister, will never wear them?'

'Nay, Celia, that is too much to ask, that I should wear trinkets to keep you in countenance. If I were to put on such a necklace as that, I should feel as if I had been pirouetting. The world would go round with me, and I should not know how to walk.'

Celia had unclasped the necklace and drawn it off. 'It would be a little tight for your neck; something to lie down and hang would suit you better,' she said, with some satisfaction. The complete unfitness of the necklace from all points of view for Dorothea, made Celia happier in taking it. She was opening some ring boxes, which disclosed a fine emerald with diamonds, and just then the sun passing beyond a cloud sent a bright gleam over the table.

'How very beautiful these gems are!' said Dorothea, under a new current of feeling, as sudden as the gleam. 'It is strange how deeply colours seem to penetrate one, like scent. I suppose that is the reason why gems are used as spiritual emblems in the Revelation of St John. They look like fragments of heaven. I think that emerald is more beautiful than any of them.'

'And there is a bracelet to match it,' said Celia. 'We did not notice this at first.'

'They are lovely,' said Dorothea, slipping the ring and bracelet on her finely turned finger and wrist, and holding them towards the window on a level with her eyes. All the while her thought was trying to justify her delight in the colours by merging them in her mystic religious joy.

'You *would* like those, Dorothea,' said Celia, rather falteringly, beginning to think with wonder that her sister showed some weakness, and also that emeralds would suit her own complexion even better than purple amethysts. 'You must keep that ring and bracelet – if nothing else. But see, these agates are very pretty – and quiet.'

'Yes! I will keep these – this ring and bracelet,' said Dorothea. Then, letting her hand fall on the table, she said in another tone – 'Yet what miserable men find such things, and work at them, and sell them!' She paused again, and Celia thought that her sister was going to renounce the ornaments, as in consistency she ought to do.

'Yes, dear, I will keep these,' said Dorothea, decidedly. 'But take all the rest away, and the casket.'

She took up her pencil without removing the jewels, and still looking at them. She thought of often having them by her, to feed her eye at these little fountains of pure colour.

'Shall you wear them in company?' said Celia, who was watching her with real curiosity as to what she would do.

Dorothea glanced quickly at her sister. Across all her imaginative adornment of those whom she loved, there darted now and then a keen discernment, which was not without a scorching quality. If Miss Brooke ever attained perfect meekness, it would not be for lack of inward fire.

'Perhaps,' she said, rather haughtily. 'I cannot tell to what level I may sink.'

Celia blushed, and was unhappy; she saw that she had offended her sister, and dared not say even anything pretty about the gift of the ornaments which she put back into the box and carried away. Dorothea too was unhappy, as she went on with her plan-drawing, questioning the purity of her own feeling and speech in the scene which had ended with that little explosion.

Celia's consciousness told her that she had not been at all in the wrong: it was quite natural and justifiable that she should have asked that question, and she repeated to herself that Dorothea was inconsistent: either she should have taken her full share of the jewels, or, after what she had said, she should have renounced them altogether.

'I am sure – at least, I trust,' thought Celia, 'that the wearing of a necklace will not interfere with my prayers. And I do not see that I should be bound by Dorothea's opinions now we are going into society, though of course she herself ought to be bound by them. But Dorothea is not always consistent.'

Thus Celia, mutely bending over her tapestry, until she heard her sister calling her.

'Here, Kitty, come and look at my plan; I shall think I am a great architect, if I have not got incompatible stairs and fireplaces.'

As Celia bent over the paper, Dorothea put her cheek against her sister's arm caressingly. Celia understood the action. Dorothea saw that she had been in the wrong, and Celia pardoned her. Since they could remember, there had been a mixture of criticism and awe in the attitude of Celia's mind towards her elder sister. The younger had always worn a yoke; but is there any yoked creature without its private opinions?

George Eliot, 1872

Virginia since early childhood has made it her business to create a character for me according to her own wishes and has now so succeeded in imposing it upon the world that these preposterous stories are supposed to be certainly true because so characteristic.

Vanessa Bell to Clive Bell, 1910

Manon rang her father to be told that Ffion was marrying William [Hague]. Admitting defeat she replied: 'Well, that's the end of sibling rivalry.'

Press report, 1997

From The Cage Birds

Gay and confiding, she took Grace back to the bedroom and looked at the dresses spread out on the bed. She held up a blue one.

'It's funny, I used to be jealous of your clothes. When we went to church,' Elsie said. 'Do you remember your blue dress, the dark blue one with the collar? I could have killed you for it and the bank manager saying, "Here comes the bluebird of happiness." Aren't kids funny? When you grew out of it and it came down to me, I hated it. I wouldn't put it on. It was too long. You were taller than me then, we're the same now. Do you remember?'

'And here is a black,' she said, holding up another. 'Well, every picture tells a story. Mr Williams threw it out of the window when we were in Nice. He has a temper. I was a bit naughty. This one's Italian. It would suit you. You never wear anything with flowers though, do you?'

She was pulling the dresses off the bed and throwing them back again.

'Reg was generous. He knew how to spend. But when his father died and he came into all that money, he got mean – that's where men are funny. He was married – well, I knew that. Family counted for Reg. Grace, how long have you been married?'

'Ten years,' said Grace.

Elsie picked up a golden dress that had a paler metallic sheen to it, low in the neck and with sleeves that came an inch or two below the elbow. She held it up.

'This would suit you, Grace. You could wear this colour with your hair. It's just the thing for cocktails. With your eyes it would be lovely. Mr Williams won't let me wear it, he hates it, it looks hard, sort of brassy on me – but you, look!'

She held it against her sister.

'Look in the mirror. Hold it against yourself.'

Against her will Grace held it to her shoulders over her navy woollen dress. She saw her body transformed into a sunburst of light.

'Grace,' said Elsie in a low voice. 'Look what it does to you. It isn't too big.'

She stepped behind and held the dress in at the waist. Grace stood behind the dress and her jaw set and her bones stiffened in contempt at first and then softened.

'There's nothing to be done to it. It's wonderful,' said Elsie.

'I never go to cocktail parties,' said Grace.

'Look. Slip it on. You'll see.'

'No,' said Grace and let go of a shoulder. Elsie pulled it back into place.

'With the right shoes,' Elsie said, 'that will lift it. Slip it on. Come on. I've never seen anything like it. You remember how things always looked better on you. Look.'

She pulled the dress from Grace and held it against herself. 'You see what I look like.'

'No,' she went on, handing it back. She went to the bedroom door and shut it and whispered, 'I paid two hundred and forty pounds for it in Paris – if you're not going to wear it yourself you can't have it. I'll give it to Mary. She's had her eye on it.'

Grace looked shrewdly at Elsie. She was shocked by her sister's life. From her girlhood Elsie had wheedled. She had got money out of their aunt; she drew the boys after her but was soon the talk of the town for going after the older men, especially the married. She suddenly called herself Augusta. It baffled Grace that men did not see through her. She was not beautiful. The blue eyes were as hard as enamel and she talked of nothing but prices and clothes and jewellery. From this time her life was a procession through objects to places which were no more than objects, from cars to yachts, from suites to villas. The Mediterranean was something worn in the evening, a town was the setting for a ring, a café was a looking-glass, a nightclub was a price. To be in the sun on a beach was to have found a new man who had bought her more of the sun.

Once she giggled to Grace: 'When they're doing it – you know what I mean – that's when I do my planning. It gives you time to yourself.'

Now, as Grace held the golden dress and Elsie said in her cold baby voice, 'If you don't keep it to wear I'll give it to Mary,' Grace felt their kinship. They had been brought up poor. They feared to lose. She felt the curious pleasure of being a girl again, walking with Elsie in the street and of being in the firm humouring position of the elder sister of a child who at that time simply amused them all by her calculations. Except for their father, they were a calculating family. Calculation was their form of romance. If I put it on, Grace thought, that doesn't mean I'll keep it for myself. I'll sell it with the rest.

'All right. I'll just try it,' she said.

'I'll unzip you,' said Elsie, but she let Grace pull her dress over her head, for the navy wool disgusted her. And Grace in her black slip pouted shyly, thinking, Thank heavens I ironed it yesterday. To be untidy underneath in an expensive flat like this – she would have been shamed.

She stepped into the golden dress and pulled it up and turned to the long mirror as she did this, and at once to her amazement she felt the gold flowing up her legs and her waist, as if it were a fire, a fire which she could not escape and which, as Elsie fastened it, locked her in. The mirror she looked in seemed to blaze.

'It's too long.'

'We're the same height. Stand on your toes. Do you see?'

Grace felt the silk with her fingers.

'Take off your scarf.'

Grace pulled it off. Her dead hair became darker and yet it, too, took on the yellow glint of the flame.

'It's too full,' said Grace, for her breasts were smaller than Elsie's.

'It was too tight on me. Look!' Elsie said. She touched the material here and there and said, 'I told you. It's perfect.'

Grace half smiled. Her face lost its empty look and she knew that she was more beautiful than her sister. She gazed, she fussed, she pretended, she complained, she turned this way and that. She stretched out an arm to look at the length of the sleeve. She glowed inside it. She saw herself in Elsie's villa. She saw herself at one of those parties she had never been to. She saw her whole life changed. The bus routes of London were abolished. Her own house vanished and inside herself she cried angrily, looking at the closed door of the bedroom, so that her breasts pushed forward and her eyes fired up with temper: 'Jim, where are you? Come here! Look at this.'

At that very moment, the bedroom door was opened. The boy walked in and a yard behind him, keeping not quite out of sight, was a man.

'Mum,' the child called, with his hands in his pockets, 'there's a man.'

The boy looked with the terror of the abandoned at the new woman he saw and said, 'Where's Mum?' looking at her in unbelief.

She came laughing to him and kissed him. He scowled mistrustfully and stepped back.

'Don't you like it?'

As she bent up from the kiss she had a furtive look at the man in the room: Was it Mr Williams? He was gazing with admiration at her.

But Elsie was quick. She left Grace and went into the sitting-room and Grace saw her sister stop suddenly and heard her say, in a voice she had never heard before – a grand stagy voice spoken slowly and arrogantly as if she had a plum in her mouth, her society voice: 'Oh, you! I didn't invite you to call this afternoon.' The man was dark and young and tall, dandified and sunburned. He was wearing a white polo-neck jersey and he was smiling over Elsie's golden head at Grace, who turned away at once.

Elsie shut the bedroom door. As she did so, Grace heard her sister say, 'I have got my dressmaker here. It's very inconvenient.'

V. S. Pritchett, *Collected Stories*, 1982

From A Queer Heart

'Mother, she's asking for you.'

'Oh, dear – do you mean she's – ?'

'She's much more herself this evening,' Lucille said implacably.

Mrs Cadman, at the kitchen table, had been stirring sugar into her third cup. She pushed her chair back, brushed crumbs from her bosom and followed Lucille like a big, unhappy lamb. The light was on in the hall, but the stairs led up into shadow: she had one more start of reluctance at their foot. Autumn draughts ran about in the top storey: up there the powers of darkness all seemed to mobilize. Mrs Cadman put her hand on the banister knob. 'Are you sure she *does* want to see me? Oughtn't she to stay quiet?'

'You should go when she's asking. You never know . . .'

Breathless, breathing unevenly on the top landing, Mrs Cadman pushed open the spare-room – that was the sick-room – door. In there – in here – the air was dead, and at first it seemed very dark. On the ceiling an oil-stove printed its flower pattern; a hooded lamp, low down, was turned away from the bed. On that dark side of the lamp she could just distinguish Rosa, propped up, with the sheet drawn to her chin.

'Rosa?'

'Oh, it's you?'

'Yes; it's me, dear. Feeling better this evening?'

'Seemed funny, you not coming near me.'

'They said for you to keep quiet.'

'My own sister . . . You never liked sickness, did you? Well, I'm going. I shan't trouble you long.'

'Oh, don't talk like that!'

'I'm glad to be going. Keeping on lying here . . . We all come to it. Oh, give over crying, Hilda. Doesn't do any good.'

Mrs Cadman sat down, to steady herself. She fumbled in her lap with her handkerchief, perpetually, clumsily knocking her elbows against the arms of the wicker chair. 'It's such a shame,' she said. 'It's such a pity. You and me, after all . . .'

'Well, it's late for all that now. Each took our own ways.' Rosa's voice went up in a sort of ghostly sharpness. 'There were things that couldn't be otherwise. I've tried to do right by Lucille. Lucille's a good girl, Hilda. You should ask yourself if you've done right by her.'

'Oh, for shame, Rosa,' said Mrs Cadman, turning her face through the dark towards that disembodied voice. 'For shame, Rosa, even if you *are* going. You know best what's come between her and me. It's been you and her, you and her. I don't know where to turn sometimes –'

Rosa said: 'You've got such a shallow heart.'

'How should you know? Why, you've kept at a distance from me ever since we were tots. Oh, I know I'm a great silly, always after my fun, but I never took what was yours; I never did harm to you. I don't see what call we have got to judge each other. You didn't want my life that I've had.'

Rosa's chin moved: she was lying looking up at her sister's big rippling shadow, splodged up there by the light of the low lamp. It is frightening, having your shadow watched. Mrs Cadman said: 'But what did I do to you?'

'I *could* have had a wicked heart,' said Rosa. 'A vain, silly heart like yours. I could have fretted, seeing you take everything. One thing, then another. But I was shown. God taught me to pity you. God taught me my lesson . . . You wouldn't even remember that Christmas tree.'

'What Christmas tree?'

'No, you wouldn't even remember. Oh, I thought it was lovely. I could have cried when they pulled the curtains open, and there it was, all blazing away with candles and silver and everything –'

'Well, isn't that funny? I –'

'No; you've had all that pleasure since. All of us older children couldn't take it in, hardly, for quite a minute or two. It didn't look real. Then I looked up, and there was a fairy doll fixed on the top, right on the top spike, fixed on to a star. I set my heart on her. She had wings and long, fair hair, and she was shining away. I couldn't take my eyes off her. They cut the presents down; but she wasn't for anyone. In my childish blindness I kept praying to God. If I am not to have her, I prayed, let her stay there.'

'And what did God do?' Hilda said eagerly.

'Oh, he taught me and saved me. You were a little thing in a blue sash; you piped up and asked might you have the doll.'

'Fancy me! Aren't children awful!' said Mrs Cadman. 'Asking like that.'

'They said: "Make her sing for it." They were taken with you. So you piped up again, singing. You got her, all right. I went off where they kept the coats. I've thanked God ever since for what I had to go through! I turned my face from vanity from that very night. I had been shown.'

'Oh, what a shame!' said Hilda. 'Oh, I think it was cruel; you poor little mite.'

'No; I used to see that doll all draggled about the house till no one could bear the sight of it. I said to myself: that's how those things end. Why, I'd learnt more in one evening than you've ever learnt in your life. Oh, yes, I've watched you, Hilda. Yes, and I've pitied you.'

'Well, you showed me no pity.'

'You asked for no pity – all vain and set up.'

'No wonder you've been against me. Fancy me not knowing. I didn't *mean* any harm – why, I was quite a little thing. I don't even remember.'

'Well, you'll remember one day. When you lie as I'm lying you'll find that everything comes back. And you'll see what it adds up to.'

'Well, if I do?' said Hilda. 'I haven't been such a baby; I've seen things out in my own way; I've had my ups and downs. It hasn't been all jam.' She got herself out of the armchair and came and stood uncertainly by the foot of the bed. She had a great wish to reach out and turn the hooded lamp round, so that its light could fall on her sister's face. She felt she should *see* her sister, perhaps for the first time. Inside the flat, still form did implacable disappointment, then, stay locked? She wished she could give Rosa some little present. Too late to give Rosa anything pretty now: she looked back – it had always, then, been too late? She thought: you poor queer heart; you queer heart, eating yourself out, thanking God for the pain. She thought: I did that to her; then what have I done to Lucille?

She said: 'You're ever so like me, Rosa, really, aren't you? Setting our hearts on things. When you've got them you don't notice. No wonder you wanted Lucille ... You did ought to have had that fairy doll.'

Elizabeth Bowen, *Collected Stories*, 1980

From A Very Close Conspiracy

Vanessa never doubted their separateness. She had enjoyed her first three years of life without Virginia and as the eldest of the Stephen children bore a mantle of distinction and responsibility. Throughout their childhood, it had been she, too, who had suffered unfavourable comparisons with her irresistible younger sister, and so had striven all the more to establish her own identity. Nevertheless circumstances and their own natures combined to make the bond between them a potent one. For each, this bond could be both inhibiting and inspiring.

Virginia, however, was never as certain of her separateness from Vanessa. 'Do you think we have the same pair of eyes, only different spectacles? I rather think I'm more nearly attached to you than sisters should be,' she wrote to Vanessa when they were both nearly sixty. This attachment was at times fiercely demanding, if life-sustaining in a truly umbilical sense; throughout their adult lives, Virginia was to remind her sister that she was Vanessa's first-born, asking 'Why did you bring me into the world?' Her intimacy, her need and love for Vanessa infused every one of her days.

For Virginia there was always Vanessa. There from the beginning of consciousness, she was there too, barely five miles away, when fifty-nine years later Virginia drowned herself in the River Ouse. Virginia had never known a day which had not been underpinned with the knowledge of the existence of her sister. She pined for her when they were apart, felt 'parched', 'dried up'; her language is full of desert imagery in which Vanessa became the longed-for fountain of water, of life itself. Everywhere, in her letters, her diaries, her fiction, there is evidence of the central importance of Vanessa to Virginia: 'There is no doubt that I love you better than anyone in the world.'

Vanessa's feelings for Virginia were much less explicit. Admiration, exasperation and a strong maternal solicitude were the surface currents, but deeper and more obscure was her own emotional dependence on her sister; there were periods in her life when she was as desperate for the sisterly devotion that Virginia had demanded always so candidly for herself.

Jane Dunn, 1990

From Talking to the Dead

I keep thinking about Isabel. Being in the same house for so long is working strangely, making me think of her more rather than less. I think of us being sisters. She's like me, more like me than Susan sees, and yet not like. All those genes thrown up into the air as casually as dice have come down quite differently each time. Once I used to think Isabel had had all the sixes, but now I'm not so sure. She's three years older than me, so the family she grew up in was never quite the same as the one I knew. She remembers – or says she remembers – the time before I was born, when she walked between our parents holding a hand of each, linking them. When she talked to our parents about that time in front of me, I seemed to vanish. My not existing was as real to them as my existing. Isabel remembers our mother being pregnant. She was the big one, the sensible one, and I was the toddler who could scream and bite. For years I accepted Isabel's list of the things I had done to her, not even beginning to think that there might be other lists, other things, done to me. She told her stories with an air of adult patience, for adult ears.

'Nina cut the eyelashes off Rosina. She thought they'd grow again. She doesn't realize Rosina's only a doll.'

But she doesn't tell how every time it was my turn for the doll's pram she would calmly, firmly take out my doll and put in her own.

'You see, Nina, Mandy doesn't fit in the pram properly. Look at her legs sticking out. Rosina came with the pram, so it's hers really. But I'll let you have a turn pushing her.'

And off we went to push our doll's pram round Barnoon Cemetery, up and down the little paths, visiting our favourite graves Below us the sea glittered and the holiday people threw themselves in and out of the waves, but we took no notice of them. Our parents let us go where we liked. We'd walk as far as Wicca Pool sometimes, and swim with the seals. Once we saw a honeymoon couple bathing there naked, their fronds of pubic hairs touching.

'They'll lie down on the rocks and cuddle each other next,' said Isabel authoritatively, and they did. Isabel was so sure of things that sometimes I thought it was her certainty that made them happen. Without Isabel's predictions I'd have been lost in a world where anything might come next. She even knew when I was going to cry.

Once I slipped when we were running back along the cliff path. We'd been picking blackberries and I was watching the berries bounce in the bucket clasped in front of me, not the path. My foot caught on a stone, and I fell sideways, not safely on to the path, but sliding with horrible smoothness and speed to the lip of the cliff. I saw myself going and heard Isabel scream, and then I went over. But it was a rough slope, not the edge of the cliff itself, which was still fifteen feet away. I slid ten of them, bumping and banging, and then stopped. I began to scream, lying on my back, looking straight up at the sky. A second later a half-circle of terror broke the sky, upside down. It took me a moment to realize that this was Isabel's face. The next minute she was with me, dragging me back with both hands over the scattered blackberries. I got back to the path and sat down on it, shivering. My legs were smeared with blood and blackberry juice. There was a long burning graze up the inside of my arms.

'My bucket's gone,' I said.

'I'll have a look.' Isabel stood up and peered down. 'I can't see it. It must have gone over.'

I thought of my new bucket, silvery inside, bouncing and clanging down to the rocks, and I began to cry. Then Isabel was crying too, worse than me, shaking and hiding her face with her hands. She hardly ever cried, and this was worse than losing the bucket. I patted her shoulders but she didn't seem to feel it. 'It's all right, Isabel. I didn't fall. I'm all right.' But she cried harder and I gave up and began to pick up the fallen blackberries and eat them. I wiped off the dust carefully and popped them into my mouth, one by one. They were delicious. And then there was Isabel, facing me on hands and knees, her face fierce. She was all smeary with crying, but back to herself again.

'And don't you dare tell them, Nina. Or I'll say I told you to stop and you ran on.'

Helen Dunmore, 1996

From The Hundred Secret Senses

I was nearly six by the time Kwan came to this country. We were waiting for her at the customs area of San Francisco Airport. Aunt Betty was also there. My mother was nervous and excited, talking non-stop: 'Now listen, kids, she'll probably be shy, so don't jump all over her . . . And she'll be skinny as a beanpole, so I don't want any of you making fun of her . . .'

When the customs official finally escorted Kwan into the lobby where we were waiting, Aunt Betty pointed and said, 'That's her. I'm telling you that's her.' Mom was shaking her head. This person looked like a strange old lady, short and chubby, not exactly the starving waif Mom pictured or the glamorous teenage sister I had in mind. She was dressed in drab grey pyjamas, and her broad brown face was flanked by two thick braids.

Kwan was anything but shy. She dropped her bag, fluttered her arms, and bellowed, 'Hall-oo! Hall-oo!' Still hooting and laughing, she jumped and squealed the way our new dog did whenever we let him out of the garage. This total stranger tumbled into Mom's arms, then Daddy Bob's. She grabbed Kevin and Tommy by the shoulders and shook them. When she saw me, she grew quiet, squatted on the lobby floor, and held out her arms. I tugged on my mother's skirt. 'Is *that* my big sister?'

Mom said, 'See, she has your father's same thick, black hair.'

I still have the picture Aunt Betty took: curly-haired Mom in a mohair suit, flashing a quirky smile; our Italo-American stepfather, Bob, appearing stunned; Kevin and Tommy mugging in cowboy hats; a grinning Kwan with her hand on my shoulder; and me in a frothy party dress, my finger stuck in my bawling mouth.

I was crying because just moments before the photo was taken, Kwan had given me a present. It was a small cage of woven straw, which she pulled out of the wide sleeve of her coat and handed to me proudly. When I held it up to my eyes and peered between the webbing, I saw a six-legged monster, fresh-grass green, with saw-blade jaws, bulging eyes, and whips for eyebrows. I screamed and flung the cage away.

At home, in the bedroom we shared from then on, Kwan hung the cage with the grasshopper, now missing one leg. As soon as night fell, the grasshopper began to chirp as loudly as a bicycle bell warning people to get out of the road.

After that day, my life was never the same. To Mom, Kwan was a handy babysitter, willing, able, and free. Before my mother took off for an afternoon at the beauty parlour or a shopping trip with her gal pals, she'd tell me to stick to Kwan. 'Be a good little sister and explain to her anything she doesn't understand. Promise?' So every day after school, Kwan would latch on to me and tag along wherever I went. By the first grade, I became an expert on public humiliation and shame. Kwan asked so many dumb questions that all the neighbourhood kids thought she had come from Mars. She'd say: 'What M&M?' 'What ching gum?' 'Who this Popeye Sailor Man? Why one eye gone? He bandit?' Even Kevin and Tommy laughed.

With Kwan around, my mother could float guiltlessly through her honeymoon phase with Bob. When my teacher called Mom to say I was running a fever, it was Kwan who showed up at the nurse's office to take me home. When I fell while roller-skating, Kwan bandaged my elbows. She braided my hair. She packed lunches for Kevin, Tommy, and me. She tried to teach me to sing Chinese nursery songs. She soothed me when I lost a tooth. She ran the washcloth over my neck while I took my bath.

I should have been grateful to Kwan. I could always depend on her. She liked nothing better than to be by my side. But instead, most of the time, I resented her for taking my mother's place.

I remember the day it first occurred to me to get rid of Kwan. It was summer, a few months after she had arrived. Kwan, Kevin, Tommy, and I were sitting on our front lawn, waiting for something to happen. A couple of Kevin's friends sneaked to the side of our house and turned on the sprinkler system. My brothers and I heard the telltale spit and gurgle of water running into the lines, and we ran off just before a dozen sprinkler heads burst into spray. Kwan, however, simply stood there, getting soaked, marvelling that so many springs had erupted out of the earth all at once. Kevin and his friends were howling with laughter. I shouted, 'That's not nice.'

Then one of Kevin's friends, a swaggering second-grader whom all the little girls had a crush on, said to me, 'Is that dumb Chink your sister? Hey, Olivia, does that mean you're a dumb Chink too?'

I was so flustered I yelled, 'She's not my sister! I hate her! I wish she'd go back to China!' Tommy later told Daddy Bob what I had said, and Daddy Bob said, 'Louise, you better do something about your daughter.' My mother shook her head, looking sad. 'Olivia,' she said, 'we don't ever hate anyone. "Hate" is a *terrible* word. It hurts you as much as it hurts others.' Of course, this only made me hate Kwan even more.

The worst part was sharing my bedroom with her. At night, she liked to throw open the curtains so that the glare of the street lamp poured into our room, where we lay side by side in our matching twin beds. Under this 'beautiful American moon', as she called it, Kwan would jabber away in Chinese. She kept on talking while I pretended to be asleep. She'd still be yakking when I woke up. That's how I became the only one in our family who learned Chinese. Kwan infected me with it. I absorbed her language through my pores while I was sleeping. She pushed her Chinese secrets into my brain and changed how I thought about the world. Soon I was even having nightmares in Chinese.

In exchange, Kwan learned her English from me – which, now that I think of it, may be the reason she has never spoken it all that well. I was not an enthusiastic teacher. One time, when I was seven, I played a mean trick on her. We were lying in our beds in the dark.

'Libby-ah,' Kwan said. And then she asked in Chinese, 'The delicious pear we ate this evening, what's its American name?'

'Barf,' I said, then covered my mouth to keep her from hearing my snickers.

She stumbled over this new sound – 'bar-a-fa, bar-a-fa' – before she said, 'Wah! What a clumsy word for such a delicate taste. I never ate such good fruit. Libby-ah, you are a lucky girl. If only my mother did not die.' She could segue from just about any topic to the tragedies of her former life, all of which she conveyed to me in our secret language of Chinese.

Amy Tan, 1996

From Lost and Found

My sister lives in Angola. She has been there for eight years, first working as an agronomist for a charity, then with a non-governmental organization trying to help the thousands of displaced and maimed citizens, now running a farm just outside Lubango, a town in the south of the country. She has lived there through its terrible civil war, through the false hope of its elections and the violent unrest that followed, into its present state of poverty and betrayal. [. . .] And yet, of her own free will Jackie stays, and, now that she lives with an Angolan and their small son, she is not just in Angola but of it, part of its floundering economy. All of her peripatetic life [. . .] she has looked for a place where she felt she could belong. She has chosen to make her home in a place so far removed from her childhood that it is as if she has become an exile from her past.

It had been a long time since I had seen Jackie. At family gatherings, she is always the powerful absence – the one we raise our glasses to at Christmas dinners, remember on her February birthday, the one whom we endlessly try to interpret from afar and whose silences we fill with many meanings. Sometimes a letter, five months old, will arrive on transparent airmail paper, in looped and urgent script. Sometimes, very rarely, she manages to call us on an echoey telephone line, one in three of her words getting through: 'Hello . . . difficult . . . missing . . . loving . . . trying . . . hope . . . well . . . happy . . . sad . . . goodbye.' We hear our own voices boom back at us: 'Are you OK . . . OK . . . OK?' When I flew to Lubango, I wanted not just to find her, hug her, talk to her and see what her life was actually like, I wanted to restore her from a symbolic and painful absence in my life to my unghostly elder sister – reduce her to her proper size, five foot five in her stockinged feet. [. . .]

Jackie is the oldest of four siblings. It's always hard to be the first-born, especially for someone like her: a bit awkward, a bit dyslexic, rather shy and stubborn and unsure. And just behind her, moving along the trail that she'd had to blaze for herself, the rest of us Gerrards to whom life came a little more easily. Looking back now, I feel that I was quick and bright, like a shallow stream chattering along. She was slow and deep; the river, quiet waters. She loved nature; very early, she learnt from my father the names for birds, trees, flowers. She loved animals, and had lots of rabbits, hamsters and budgies that she buried with their twig crosses under the copper-beech tree. She had a small circle of good friends. She was dogged, even then a stoic. Sometimes she would go long-distance running and I thought she could have pounded steadily on for ever, eyes on a far horizon. But she grew up with such difficulty, as older siblings maybe usually do. She was never a flirt, she refused to wear make-up or high-heeled shoes. She was alarmed by the attentions of the boys with acne and beery breath who wriggled their pelvises to rock music, or by the earnest boys who read poems to her from Ted Hughes's *Crow*. When she went out to parties, I would watch while she dressed, while she gazed anxiously at her pale, unadorned face in the mirror. She looked lovely, blond, serious, anxious – never the pert little thing that boys would pull carelessly into a dark corner. I was the flirt, the pert little thing. She was proud of my artifice, my obnoxious, giggly cheek. Only later did I learn to be properly proud of her stalwartness and endurance.

But I always thought we'd grow middle-aged together, go shopping together, have tea with each other while our children played, meet up for birthdays, anniversaries. When we all talked about what we'd do when we were adults, my brother, youngest sister and myself would choose the obvious things: doctor, nurse, ballerina, engine driver, pilot, mummy. Jackie, though, always wanted to go round the country with a horse and cart, selling bread to the gypsies.

In Lubango and on the farm, she is a well-loved figure. People come to her when they are injured. One morning, I watch as she cleans wounds and dresses them with gentian violet. Later, we visit the second chief of the area in his mud hut [. . .] His foot, wrapped in a dirty strip of material, is suppurating and swollen. He tells Jackie he treated his sprained ankle by lancing it. She arranges to drive him to hospital in the farm's small, yellow dumper truck that bumps along at ten miles an hour. She makes sure all the workers go to a clinic regularly [. . .] Once, she rescued a very sick boy and gave some of her own blood to save his life – he stayed at her house for a few days, until his family could collect him. After they left, Tomas and Jackie discovered they had taken the farm's precious supply of nails with them. She shrugs when she talks about it: friend steals from friend, cousin from cousin, in this land of no tomorrow. [. . .]

Staying there felt like going underwater, into the emotional badlands where nothing is solid or certain any more, nothing familiar, nothing safe. And there is Jackie, trudging the many miles to market with a sack of maize on her back, hoeing the sandy soil under the hot sun, carefully sewing her only pair of sandals back together, anxiously calculating how long the rice will last, paying her debts to the last penny, giving away her last qwanza, her face blossoming like a flower when she looks at her manic little son, living a life which seems so hard, so good, and so self-denying that I am filled with an admiration that feels more like rage. Or guilt.

[. . .]

We cook together, giggling. Tommy – my shadow for a week –

helps us, chucking salt crystals into pans, stirring onions. Mealie-meal is our staple, thick and white like wallpaper paste. Dried fish, sometimes salt cod. Pulses that have to be soaked for seven days before they are cooked. Goat is a delicacy; this Christmas, Jackie will cook goat for her family and friends, though Father Christmas may not come with a very large sack. [. . .]

I teach Tommy follow-my-leader, grandmother's footsteps, hide-and-seek, Simon says. We hop round the garden together. I teach him 'Twinkle Twinkle Little Star'. He sings, in his broken English, a song Jackie must have sung to him: 'I see the moon/The moon sees me/The moon sees the one/That I want to see/God bless the moon/And God bless me/And God bless the one/That I want to see.' Then he shows me their photograph album: it is full of pictures from England: his granny Pat and grandpa John who adore him and whom he adores right back, his Auntie Katie and Uncle Timmy, all of his many cousins. [. . .] He says that he wants to come back with me for a visit. He wants to see the snow and eat cake.

[. . .]

Families are so complicated; almost all of their dramas lie between the lines, in a subtext of love, guilt, nostalgia. One of Jackie's favourite songs used to be Edith Piaf's 'Je Ne Regrette Rien' – because, of course, she does regret some things. She misses the family. 'I have a torn life,' she says to me. 'I do not know where my home is.' And sometimes, like her, I feel full of homesickness for our mythologized, reinvented, enchanted childhood, where we four played in the garden at the end of the day while our mother baked cakes and folded down our bed covers and smelt of roses and our father drove home with his briefcase, and where everything seemed possible. Now we all have children of our own, who think that they can be ballerinas or pilots when they grow up, who also think that they will always be together. A strange African journey, coming so far to say hello, to say goodbye again.

Nicci Gerrard, *Observer*, 8 December 1996

Princess Elizabeth to the Queen

16 March 1554

If any ever did try this old saying 'that a king's word was more
than another man's oath', I most humbly beseech your Majesty to
verify it in me, and to remember your last promise and my last
demand that I be not condemned without answer and due proof;
which it seems that now I am; for without cause proved, I am by
your Council from you commanded to go into the Tower, a place
more wanted for a false traitor, than a true subject; which though
I know I deserve it not, yet in the face of all this realm appears that
it is proved. I pray God I may die the shamefullest death that ever
any died, afore I may mean any such thing; and to this present hour
I protest afore God (who shall judge my truth whatsoever malice
shall devise) that I never practised, counselled, nor consented to
anything that might be prejudicial to your person in any way, or
dangerous to the State by any means. And therefore I humbly
beseech your Majesty to let me answer afore yourself, and not
suffer me to trust to your councillors; yea, and that afore I go to
the Tower (if it be possible) if not, afore I be further condemned;
howbeit, I trust assuredly your Highness will give me leave to do
it afore I go, for that thus shamefully I may not be cried out on as
I now shall be, yea and without cause; let conscience move your
Highness to take some better way with me than to make me be
condemned in all men's sight afore my known desert. Also I most
humbly beseech your Highness to pardon this my boldness, which
my innocency procures me to do, together with hope of your natural
kindness, which I trust will not see me cast away without desert,
which what it is I would desire no more of God but that you truly
knew. Which thing I think and believe you shall never by report
know, unless by yourself you hear. I have heard in my time of many
cast away, for want of coming to the presence of their prince; and
in late days I heard my Lord of Somerset say that if his brother
had been suffered to speak with him he had never suffered, but
persuasions were made to him so great that he was brought in belief
that he could not live safely if the admiral lived; and that made him

give his consent to his death. Though these persons are not to be compared to your Majesty, yet I pray God that evil persuasions persuade not one sister against the other, and all for that they have heard false report, and not hearken to the truth known. Therefore, once again kneeling with humbleness of my heart, because I am not suffered to bow the knees of my body, I humbly crave to speak with your Highness, which I would not be so bold as to desire, if I knew not myself most clear, as I know myself most true. And as for the traitor Wyatt he might peradventure write me a letter, but on my faith I never received any from him. And as for the copy of my letter sent to the French King, I pray God confound me eternally if ever I sent him word, message, token, or letter, by any means. And to this truth I will stand in till my death.

I humbly crave but only one word of answer from yourself.

Your Highness's most faithful subject, that hath been from the beginning, and will be to my end.

Elizabeth

From Frederick Chamberlain, *The Sayings of Queen Elizabeth*, 1923

From An Accident of Birth

I am a natural-born eldest child: responsible, hard-working, rather conventional. I worry about my siblings and have a tendency to cluck around everyone I know, feeling it's my duty to look after them. Only I'm not an eldest child. I'm the youngest of three. Current lore (and psychology) dictates that because I was spoilt, indulged, allowed to do my own thing – all true – I should be an adult baby: wilful and seeking to be nurtured throughout my life.

I'm not a fan of statistics, generalizations or rules – probably the only vestige of youngest-child waywardness remaining. There is logic in the convention that the eldest, burdened by the expectations of excited, new parents, becomes a pillar of society, that the youngest, unfettered, becomes an emotional and professional dilettante, and that the middle, caught between the two, feels a bit of an outsider and becomes an expert in compromise.

But the glorious thing about humans, versus the tidy predictability of machines, is that no one really knows how we will turn out. Birth order works well as a general rule of thumb, but there are exceptions [. . .]

I'm fortunate that my sister Vida, ten years older than me, felt similarly misplaced in the birth order. 'I was born at the wrong time, like people born the wrong sex. The only perk was being the one who could stay up latest. Nothing else was worth it.' You only have to look at our work to see that fate got our roles mixed up. From my early twenties I've been writing earnest self-help stuff about getting your life in order and repairing your relationships. People who meet me for the first time often say I'm 'different' from what they envisaged. Sometimes they mean 'younger'. Most people who've read me expect me to be older, by quite a bit, than themselves.

Vida, on the other hand, is an anarchic and achingly funny novelist. In *Sons, Lovers, Etcetera*, her heroine, Kate, a heightened and fictionalized version of herself, careers through life and love disasters as a child would – despite having a grown-up son herself – protected, as life's innocents are, by zest, optimism and a big heart. She copes with tawdry reality by dialling into her imagination and by doing the kinds of things most 'grown-ups' believe are past them. [. . .]

Vida was the mother of two children before she spotted my potential to take over as her older sister. 'One day I was telling you to go fetch my handbag, because you were the littlest, and the next you turned eighteen, and I saw the answer to my prayers. I'd spent my life looking for people to look after me and there you were. I could say "these are my problems, solve them". We swapped roles seamlessly. It only brings me up short when, by mistake, I call you "mummy". From the moment we had the realization that you'd be the eldest and I'd be the baby, we didn't jostle, as some siblings do. We'd found the balance that suited us both.'

Sarah Litvinoff, *Independent on Sunday*, 2 November 1997

I always thought I had to be an Elinor. But now I realize I'm really a Marianne.

Cry by eldest sister of four after coming through a personal crisis

Now being older just means I'm getting saggy faster, and it's downhill all the way . . .

Claire Seeber, *Independent on Sunday*, 26 April 1998

5
Three Sisters

INTRODUCTION

In myth three sisters turn up everywhere; terrible ones – the Gorgons; prophetic ones – the Fates and their Norse equivalents, the Norns; young ones – the Three Graces, the Rhine Maidens, with whom Wagner's Ring cycle opens; old ones – the Grey Sisters, the Graeae, here shown confronted by Perseus. Chekhov's play *Three Sisters* depicts the reality of sisterhood, rather than such myths. But just as the myths give the title of that play its force, so they also affect the way any three sisters are seen by others, and the way we see ourselves.

The number three is significant everywhere, of course, not just among sisters. The Trinity in Christian theology – the Holy Ghost mediating the Father and the Son; Marx's 'thesis, antithesis, synthesis'; even the rhetoric of most political speeches, composed of arguments or statements each incorporating three points. The 'embracing synthesis' one writer calls it, going on to quote another who claims that 'the triad leads to a new integration, one that does not negate the duality proceeding it, but, rather, overcomes it'. This, I guess, is an elaborate way of saying that a third party, taking the views of two opponents into account, can restore order: the basis of all arbitration. Perhaps it is significant that it's the third sister Beth, in *Little Women*, who pours the oil on troubled family waters. Would my two inimical aunts have got on better had there been a third sister to explain each of them to the other?

On the other hand, there is the adage, 'Two's company, three's a crowd.' And, in some families, for sure, the existence of three sisters means two of them ganging up against the lonely third; a common problem with sisters born as triplets, I am told. Yet I suspect that quite often fluctuating alliances between three sisters make it easier to avoid fights; with two alone there's no relief from confrontation. Would the Beverley Sisters have achieved the harmony they did, let alone the fame, had they been two, not three, I wonder?

In my own family, during our little sister's childhood, it was inevitably two against one. We were the twins, a fortress impossible to breach. She, meanwhile, was the classic younger sister of fairy tale, and of *King Lear* for that matter, which of course started out as a folk tale (and ended up, via Jane Smiley, as a novel). A fair-haired, beautiful child, admired by our brother the way we were not, she might have been a classic source of resentment for her elders; not that we did resent her that way often, maybe because she was so much younger. In adulthood no resentment was necessary: our little sister got on with both of us far better than we twins did with each other. It helped, of course, that she saw two very different people from the ones we showed each other. Getting to know our younger sister as adults, we could be adults around her. Whereas with each other, we twins could not help reverting to childhood resentment and hostility – alternating, in times of trouble, with bouts of passionate affection. Because of this, because of how different we were with her, our younger sister often found herself having to explain my twin to me and me to my twin. The role of peacemaker into which she was cast made her thankful, I think, that she lived 12,000 miles away.

As for all three of us sisters together, that was quite another matter, that was pure pleasure, all the more so, maybe, because it so rarely came about. (Margaret Mead makes the same points about the meetings between her and her two sisters.) It was not a pleasure we discovered, of course, till we were well grown up. But I suspect that even in families where sisters aren't so separated by age and circumstance as we were, it is only in adulthood that the pleasure of the three-sister relationship can fully reveal itself.

I remember two such meetings especially. One was in April, in a year when, unbeknown even to my twin at that stage, I was awaiting the result of a biopsy. My terror sharpened my awareness of everything else; made what was sweet still very much sweeter. We met at my father's house in Surrey for Saturday lunch, us three sisters and my sisters' children, ranging in age from twelve down to two, a boy and a girl in each case. Overwhelmed by so many of our father's first family, our stepmother absented herself as soon as she'd sat the four children down to fish fingers and ice-cream. We and our father ate cheese and pâté and sliced bread straight out of their greaseproof packets – I can see the dull shine of the paper even now. Afterwards, on one of those blue, bright yet hazy April days, the branches of the trees still naked, the daffodils careless and brilliant, the fields very green, we wandered up the rutted track behind his house, towards the bare woods on top of the ridge, talking desultorily, my twin's twelve-year-old coaxing on his two-year-old cousin, the children's voices filling the air. I remember the sounds of the voices, even the feel of the ruts under my feet. I remember it as heaven.

In a more painful way, too, it was heaven the last time we met as three; on yet another bright spring day, Holy Thursday, just before Easter, shortly before my twin died. Our younger sister had come over from Australia to spend time with her, but was now due to go home, and I had driven up to Oxford to fetch her. We sat in the radiotherapy ward in which my sister was to die – she'd been summoned as an out-patient for a blood transfusion to raise her white-cell blood count. The ward much depleted by the coming holiday, we had one end of it almost to ourselves. My younger sister and I perched on an empty bed, hearing behind drawn curtains the protests of my twin as the doctor attempted to find an unused vein for the transfusion; we looked at each other, tensed up, said nothing. And then for a while, the curtain drawn back again, we sat there together, all of us knowing that this was the last time we sisters could meet as three. It made the familiar sweetness of our meeting agony; at the same time, like my fear that other spring day, it made it sweeter. Despite the tubes in my sister's arm, despite her swellings and her worn, white, aged look, what was to happen did not seem real. Only this, now, seemed real – the ward I remember as full of space and light and sun. My twin and my sister hugged and cried on parting. I watched, still locked in our eternal threeness, part of them, yet detached at the same time. Two weeks later my twin was dead; leaving just two of us.

Three . . . 'Heaven's dearest number [. . .] the first that has a beginning, middle and end.'

Du Bartas, *La Semaine*, translated by Joshua Sylvester, 1578

From Cap o' Rushes

Well, there was once a very rich gentleman, and he'd three daughters, and he thought he'd see how fond they were of him. So he says to the first, 'How much do you love me, my dear?'

'Why,' says she, 'as I love my life.'

'That's good,' says he.

So he says to the second, 'How much do *you* love me, my dear?'

'Why,' says she, 'better nor all the world.'

'That's good,' says he.

So he says to the third, 'How much do *you* love me, my dear?'

'Why, I love you as fresh meat loves salt,' says she.

Well, but he was angry. 'You don't love me at all,' says he, 'and in my house you stay no more.' So he drove her out there and then, and shut the door in her face. [. . .]

Retold by Joseph Jacobs, 1898

From A Thousand Acres

I said, 'What's the plan, Daddy?'

He glanced at me, then at Caroline, and, looking at her all the while, he said, 'We're going to form this corporation, Ginny, and you girls are all going to have shares, then we're going to build this new Slurrystore, and maybe a Harvestore, too, and enlarge the hog operation.' He looked at me. 'You girls and Ty and Pete and Frank are going to run the show. You'll each have a third part in the corporation. What do you think?'

I licked my lips and climbed the two steps on to the porch. Now I could see Harold through the kitchen screen, standing in the dark doorway, grinning. I knew he was thinking that my father had had too much to drink – that's what I was thinking, too. I looked down at the paper plates in my hands, bluing in the twilight. Ty was looking at me, and I could see in his gaze a veiled and tightly contained delight – he had been wanting to increase the hog operation for years. I remember what I thought. I thought, okay. Take it. He is holding it out to you, and all you have to do is take it. Daddy said, 'Hell, I'm too old for this. You wouldn't catch me buying a new tractor at my age. If I want to listen to some singer, I'll listen in my own house. Anyway, if I died tomorrow, you'd have to pay seven or eight hundred thousand dollars inheritance taxes. People always act like they're going to live for ever when the price of land is up' – here he threw a glance at Harold – 'but if you get a heart attack or a stroke or something, then you got to sell off to pay the government.'

In spite of that inner clang, I tried to sound agreeable. 'It's a good idea.'

Rose said, 'It's a great idea.'

Caroline said, 'I don't know.'

When I went to first grade and the other children said that their fathers were farmers, I simply didn't believe them. I agreed in order to be polite, but in my heart I knew that those men were impostors, as farmers and as fathers, too. In my youthful estimation, Laurence Cook defined both categories. To really believe that others even existed in either category was to break the First Commandment.

My earliest memories of him are of being afraid to look him in the eye, to look at him at all. He was too big and his voice was too deep. If I had to speak to him, I addressed his overalls, his shirt, his boots. If he lifted me near his face, I shrank away from him. If he kissed me, I endured it, offered a little hug in return. At the same time, his very fearsomeness was reassuring when I thought about things like robbers or monsters, and we lived on what was clearly the best, most capably cultivated farm. The biggest farm farmed by the biggest farmer. That fit, or maybe formed, my own sense of the right order of things.

[. . .]

When my father turned his head to look at Caroline, his movement was slow and startled, a big movement of the whole body, reminding me how bulky he was – well over six feet and two hundred thirty pounds.

Caroline would have said, if she'd dared, that she didn't want to live on the farm, that she was trained as a lawyer and was marrying another lawyer, but that was a sore subject. She shifted in her chair and swept the darkening horizon with her gaze. Harold turned on the porch light. Caroline would have seen my father's plan as a trapdoor plunging her into a chute that would deposit her right back on the farm. My father glared at her. In the sudden light of the porch, there was no way to signal her to shut up, just shut up, he'd had too much to drink. He said, 'You don't want it, my girl, you're out. It's as simple as that.' Then he pushed himself up from his chair and lumbered past me down the porch steps and into the darkness.

Caroline looked startled, but no one else did. I said, 'This is ridiculous. He's drunk.' But after that, everyone got up and moved off silently, knowing that something important had just happened, and what it was, too. My father's pride, always touchy, had been injured to the quick. It would be no use telling him that she had only said that she didn't know, that she hadn't turned him down, that she had expressed a perfectly reasonable doubt, perhaps even doubt a lawyer must express, that his own lawyer would express when my father set this project before him. I saw that maybe Caroline had mistaken what we were talking about, and spoken as a lawyer when she should have spoken as a daughter. On the other hand, perhaps she hadn't mistaken anything at all, and had simply spoken as a woman rather than as a daughter. That was something, I realized in a flash, that Rose and I were pretty careful never to do.

Jane Smiley, 1992

From King Lear

Sennet. Enter Lear, Cornwall, Albany, Goneril, Regan, Cordelia and Attendants

LEAR. Attend the Lords of France and Burgundy, Gloucester.

GLOUCESTER. I shall, my liege.

Exeunt Gloucester and Edmund

LEAR. Tell me, my daughters
Since now we will divest us both of rule,
Interest of territory, cares of state, –
Which of you shall we say doth love us most?
That we our largest bounty may extend
Where nature doth with merit challenge. Goneril,
Our eldest-born, speak first.

GONERIL. Sir, I love you more than words can wield the matter;
Dearer than eyesight, space, and liberty;
Beyond what can be valu'd, rich or rare;
No less than life, with grace, health, beauty, honour,
As much as child e'er lov'd, or father found;
A love that makes breath poor and speech unable;
Beyond all manner of so much I love you.

CORDELIA (*aside*). What shall Cordelia do? Love, and be silent.

LEAR. Of all these bounds, even from this line to this,
With shadowy forests and with champains rich'd,
With plenteous rivers and wide-skirted meads,
We make thee lady: to thine and Albany's issue

Be this perpetual. What says our second daughter,
Our dearest Regan, wife to Cornwall? Speak.

REGAN. I am made of that self metal as my sister,
And prize me at her worth. In my true heart
I find she names my very deed of love;
Only she comes too short: that I profess
Myself an enemy to all other joys
Which the most precious square of sense possesses
And find I am alone felicitate
In your dear highness' love.

CORDELIA (aside). Then, poor Cordelia!
And yet not so; since, I am sure, my love 's
More richer than my tongue.

LEAR. To thee and thine, hereditary ever,
Remain this ample third of our fair kingdom,
No less in space, validity, and pleasure,
Than that conferr'd on Goneril. Now, our joy,
Although our last, not least; to whose young love
The vines of France and milk of Burgundy
Strive to be interess'd; what can you say to draw
A third more opulent than your sisters? Speak.

CORDELIA. Nothing, my lord.

LEAR. Nothing?

CORDELIA. Nothing.

LEAR. Nothing will come of nothing: speak again.

CORDELIA. Unhappy that I am, I cannot heave
My heart into my mouth: I love your majesty
According to my bond; nor more nor less.

LEAR. How, how, Cordelia! mend your speech a little,
Lest you may mar your fortunes.

CORDELIA.   Good my lord,
You have begot me, bred me, lov'd me: I
Return those duties back as are right fit,
Obey you, love you, and most honour you.
Why have my sisters husbands, if they say
They love you all? Haply, when I shall wed,
That lord whose hand must take my plight shall carry

Half my love with him, half my care and duty:
Sure I shall never marry like my sisters,
To love my father all.
LEAR. But goes thy heart with this?
CORDELIA.   Ay, good my lord.
LEAR. So young, and so untender?
CORDELIA. So young, my lord, and true.
LEAR. Let it be so; thy truth then be thy dower!

William Shakespeare, 1605?

When two fight for an egg, the third will get it.

German rhyme

From Isak Dinesen

For the early part of her childhood, Tanne was one of a triptych
of sisters, extremely close in age, with the same fine Westenholz
features and always – or at least in all their photographs – identically
dressed. They pose in the snow by their mother's sleigh, in hooded
capelets with fox scarves. They stand in a row, hands clasped, lips
pursed, in pinafores and polka dots. They sit on the steps of a
garden in fine smocking, and on a blanket with an infant brother,
wearing shifts and straw boaters. They all receive the same little
strand of pearls, the same gamin bob, the same pompon hat. And
even at the ages of seventeen, fifteen, and fourteen respectively,
they face the camera wearing the same dark Sunday frock of dotted
swiss with a high white collar. Tanne, in the middle, is the one with
a wry smile.

Later in her life, Isak Dinesen hated to be told that she resembled
anyone, particularly anyone in her family. She became famous for
her chic, her love of dramatic costumes, the way she wore hats and

scarves, and for shooting her own fur coats. That originality was perhaps partly inspired by the memory of a childhood in uniform.

Ea, Tanne, and Elle were referred to as a unit – *Pigerne*, the girls – and shepherded about as one. They were all equally well educated and encouraged to become 'accomplished', but there was very little recognition for individual superiorities. Competition, except in the abstract – as 'spiritual struggle' – was forbidden. Praise was meted out generously but somewhat indiscriminately. Even a half century later, when Isak Dinesen published *Seven Gothic Tales*, she 'had the impression' her family expected her to 'play down' its success because a book of Elle's, published previously, had not done very well. 'Little Tanne' found the scrupulous equality of the nursery inane and infuriating. She had a precocious confidence in her own singularity.

Judith Thurman, 1982

Lady Sarah Lennox to Lady Susan O'Brien (on her brother George's daughters)

5 March 1780

I hope you will hear of the merits of her daughters by more impartial people than me, for I'm afraid the just commentation I must give them looks like prejudice. The eldest, Louisa, is middle-sized, elegant to the greatest degree in her form and rather plump; she has a true Lennox complexion, rough and shewy, her hair is fair, her eyes little & lively, her nose is like her mothers, which is pretty, and her mouth & countenance like my sister Leinsters, full of ten thousand graces; her teeth good but not superlatively fine. Her sense quick, strong & steady; her character is reserved & prudent, but so very complaisant that it's hard to discover she has a choice, & yet she has her prejudices & is firm in them. She likes the world as one does a play, for the amusement of the moment, but her turn is a jolly country life with society, where walking, working & a flower garden are her chief amusements; she don't love reading, calls everybody wise or affected that is in the least learned; she is herself free from the least tincture of affectation or of vanity, not seeming to know how pretty she is. She is feminine to the great degree, laughs most heartily at a dirty joke, but never makes one. Louisa is as you know nineteen. The next whose name is Emily, is seventeen, & the next, Georgina, fifteen. Their characters are all three as different as it is in nature to be. Emily is a fine, tall, large woman with a Lennox complexion, but red or auburn hair; her features coarse, her mouth ugly, & yet her teeth excessive white; her countenance very pleasing & all goodness like her character, which is more like my sister Louisa's than anybody I know, but for want of the same cultivation it will not be so useful perhaps. Her taste for amusement is very great, but her adoration of her sister, and the same complaisance of temper makes them appear but little different in their manners; for what Louisa does is a law to Emily. Georgina is rather little & strong made; her countenance is reckon'd very like mine, for she has little eyes, no eyebrows, a long nose, even teeth & the merriest of faces; but all her livelyness comes from her mother's side. She has all her witt, all her power of satyre, & all her goodnature too so that if she is not led to give way to the tempting vanity of displaying it, she will be delightful, but you know by experience the dangers attending on witt, & dear little Georgina I fear will experience them. Her manners are of course more lively or rather less prudent than her sisters', but the same goodhumour and complaisance reigns among them all; which considering the variety of characters is something extraordinary. I am astonished that Ly Louisa is not dying with impatience to produce girls she has so much reason to be proud of, for she is excessively fond of them, & they live like sisters with her . . .

The Life and Letters of Lady Sarah Lennox (1745–1826),
published 1901

From Christmas Jezebels

*(A seasonal story dedicated to St Nicholas, patron saint of
(among others) prostitutes)*

The three sisters lay curled asleep together like cats in a basket.
They had always shared this truckle bed; and, as they had grown
older and larger, it had become increasingly crowded. There seemed
little hope of an improvement in the situation, however, since the
family's cash-flow problems were by now quite hair-raising.

Beatrice was the first to wake, frowning and snarling her way
out of some dream argument. At eighteen she was the oldest of
the sisters, and the most worried. Opposite her snored Isobel, a
better pragmatist at sixteen than she would ever be; and in the
middle lay her favourite, Jessica, an unnervingly brainy child of
twelve.

It was still very early, but already Beatrice could hear the fishermen
down on the beach. The uncurtained window showed December
stars fading into another fourth-century Lycian morning.

'Time to get up,' she announced at last, throwing off their blanket
of patchwork sacking. Not being able to afford nightdresses, they
slept in their underwear, though they were fastidious girls and
always hung their stockings to dry at the fireplace before going to
bed.

'Oh no,' said Beatrice.

'What's the matter?' asked her sisters as they shuffled out of
bed.

'He's finally lost his reason,' said Beatrice, staring at the pile of
unfamiliar garments on the chair.

'Look at *these*,' said Jessica, holding up a pair of transparent
frilly drawers edged with red ribbon.

Isobel sniggered to herself as she buckled on a stiffly boned satin
bra.

'Don't you dare *touch* these filthy rags!' thundered Beatrice.

'Why not?' asked Isobel. 'We can't go round in our pants and
vests all day, and he's obviously pawned our usual clothes.' She

pranced over to the little mirror and started to wind a feather boa around her neck.

'Such *obvious* garments almost parody his intention,' observed Jessica. 'I suppose he expects *me* to wear this babyishly short smock with the teddy-bear appliqués.'

'Oh, my poor lamb,' moaned Beatrice, hugging her sister. 'Little do you realize.'

'I think I do, you know,' said Jessica. 'He wants you two to dress as *filles de joie*, but he's decided to aim me at the paedophile market.'

Isobel had by now wriggled into a leather jerkin and was squeezing her feet into a pair of high fur-rimmed mules.

'It's a disgrace,' said Beatrice, and sat down on the edge of the bed in tears.

'Don't worry, Beet,' called Isobel from the mirror. 'I'm not going to fall in with his wicked plans. I just like dressing up.'

Jessica put her arm round Beatrice's heaving shoulders.

'You know what he's like when he gets a bee in his bonnet,' she said soothingly.

'But he's serious this time,' sobbed Beatrice. 'And we haven't got any money at all. And he's taken our clo-othes!'

'Well, I'm certainly not going to wear that baby's dress,' said Jessica decisively. 'And you would look as ridiculous in a *guêpière* as he would. So I suggest we tear the bedspread in half and share it. We can cut head holes in the middle, and pull it all together with string belts.'

'Do cheer up,' said Isobel. 'We're going to have to stay cool and present a united front, or we're done for.'

'Meanwhile, I'll send a letter of protest to the Bishop,' said Jessica.

'Oh, well, *that's* all right then,' said Isobel.

Helen Simpson, 1990

From The Makioka Sisters

'What would be keeping her?'

Taeko and Yukiko were at the gate. There was no sign of Sachiko.

'It is almost two.' Taeko stepped toward the cab. The driver held the door open.

'They have been talking for hours.'

'She might just try hanging up.'

'Do you think Itani would let her? I can see her trying to back away from the telephone.' Yukiko's amusement suggested again that the affair was no concern of hers. 'Etsuko, go tell your mother to hang up.'

'Shall we get in?' Taeko motioned to the cab.

'I think we should wait.' Yukiko, always very proper, would not get into the cab ahead of an older sister. There was nothing for Taeko to do but wait for her.

'I heard Itani's story.' Taeko took care that the driver did not overhear her. Etsuko had run back into the house.

'Oh?'

'And I saw the picture.'

'Oh?'

'What do you think, Yukiko?'

'I hardly know, from just a picture.'

'You should meet him.'

Yukiko did not answer.

'Itani has been very kind, and Sachiko will be upset if you refuse to meet him.'

'But do we really need to hurry so?'

'She said she thought it was the hurrying that bothered you.'

Someone ran up behind them. 'I forgot my handkerchief. My handkerchief, my handkerchief. Bring me a handkerchief, someone.' Still fussing with the sleeves of her kimono, Sachiko flew through the gate.

'It was quite a conversation.'

'I suppose you think it was easy to think up excuses. I only just managed to throw her off.'

'We can talk about it later.'

'Get in, get in.' Taeko pushed her way into the cab after Yukiko.

It was perhaps a half mile to the station. When they had to hurry they took a cab, but sometimes, half for the exercise, they walked. People would turn to stare at the three of them, dressed to go out, as they walked toward the station. Shopkeepers were fond of talking about them, but probably few had guessed their ages. Although Sachiko had a six-year-old daughter and could hardly have hidden her age, she looked no more than twenty-six or twenty-seven. The unmarried Yukiko would have been taken for perhaps twenty-two or three, and Taeko was sometimes mistaken for a sixteen- or seventeen-year-old. Yukiko had reached an age when it was no longer appropriate to address her as a girl, and yet no one found it strange that she should be 'young Miss Yukiko'. All three, moreover, looked best in clothes a little too young for them. It was not that the brightness of the clothes hid their ages; on the contrary, clothes in keeping with their ages were simply too old for them. When, the year before, Teinosuke had taken his wife and sisters-in-law and Etsuko to see the cherry blossoms of the Brocade Bridge, he had written this verse to go with the souvenir snapshot:

> Three young sisters,
> Side by side,
> Here on the Brocade Bridge.

The three were not monotonously alike, however. Each had her special beauties, and they set one another off most effectively. Still they had an unmistakable something in common – what fine sisters! one immediately thought. Sachiko was the tallest, with Yukiko and Taeko shorter by equal steps, and that fact alone was enough to give a certain charm and balance to the composition as they walked down the street together. Yukiko was the most Japanese in appearance and dress, Taeko the most Western, and Sachiko stood midway between. Taeko had a round face and a firm, plump body to go with it. Yukiko, by contrast, had a long, thin face and a very slender figure. Sachiko again stood between, as if to combine their best features. Taeko usually wore Western clothes, and Yukiko wore only Japanese clothes. Sachiko wore Western clothes in the summer and Japanese clothes the rest of the year. There was something bright and lively about Sachiko and Taeko, both of whom resembled their father. Yukiko was different. Her face impressed one as somehow sad, lonely, and yet she looked best in gay clothes. The sombre kimonos so stylish in Tokyo were quite wrong for her.

. One of course always dressed for a concert. Since this was a private concert, they had given more attention than usual to their clothes. There was literally no one who did not turn for another look at them as they climbed from the cab and ran through the bright autumn sunlight toward the station. Since it was a Sunday afternoon, the train was nearly empty. Yukiko noticed that the middle-school boy directly opposite her blushed and looked at the floor as they sat down.

Junichiro Tanizaki, translated by Ewan G. Seidensticker, 1957

From Three Sisters

A band plays a military march off-stage; all listen

OLGA. They're going.

Enter Chebutykin

MASHA. The soldiers are going. Well . . . Happy journey to them! (*To her husband*) We must go home . . . Where's my hat and cape? . . .

KOOLYGHIN. I took them indoors. I'll bring them at once.

OLGA. Yes, we can go home now. It's time.

CHEBUTYKIN. Olga Serghyeevna!

OLGA. What is it? (*A pause.*) What?

CHEBUTYKIN. Nothing . . . I don't know quite how to tell you . . . (*Whispers into her ear.*)

OLGA (*frightened*). It can't be true!

CHEBUTYKIN. Yes . . . a bad business . . . I'm so tired . . . quite worn out . . . I don't want to say another word . . . (*With annoyance*) Anyway, nothing matters! . . .

MASHA. What's happened?

OLGA (*puts her arms round Irena*). What a dreadful day! . . . I don't know how to tell you, dear . . .

IRENA. What is it? Tell me quickly, what is it? For Heaven's sake! . . . [*Cries.*]

CHEBUTYKIN. The Baron's just been killed in a duel.

IRENA (*cries quietly*). I knew it, I knew it . . .

CHEBUTYKIN (*goes to the back of the stage and sits down*). I'm tired . . . (*Takes a newspaper out of his pocket.*) Let them cry for a bit . . . (*Sings quietly to himself*) Tarara-boom-di-ay, I'm sitting on a tomb-di-ay . . . What difference does it make? . . .

The three sisters stand huddled together

MASHA. Oh, listen to that band! They're leaving us . . . one of them's gone for good . . . for ever! We're left alone . . . to start our lives all over again. We must go on living . . . we must go on living . . .

IRENA (*puts her head on Olga's breast*). Some day people will know why such things happen, and what the purpose of all this suffering is . . . Then there won't be any more riddles . . . Meanwhile we must go on living . . . and working. Yes, we must just go on working! Tomorrow I'll go away alone and teach in a school somewhere; I'll give my life to people who need it . . . It's autumn now, winter will soon be here, and the snow will cover everything . . . but I'll go on working and working! . . .

OLGA (*puts her arms round both her sisters*). How cheerfully and jauntily that band's playing – really I feel as if I wanted to live! Merciful God! The years will pass, and we shall all be gone for good and quite forgotten . . . Our faces and our voices will be forgotten and people won't even know that there were once three of us here . . . But our sufferings may mean happiness for the people who come after us . . . There'll be a time when peace and happiness reign in the world, and then we shall be remembered kindly and blessed. No, my dear sisters, life isn't finished for us yet! We're going to live! The band is playing so cheerfully and joyfully – maybe, if we wait a little longer, we shall find out why we live, why we suffer . . . Oh, if we only knew, if only we knew!

The music grows fainter and fainter. Koolyghin, smiling happily, brings out the hat and the cape. Andrey enters; he is pushing the pram with Bobik sitting in it

CHEBUTYKIN (*sings quietly to himself*). Tarara-boom-di-ay . . . I'm sitting on a tomb-di-ay . . . (*Reads the paper.*) What does it matter? Nothing matters!

OLGA. If only we knew, if only we knew! . . .

Anton Chekhov, 1901

'We had our jealously guarded perks – who scraped out which pan, for instance. (Sarah had mashed potato, Alex had chocolate mix and I had cake mix.)'

Deborah Moggach, interview in *Radio Times*, June 1998

From The Sisters Rosensweig

GORGEOUS. Well, did you like him?

SARA. Actually, I had a nice time.

GORGEOUS. Did you tell him that?

SARA. No. I told him he was a very nice man instead.

GORGEOUS
PFENI } (*together*). Ugh.

GORGEOUS. How did our nice Jewish mother do such a lousy job on us?

SARA. Why is it her fault? She always told me to say thank you for having me.

PFENI (*getting up*). Personally, I feel that teatime is over. And we can now move into wine.

SARA. Such a good baby sister.

GORGEOUS. Very good. And gifted.

PFENI (*taking a bottle from the wine rack*). This Bordeaux has a reputation for being rather versatile.

GORGEOUS. Pish-pish.

SARA (*giggles*). Double pish-pish.

PFENI (*finding three glasses and pouring out the wine*). What does pish-pish actually mean?

SARA. Gorgeous, have you met my sister the wandering Gentile?

GORGEOUS. Pfeni, when Geoffrey told you he missed men, what did you do?

PFENI. I said I missed them, too.

They laugh

GORGEOUS. Good girl!

SARA. Brilliant girl! Maybe Rita Rosensweig didn't do so badly by us after all. (*She lifts her glass.*)

PFENI. To Rita!

GORGEOUS. To Rita!

SARA. To Rita! And her stunningly brilliant daughters.

GORGEOUS ⎱ (*together*). And her stunningly brilliant daughters.
PFENI ⎰ (*They sip the wine.*) Mmmm. Versatile.

GORGEOUS. Drinking goes directly to my feet. Does it go to your feet, Pfeni?

PFENI. No my head. Directly to my head. What about you, Sara?

SARA. In my hair. I feel it in my hair.

GORGEOUS. I'm exhausted.

PFENI. Me too. Very tired.

Pfeni and Gorgeous lie down next to Sara on the sofa

GORGEOUS. Sara, didn't Mama always say you were a shtarker? Maybe you should take care of us now.

PFENI. That would be very nice.

GORGEOUS. Pfeni, do you know what a shtarker is?

PFENI. A person who takes charge. A general in the Cossack army.

SARA. That must be why I'm so popular.

GORGEOUS. You have nice hands, Sara. But you should use hot oil treatments. It would loosen your cuticles. What do you think, Pfeni?

PFENI. I think Sara was a shtarker to that nice Merlin.

SARA. Shtarker. But I really hardly even knew him.

GORGEOUS. You could get to know him. Call him.

PFENI
GORGEOUS } (*together; chanting*). Call him. Call him. Call him.

SARA. Please. Girls, girls, girls. (*She holds both their faces in her hands.*) My two little sisters. Gorgeous and also Gorgeous. We are.

ALL. The sisters Gorgeous.

They laugh

GORGEOUS. You know what I wish with all my heart?

SARA. What?

PFENI. What?

GORGEOUS. I wish that on one of our birthdays, when all the children and men have gone upstairs to sleep!

SARA. What men?

GORGEOUS. And we finally sit together – just us three sisters –

PFENI. Around the samovar.

SARA. Sh!

GORGEOUS. And we talk about life!

PFENI. And art.

SARA. Pfeni!

GORGEOUS. Thank you, Sara. (*She kisses Sara's hand.*) That each of us can say at some point that we had one moment of pure, unadulterated happiness! Do you think that's possible, Sara?

SARA. Brief. But a moment or two.

PFENI. I like that.

GORGEOUS. Me too.

Pause

SARA. Gorgeous, there's something I've been meaning to share with you. Your neck is very dry.

GORGEOUS. No.

SARA. Don't you think her neck is dry, Pfeni?

PFENI. Let me see. Let me see. (*She touches Gorgeous's neck.*) Oh, yes, very dry!!

SARA. Don't you think she should use that special rejuvenation treatment? The deluxe pish-pish one!

PFENI. Oh that pish-pish rejuvenation treatment! I think so.

Sara and Pfeni suddenly jump on Gorgeous and begin tickling her

Rabbi Pearlstein says more collagen shots!

GORGEOUS. No! No! Pfeni, stop and you can have my remaining shoe! (*She jumps up from the sofa.*)

PFENI (*chasing Gorgeous upstairs*). I want that shoe. Gorgeous, gimme that shoe! Gorgeous!

Black-out

Wendy Wasserstein, 1996

From The Rhine Maidens

ALBERICH. Hey, hey, you nymphs!
How pretty you are,
desirable creatures!
From Nibelheim's night
I'd like to draw near you
if only you would be kind to me.
The girls stop their game as soon as they hear Alberich's voice

WOGLINDE. Hey, who's there?

FLOSSHILDE. It's darker and someone's calling.

WELLGUNDE. Look who's listening to us!
They dive further down and recognize the Nibelung

WOGLINDE and WELLGUNDE. Ugh! how loathsome!

FLOSSHILDE (*diving upwards quickly*). Guard the gold!
Father warned us
of such a foe.
The other two follow her and all three gather quickly round the rock in the middle

ALBERICH. You up there!

WOGLINDE, WELLGUNDE and FLOSSHILDE. What d'you want, down there?

ALBERICH. Do I disturb your game
if I stand and stare here quietly?
If you'd dive down,
a game with you

and a joke would be fun for a
Nibelung.

WOGLINDE. Does he want to play with us?

WELLGUNDE. Is he making fun?

ALBERICH. In this light how
bright and fair you look!
How I'd love to hold
one of you sylphs in my arms,
if only she'd slip down here.

FLOSSHILDE. Now I laugh at my fears,
our enemy is in love.
They laugh

WELLGUNDE. The bawdy old goat!

WOGLINDE. We'll teach him!
*She lowers herself on to the top of the rock whose base Alberich
has now reached*

Richard Wagner, 1853

From More than Just a House

'. . . I'm the best dancer of the three and I'm much the smartest one.
Jean is the jazzy one, the most chic, but I think it's *passé* to be jazzy
and play the traps and neck every second boy. Amanda is the
beauty, of course. But I'm going to be the Cinderella, Mr Lowrie.
They'll be the two wicked sisters, and gradually you'll find I'm the
most attractive and get all hot and bothered about me.'

F. Scott Fitzgerald, *The Price was High: Last Collected Stories*, 1989

Cinderella

This new wife had two daughters of her own, that she brought home with her. 'What does the good-for-nothing thing want in the parlour?' said they; 'they who would have bread should first earn it; away with the kitchen maid!' Then they took away her fine clothes, and gave her an old grey frock to put on, and laughed at her and turned her into the kitchen.

The Brothers Grimm

. . . her wretched clothes did not prevent Cinderella from being a hundred times more beautiful than her sisters, for all their resplendent garments.

Perrault

From The Beverley Sisters

Of my three interviewees there was no sign. Or was there? On one of the round tables were three teacups, two black patent leather handbags and a faint whiff of *eau de toilette*. If the *Marie Celeste* had run to a stateroom, it would have looked like this. And just as I was wondering if, overwhelmed by sudden nerves, they were hiding behind a pillar, they suddenly emerged. Through the Stygian murk, three sixtysomething blond women in identical tuxedos and rhinestone jockey caps processed towards me, uttering random but wholly phatic cries of welcome. As they drew level with our table, the leader, without preamble or invitation, abruptly kicked one elegant, black-trousered leg in the air, to about the level of my ear. 'I'm Teddy,' she said, softly as a courtesan, and kissed me on the cheek. So did Joy, the leonine elder sister, a few seconds later. So did Babs, the other twin. ('Isn't he *tall*?' she murmured to her siblings, as though admiring a lampstand at an antiques market.) Then the Beverley Sisters sat down, their sequined heads iridescently glowing in blues and pinks and greens as the facets of their caps caught the muted lights from the bar. 'We thought we'd better dress up,' said Joy. 'We were afraid you might not recognize us.'

This is what is known as Making An Entrance. The Bevs are rather good at entrances. Also at close harmonies, cross-dressing, comebacks and telling you how utterly divine their lives are. They are, on the other hand, hopeless at growing old. The hair that curls from under their rhinestone lids is a triumph of the Barbie-doll accessorizer's art. They are all weirdly slim. Their eyes shine with an unearthly, belladonna glint. Joy, older than the twins by three years (they all spookily share a birthday), sits in the middle, as when they're singing, and talks the most. She is the conciliator, Teddy the stroppy one, Babs the quietest and prettiest. They all talk incessantly, interrupting each other, finishing each other's remarks, backtracking in mid-sentence, changing their minds, fishing their memory banks for appropriate replies, and always, always insisting on their devotion to each other, their parents, their children, their public. In addition, they will sing to you, act out embarrassing on-stage pratfalls that have befallen them, hold your hand, flirt like madwomen, and even, occasionally, insult you. 'Tell me, John,' said Teddy during a rare lull in the girlish blizzard, 'Are you colour-blind?' No, I said. Why? 'How did you come to wear that tie with that shirt?' Instantly (and typically) the others joined in. 'It makes him look boyish,' said Babs. 'I didn't even notice,' said Joy reassuringly, 'Teddy must have thought things had gone a bit quiet for a moment.' 'No, no,' said Teddy with dismaying finality, 'I'd been thinking it for some time . . .'

The Beverleys' career trajectory is well-known – how they were little East End kids who in 1945 were scooped in an Ovaltine commercial, where their piping harmonies were heard by a BBC scout, who signed them up; how they went to America, came back with Danny Kaye and hit the London Palladium, had their own live television show for seven years, made a string of 'novelty' records of emetic sweetness ('I Saw Mommy Kissing Santa Claus', 'How Much is that Doggy in the Window?', 'Little Drummer Boy', 'Little Donkey', and their ineffable signature tune, 'Sisters') before being overtaken by the winged chariot of rock 'n' roll; how they retired in 1967 (eight years after their last appearance in the charts) to raise families, and reappeared on the scene two decades later as icons to a new audience of gay men they would not have dreamed existed in their tomboyish heyday. For an act whose natural sell-by date was 1959, they are doing all right.

John Walsh, *Independent*, 26 October 1996

From Marital Frustrations

Finally Tzu-ku entered the bridal chamber. He quickly undressed his bride and brought her to the bed. As he started to consummate the union, he became suddenly aware that he was on the threshold of a mystery most unexpected and extraordinary. What was to have been the greatest pleasure in life had, without any warning, turned into a state of bewilderment.

A ditty 'To the tune of Yellow Oriole' serves to describe the moment of discovery:

> [. . .]
> But the jade ravine, alas, is wanting;
> The architects have been remiss.
> I call this a riddle,
> Why should Nature,
> Having bountifully endowed,
> Withhold one single gift?

He embraced her in great sadness and wondered why he should be so tortured and why such a beauty could have such a defect. But there was nothing he or she could do. After a long, deep sigh, his initial excitement changed to a solemn silence.

'I know how you must feel, but there is nothing I can do about it. I beg you to treat me as a plaything or perhaps as a pet dog. Take a few concubines. Surely they will bear you children. But whatever you do, please don't send me back to my parents,' his wife pleaded.

Turning his head to face his wife, Tzu-ku answered, 'Your face is beyond compare. I would like to keep you for ever as a beautiful object, to be looked at and admired. But whenever I see you, I am consumed by passion. I want to devour you completely. How can I go on this way?'

[. . .]

The next morning Tzu-ku told his parents his unusual and unpleasant experience. His parents sought to divert him by inviting several friends to accompany him on a trip to various places. At the same time, they angrily called in the matchmaker and accused her of withholding vital information with fraudulent intent. They threatened a lawsuit against the girl's parents. But after some discussion, they suggested that the girl's parents provide another daughter to complete the job which their 'useless' first daughter couldn't finish. It so happened that the T'us still had two unmarried daughters.

The matchmaker feared further trouble, and obediently delivered the message to the T'us. Simple and honest, the T'us sent over their youngest daughter as requested. After all, life had taught them that the poor should never argue with the rich. Tzu-ku's ruthless parents forced their son's wife to leave their home and accepted the youngest T'u girl as their latest acquisition. The exchange was completed before their son returned from his trip.

II

[. . .] In considering the substitution of one sister for the other, the Yaos thought only of safeguarding the family name and the need for an heir. Therefore, they accepted the youngest T'u girl though they were not pleased with her looks, with the assumption that no family could have two daughters with that particular defect.

Tzu-ku returned home late the night when the substitution took place. Drunk, tired and sleepy he crawled into bed and fell asleep instantly. When he had slept off his drunkenness, he began to 'work' on the girl in his bed thinking that it was the one he had married.

It was only after intercourse had actually taken place that he realized he had a different girl in his arms. In the dark, his hands examined her body the best they could and found her skin as 'coarse as leather'. When the first light of dawn came, he looked at her and found she was extremely homely. Furious, he said to himself: 'The woman I married is at least pleasant to look at. I could have concubines to bear me children. Now I have this ugly woman. What shall I do with her?' Resentment mounting by the minute, he went to his parents and objected strongly to their not having consulted him about the exchange.

To make the situation intolerable, Tzu-ku discovered that she had the habit of urinating in bed when asleep. When she was awake, she had little need to use the toilet; she made up for it when she was asleep. For a few nights she was able to cover up her bad habit one way or another. But one night, Tzu-ku suddenly felt wet and in a few minutes the wetness became a flood which brought with it a pungent odour. When he had discovered the source of the flood, he got out of bed and rushed to his parents' room, demanding that they arrange for his first wife to be immediately returned.

Frightened by his anger, Tzu-ku's parents called in the matchmaker that very morning for an emergency session. They demanded that the T'us return their eldest daughter. To this request the matchmaker replied, 'You should have thought about this a few days ago. Their eldest girl has been married to someone else. But their second daughter is still unmarried, and she looks more or less like the eldest one. You should have asked for their second daughter last time. Do you really want to go through with another exchange?'

'We are afraid that we will have to,' answered Mr Yao. 'If the T'us object, we will sue them.'

The matchmaker went to the T'us once more and pressured them to agree to still another exchange. Poor and unimportant, the T'us felt they had to agree.

The T'us' second daughter actually looked exactly like the first one and Tzu-ku's parents let him think that his first wife had returned as he had requested. Tzu-ku was also unable to tell the difference until he got into bed with her. Soon he discovered that this girl was not a virgin but a very experienced bed-mate. She had lost her virginity a long time ago, and when she entered the Yao's house, she was already five months pregnant.

Soon everyone in the family knew that the newest bride was heavy with child, with someone else's child. The family reputation was again at stake, so the Yaos sent the girl back to her parents, thus revealing to the neighbours without words that the shame stemmed from the girl and her family.

Li Yu, 1979

Elizabeth Barrett Browning to her sister, 27 January 1853

My ever dearest Henrietta,
It haunts me, dearest Henrietta, I know it is much the same thing when I write to Arabel – and you do remember that Arabel has no two babies as you do have. You are the richest of us three in that respect, and have enough to do that you say I send you few letters. Remember, dearest, I daresay, in counting your monies. That I love you, dearly, fruitfully, unforgettingly, you know well besides, and we really ought (both you and I) to send most of our letters to that darling Arabel who wants them.

Letters to Her Sisters, ed. L. Huxley, 1929

From Marriage

I shall endeavour to give a slight sketch of the female *dramatis personae* of Glenfern Castle.

Miss Jacky, the senior of the trio, was what is reckoned a very sensible woman – which generally means, a very disagreeable, obstinate, illiberal director of all men, women, and children – a sort of superintendent of all actions, time, and place – with unquestioned authority to arraign, judge, and condemn, upon the statutes of her own supposed sense. Most country parishes have their sensible woman, who lays down the law on all affairs spiritual and temporal. Miss Jacky stood unrivalled as the sensible woman of Glenfern. She had attained this eminence, partly from having a little more understanding than her sisters, but principally from her dictatorial manner, and the pompous, decisive tone in which she delivered the most commonplace truths. At home, her supremacy in all matters of sense was perfectly established; and thence the infection, like other superstitions, had spread over the whole neighbourhood. As sensible woman, she regulated the family, which she took care to let everybody see; she was conductor of her nieces' education, which she took care to let everybody hear; she was a sort of postmistress general – a detector of all abuses and impositions; and deemed it her prerogative to be consulted about all the useful and useless things, which everybody else could have done as well. She was liberal of her advice to the poor, always enforcing upon them the iniquity of idleness, but doing nothing for them in the way of employment – strict economy being one of the many points in which she was particularly sensible. The consequence was, while she was lecturing half the poor women in the parish for their idleness, the bread was kept out of their mouths, by the incessant carding of wool and knitting of stockings, and spinning, and reeling, and winding, and pirning, that went on amongst the ladies themselves. And, by the by, Miss Jacky is not the only sensible woman who thinks she is acting a meritorious part, when she converts what ought to be the portion of the poor into the employment of the affluent.

In short, Miss Jacky was all over sense. A skilful physiognomist would, at a single glance, have detected the sensible woman, in the erect head, the compressed lips, square elbows, and firm judicious step. Even her very garments seemed to partake of the prevailing character of their mistress: her ruff always looked more sensible than any other body's; her shawl sat most sensibly on her shoulders; her walking shoes were acknowledged to be very sensible; and she drew on her gloves with an air of sense, as if the one arm had been Seneca, the other Socrates. From what has been said, it may easily be inferred, that Miss Jacky was in fact any thing but a sensible woman; as indeed no woman can be, who bears such visible outward marks of what is in reality the most quiet and unostentatious of all good qualities. But there is a spurious sense, which passes equally well with the multitude: it is easily assumed, and still easier maintained, common truths and a grave dictatorial air being all that is necessary for its support.

Miss Grizzy's character will not admit of so long a commentary as that of her sister: she was merely distinguishable from nothing by her simple good nature, the inextricable entanglement of her thoughts, her love of letter-writing, and her friendship with Lady Maclaughlan. Miss Nicky had about as much sense as Miss Jacky; but, as no kingdom can maintain two kings, so no family can admit of two sensible women; and Nicky was, therefore, obliged to confine hers to the narrowest possible channels of housekeeping, mantua-making, &c., and to sit down for life (or at least till Miss Jacky should be married) with the dubious character of 'not wanting for sense either'. With all these little peccadilloes, the sisters possessed some good properties: they were well-meaning, kind-hearted, and, upon the whole, good-tempered; they loved one another, revered their brother, doated upon their nephews and nieces, took a lively interest in the poorest of their poor cousins, a hundred degrees removed, and had a firm conviction of the perfectibility of human nature, as exemplified in the persons of all their own friends. 'Even their failings leaned to virtue's side'; for whatever they did was with the intention of doing good, though the means they made use of generally produced an opposite effect. But there are so many Miss Douglases in the world, that doubtless every one of my readers is as well acquainted with them as I am myself. I shall, therefore, leave them to finish the picture according to their own ideas, while I return to the parlour, where the worthy spinsters are seated in expectation of the arrival of their friend.

Susan Ferrier, 1818

From The Heroes

[Perseus] walked across the Ister dry-shod, and away through the moors and fens, day and night towards the bleak north-west, turning neither to the right hand nor the left, till he came to the Unshapen Land, and the place which has no name.

And seven days he walked through it, on a path which few can tell [. . .] till he came to the edge of the everlasting night, where the air was full of feathers, and the soil was hard with ice; and there at last he found the three Grey Sisters, by the shore of the freezing sea, nodding upon a white log of driftwood, beneath the cold white winter moon; and they chaunted a low song together, 'Why the old times were better than the new.'

There was no living thing around them, not a fly, not a moss upon the rocks. Neither seal nor seagull dare come near, lest the ice should clutch them in its claws. The surge broke up in foam, but it fell again in flakes of snow; and it frosted the hair of the three Grey Sisters, and the bones in the ice-cliff above their heads. They passed the eye from one to the other, but for all that they could not see; and they passed the tooth from one to the other, but for all that they could not eat; and they sat in the full glare of the moon, but they were none the warmer for her beams. And Perseus pitied the three Grey Sisters; but they did not pity themselves.

So he said, 'Oh, venerable mothers, wisdom is the daughter of old age. You therefore should know many things. Tell me, if you can, the path to the Gorgon.'

Then one cried, 'Who is this who reproaches us with old age?' And another, 'This is the voice of one of the children of men.'

And he, 'I do not reproach, but honour your old age, and I am one of the sons of men and of the heroes. The rulers of Olympus have sent me to you to ask the way to the Gorgon.'

Then one, 'There are new rulers in Olympus, and all new things are bad.' And another, 'We hate your rulers, and the heroes, and all the children of men. We are the kindred of the Titans, and the Giants, and the Gorgons, and the ancient monsters of the deep.' And another, 'Who is this rash and insolent man who pushes unbidden into our world?' And the first, 'There never was such a world as ours, nor will be; if we let him see it, he will spoil it all.'

Then one cried, 'Give me the eye, that I may see him'; and another, 'Give me the tooth, that I may bite him.' But Perseus, when he saw that they were foolish and proud, and did not love the children of men, left off pitying them, and said to himself, 'Hungry men must needs be hasty; if I stay making many words here, I shall be starved.' Then he stepped close to them, and watched till they passed the eye from hand to hand. And as they groped about between themselves, he held out his own hand gently, till one of them put the eye into it, fancying that it was the hand of her sister. Then he sprang back, and laughed, and cried –

'Cruel and proud old women, I have your eye; and I will throw it into the sea, unless you tell me the path to the Gorgon, and swear to me that you tell me right.'

Then they wept, and chattered, and scolded; but in vain. They were forced to tell the truth, though, when they told it, Perseus could hardly make out the road.

'You must go,' they said, 'foolish boy, to the southward, into the ugly glare of the sun, till you come to Atlas the Giant, who holds the heaven and the earth apart. And you must ask his daughters, the Hesperides, who are young and foolish like yourself. And now give us back our eye, for we have forgotten all the rest.'

So Perseus gave them back their eye; but instead of using it, they nodded and fell fast asleep, and were turned into blocks of ice, till the tide came up and washed them all away.

Charles Kingsley, 1856

Macbeth's Witches

'When shall we three meet again . . .'

William Shakespeare

6

Sisters in the Limelight

INTRODUCTION

Having opted for a somewhat more public career than either of my sisters, I thought I should include a section on sisters who have high-profile lives. Unlike many of them, however, I did not suffer sisterly competition in my field. My twin sister, on the contrary, avoided competing with me altogether, even disregarding talents of her own thereby. Not that she ever wanted to be a writer. As a publisher, briefly, she'd seen what life was like for writers, she said, and it was the last kind of life she wanted for herself. As for my younger sister, having fixed on being a nurse at the age of five, she wasn't interested, either.

Given genetic likeness, and the access to people and institutions with which one sibling's career can provide another, it's not surprising that talent should emerge in more than one member of a family. Yet it's not always talent that drives the ensuing competition, and in any case, the chances of two being equally successful are low. Even where they are, if Joan Fontaine and Olivia de Havilland are anything to go by, it may not reduce their rivalry one jot. Most likely, the relative success of one sister as against another isn't quite the point. Most likely the competition is just the form that rivalry takes with these particular siblings. It's a form that augments bitterness, unfortunately, whether a younger sister is trying to make good in a world where her elder sister stars, or an older one finds her younger sister outstripping her, or two sisters are running side by side and forever looking across at each other to make sure they stay that way. The only escape is to be exceptionally nice and long-established like the Cusack sisters. Or to be musical rather than theatrical, and form duos or trios.

Sisters whose competition is literary have, of course, a means of expressing it that other high-profile sisters lack. A. S. Byatt is now rather better known than her once more illustrious younger sister, Margaret Drabble. But in what would have been, for her, the bad old days, Byatt wrote a novel about writer sisters in which one destroys the other by using her as subject for a novel. The claustrophobia induced by a closed circle made up of real and fictional sisters is profound, yet at the same time merely an extreme version of what any writer knows a little about, and in particular, here, any literary sister. I know about it. What am I doing, for instance, but using *my* sisters as a leitmotif for this book? My younger sister claims, via e-mail from Australia, to forgive me; someone has to tell the family stories, she says. I am not at all sure that my dead twin would have said the same, but I don't, for one moment, let it stop me. It's the danger of writers in the family, always. Writers are cannibals, they munch bloodily on whatever and whoever is around them, beginning with their families, of course. And who's to say that this isn't, subconsciously, a way of letting out the resentment, the hatefulness, aroused by even the nicest of families; and of sisters.

I hope that there's no element of that here. Of course, I'm not recreating my sisters as fiction as, in *The Game*, A. S. Byatt's fictional younger sister recreates hers, or as the sister in the Elizabeth Taylor story quoted recreates her hapless – but charmless – elder sister. In fiction, hiding behind the plot, you can be much crueller than I can afford to be, or think I want to be; but God knows what might come out if I fictionally let rip. That's one reason why, so far as my sisters are concerned, I don't.

Next to fights over men, I suspect, this kind of competition can rouse the most primitive of the feelings. Which is why, I guess, the press is so fascinated with high-profile sisters, forever looking beneath and behind, forever stirring them up to get them to express hostility or – in the case of the Beverley sisters, say – sweetness. The press doesn't quite invent them but they try to, aided and abetted by the sisters themselves and their publicists, and by the curiosity of the world outside. At the same time, feeding into all the myths and fairy tales invoking sisters, these sisters are also – or at least appear to be – the most mythical. They're not up to it, of course, with the exception of the Grand Guignol Hollywood pairs like Fontaine and de Havilland (or, just possibly, given their own and their family history, Lynn and Vanessa Redgrave). The Collins sisters, Joan and Jackie, actress and writer, aren't up to it for sure, larger than life though they may be. Yet they're all we've got now. Maybe media hype really has made them, maybe by now these sister rivals *are* the Helens and Clytemnestras, the Regans, *Gonerils and Cordelias* of our times. The Beverley Sisters as Three Graces? Or Gorgons? *Take your pick.*

From Preface to the new edition of
Wuthering Heights

It becomes my duty to explain briefly the origin and authorship of the books written by Currer, Ellis, and Acton Bell.

About five years ago, my two sisters and myself, after a somewhat prolonged period of separation, found ourselves reunited, and at home. Resident in a remote district, where education had made little progress, and where, consequently, there was no inducement to seek social intercourse beyond our own domestic circle, we were wholly dependent on ourselves and each other, on books and study, for the enjoyments and occupations of life. The highest stimulus, as well as the liveliest pleasure we had known from childhood upwards, lay in attempts at literary composition; formerly we used to show each other what we wrote, but of late years this habit of communication and consultation had been discontinued; hence it ensued, that we were mutually ignorant of the progress we might respectively have made.

One day, in the autumn of 1845, I accidentally lighted on a MS volume of verse in my sister Emily's handwriting. Of course, I was not surprised, knowing that she could and did write verse: I looked it over, and something more than surprise seized me – a deep conviction that these were not common effusions, nor at all like the poetry women generally write. I thought them condensed and

terse, vigorous and genuine. To my ear, they had also a peculiar
music – wild, melancholy, and elevating.

My sister Emily was not a person of demonstrative character,
nor one on the recesses of whose mind and feelings, even those
nearest and dearest to her could, with impunity, intrude un-
licensed; it took hours to reconcile her to the discovery I had made,
and days to persuade her that such poems merited publication. I
knew, however, that a mind like hers could not be without some
latent spark of honourable ambition, and refused to be discouraged
in my attempts to fan that spark to flame.

Meantime, my younger sister quietly produced some of her own
compositions, intimating that, since Emily's had given me pleasure,
I might like to look at hers. I could not but be a partial judge, yet
I thought that these verses, too, had a sweet sincere pathos of their
own.

We had very early cherished the dream of one day becoming
authors. This dream, never relinquished even when distance divided
and absorbing tasks occupied us, now suddenly acquired strength
and consistency: it took the character of a resolve. We agreed to
arrange a small selection of our poems, and, if possible, get them
printed. Averse to personal publicity, we veiled our own names
under those of Currer, Ellis and Acton Bell; the ambiguous choice
being dictated by a sort of conscientious scruple at assuming Chris-
tian names positively masculine, while we did not like to declare
ourselves women, because – without at that time suspecting that
our mode of writing and thinking was not what is called 'feminine'
– we had a vague impression that authoresses are liable to be looked
on with prejudice [. . .]

The bringing out of our little book was hard work. As was to be
expected, neither we nor our poems were at all wanted; but for this
we had been prepared at the outset; though inexperienced ourselves,
we had read the experience of others. The great puzzle lay in the
difficulty of getting answers of any kind from the publishers to
whom we applied. Being greatly harassed by this obstacle, I ventured
to apply to the Messrs Chambers, of Edinburgh, for a word of
advice; *they* may have forgotten the circumstance, but *I* have not,

for from them I received a brief and business-like, but civil and sensible reply, on which we acted, and at last made a way.

The book was printed; it is scarcely known, and all of it that merits to be known are the poems of Ellis Bell. The fixed conviction I held, and hold, of the worth of these poems has not indeed received the confirmation of much favourable criticism; but I must retain it notwithstanding.

Ill-success failed to crush us: the mere effort to succeed had given a wonderful zest to existence; it must be pursued. We each set to work on a prose tale: Ellis Bell produced *Wuthering Heights*, Acton Bell *Agnes Grey*, and Currer Bell also wrote a narrative in one volume. These MSS were perseveringly obtruded upon various publishers for the space of a year and a half; usually, their fate was an ignominious and abrupt dismissal.

At last *Wuthering Heights* and *Agnes Grey* were accepted on terms somewhat impoverishing to the two authors; Currer Bell's book found acceptance nowhere, nor any acknowledgement of merit, so that something like the chill of despair began to invade his heart. As a forlorn hope, he tried one publishing house more – Messrs Smith Elder and Co. Ere long, in a much shorter space than that on which experience had taught him to calculate – there came a letter, which he opened in the dreary expectation of finding two hard hopeless lines, intimating that Messrs Smith Elder and Co. 'were not disposed to publish the MS', and, instead, he took out of the envelope a letter of two pages. He read it trembling. It declined, indeed, to publish that tale, for business reasons, but it discussed its merits and demerits so courteously, so considerately, in a spirit so rational, with a discrimination so enlightened, that this very refusal cheered the author better than a vulgarly expressed acceptance would have done. It was added, that a work in three volumes would meet with careful attention.

I was just then completing *Jane Eyre*, at which I had been working while the one-volume tale was plodding its weary round in London: in three weeks I sent it off; friendly and skilful hands took it in. This was in the commencement of September 1847; it came out before the close of October following, while *Wuthering Heights* and *Agnes Grey*, my sisters' works, which had been in the press for months, still lingered under a different management.

They appeared at last. Critics failed to do them justice. The immature but very real powers revealed in *Wuthering Heights* were scarcely recognized; its import and nature were misunderstood; the identity of its author was misrepresented; it was said that this was an earlier and ruder attempt of the same pen which had produced *Jane Eyre*. Unjust and grievous error! We laughed at it at first, but I deeply lament it now. Hence, I fear, arose a prejudice against the book. [. . .]

It is my duty, as well as my pleasure, to acknowledge one exception to the general rule of criticism. One writer (*The Palladium* for September 1850), endowed with the keen vision and fine sympathies of genius, has discerned the real nature of *Wuthering Heights*, and has, with equal accuracy, noted its beauties and touched on its faults. [. . .]

Yet even the writer to whom I allude shares the mistake about the authorship, and does me the injustice to suppose that there was equivoque in my former rejection of this honour (as an honour I regard it). May I assure him that I would scorn in this and in every case to deal in equivoque; I believe language to have been given us to make our meaning clear, and not to wrap it in dishonest doubt.

The Tenant of Wildfell Hall, by Acton Bell, had likewise an unfavourable reception. At this I cannot wonder. The choice of subject was an entire mistake. Nothing less congruous with the writer's nature could be conceived. The motives which dictated this choice were pure, but, I think, slightly morbid. She had, in the course of her life, been called on to contemplate, near at hand, and for a long time, the terrible effects of talents misused and faculties abused; hers was naturally a sensitive, reserved, and dejected nature; what she saw sank very deeply into her mind; it did her harm. She brooded over it till she believed it to be a duty to reproduce every detail (of course with fictitious characters, incidents, and situations), as a warning to others.

Charlotte Brontë ('Currer Bell'), 1850

Margaret Drabble and A. S. (Antonia) Byatt

The writers Margaret Drabble and A. S. Byatt are often assumed to hate each other because both have written eloquently about the pangs of sisterly rivalry in novels such as Drabble's *A Summer Birdcage* and Byatt's *The Game*. Byatt knew she wanted to write 'on hearing my first fairy tale', while Drabble 'never thought I would be a writer – it seemed such a pretentious and lofty thing to think'. Nevertheless, it was Drabble, the younger, who published first (at the age of twenty-three) and became a darling of the literary chattering classes. It was only when Byatt won the Booker Prize in 1990 with her literary novel *Possession* that she outclassed her more famous younger sister. 'Sibling rivalry is the most natural experience in the world,' Drabble says. 'To pretend that sisters or brothers love each other is just rubbish. They are always fighting. What annoys me is the idea that Antonia and I should be lovey-dovey. We respect and admire each other, have fascinating conversations, but of course there was competition when we were children which we've tried to grow out of. We were pitted against each other by my mother largely. So the pressure on us was to be clever. Any sign of intelligence was praised, any interest in girly things ignored. We grew up not knowing how to dress, but very good at exams.'

Amanda Craig, *Good Housekeeping*, August 1998

From A Summer Birdcage

At Louise's I drank gin and tonic and talked a little bad Italian and soaked myself in the air of worldly well-being that emanated from that flat. Unobtrusive warmth, a choice of drinks, well-deployed lights, cigarettes in all the cigarette-boxes, books on all the book-shelves, and choice duck-egg blue towels on the towel-rails in the bathroom. This really feels like life, I said to myself. It was a pity the people were dull, but then one can't have everything. Anyway, they very shortly left, and left Louise and me confronting each other among the ashtrays. We were talking fairly easily, having been broken in by the presence of others, about films and people and Oxford. She was wearing a lilac-coloured silky jersey. After an idle hour or so, in which we played Frank Sinatra and drank another drink – odd how the very thought of such idle boredom can later cause such pangs of nostalgia and desire – we decided to go and look for something to eat. The kitchen was indeed impressive, as Wilfred had told me at the party – it wasn't in any way modern or streamlined, but very oldy-worldy, with pestles and mortars and jars of herbs and copper pans. It gave the impression of French country cooking. I was pleasantly surprised when Louise opened a cupboard and displayed such normal fare as tins of sardines and beans and ravioli. However, Louise said she felt like cooking, so we had spaghetti: I stood aghast as she tipped wine and garlic recklessly into the sauce, and splashed tomato purée on to her smart shirt affair. Life must be totally different if one doesn't have to think about cleaners's bills. And grocer's bills.

'The funny thing is,' she said, 'that I really love cooking. I'm just greedy, I suppose, but I really love it. The smells and the mixtures. But I won't do it, you know, because it's beneath my dignity. So I have to let Françoise do it most of the time.'

'That's ridiculous. I hate it, and I have to. Let's swap.'

'Why don't you eat out?'

'I don't like eating out alone.'

'Why not?'

'People stare.'

'You little timid. Why don't you just let them?'

'I don't like being stared at. I would like to be ignored.'

'*I* don't mind being stared at.'

'I know. That's because you're always bloody sure of the reason why.'

'Well, what's wrong with that?'

She started to strain the spaghetti through an enormous sieve. I always have to use a small red plastic colander, and everything eels into the sink as often as not. We sat down to eat at the kitchen table, which was covered with a choice orange tablecloth.

'It doesn't go with your blouse,' I said.

'Oh for Christ's sake,' she said furiously. 'You can't have everything matching all the time.'

The spaghetti was most delicious, and when we had finished it we went back into the sitting-room and played Frank Sinatra again. I was struck as we sat there by the charming convention of the scene – sisters idling away an odd evening in happy companionship. It was like something out of *Middlemarch* or even Jane Austen.

Margaret Drabble, 1962

From The Game

Cassandra's Journal

So I have become a doll to stick pins in? Or a mirror on the wall to be asked what she, what either of us, means? At first I felt simply dirtied. My shoes, my nightdress, my pens, my papers, little dirty details of me lifted. Pinned out – oh yes, even my underwear – like a limp doll to be filled with puffs of her breath. What was missing filled in by her with dotted lines, pieces of new string to jerk the joints, or wood to replace limbs, as they do in museums, and never a footnote to say, this material is conjectural. This is an eclectic and conflated text.

Our normal intercourse is made up of this, all the time, I know. I know. We hide our knowledge of it. We could not live if we were made to see ourselves more than conjecturally as others see us. At best we translate their vision back into our own terms. But she does a little more than simply see me, and that little is intolerable.

When we were children, we were not quite separate. We shared a common vision, we created a common myth. And this, maybe, contained and resolved our difficulties. This is that primitive state that has been called innocence. We wove a web in childhood, a web of sunny air ... But there is no innocent vision, we are not indistinguishable. We create each other, separate. It is not done with love. Or not with pure love. Nor with detachment. We are not simply specimens, under the bright light, in the glass case, in the zoo, in the museum. We are food for thought. The web is sticky. I trail dirty shreds of it.

I do not choose to stay to be pitied for that rag doll's passions. They are not mine. But they were fed and watered by me, too much of my energy went into their growth for me to be able to clear them away, or make myself a space to inhabit.

There is nowhere I shall not drag this grotesque shadow, our joint creature. I can choose, at least, to put out the light that throws it. I want no more reflections.

A. S. Byatt, 1968

From Sisters

Watching Mrs Mason's face slowly flushing all over to blend with her rouged cheekbones, the young man, leaning back easily, felt he had bided his time long enough. Something was obviously being stirred up. He said gently – so that his words seemed to come to her like her own thoughts – 'A few stories now, please. Was it a happy childhood?'

'Yes. No. It was just an ordinary childhood.'

'With such a genius amongst you? How *awfully* interesting!'

'She was no different from any of the rest of us.' But she *had* been, and so unpleasantly, as it turned out.

'Really *extraordinarily* interesting.' He allowed himself to lean forward a little, then, wondering if the slightest show of eagerness might silence her, he glanced about the room again. There were only two photographs – one of a long-ago bride and bridegroom, the other of a pompous-looking man with some sort of chain of office hanging on his breast.

It was proving very hard-going, this visit; but all the more of a challenge for that.

Mrs Mason, in her silvery-grey wool dress, suddenly seemed to him to resemble an enormous salmon. She even had a salmon shape – thick from the shoulders down and tapering away to surprisingly tiny, out-turned feet. He imagined trying to land her. She was demanding all the skill and tenacity he had. This was very pleasurable. Having let him in, and sat down, her good manners could find no way of getting rid of him. He was sure of that. Her good manners were the only encouraging thing, so far.

'You know, you are really not at all what I expected,' he said boldly, admiringly. 'Not in the very least like your sister, are you?'

What he had expected was an older version of the famous photograph in the Collected Edition – that waif-like creature with the fly-away fringe and great dark eyes.

Mrs Mason now carefully lifted off her hat, as if it were a coronet. Then she touched her hair, pushing it up a little. 'I was the pretty one,' she did not say; but, feeling some explanation was asked for, told him what all the world knew. 'My sister had poor health,' she said. 'Asthma and migraines, and so on. Lots of what we now call allergies. I never had more than a couple of days' illness in my life.' She remembered Marion always being fussed over – wheezing and puking and whining, or stamping her feet up and down in temper and frustration, causing scenes, a general rumpus at any given moment.

He longed to get inside her mind; for interesting things were going on there he guessed. Patience, he thought, regarding her. She was wearing opaque grey stockings; to hide varicose veins, he thought. He knew everything about women, and mentally unclothed her. In a leisurely fashion – since he would not hurry anything – he stripped off her peach-coloured slip and matching knickers, tugged her out of her sturdy corselette, whose straps had bitten deep into her plump shoulders, leaving a permanent indentation. He did not even jib at the massive, mottled flesh beneath, creased, as it must be, from its rigid confinement, or the suspender imprints at the top of her tapering legs. Her navel would be full of talcum powder.

'It was all so long ago. I don't want to be reminded,' she said simply.

'Have you any photographs – holiday snapshots, for instance? I adore looking at old photographs.'

There was a boxful upstairs, faded sepia scenes of them all paddling – dresses tucked into bloomers – or picnicking, with sandwiches in hand, and feet out of focus. Her father, the Rector, had developed and printed the photographs himself, and they had not lasted well. 'I don't care to live in the past,' was all she said in reply.

'Were you and Marion close to one another?'

'We were sisters,' she said primly.

'And you kept in touch? I should think that you enjoyed basking in the reflected glory.' He knew that she had not kept in touch, and was sure by now that she had done no basking.

'She went to live in Paris, as no doubt you know.'

Thank heavens, Mrs Mason had always thought, that she *had* gone to live in Paris, and that she herself had married and been able to change her name. Still quite young, and before the war, Marion had died. It was during Mr Mason's year as mayor. They had told no one.

'Did you ever meet Godwin? Or any of that set?'

'Of course not. My husband wouldn't have had them in the house.'

The young man nodded.

Oh, that dreadful clique. She was ashamed to have it mentioned to her by someone of the opposite sex, a complete stranger. She had been embarrassed to speak of it to her own husband, who had been so extraordinarily kind and forgiving about everything connected with Marion. But that raffish life in Paris in the thirties! Her sister living with the man Godwin or, turn and turn about with others of her set. They all had switched from one partner to the other; sometimes – she clasped her hands together so tightly that her rings hurt her fingers – to others of the same sex. She knew about it; the world knew; no doubt her friends knew, although it was not the sort of thing they would have discussed. Books had been written about that Paris lot, as Mrs Mason thought of them, and their correspondence published. Godwin, and Miranda Braun, the painter, and Grant Opie, the American, who wrote obscene books; and many of the others. They were all notorious: that was Mrs Mason's word for them.

'I think she killed my father,' she said in a low voice, almost as if she were talking to herself.' He fell ill, and did not seem to want to go on living. He would never have her name mentioned, or any of her books in the house. She sent him a copy of the first one – she had left home by then, and was living in London. He read some of it, then took it out to the incinerator in the garden and burned it. I remember it now, his face was as white as a sheet.'

'But *you* have read the books surely?' he asked, playing her in gently.

She nodded, looking ashamed. 'Yes, later, I did.' A terrified curiosity had proved too strong to resist. And, reading, she had discovered a childhood she could hardly recognize, although it was all there: all the pieces were there, but shifted round as in a kaleidoscope. Worse came after the first book, the stories of their girlhood and growing up and falling in love. She, the Cassie of the books, had become a well-known character, with all her secrets laid bare; though they were really the secrets of Marion herself and not those of the younger sister. The candour had caused a stir in those far-off days. During all the years of public interest, Mrs Mason had kept her silence, and lately had been able to bask indeed – in the neglect which had fallen upon her sister, as it falls upon most great writers at some period after their death. It was done with and laid to rest, she had thought – until this morning.

'And you didn't think much of them, I infer,' the young man said.

She started, and looked confused. 'Of what?' she asked, drawing back, tightening his line.

'Your sister's stories.'

'They weren't true. We were well-brought-up girls.'

'Your other sister died, too.'

He *had* been rooting about, she thought in dismay. 'She died before all the scandal,' Mrs Mason said grimly. 'She was spared.'

Elizabeth Taylor, 1975

From My Life as a Twin

When I had started fire-fighting, Alexandra landed a role on the television show *Baywatch*. It features lifeguards on impeccably sunny California days making surf rescues. Also known as 'Babewatch', the show is famous for its beautiful people with large smiles and larger mammaries. [. . .]

Alexandra has been working steadily since she first started acting. The result is that people often seem to think they have met me before. Sometimes I catch them staring; at other times, there is a faraway look in their eyes when they talk to me, and I know that they are trying to puzzle out why I look so familiar. When Alexandra began appearing weekly as *Baywatch*'s Stephanie Holden, the stares multiplied. Every other day or so someone will say that I look uncannily like that woman on *Baywatch*. Or, out of the corner of my eye, I will see the unmistakable signs of someone mustering up the courage to ask for my autograph. First, the reflexive double take, then the refocus of the eyes as I am imagined into a slim red bathing-suit.

As Alexandra becomes more famous, the encounters become more comical: a fire drill that my crew conducts at a nearby grammar school is disrupted when kids break from the line to get my autograph; while flying to Canada, I am put in first class without a word of explanation, just a small wink by the flight attendant to indicate that she won't tell anyone else who I am. With the *Baywatch* job, our twinship takes on a cartoonish similarity. Alexandra rescues people on television, while I rescue them in real life. How much more all-American can you get?

Caroline Paul, 1998

From Isn't That You Know Who?
Not Quite

Over the past week two young women, Wendy Turner, sister of Anthea, and Beth Winslet, sister of Kate, have leapt to public prominence. Turner gave herself a role in Anthea's recent love drama by telling the press exactly what she thought of Anthea's ex-lover, Grant Bovey.

Meanwhile Beth Winslet, a younger, slightly diminished version of her sumptuous sister, was featured in several newspaper articles previewing her debut [. . .] The temptation to mention Kate in every other sentence was not resisted.

[. . .]

Of course, siblings should have the right to pursue whatever career they choose. If they have a talent, how unfair it would be to bar them on the grounds that someone else in the family got there first. [. . .]

And yet you cannot help wondering what it is that motivates them to follow so closely – slavishly even – in their sibling's footsteps? How can the more successful of the two refrain from mistrust at the sight of the other's attempts to muscle in on their territory? How can the aspirant not be motivated by a powerful desire to compete with, upstage, the other?

[. . .]

Sibling rivalry is largely unavoidable, even in the most banal of circumstances. If it can happen over who gets the last Wagon Wheel, imagine how it might escalate when an Oscar is the prize (indeed, when Joan Fontaine won one, her sister Olivia de Havilland refused to speak to her for about a decade).

[. . .]

Of course, there are those siblings who, while pursuing the same high-profile careers, manage not to encroach upon each other. [. . .]

On the whole, however, the sudden emergence into the public sphere of that younger brother or sister, spinning those breathless tales of 'Oh, I've always wanted to act as well', 'Oh, there's no rivalry between us', 'Oh, my name has never helped me at auditions', is met nowadays with a cynical groan. If the talent is strong enough, or different enough, then the celebrity sibling can win through. If not – and usually it isn't – it is back to the *OK!* magazine fashion shoots.

For celebrity is concerned with the pursuit of singleness, or individuality. It is perhaps the most solipsistic state known to humanity, and this is what audiences both perceive and adore. They are compelled by that celebration of the individual and they don't really want to see a lesser, diluted, unoriginal version of what they know and love.

They don't want to see a familiar face looking the same, but somehow *wrong*. They don't want to be reminded that here is the earthbound clay from which a more magical being was created. They feel, obscurely, that the celebrity's sibling is taking away some of what makes the celebrity special; and if they feel that, how much more might the celebrities themselves?

Laura Thompson, *Guardian*, 11 April 1998

From No Bed of Roses

It was during the making of *The Constant Nymph* that I read in the *Hollywood Reporter* on the set one morning that I was one of five actresses nominated for an Academy Award under the category of leading lady. As *Suspicion* was not the classic that *Rebecca* was, I felt my chances of winning this time were negligible. Another of the five candidates was Olivia de Havilland!

Jean Hersholt, that gentle Danish actor who was best known for playing the *Dr Christian* film series, was at that time president of the Academy. He telephoned me at the studio the day of the award dinner. Surely, I was attending the banquet? I told him it wasn't possible. Being in the middle of a film, I didn't want to have a late night only to get up at six-thirty next morning for the drive from

Beverly Hills across the Hollywood Hills to the studio in Burbank in time for the eight o'clock session.

The next phone call to the set came from Olivia. I *had* to attend the dinner. My absence would look odd. The contestants in all categories were expected to be there, and, moreover, I was an Academy member. 'But I haven't anything to wear!' I wailed.

Within an hour, Olivia arrived with our usual saleslady from I. Magnin. They deposited in my dressing-room tan and white striped boxes containing all the size sixes the store possessed. Between takes, I tried on the dresses, finally selecting a ballet-length black number with a lace skirt and mantilla, which was hastily basted to fit me. The studio hairdresser and make-up man obligingly stayed after work to do away with my pigtails and hide my freckles.

At the Biltmore Hotel that evening we sat at David Selznick's table through the usual fruit cocktail-to-parfait dinner. Hardly anyone touched the meal. Excitement mounted steadily as the presentation time grew near. Finally, the programme began with categories such as special effects and shorts. At last came the principal awards: the best film of the year, best producer, best director, best actor, and best actress.

[. . .]

From the dais, Ginger Rogers, to whom I had lost the previous year, slowly read the list of nominees for the best-actress award:

1. Bette Davis for *The Little Foxes*
2. Greer Garson for *Blossom in the Dust*
3. Barbara Stanwyck for *Ball of Fire*
4. Olivia de Havilland for *Hold Back the Dawn*
5. Joan Fontaine for *Suspicion*

And then she said, 'The envelope, please.' The banquet room was silent. The gentleman from Price, Waterhouse slithered on to the stage. With trembling hand he presented Ginger with the sealed document. The mike amplified the sound of the ripping of paper. Ginger cleared her throat. 'The winner is . . . Joan Fontaine for *Sus*—' The last syllables were drowned in gasps, whistles, applause.

I froze. I stared across the table, where Olivia was sitting directly opposite me. 'Get up there, get up there,' she whispered commandingly. Now what had I done! All the animus we'd felt toward each other as children, the hair-pullings, the savage wrestling matches, the time Olivia fractured my collar-bone, all came rushing back in kaleidoscopic imagery. My paralysis was total. I felt Olivia would spring across the table and grab me by the hair. I felt age four, being confronted by my older sister. Damn it, I'd incurred her wrath again!

Joan Fontaine, 1978

From Sisters

Of course I had been fortunate in my two meetings with Maria – she was on top form on both occasions. Her appearances had been a huge success and no doubt Onassis, who longed to be accepted as a major figure in his native land, was very satisfied with her. As her life revolved round his whims that would explain her sunny disposition when we'd met. But I ought to have known that I could not expect so smooth a ride every time, and when we next met I could read the storm warnings from the start. Father and I had been invited to lunch at the Glyfada home of Onassis' brother-in-law [. . .] Maria arrived for the lunch looking cross; clearly something had happened on the yacht that had spoiled her mood. Everyone was slightly on edge, having sensed the situation and no one wanted to be in the firing-line. [. . .] The lunch began cautiously with rather stilted conversation as everyone kept to safe topics. I tried to make myself as inconspicuous as possible, fearing the worst, and was duly appalled when the doctor leant across to me.

'Jackie,' he said. 'Where I heard it I don't remember, but someone told me you had a lovely voice. What did you do with your voice?'

Fortunately Maria appeared to be talking to someone else at the other end of the table and there might just be time to close the matter.

'I left it,' I replied. 'I gave a concert but my fiancé was ill so I couldn't go on and I left it.'

But it was no good. Maria had heard the word 'voice'. 'Are you talking about me?' she asked, equally at first.

'No,' said the doctor smiling. 'It's your sister here. I heard she had a voice.'

'Doctor,' said Maria coldly, 'the donkeys bray and think they have a voice.' She turned towards me and let fly. 'It was your crazy mother who thought you had a voice. She was behind those lessons. Don't you know how old you are? Don't you know you're too old to train your voice? Singing is for young people, it needs years of study, not just braying like a donkey.'

It was no use trying to keep out of it. Silence would only provoke her further. I knew the signs, she wanted a row and must have one.

'Maria,' I said, 'anyone can have a voice, a maid, a painter, anyone. It's what you do with it. I had a voice but I threw away the chance to do something because of Milton. You know that.'

'You a voice,' she yelled. 'Do you want me to start breaking dishes?'

The doctor quickly got to his feet. 'I have to go and rest,' he said. 'I have surgery later so I must lie down for a while but do go on with your family talk.' He shook my hand and said how happy he was to have met me.

The interruption seemed to take the steam out of Maria, her discontent evaporated. As we moved from the table to the salon she came over and was friendly again.

'So how is Milton?' she asked.

'At an end. Like a skeleton. It's making me ill, too. Yet if he dies what am I going to do? I'm going to be so lonely. He's been a father and a husband since I was eighteen. Who else can I trust now?'

The outburst must have been too intimate for her, the reality of my sorrow was not something she wanted to be confronted with.

'You have to cope,' she said, turning away. 'Hope is a wonderful thing. God gives us hope.'

I looked at her and realized there was no point in saying any more. Father, too, was staring at her, a look of pity on his face as if to say here is someone who has forgotten how to feel for another and that is a terrible thing. I felt sorry for her: she was so wrapped up in her own daily worries no one else except she and Onassis existed.

We said goodbye and left her there.

In the taxi Father held my hand and shook his head. 'She cannot change now,' he said. 'It's too late.'

Jackie Callas, 1989

From A Genius in the Family

At the concert hall, Dad found seats near the front and put programmes on them for reservation. There was lively chatter as families arrived, the prizewinners in their best clothes, everyone jostling for seats and scanning programmes to see when they were playing. Gradually, as people settled, a hush descended over the packed hall. The diminutive Mr Bluett, Chairman of the festival, walked on to the stage to welcome the great Dorothy Grinstead, who was to present the prizes. The concert began.

My turn came and I went excitedly on to the platform. I couldn't wait to play. I adjusted the height of the piano stool, and began. This was the culmination of all the preparation, the moment I had been waiting for, and I loved it.

First, the Minuet in G by Bach. I had to paint a picture of the dancers, where they were dancing, and who they were. I instantly found myself in my own musical world, unaware of anyone or anything else. I felt free and totally involved in what I was doing. I was in charge and the piano and the music were there for me.

Next came the Bach Invention and I embarked on my gossipy conversation running around the keys, listening to the sounds and the story in my head. It worked.

My pieces came to an end and I bowed to noisy applause and ran back to my glowing parents. The clapping continued.

'Go and bow again, Hil, go on,' Mum said, as she pushed me back towards the platform.

Up I ran, my heart pounding with the thrill of success, and gave a sweeping bow to a sea of beaming faces. I knew I had played well and now *I* was walking on air, and Mum was extremely pleased with me. I *had* enjoyed myself.

I was in such a state of elation that, instead of returning to my seat beside Mum and Dad, I skipped off the platform and down to the end of the hall. Shortly after my turn, it was Jackie's. She was to perform the set piece, Purcell's Air in D minor. Mum climbed on to the platform with her and played the 'A' on the piano for Jackie to tune. Silence descended, and Jackie began. Her concentration was so intense that it seemed as though the whole hall had stopped breathing while she was performing for them.

I loved her playing and had already heard this piece while I was on the swing, but now there was an electric feeling in the air. As the final note died away, the audience burst into spontaneous cheering.

When the clapping died down, the talking about her took over. Jackie returned to her seat, and she and Mum and Dad were quickly surrounded by a press of people offering their praises and asking questions. I knew that Dad would be the proudest man in the world that night and I wanted to be with them but was too shy to push my way through the crowd.

Dorothy Grinstead was now on the platform. What a commanding presence she was, towering above us in a glamorous long, green evening dress, the colour set off by her silvery white hair. Mr Bluett stood next to her and called out the winners' names. One by one, we received our prizes, shook Miss Grinstead's hand, and bowed. I was still so excited that, again, I skipped off the platform and carried on to the back of the hall.

And then it was Jackie's turn. Instead of immediately giving her the medals, Miss Grinstead beamed and launched into a speech about this remarkable child, her outstanding and rare playing and how lucky we were to hear her. A photographer was called on to the stage and Jackie was surrounded by important people as she was presented with her medals and a special prize for outstanding achievement. The audience rose to its feet as the cameras clicked.

Why wasn't I there too? Mummy was pleased with me and I knew that I had played well. Surely I should be there for the photos? Miss Grinstead must have forgotten to make a speech about me.

Why didn't she call me back now? But she didn't. I stood on tiptoe, hoping to make myself seen, but no one saw me. Suddenly I felt very alone. Every muscle in my body was straining for recognition but it didn't come.

All eyes and all attention were on Jackie. We had always done everything together, but now we were separated and I felt frantic. I turned and ran: ran out of the door at the back of the hall, and along a dark corridor. Applause seemed to follow me but no one was calling me back. I was crying and felt bereft and completely forgotten. I dashed through an open door into a huge kitchen and shot under a table, dropping my medals on the floor. I buried my head against my knees and sobbed and sobbed. My mind raced in a whirl of loneliness, dismay, failure. I was lost.

I don't know how long I stayed there, but after a while my crying lessened and I knew the only way I could cope would be to go back, smiling and joining in. I came out from under the table, shook my frock to uncrumple it and drank some cold water. Gran had always given me a glass of water and washed my face if I had been crying. So I did that now. I gathered up my medals and retraced my steps.

The concert and prize-giving were over, and there was a jostle of people chatting and preparing to leave.

No one had missed me.

When eventually I found Mum and Dad, I told them I had a headache – which was true. I don't think they ever found out what had actually happened.

Hilary and Piers du Pré, 1997

From Superwomen Sisters

The lives of Spain's glamorous Koplowitz sisters, Esther and Alicia, rated by *Harper's & Queen* the eighth and ninth richest women in Europe, have been closely entwined since childhood. Their dazzling progress as heiresses, wives, mothers, divorcées and multi-millionaire business empresses has unfolded with a symmetry so perfect that a pulp novelist would dismiss their tale as too improbable.

But now the inseparable pair are breaking up, in a move that is rocking the Spanish financial world and thrilling those who have followed their technicolour career for more than a decade. Hand in hand, the sisters saw a cement business inherited in 1966 from their Polish refugee father become a conglomerate that built roads and reservoirs throughout Spain. The company, Fomento de Construcciones y Contratas (FCC), is the flagship of their joint fortune, estimated at $2.2bn (£1.3bn), among the world's top two hundred.

Through skilful diversification steered by the two, and shrewd international deals (from building motorways in Canada to cleaning Brighton beach), the company rode the recession and prospered. But Alicia, forty-five, blond and beautiful, has announced that she is fed up with business and wants to quit.

[...]

None of this would amount to more than a ripple in the financial press were it not for the fact that these two discreet and brilliant women have challenged every stereotype. Orphaned when their father, Ernesto, fell from his horse in 1962, both married young – at eighteen and twenty – to two cousins, both called Alberto. The so-called 'two Albertos' took over the running of FCC in the 1970s and the sisters kept in the background as dutiful wives and mothers.

By the late 1980s the company had prospered and the Albertos became powerful industrialists. But in 1988, Alicia was shattered to discover that her Alberto (Cortina) was carrying on with a marquesa, Marta Chavarri. Shortly afterwards, Esther found that *her* Alberto (Alcoer) was seeing a former model, Margarita Hernandez [...]

Each sister divorced her husband – simultaneously, naturally – and on International Women's Day, 8 March 1990, they took over the running of FCC. The two Albertos slunk from the forty-two-storey company headquarters in the heart of Madrid, each pocketing £2.7m, a fraction of what they claimed.

Esther and Alicia emerged from seclusion to supervise directors' meetings of Spain's top construction company, in a no-nonsense style, with their trademark elegant suits, smart earrings and *décollet-*

ages. They operated as one, but it is now said that Alicia never took to business with quite the relish of her sister.

No one really knows why they have parted company, but problems about the succession are thought to be at stake. [. . .] Esther Jr works in the company and is shaping up as a possible successor to her mother, while Alicia's eldest son, Alberto Jr, works in the Banco Zaragozano bank.

The hard-nosed gossip is that Alberto Jr has persuaded his mother to catch the peak of Spain's stock-market boom, sell up now and make a killing. Softer-focus whispering says that Alicia, always the less gregarious sister, is tired of making headlines and wants to withdraw from the limelight into rich obscurity.

Elizabeth Nash, *Independent on Sunday*, 15 January 1998

7

Brothers and Sisters

INTRODUCTION

When our little brother was born in the seventeenth-century house next to the church where we spent the first six years of our life, my twin sister and I were not at home; we'd been sent into Surrey to stay with our Aunt Ruth. Since we were still ensconced in Aunt Ruth's gloomy Victorian house when he died a week later, the only evidence for us that he'd ever existed was the tiny grave in the shadow of the wall that divided the graveyard from the garden lying below it, behind what was then our house. Yet I still think of him quite often. When I visit him, on rare visits to our mother's grave, I can also check up on the chestnut tree that introduced us to conkers, and the low, lichen-covered roof that backed the lawn on which we played, but he never had a chance to. It makes me wonder what kind of man he would have made; he'd be roughly the same age now, I realize, amazedly, as the men of fifty odd I see these days – would I have had more in common with him than I have with our older, surviving brother? And though there would have been no little sister had he lived, and though most likely the money spent on sending me to Oxford would have been kept for him, I still regret him sometimes, deeply.

He would have been put through the same crippling processes as our elder brother, without doubt; sent away to school at eight, beaten when he misbehaved, encouraged to limit expressions of fear and pain and love. 'I am homsick and lonly' wrote my brother, heartbreakingly, in his first letter from prep school. Two years or so later, when he made a fuss about having a smallpox vaccination, not something permitted in a future English gentleman, I saw my father march him upstairs, cane in hand, to administer the appropriate punishment. Even then it seemed to me quite outrageous. I followed behind, hammering on my father's bottom, shouting 'How dare you beat my brother!' What made it all still sadder was that my parents, both, would have hated the whole business; but the training of my father, at least, made him think he owed his son such a training.

Much has been written about the limited roles offered sisters in such a world. All three of us had to fight our way out from such restrictions, much to the bewilderment of my sweet father. He still remarks, wistfully, 'I can't think why you three girls all wanted to go to university.' But we did, and we went, even if two of us got there belatedly, and I managed it at eighteen simply because my brother wasn't academic, leaving the money available for me instead. A century back, undoubtedly, I'd have suffered the same fate as Maggie Tulliver. As it was, given the chance, I took it. And now I think, after all, that the insidiousness of his training – as well as the pressure of being the eldest – made it much harder for my brother to escape socially and educationally than it was for his sisters. Not least it seemed to have prevented him from wanting to escape.

My father's – and so my brother's world – was one in which men were very much head of the family, responsible for their daughters till they married, when they would hand over responsibility to the husband. If the father were to die before his daughters married, his son – the brother – would take on the same responsibility. Both my father's older brothers were killed in the First World War, leaving him after his father's death the senior male in their family, a responsibility he felt keenly, continuing to visit both his widowed sisters till they died. (In the case of the younger, Ruth, a dear woman, who had mothered him in his youth, there was real feeling as well as duty.) Presumably a similar sense of duty directed Charles Lamb to forgo marriage to take care of his periodically mad sister, Mary; a relationship which turned, though, into its own kind of celibate – and very affecting – marriage, as can happen.

The world has changed now for us Anglo-Saxons. Family structures are much less formal; feelings between people signify more than duty, and if a sense of duty prevails in some cases it's out of choice. Brothers – males – are no longer paramount. Elder-brother-takes-all no longer operates except in the matter of titles and family seats; though there was always some discretion in that. (Even in the 1920s, my rich grandfather intended leaving my mother and her sister, offspring of his dead daughter, half his estate; alas, the wiles of his second – American – wife prevailed, and my grandmother's half-brother got something close to the lot. However, he did pay for my mother's wedding.) Yet the way my father saw his family and his male duty, even his regrets that his grandchildren have so far produced only great-granddaughters, reflects the former ways of thinking so often described in eighteenth- and nineteenth-century novels, and which persist, still, in other communities and in other parts of the world, at least in patriarchal or patrilineal societies. The extract from Jane Austen's early novel, finished by her niece, shows the unmarried sister as the unwilling brother's responsibility. You see echoes of the same thing in Virginia Woolf's and Vanessa Bell's relationship's with their stepbrother George; the amazing thing to us now is that such a pair felt obliged to comply with his demands, though they rebelled finally. Over the centuries, in worlds where middle-class women didn't work and had no money except from their families, only heiresses, by definition brotherless women, have, sometimes, been able to avoid submitting. In the aristocratic and royal worlds of Europe, as elsewhere, women were property, married off by fathers and brothers for political purposes, to bring dynasties together, or to bring money into the family. In all events, reverence had to be given to a brother as head of a family, no matter how young, sometimes to help preserve a sister's skin. Elizabeth Tudor's obsequious letter to her brother, Edward VI, makes the point.

Matters of family honour can make brothers dangerous even now, when they are responsible for their sisters' marriages and their behaviour before and after. Among Muslims, in England and elsewhere, a sister's loss of virginity or elopement with a husband of her own choice rather than her family's so reflects on family honour that brothers can think it their duty to murder her and him, as in the appalling story of Jack and Zena. Another piece, from Oceania, describes in graphic detail the brothers' obligation to kill their widowed sister ritually, so that she can accompany her husband to the grave.

In some societies it may even be a brother's duty to oversee their sisters' first menstruation; in others – as in the account included here of ritual honour paid to brothers in Hindu Nepal – the economic power of brothers may be balanced by the ritual power of women, yet accounts by anthropologists of family structures and relationships rarely mention sisters. This is not to say that deep sororal relationships don't exist. But, as purely informal matters, they were not referred to by informants. In some cases, girls had lost all contact with their genetic sisters from early adolescence, after removal to the husbands' families. (The effect of further education in delaying marriage is changing this – in some parts of India, for instance.) In such circumstances a woman's brother was often her contact with her family, her significant relationship. The affection between them could be real – as is shown in some pieces here; a brother feeling more at ease with a sister than a wife, and trusting her a great deal more. In the West, equally, the love and loyalty of a woman for her brother, which could lead her as a child into forced complicity with naughty siblings, could lead her as an adult to give up her life to fraternal talents or activities, as with Dorothy Wordsworth and Caroline Herschel – or the mafia sister described here, come to that.

One other aspect of the relationship between brothers and sisters, seen universally, is a kind of teasing irreverence unthinkable between other members of the opposite sex, even spouses. In the structured societies described by anthropologists, these 'joking relationships' were and are formally defined, and arose out of relationships precisely determined by social norms. Nevertheless they bear a strong resemblance to the scatalogical freedom shown in the letters between Mozart and his sister, or the more decorous mocking of Charles by Mary Lamb, either of which would have been unthinkable between spouses then, let alone between friends of the opposite gender. The universality of the ribbing between brother and sister doesn't always mean it's fun, of course: apart from being a vehicle of patronage on a brother's part, as in the affectionate belittlement of 'little' Alice James by her brothers William and Henry, it carries, or can carry, much less kindly family baggage. My brother's propensity to tease me for the size of my backside went on till long after I was married and thin, by my standards, and I didn't think it the least amusing. But then I wouldn't, would I?

In all societies brothers and sisters can love as well as tease each other, now as much as ever. What they may not indulge in at any time or in any society is sexual love or teasing. No one knows or will ever know the precise incidence of brother–sister incest. But it's probably far higher than ever gets reported, much of it simple sexual abuse, rather than consensual (but still deeply complicated) pleasure. The cavortings of the pair in *'Tis Pity She's a Whore*, is one thing; the touching up of the six-year-old Virginia Woolf by her half-brother, Gerald, is quite another. It may or may not have been a factor in her mental problems. But from her account it was certainly a matter of profound shame. I place it alongside an account of the and half-mad sister of the seventeenth-century Scottish witch, Major Weir, who had 'the incestuous use of her' between the ages of sixteen and fifty. This piece, incidentally, contains the two most shocking statements in this book: Major Weir rejected his sister, finally, because 'he loathed her for her age'; while poor Grizel insisted on being hung naked, to reveal *her* shame at what had been so long inflicted on her by her brother.

Electra

You were my faith, my brother –
You alone restore my self-respect.

Aeschylus, *The Libation Bearers*

A sister knows what you like.

Comment from the Gilbert Islands

Happy is that brother who has such a good sister.

> Mozart to N7, March 1778, translated by Emily Anderson, 1966

My brother then, my fosterer then
My source of friendly invitation in the land.

> Traditional verses from *We the Tikopia*,
> by Raymond Firth, 1936

She was harbour or refuge in all the storms of my life, & I hoped she would have closed my eyes.

> Benjamin Disraeli to his brother Ralph, 1859,
> on the death of their sister

To Mary Anne Lamb, the author's best friend and sister.

> Dedication of C. Lamb's poems in Coleridge's
> *Poems on Various Subjects*, 2nd edition, 1797

The pivot of the Ashanti kinship system in its function as a system of jural relations is the tie between brother and sister . . .

> M. Fortes, 'Kinship and Marriage among the Ashanti'

About the Great Strength of Ōi Mitsutō's Younger Sister

Long ago, there was a wrestler from the province of Kai named Ōi Mitsutō. A stocky, tough, powerful, fleet-footed man, he excelled all round – in appearance, character, in fact in everything. He had a younger sister of about twenty-six or twenty-seven, a slim girl who was also well-favoured in her looks and character and bearing. She lived in a house that stood apart from his, and one day a man who was being hotly pursued rushed inside the gate with drawn sword, seized her as a hostage and took up a position with his sword held against her belly.

When someone ran to tell Mitsutō that his sister had been seized as a hostage, he was quite unperturbed and said, 'It would need a man like Ujinaga from Satsuma to seize her as a hostage.' Very puzzled, the man who had come to warn him went back to the house and peered in. There was the girl, wearing a crimson skirt with a single robe of pale mauve (since it was in the ninth month) and sitting with her hand held over her mouth. The man was a big, fierce-looking fellow holding the point of a big sword upwards against her belly, while his legs gripped her from behind in a scissor grip.

The girl was hiding her face with her left hand and crying. With the right hand she was picking up some of the twenty or thirty half-finished arrow shafts which lay in front of her and with studied casualness – gripping them just below the joints, pressing them against the floorboards and giving a twist – she was snapping them as easily as you would snap a soft piece of rotten wood. As he watched her, the thief felt his blood run cold. 'This girl's brother is supposed to be pretty strong,' he thought, 'but even if he tried to smash those arrow shafts with a hammer, he couldn't do it as easily as this. What tremendous strength! If that's how things are, I shall soon get smashed up myself. I'm not having that. I'm not staying here.' And watching for an opportunity, he dashed out of the house and ran away. But there was a crowd of pursuers on his tail and they captured him and took him back, securely tied up, to Mitsutō's house.

When Mitsutō asked him what had made him run away, he said, 'I did it because I was so flabbergasted and scared when the lady broke those arrow shafts at the joints as easily as if they were rotten wood.' Mitsutō burst out laughing. 'Whatever happens, she'll never be run through,' he said. 'If anyone thrust at her, she'd grab his hand and with a twist she'd jerk it upwards till the shoulder was wrenched right out of its socket. You'd have had your shoulder nicely dislocated. Fate must have been on your side – you're lucky she didn't twist your arm. Even I could have killed you with my bare hands. I doubt if you'd have lived to tell the tale if I had twisted your arm and trampled on your belly and your chest. But she is as strong as two of me put together. She is still very slim and feminine, but if I playfully get hold of her arm, I find she gets hold of mine, and I have to slacken my grip and let go. Really, if she were a man, there would be no one to match her. What a pity she's a girl!' This recital made the thief's heart stand still. He had believed he was securing a fine hostage, thinking it was only a woman – but he was wrong. 'I ought to kill you,' said Mitsutō. 'If my sister's life really had been in danger, I certainly would have killed you. It was a good thing for you that you made yourself scarce, or you'd have got yourself killed. You know, she breaks big deer antlers across her knee just as if she were breaking little bits of dead wood.' With that, he let the thief go.

A Collection of Tales from Uji, translated by D. E. A. Mills, 1970

From Mafia Women

Since he couldn't do everything from inside prison, Cutolo put together a trusted group of directors, led by his sister Rosetta. Known as 'eyes of ice', Rosetta, five years his senior, became his manager. He gave her orders, and she ran the organization.

Rosetta Cutolo was the power behind her notorious brother for over fifteen years. She became a legendary figure during the dozen years she was in hiding, and was further glamorized by Giuseppe Tornatore's film *Il Camorrista*, until she gave herself up to the police in 1993. She is currently serving a five-year sentence for mafia association.

When young, she was a dumpy, plain creature, with a big nose and long straight hair which she tied in a pony-tail; the rare photographs of her taken in the 1970s show her dressed mannishly in a patterned shirt over a T-shirt, without make-up. It is said that she was once engaged, but gave up the love of her life to dedicate herself to her brother. Giuseppe Marrazzo, the writer who helped create the Cutolo myth with his fictionalized version of the *camorrista*'s life, implied an incestuous relationship between brother and sister. 'Rosa Cutolo is the true, faithful right arm of the boss of Ottaviano . . . she has remained a spinster to dedicate her life to him.'

She was pious as a young woman and, while she was in hiding, spent her time in the company of a priest [. . .] But the moral universe was swallowed up by the cult of Raffaele Cutolo. Even as a small boy he had grand ideas: his father was a man of such piety he was known as *'o monaco*, 'the monk' [. . .]

While Raffaele has created scandal, giving interviews and making speeches in the courtroom, his sister has kept a low profile. Rosetta ran her younger brother's organization with a selfless dedication that added to his cult status. She collected money from local businesses with missionary zeal, and painted him as a kind of saint: 'We do good in my brother's name. Do you see these people here? They come to us for many reasons; if there are jobs to be allocated in the local town or elsewhere, we are given a quota to fill. We also help prisoners: every trader gives us a contribution, of his own accord, to support prisoners' families.'

[. . .]

Rosetta passed on her brother's orders and cultivated his devoted following. One resident of Ottaviano told a reporter that without her, the organization would have collapsed. Shortly after Cutolo succeeded in getting himself transferred to a mental hospital, a bomb blew a hole in the perimeter wall and he escaped. Rosetta and her mother – the last people to see him before the escape –

were arrested and charged with engineering Raffaele's escape, but were released after three days.

Some say that, in spite of his evident megalomania, 'the professor' was always in awe of his older sister. According to Antonio Laudati, prosecutor at the National Anti-mafia Department, who has questioned Cutolo many times, Rosetta was the true force behind the organization. [. . .]

In October 1981, police raided her house in Orlando, and broke in on a meeting of fifteen of Cutolo's aides, including a local councillor and Cutolo's nineteen-year-old son, Robertino. Rosetta, who had been chairing the meeting, escaped with two of her men. She was not seen in public again for over ten years, during which time she directed operations from a series of safe houses in different cities.

[. . .]

Rosetta has always had a love–hate relationship with her brother. 'Their relationship is very stormy,' says Trofino. 'They often have rows. She thinks he talks too much. She wishes he wouldn't give interviews.' [. . .]

When [she] gave herself up to the police in February 1993, after ten years in hiding, the papers described her as looking like a dowdy housewife. The Italian press describes almost anything in a skirt as *bella* – it helps keep the readers interested – but Rosetta, never. At fifty-five, her grey hair was neatly trimmed and curled, her famous 'eyes of ice' had melted with age. The police chief who went to arrest her said later that as he opened the door, she burst into tears. (Her lawyer, who was also present, says she was perfectly calm and resigned.) The police claimed she had given herself up because she was afraid her enemies were trying to kill her. Others said that, faithful to the last, Rosetta had been sacrificed to her brother, that her capture was part of a bargain between Cutolo and the magistrates, but on this subject her lawyer reserves comment.

Clare Longrigg, 1997

From Quite Unexpected

Geoff is the robber king, Jim is the second in command, and they take it in turns to represent the whole gang [. . .] Maidie is a beautiful maiden whom they have carried into captivity, and she consents to allow herself to be tied with a skipping-rope.

Geoff, however, is not entirely satisfied with tying her, but insists that she must be tied to something to prevent her escape; and between them Geoff and Jim fasten her round the waist to a pedestal, in a corner of the boxroom, on which stands a large plaster bust. Maidie makes them promise only to tie the rope once, but as Geoff passes it twice round her waist, it keeps her fastened rather tight, and the wooden handles prevent all possibility of the knot slipping. This done they play their game with great earnestness for a few minutes, when suddenly Geoff says:

'Oh! just wait a minute – I want to see something,' and off he goes, leaving Maidie powerless to stop him.

'Oh, Jim, let me go! Untie this horrid rope, for I must see what Geoff is doing.'

'I are going to see for you,' says Jim, cheerfully, and forthwith follows in Geoff's footsteps, and Maidie is left alone.

What ought she to do? Every time she tries to move the pedestal shakes and the great bust overhead begins to rock, so that she does not dare make any effort to free herself.

[. . .] At length the door opens, and two of the strangest figures appear. The first has on a long black satin gown, so long as to be very inconvenient length for walking; a cape falls from the shoulders halfway down the dress, and Geoff's laughing face looks out from one of Aunt Bethia's best caps.

The other figure is almost more peculiar, for a gentleman's light drab coat trails on the ground, a necktie is twisted in a very wonderful manner round the throat, while upon the head is Uncle James's new wig, and his high white hat on top of all. [. . .] Maidie would like to laugh – only she is far too dismayed, and gives a little cry instead.

'Oh! you dreadful boys! Go away and put these things back at once and when Uncle James come home – hush! Listen! THERE HE IS!'

A thrill of horror runs through the children as they listen, for sure enough Uncle James is speaking in the hall below.

A struggle to get to the door and back to the rooms to replace their borrowed plumes occurs at once, but too late, for Uncle James is mounting the stairs and faces them as they rush wildly out of the boxroom.

There is a sudden stop and exclamation – and then a silence so awful that Maidie wriggles wildly, and nearly brings the big bust down on top of her. What will Uncle James say? And Maidie, whose tender conscience feels responsible for them, cannot get there to take a share of the blame – which she generally manages shall be the lion's share – and Uncle James will punish them, and then – Maidie listens, but she only hears footsteps, a door shut, and all is still.

Presently the steps come nearer again, and oh, terror! Uncle James himself comes into the room, and stands still to look at her.

'Come to me at once!' he says decidedly; but poor Maidie can only shrink and whisper,

'I can't – I'm tied!'

'Try to get free then!' says Uncle James, still very severely, and Maidie makes a tremendous effort.

It is without effect as far as she is concerned, but the bust rocks more violently than before, and Maidie feels sure that it is going to fall. She feels a little frightened shiver, and sees her uncle start towards her, then there is a loud crash, and Maidie knows no more.

Ismay Thorn, 1889

From Bhai Tika and the Sacred Status of Sisters

There is one more major ritual celebrating the filiafocal dimension of kinship: the calendrical festival of Bhai Tika (brother-tika).

The ceremony takes place in the morning before anyone has eaten. A space on the mud floor of the house is purified with gobar and a straw mat and cushions or woollen rugs are placed in the centre, where the brother will sit. A betel nut in a leaf cup of rice is set out to represent Ganes. There are a brass vessel filled with water that has a piece of holy kus grass in the spout, a wick soaked in clarified butter placed in a leaf plate, and other plates containing fruits, flowers, and items needed for worship. On the edge of the gobar circle are a walnut and a stone.

The brother (or brothers) must sit in the centre of the circle while the sister worships Ganes and all the other gods and finally the walnut which represents Yama [the god of death]. Then she lights the votive lamp in the circle and, taking the spouted vessel in hand, walks three times around the edge of the circle evenly spilling out a little of the water as she goes. Next she makes another triple circumambulation of her brother, this time dripping a steady line of oil from a sprig of kus grass. She then sprinkles oil seven times on her brother's head and once in each ear. Then she puts flowers on his head, shoulders, knees, and hands and garlands him with a necklace of amaranth flowers. These special purple flowers retain their colour and shape as they dry and are virtually everlasting; so like the boy in the myth, the brother will be safe from Yama as long as these flowers look fresh. As a sign of her blessing and protection, she now gives the special tika mark on his forehead which only a sister can give on Bhai Tihar. With her little finger she makes a long vertical line of yellow. On this she carefully places dots of red, green, blue, and white. Then she must go to the edge of the ceremonial circle and with one blow smash the walnut with the stone, thus vanquishing Yama. Finally, she gives her brother his *bhag*, or 'share' – a gift of food which must contain curds, mustard greens, dried fish, and *sel roti* (a doughnut-like fried bread), along with as many other sweets and delicacies as she can afford. The brother must eat some of the yoghurt and sel roti, after which his sister washes his hands. Then the brother gives tika to his sister, touches his forehead to her foot, and presents her with daksina. The daksina which grown men give to their sisters can be quite substantial, including gifts of clothes and sometimes even a cow, along with considerable amounts of cash.

Lynne Bennett, 1983

From Letters from Africa

To *Thomas Dinesen*

Ngong, 13 December 1918

My own beloved, wonderful Tommy.

I don't know how to congratulate you enough on your VC – Living among the English I do know how immeasurably much it means, 'the only order in the world'; perhaps that is not really properly understood at home. I have heard that yours was about the thousandth to be awarded, so that means that you are among the thousand bravest men in the world, – which of course I have never doubted, but it is good to have it in black and white! I am so proud of you and so *overjoyed* at how it has gone that every single day I wake up in the morning as one did on one's birthday when one was small! Some of the hero's glory does indeed descend on his sister, and people out here have been so kind as to say that courage is a feature of the family. Apart from the honour – which is *le superflu*, that is, *le nécessaire*, – you have benefited us greatly with your cross. It has been announced in the local papers and really put a stop to the continuous gossip that some people were spreading with incredible persistence about our being pro-German . . .

If only you would come out here. You are probably being well fêted where you are, but we would prepare a grand reception for you, I can tell you. But in any case I am more grateful to you than I can say; for your VC came at a time when I had been suffering much adversity and was beginning to lose faith in the eternal gods, and there is no greater misfortune than that. Now I have regained my belief in both gods and heroes, indeed, even in their very close presence.

Now I am going to tell you something remarkable. When you first went to war I was terribly worried about you, and I used to talk to Fara about it, and he suggested that we should get the old Somali or rather, Arab sheik, i.e., priest, to cast a spell to keep you safe in all the danger. This was done on three successive Fridays, and consisted of a small piece of paper covered with passages from the Koran, which Fara and I had to bury, and not tell anyone where we had buried it or anything about it; we obeyed this command. Probably you will laugh when I say that it was often a great comfort to me, and still more when you hear that, despite the fact that it was a period of straitened finances for me, I paid the old sheik 1,000 rupees to make it up. But now listen and stop your mocking. The sheik's sorcery called not only for you to come safely through the war unharmed by enemy fire but for you to SLAY TWELVE OF THE ENEMY, BE AN EXAMPLE TO ALL AND GAIN GREAT HONOUR! – And yesterday I received a clipping from the *Times* that said the same thing in identical words! Don't ever let me hear you deny that we are in league with the higher powers!

Isak Dinesen

From The Little Boy 'Nurse'

I was not yet four years old when my sister was born. I had got used to sleeping away from my mother's care, having been so long with my uncle. On my return, together with other male youngsters of very nearly the same age, I began to sleep in my grandfather's hut. (The girls of this age also would sleep away from their parents' homes and at some grandmother's house.) Because there was no older sister in the family, and my mother had to go off to work in the *shamba* every day, it wasn't long before I was obliged, though still a very young child myself, to become the day-to-day 'nurse' for my baby sister. For my mother to make me succeed in this function, she had to train me – to give me instructions and to see how well I carried them out. I had at first to do some of the things while she watched – feed the child on porridge, for example. Such training took us into the planting season of the following year. As her *shamba* work increased, so did my nursing duties.

In our home the day would start with early-morning duties for all the members of our household except the baby, Mang'ong'o Alusa. [. . .] On my arrival from Grandfather's hut, which used to be at sunrise, I would be sent to look for fire from other homes; if, that is, my mother had been careless about keeping hers burning through the night. I would build or stir up the fire in the fireplace, and leave it for my mother to make breakfast. [. . .] My mother would check Alusa's porridge, which had been made out of millet flour and stored in a gourd for ready use. Sometimes the porridge turned out to be sour, but it would still serve the purpose, my mother believed. She would then wake up the baby to give her the last feed for the morning. And lastly, before moving off to the *shamba*, she would give me instructions: Do not leave the home unguarded, she would tell me, for fear that thieves would steal our property. Do not leave Alusa crying for long periods of time, for that would be dangerous to her health. Feed her when she cries. Guard the chickens from wild cats and the chicks from wild birds. Be helpful to visitors and strangers who ask you for information. Finally, she would promise to bring me a present – a piece of fruit, a potato – when she returned from work. Then she would leave, not to return until very late in the evening.

As soon as my mother left, loneliness would set in. I was in charge of a huge house and, judged by present-day standards, it was a very dark, extremely untidy and even filthy house. The outside was frightful, too. There were known to be wild cats which would come to catch our chickens. Thieves might come at any moment, too. All of these thoughts would frighten me constantly in my early days of home-guarding and baby-nursing.

As Alusa slept for long hours, I would decide to do some of the things I had seen my mother do, but which she had not particularly asked me to do. I had seen her grind millet and prepare and cook bananas; so I would keep busy with one or two of these jobs until Alusa would wake up. Then I would feed her according to instructions: shake the gourd that contained the porridge, lay Alusa on my lap with the head resting on my stomach, fold my left palm and fingers so as to make a curved cup to be placed below her mouth. Into this curve I would pour porridge until her mouth was submerged. As soon as the porridge touched her mouth, Alusa would suck it in. If she refused to suck it, I had been told to stop feeding her. But, of course, I had noticed my mother force the baby to suck by closing her nostrils with a finger, thereby forcing her to breathe through the mouth. As the mouth was submerged in porridge, the breathing would inevitably force the porridge down the gullet. At first I feared trying this trick; I would simply hold her until my mother returned from work.

Sooner or later, I discovered that in the meantime I could go away and – when Alusa was sleeping – play with other 'nurses' from the neighbouring homes. At first we were afraid to go because our parents had given us strict orders to remain at home. But having established among us the place where we would play whenever a chance came, we would gather there as soon as possible after the parents had gone to the *shambas*.

Here we would come with our siblings. We would sit them or lay them on the ground and the five of us would go on playing. We would attend to our babies only when they cried excessively. Then we would sing lullabies to make them go to sleep quickly, hurriedly feed them, or perhaps tie them, still crying, on our backs and continue playing. Neither our babies nor we ourselves had any clothes to put on, so there was no problem of washing napkins! Neither were children and babies supposed to be bathed lest they catch disease. [. . .]

It was my duty as Alusa's nurse to offer her toilet 'training'. For toilet paper, I was instructed to use *mavuya*, a special type of leaf, soft enough to resemble the feel of our present-day toilet paper. Nurses were all instructed to use *mavuya* whenever babies defecated. As Alusa grew older she was usually told, either by my mother or by myself, to excrete on the grass. But many children in our location, fearing the cool dew in the early morning, would go alongside the house, or even in the house itself. There were no latrines as such; grown-ups went into the bush. Hence there was always an uncultivated piece of land near the home for this purpose.

When my mother returned from work, she would look round the house and at the baby to see if I had done my duty well. If Alusa's eyes were red, she would know Alusa had cried a lot during the day. If the gourd was still full of porridge, she would know Alusa had not been fed. She would then deduce that I had left her uncared for and had gone off to play. I would be reported to my father who would decide the punishment for the offence and who would inflict that punishment, usually a beating. If all was well, on the other hand, my mother would breast-feed Alusa, lay her down to rest, and begin to prepare our evening meal. I would be released to go out and play with the other children.

Joseph A. Lijembe, 1967

Charles and Mary Lamb

But Lamb's life was to be devoted to a different and to a higher purpose. He was to become a sacrificer at the altar of love; but this was a loftier and purer godhead than that pagan Cupid who links the hearts of men and women so fast together. His was another sort of marriage; contracted by him in early youth, it was the only union he ever knew: and no hymeneal rites could have been more religiously observed than the bond which knit together the son and daughter of John Lamb.

[. . .]

There was a certain old-world fashion in Mary Lamb's diction which gave it the most natural and quaintly pleasant effect, and which heightened rather than detracted from the more heartfelt or important things she uttered. She had a way of repeating her brother's words assertingly when he spoke to her. He once said (with his peculiar mood of tenderness, beneath blunt, abrupt speech), 'You must die first, Mary.' She nodded, with her little quiet nod and sweet smile: 'Yes, I must die first, Charles.'

[. . .]

At another time, he said, in his whimsical way, plucking out his words in gasps, as it were, between the smiles with which he looked at her: 'I call my sister "Moll" before the servants: "Mary" in the presence of friends; and "Maria" when I am alone with her.'

W. Carew Hazlitt, *The Life and Character of Charles Lamb*, 1874

'You would laugh, or you would cry, perhaps both, to see us sit together, looking at each other with long and rueful jaws, and saying "How do you do", and "How do you do?" And then we fall a-crying and say we will be better on the morrow.'

Mary Lamb, letter, 1805
[They used to call each other Toothache and Gumboil.]

Whenever the approach of her fits of insanity were announced, by some irritability or change of manner, Lamb would take her, under his arm, to Hoxton Asylum. It was very affecting to encounter the young brother and sister walking together (weeping together) on this painful errand; Mary herself, although sad, very conscious of the necessity of temporary separation from her only friend. They used to carry a strait-jacket with them.

Barry Cornwall, *Charles Lamb: A Memoir*, 1876

I have every reason to suppose that this illness, like all her former ones, will be but temporary: but I cannot always feel so. Meantime she is dead to me, and I miss a prop. All my strength is gone and I am like a fool, bereft of her cooperation. I dare not think, lest I shall think wrong: so used am I to think up to her in the least and biggest complexity.

Charles Lamb, letter to Dorothy Wordsworth, 14 June 1805

Marjorie Wilson

It is difficult to be the male spouse of a leading lady politician. I suspect it is no less difficult being the big sister of a Prime Minister. Marjorie Wilson succeeded in being a lady of considerable worth in her own right. After studying chemistry at Leeds University, she became a teacher, later moving to Cornwall, where she spent many years as headmistress of St Blazey's Infants School and, from 1966 to 1971, of Biscovey Infants School.

David Blackford, Secretary of the Cornwall branch of the National Association of Head Teachers, describes her as 'caring'. Nothing, he says, was too much trouble for her. She was respected by staff and parents alike and a keen member of his association. 'Nobody would ever have been aware of the special circumstances of her relationship with the Prime Minister.'

Marjorie used to bring their father, Herbert Wilson, a widower, to Labour Party conferences, where they both became something of a benign institution. I remember her irreverent outpourings at Scarborough in 1967. Harold, she told us, was born the day before her seventh birthday. 'I suppose he was a sort of birthday present.' Marjorie would talk about him as if he were half baby and half doll, someone to be protected.

Actually Harold Wilson owed Marjorie a great deal, as she it was who was to look after his father and carry many of the family responsibilities. Without her he might not have had the time so assiduously to climb the Labour Party tree.

All was not sweetness and light. As the secretary of the Labour Party Standing Conference on the Sciences and a young MP, Harold Wilson wanted me to talk at length to his father Herbert, who had been a chemist, about the science policy, during the white heat of the technological revolution.

Later, when I told him genuinely that his father had been interesting and his sister charming, he looked quizzically, in a particular Harold Wilson way, as if to say, 'That's only half the story.' Ever a gossip, he told me that Marjorie had bullied him and recalled that during one summer holiday – I think in Morecambe – he had nearly lost his life at her hands. Going for a walk along the sea front he and his sister had had a fight. Marjorie overpowered him and hurled him with all his clothes on into the sea. He was terrified and his heavy garments were soaked through. He had to be taken to a shop to get new clothes.

This may have been Marjorie's revenge for all the attention that came to her young brother. As Ben Pimlott put it in his brilliant and perceptive biography, *Harold Wilson* (1992), 'Marjorie was expected to watch Harold's brilliant successes and to be enthusiastic about them, almost as a third parent.'

Marjorie's successes were automatically regarded as less of an achievement. There is an oft-repeated story which Harold Wilson would tell against himself. When Marjorie told her parents excitedly that she had won a scholarship to Huddersfield Girls High School, Harold, then four years of age, complained, 'I want a "ship" too.' When Herbert Wilson made a celebrated sightseeing trip to London and visited Downing Street, it was Harold and not Marjorie who had a photograph taken outside the door of No. 10.

The relationship between brother and sister, however, became very good. When Harold was called to Chequers to see Clem Attlee in 1947, he was staying with Marjorie at her St Austell bungalow (she had moved to Cornwall with her mother shortly after her father started to work there in 1938); they spent the evening making guesses about what Attlee would offer.

Marjorie wanted to know on Monday morning where her brother was to go in the government, so he arranged to leave a symbolic message on her breakfast table on his way back to Mullion Cove in Cornwall where he used to stay. A lump of coal would mean that he was to be Minister of Fuel and Power, a strip of metal would mean Minister of Supply and a slice of bread Minister of

Food. Neither of them had imagined that he would be given the presidency of the Board of Trade.

Tam Dalyell, *Independent*, 11 April 1998

Brothers are to sisters what sisters can never be to brothers as objects of engrossing and devoted affection. The law of their frames is answerable for this: and that other law – of equity – which sisters are bound to obey, requires that they should not render their account of their disappointments when there can be no fair reply. Under the same law, sisters are bound to remember that they cannot be certain of their own fitness to render an account of their own disappointments, or to form an estimate of the share of blame which may be due to themselves on the score of unreasonable expectations.

Harriet Martineau, *Autobiography*,
with memorials by Maria Weston, 1877

Let the delicious little grey-eyed Alice be locked up alone . . . with paper and envelopes to write a letter unassisted, uncorrected and unpunctuated to her loving brothers who would send her novels and peaches if they could. What a blessing it is to have such [. . . a] splendid little sister!

William James to his parents, 1866

My sister's poems are homely, but just what they should be; I send them not for their poetry but the good sense and good will of them.

Charles Lamb to Barron Field Esq, 4 October 1827

My sister indeed, is all I can wish in a companion; but our spirits are alike poorly, our reading and knowledge from the self-same sources, our communication with the scenes of the world alike narrow: never having kept separate company, or any 'company' 'together' – never having read separate books, and few books together – what knowledge have we to convey to each other?

Charles Lamb

Girl, aged ten, on her younger brother: 'Well, he's nice to me. I'd be very lonely without [him and] I play with him a lot.'

Boy, aged six, on his older sister. 'She's pretty disgusting and we don't talk to each other much.' [What do you like about her?] 'Nothing.'

Source unknown, 1980s

From the age of fifteen, the surrealist Max Ernst was deeply affected by the simultaneous death of a favourite pink cockatoo and the birth of his sister. From that moment, he felt a confusion between birds and mankind ...

Observer, Review, 16 May 1999

From The Mill on the Floss

Now, then, Magsie, give us the Grammar!'

'O Tom, it's such a pretty book!' she said, as she jumped out of the large armchair to give it him, 'it's much prettier than the Dictionary. I could learn Latin very soon. I don't think it's at all hard.'

'O I know what you've been doing,' said Tom, 'you've been reading the English at the end. Any donkey can do that.'

Tom seized the book and opened it with a determined and business-like air as much as to say that he had a lesson to learn which no donkeys would find themselves equal to. Maggie, rather piqued, turned to the bookcases to amuse herself with puzzling out the titles.

Presently Tom called to her: 'Here, Magsie, come and hear if I can say this. Stand at that end of the table, where Mr Sterling sits when he hears me.'

Maggie obeyed and took the open book.

'Where do you begin, Tom?'

'O, I begin at *Appellativa arborum*, because I say all over again what I've been learning this week.'

Tom sailed along pretty well for three lines; and Maggie was beginning to forget her office of prompter, in speculating as to what *mas* could mean, which came twice over, when he stuck fast at *Sunt etiam volucrum*.

'Don't tell me, Maggie; *Sunt etiam volucrum . . . Sunt etiam volucrum . . . ut ostrea, cetus . . .*'

'No,' said Maggie, opening her mouth and shaking her head.

'*Sunt etiam volucrum,*' said Tom, very slowly, as if the next words might be expected to come sooner, when he gave them this strong hint that they were waited for.

'C, e, u,' said Maggie, getting impatient.

'O, I know – hold your tongue,' said Tom. '*Ceu passer, hirundo, ferarum . . . ferarum . . .*' Tom took his pencil and made several hard dots with it on his book-cover . . . '*ferarum . . .*'

'O dear, O dear Tom,' said Maggie, 'what a time you are! *Ut . . .*'

'*Ut, ostrea . . .*'

'No, no,' said Maggie, '*ut, tigris . . .*'

'O yes, now I can do,' said Tom, 'it was *tigris, vulpes*, I'd forgotten: *ut tigris, vulpes, et piscium.*'

With some further stammering and repetition, Tom got through the next few lines.

'Now then,' he said, 'the next is what I've just learnt for tomorrow. Give me hold of the book a minute.'

After some whispered gabbling, assisted by the beating of his fist on the table, Tom returned the book.

'*Mascula nomina in a*,' he began.

'No, Tom,' said Maggie, 'that doesn't come next. It's *Nomen non creskens genittivo* . . .'

'*Creskens genittivo*,' exclaimed Tom, with a derisive laugh, for Tom had learned this omitted passage for his yesterday's lesson, and a young gentleman does not require an intimate or extensive acquaintance with Latin before he can feel the pitiable absurdity of a false quantity. '*Creskens genittivo!* What a little silly you are, Maggie!'

'Well, you needn't laugh, Tom, for you didn't remember it at all. I'm sure it's spelt so. How was I to know?'

'Phee-e-e-h! I told you girls couldn't learn Latin. It's *Nomen non crescens genitivo*.'

'Very well, then,' said Maggie, pouting. 'I can say that as well as you can. And you don't mind your stops. For you ought to stop twice as long at a semicolon as you do at a comma, and you make the longest stops where there ought to be no stop at all.'

'O well, don't chatter. Let me go on.'

They were presently fetched to spend the rest of the evening in the drawing-room, and Maggie became so animated with Mr Stelling, who, she felt sure, admired her cleverness, that Tom was rather amazed and alarmed at her audacity. But she was suddenly subdued by Mr Stelling's alluding to a little girl of whom he had heard that she once ran away to the gypsies.

'What a very odd little girl that must be!' said Mrs Stelling, meaning to be playful, but a playfulness that turned on her supposed oddity was not at all to Maggie's taste. She feared Mr Stelling, after all, did not think much of her, and went to bed in rather low spirits. Mrs Stelling, she felt, looked at her as if she thought her hair was very ugly because it hung down straight behind.

Nevertheless it was a very happy fortnight to Maggie – this visit to Tom. She was allowed to be in the study while he had his lessons, and in her various readings got very deep into the examples in the Latin Grammar. The astronomer who hated women generally caused her so much puzzling speculation that she one day asked Mr Stelling if all astronomers hated women, or whether it was only this particular astronomer. But, forestalling his answer, she said.

'I suppose it's all astronomers: because you know, they live up in high towers, and if the women came there, they might talk and hinder them from looking at the stars.'

Mr Stelling liked her prattle immensely, and they were on the best terms. She told Tom she should like to go to school to Mr Stelling, as he did, and learn just the same things. She knew she could do Euclid, for she had looked into it again, and she saw what ABC meant: they were the names of the lines.

'I'm sure you couldn't do it, now,' said Tom. 'And I'll just ask Mr Stelling if you could.'

'I don't mind,' said the little conceited minx. 'I'll ask him myself.'

'Mr Stelling,' she said, that same evening, when they were in the drawing-room, 'couldn't I do Euclid, and all Tom's lessons, if you were to teach me instead of him?'

'No; you couldn't,' said Tom, indignantly. 'Girls can't do Euclid: can they, sir?'

'They can pick up a little of everything, I daresay,' said Mr Stelling. 'They've a great deal of superficial cleverness, but they couldn't go far into anything. They're quick and shallow.'

Tom, delighted with this verdict, telegraphed his triumph by wagging his head at Maggie behind Mr Stelling's chair. As for Maggie, she had hardly ever been so mortified: she had been so proud to be called 'quick' all her little life, and now it appeared that this quickness was the brand of inferiority. It would have been better to be slow, like Tom.

'Ha, ha! Miss Maggie!' said Tom, when they were alone, 'you see it's not such a fine thing to be quick. You'll never go far into anything, you know.'

And Maggie was so oppressed by this dreadful destiny that she had no spirit for a retort.

But when this small apparatus of shallow quickness was fetched away in the gig by Luke, and the study was once more quite lonely for Tom, he missed her grievously. He had really been brighter and had got through his lessons better since she had been there; and she had asked Mr Stelling so many questions about the Roman Empire, and whether there really ever was a man who said in Latin, 'I would not buy it for a farthing or a rotten nut,' or whether that had only been turned into Latin – that Tom had actually come to a dim understanding of the fact that there had once been people upon the earth who were so fortunate as to know Latin without learning it through the medium of the Eton Grammar. This luminous idea was a great addition to his historical acquirements during this half year which were otherwise confined to an epitomized History of the Jews.

George Eliot, 1860

From Isak Dinesen

The three sisters were 'educated privately', an expression that has a certain undeserved patrician glamour. Tanne lamented the fact that she was permitted to grow up 'totally ignorant of many things that are common knowledge to other people' – mathematics, for instance, for which she felt she had a flair. Like most women of their class, the Dinesen sisters were not prepared to earn a living – it was assumed that they would marry – although Tanne was indignant that they were not even taught about housekeeping or entertaining. Later she would express a fine, feminist indignation at a system that could allow 'practically all my abilities to lie fallow and [that] passed me on to charity or prostitution in some shape or other . . .' In Africa, living among English public-school alumni, she came to look upon their strenuous, aristocratic colleges as an ideal. 'If I had a son,' she told her brother, 'I would send him to Eton.'

Her own brothers had left for boarding-school – not so illustrious a one as Eton – at the ages of eight and six respectively. Their older sister, who was then begging to be sent to the Royal Academy of Art, watched them go with a deep and justified envy. The boys were given guns, soldiers' uniforms, boats, permitted to wander through the park at night, or to fish on the ice when the Sound froze. Thomas marvelled as an old man at the indulgence Ingeborg had shown them. Over-protective of her daughters, she was committed to raise her sons as 'their dead father would have wished'. Tanne secretly believed that Wilhelm would have wished a richer scope for her, as well. But there was no way she could prove it.

Judith Thurman, 1982

Prince Edward to His Sister
Elizabeth

5 December 1546

Change of place, in fact, did not vex me so much, dearest sister, as your going from me. Now, however, nothing can happen more agreeable to me than a letter from you; and especially as you were the first to send a letter to me, and have challenged me to write. Wherefore I thank you both for your goodwill and dispatch. I will then strive, to my utmost power, if not to surpass, at least to equal you in goodwill and zeal. But this is some comfort to my grief, that I hope to visit you shortly (if no accident intervene with either me or you), as my chamberlain has reported to me. Farewell, dearest sister!

Edward the Prince

To King Edward VI,
Her Boy Brother

Elizabeth about seventeen and the King thirteen. This is a fair example of her early style of composition

Your letter, most illustrious King, has cheered my mind for many reasons; in the first place, that it certified me of your sound health, which has ever been my chief care; in the second, that it exhibited no common marks of your love for me; and in the last that it showed satisfactorily with how kind feeling you accepted my bounden duty, by the messenger sent by me to inquire of your health. Amidst all which, while I was pondering on what was the most important, your majesty's prosperous health struck me at the first glance, than which nothing can ever happen more desirable or more necessary to this realm. For, what a family is without a steward, a ship without a pilot, a flock without a shepherd, a body without a head, the same, I think, is a kingdom without the health and safety of a good monarch. Since then so much weight rests on the prosperity of princes, your majesty's well-being ought to be desired and wished for by all with the heartiest prayers; and without it, in fact, the subjects of this kingdom can in no wise be safe and secure. For, as sheep cannot be guarded against, or escape from the snares of wolves without the shepherd's care and foresight, so without the foresight of kings (whom Homer calls 'Shepherds of the people' and Isaiah, 'Feeders of the Church') neither can states be sufficiently guarded and fortified against the inroads and attacks of tyrants, nor can the Church be rightly fed and satisfied with food for the spirit, that is, with the word of God. Moreover, lest I should seem unmindful of my duty, I give my thanks to your majesty for having conceived such an opinion of me, as you have fully expressed in your letters. And that this opinion may remain settled in your majesty's mind perpetually, I have hitherto striven earnestly, and I promise that I will hereafter strive as sedulously. May God long preserve your highness in safety, to the glory of his name, and the advantage of your kingdom.

From Manus Kinship

Brother and Sister

Children will say of this relationship, 'He is my brother. He hits me and I hit him.' 'She is my sister. I take her canoe [play canoe] and she takes mine.' Later in life an adult will say, 'She is my sister. Her *metcha* became my *metcha*' (i.e., the great late marriage payment for her marriage was paid to me, and with it I made a similar payment for my wife). 'She is my sister, when I die she will weep for me.' 'A man likes to marry a woman who has wept long for her brothers. She is a good woman.' 'He is my brother. He gives me sago. I give him beadwork. When he dies I will weep for him.' [. . .]

Ideologically, an unmarried girl has no special relationship to her brother. If her brother, or any male relative of her own generation whom she would normally call brother, arranges a betrothal or gives the *mwelamwel* for her marriage, she calls him, thereafter, 'father', i.e., he is regarded as having played a 'father' role. The wife of such a man is called 'mother'. [. . .] When, however, a woman becomes pregnant for the first time there is a shift in kinship function. Henceforth the responsibility for her part of the affinal exchange is assumed by her 'brother'. [. . .]

In addition to making a series of birth feasts, beginning as soon as pregnancy is known and culminating in the large feast when the mother is returned to her husband, the brother assumes the care of his sister from a few days before delivery until thirty days after the birth of the child. The method of carrying out this charge rests in the brother's discretion. He divines as to whether the spirits prefer that his sister be moved to his house, or that she remain in her husband's house. If the latter reply is given, the husband vacates his own house and the brother and his wife and children move into it. The husband and his children go to live with the husband's sister. [. . .] During this month the brother provides food for his sister and her children.

This economic relationship is repeated for each childbirth. [. . .]

When a boy or girl has the ears pierced, the mother's brother is again responsible. The mother's brother and the mother's brothers' wives come to live in the house, but in this case the father is not excluded. [. . .]

Furthermore there are certain other economic contacts between brothers and sisters. A man keeps his ceremonial property – charms, war charms, the skull and bones of his Sir Ghost, in his own house, but his most valuable secular property, shell money and dogs' teeth, is kept for him by his sisters. It is their task to keep the shell money aprons in repair, to work strands of shell money into belts, and new aprons, and to string dogs' teeth in distinctive ways so that one string will be known from another. As a man accumulates small amounts of currency towards a large payment, such as a marriage payment for a son, he takes them to his sisters who put them away for him.

[. . .]

In addition to the ceremonial and the economic contacts, there are many slight day-by-day contacts between brother and sisters. Although the peaceful cooperation of husband and wife is often threatened by a brother's economic demands on his sister and her demands on him, it is the small intimacies between brother and sister (the mood of complete reciprocity and understanding which the little girl described in the phrase, 'He is my brother, he hits me and I hit him') which interfere most with marriage. It is the only completely reciprocal relationship uncomplicated by age. [. . .] The same attitude of utter trust is expressed by young girls who, after they have discussed their fear of young men with imported love magic, will add of A and B and C: 'They are my brothers, I can talk to them. I am not afraid of them.'

Between brother and sister there is no taboo, only an enjoined reserve in matters pertaining in any way to the body. This reserve acts as a guarantee of safety, of pleasant confidence, to a people as puritanical and shame-faced as the Manus. It must be regarded in Manus, as making for better relations rather than detracting from them. [. . .] Between brothers and sisters there is also an enjoined seriousness. The gravity of the relationship may even sanction otherwise interdicted intimacy, as when a brother may mention his sister's immodest dress in serious rebuke. Throughout, it is a relationship concerned with property, with obligations, with material and ceremonial interdependence. The Manus are not over given to laughter, and the segregation of the play element to the cross-cousin relationship does not detract from the pleasantness of the brother and sister relationship. In his sister's house a man can be sure of a welcome. She will not indulge in unseemly jests, she will never embarrass him by any reference to sex, she will listen gravely to his requests, and carry them out with becoming seriousness.

So, day after day, a man seeks out his sister in his free hours, he takes his baby to his sister's house to play, he goes to his sister's after successful fishing and leaves some of his choicest fish for her cooking. His sister sees him in his best mood, and often gets first choice of his fishing catch. When he eats in his sister's house, his sister eats with him, an intimate family meal, while her husband sits apart or leaves the house altogether, for brothers-in-law may not eat in each other's presence. And when a woman is sick it is her brother who sits and holds her head, while her husband sits at a distance, unwanted.

Margaret Mead, 1934

From Moments of Being

George, as I say, could have mounted alone to the highest pinnacles of London society. His mantelpiece was a gallery of invitation cards from every house in London. Why then did he insist upon cumbering himself with a couple of half-sisters who were more than likely to drag him down? It is probably useless to inquire. George's mind swam and steamed like a cauldron of rich Irish stew. He believed that aristocratic society was possessed of all the virtues and all the graces. He believed that his family had been entrusted to his care. He believed that it was his sacred duty – but when he reached that point his emotions overcame him; he began to sob; he flung himself on his knees; he seized Vanessa in his arms; he implored her in the name of her mother, of her grandmother, by all that was sacred in the female sex and holy in the traditions of our family to accept Lady Arthur Russell's invitation to dinner, to spend the weekend with the Chamberlains at Highbury.

I cannot conceal my own opinion that Vanessa was to blame; not indeed that she could help herself, but if, I sometimes think, she had been born with one shoulder higher than another, with a limp, with a squint, with a large mole on her left cheek, both our lives would have been changed for the better. As it was, George had a good deal of reason on his side. It was plain that Vanessa in her white satin dress made by Mrs Young, wearing a single flawless amethyst round her neck, and a blue enamel butterfly in her hair – the gifts, of course, of George himself – beautiful, motherless, aged only eighteen, was a touching spectacle, an ornament for any dinner table, a potential peeress, anything might be made of such precious material as she was – outwardly at least; and to be seen hovering round her, providing her with jewels, and Arab horses, and expensive clothes, whispering encouragement, lavishing embraces which were not entirely concealed from the eyes of strangers, redounded to the credit of George himself and invested his figure with a pathos which it would not otherwise have had in the eyes of the dowagers of Mayfair. Unfortunately, what was inside Vanessa did not altogether correspond with what was outside. Underneath the necklaces and the enamel butterflies was one passionate desire – for paint and turpentine, for turpentine and paint. But poor George was no psychologist. His perceptions were obtuse. He never saw within. He was completely at a loss when Vanessa said she did not wish to stay with the Chamberlains at Highbury; and would not dine with Lady Arthur Russell – a rude, tyrannical old woman, with a bloodstained complexion and the manners of a turkey cock. He argued, he wept, he complained to Aunt Mary Fisher, who said that she could not believe her ears. Every battery was turned upon Vanessa. She was told that she was selfish, unwomanly, callous and incredibly ungrateful considering the treasures of affection that had been lavished upon her – the Arab horse she rode and the slabs of bright blue enamel which she wore. Still she persisted. She did not wish to dine with Lady Arthur Russell. As the season wore on, every morning brought its card of invitation for Mr Duckworth and Miss Stephen; and every evening witnessed a battle between them. For the first year or so George, I suppose, was usually the victor. Off they went, in the hansom cab of those days and late at night Vanessa would come into my room complaining that she had been dragged from party to party, where she knew no one, and had been bored to death by the civilities of young men from the Foreign Office and the condescensions of old ladies of title. The more Vanessa resisted, the more George's natural obstinacy persisted. At last there was a crisis. Lady Arthur Russell was giving a series of select parties on Thursday evenings in South Audley Street. Vanessa had sat through one entire evening without opening her lips. George insisted that she must go next week and make amends, or he said,

'Lady Arthur will never ask you to her house again.' They argued until it was getting too late to dress. At last Vanessa, more in desperation than in concession, rushed upstairs, flung on her clothes and announced that she was ready to go. Off they went. What happened in the cab will never be known. But whenever they reached 2 South Audley Street – and they reached it several times in the course of the evening – one or the other was incapable of getting out. George refused to enter with Vanessa in such a passion; and Vanessa refused to enter with George in tears. So the cabman had to be told to drive once more round the Park. Whether they ever managed to alight I do not know.

But next morning as I was sitting spelling out my Greek George came into my room carrying in his hand a small velvet box. He presented me with the jewel it contained – a Jews' harp made of enamel with a pinkish blob of matter swinging in the centre which I regret to say only fetched a few shillings when I sold it the other day. But his face showed that he had come upon a different errand. His face was sallow and scored with innumerable wrinkles, for his skin was as loose and flexible as a pug dog's, and he would express his anguish in the most poignant manner by puckering lines, folds, and creases from forehead to chin. His manner was stern. His bearing rigid. If Miss Willett of Brighton could have seen him then she would certainly have compared him to Christ on the cross. After giving me the Jews' harp he stood before the fire in complete silence. Then, as I expected, he began to tell me his version of the preceding night – wrinkling his forehead more than ever, but speaking with a restraint that was at once bitter and manly. Never, never again, he said, would he ask Vanessa to go out with him. He had seen a look in her eyes which positively frightened him. It should never be said of him that he made her do what she did not wish to do. Here he quivered, but checked himself. Then he went on to say that he had only done what he knew my mother would have wished him to do. His two sisters were the most precious things that remained to him. His home had always meant more to him – more than he could say, and here he became agitated, struggled for composure, and then burst into a statement which was at once dark and extremely lurid. We were driving Gerald from the house, he cried – when a young man was not happy at home – he himself had always been content – but if his sisters – if Vanessa refused to go out with him – if he could not bring his friends to the house – in short, it was clear that the chaste, the immaculate George Duckworth would be forced into the arms of whores. Needless to say he did not put it like that; and I could only conjure up in my virgin consciousness, dimly irradiated by having read the *Symposium* with Miss Case, horrible visions of the vices to which young men were driven whose sisters did not make them happy at home. So we went on talking for an hour or two. The end of it was that he begged me, and I agreed, to go a few nights later to the Dowager Marchioness of Sligo's ball. I had already been to May Week at Cambridge, and my recollections of gallopading round the room with Hawtrey, or sitting on the stairs and quizzing the dancers with Clive, were such as to make me wonder why Vanessa found dances in London so utterly detestable. A few nights later I discovered for myself. After two hours of standing about in Lady Sligo's ballroom, of waiting to be introduced to strange young men, of dancing a round with Conrad Russell or with Esmé Howard, of dancing very badly, of being left without a partner, of being told by George that I looked lovely but must hold myself upright, I retired to an ante-room and hoped that a curtain concealed me. For some time it did. At length old Lady Sligo discovered me, judged the situation for herself and being a kind old peeress with a face like a rubicund sow's carried me off to the dining-room, cut me a large slice of iced cake, and left me to devour it by myself in a corner.

Virginia Woolf, published 1978

From The Mill on the Floss

'Yet you might have sense enough to see that a brother who goes out into the world and mixes with men, necessarily knows better what is right and respectable for his sister than she knows herself . . .'

George Eliot, 1860

From William the Match-maker

'Let's go an' sit on the stile and see who can throw stones farthest,' [said William.]

They sat in a row on the stile. It counted ten to hit the telegraph post and fifteen to reach the further edge of the opposite field.

Ethel, who had been to the village to do the household shopping, came past when the game was in full swing.

'I'll tell father,' she said grimly to William. 'He said you oughtn't to throw stones.'

William looked her up and down with his most inscrutable expression.

''F it comes to that,' he said distantly, 'he said you oughtn't to wear high heels.'

Ethel flushed angrily and walked on.

William's spirits rose. It wasn't often he scored over Ethel and he feared that even now she would have her revenge.

He watched her go down the road. Coming back along the road was Mr March. As he met Ethel a deep flush and a sickly smile overspread his face. He stopped and spoke to her, gazing at her with a sheep-like air. Ethel passed on haughtily. He had recovered slightly when he reached the Outlaws, though traces of his flush still remained.

'Well,' he said with a loud laugh. 'Divorce or bigamy? Which is it to be? Ha, ha! Excellent!'

He put his walking stick against Ginger's middle and playfully pushed him off the stile backwards. Then he went on his way laughing loudly.

'I said he was cracked!' said Ginger climbing back to his perch.

'He'd jus' about suit Ethel then,' said William bitterly.

They sat in silence a few minutes. There was a far-away meditative look in William's eyes.

'I say,' he said at last, ''f Ethel married him she'd go away from our house and live in his, wun't she?'

'U-hum,' agreed Ginger absently as he tried to hit the second tree to the left of the telegraph post that counted five.

'I wish there was some way of makin' them fall in love with each other,' said William gloomily.

'Oh, there is, William,' said Joan. 'We've been learning it at school. Someone called Shakespeare wrote it. You keep saying to both of them that the other's in love with them and they fall in love and marry. I know. We did it last term. One of them was Beatrice and I forget the other.'

'You said it was Shakespeare,' said William.

'No, he's the one that tells about it.'

'Sounds a queer sort of tale to me,' said William severely. 'Couldn't you write to him and get it a bit plainer what to do?'

'Write to him!' jeered Ginger. 'He's dead. Fancy you not knowin' that! Fancy you not knowin' Shakespeare's dead!'

'Well, how was I to know he was dead? I can't know everyone's name what's dead, can I? I bet there's lots of dead folks' names what you don' know!'

'Oh, do you?' said Ginger. 'Well, I bet I know more dead folks' names than you do!'

'He said that anyway,' interposed Joan hastily and pacifically. 'He said that if you keep on making up nice things and saying that the other said it about them they fall in love and marry. It must be true because it's in a book.'

There was a look of set purpose in William's eyes.

'It'll take a bit of arrangin',' was the final result of his frowning meditation, 'but it might come off all right.'

Richmal Crompton, 1924

From The Younger Sister

'I'm sorry Jane sees anything to blame in my conduct,' replied Emma, meekly; 'but I do not know what she expected of me.'

'I told her she was far too sanguine,' continued Robert; 'but she would have it, that with proper attention, you might have succeeded in securing the young lord; [. . .] and, certainly, for an unprovided girl like you, it becomes an important duty to omit no opportunity of advancing your own interests, and those of your own family, by securing a good establishment when in your power.'

[. . .]

It was Penelope's turn to remain during dinner with her father, and Emma was once more in company with her repulsive brother. It was really with sensible reluctance that she sat down at the same table with him – but she struggled against the feeling, aware that it ought to be overcome if there was to be any future peace or comfort for her.

The dinner was more than plain – unfortunately it was almost entirely cold; but, in the hurry occasioned by the [last] illness of Mr Watson, the rest of his family might reasonably expect to be less comfortably accommodated than usual. Elizabeth had hardly given the subject a thought; and not at all indeed, until it was too late for amendment, beyond a steak hurriedly cooked for Robert's sake. But this was tough – tough as the table, so Robert said, and he had a particular dislike to cold mutton. His plate was pushed away with an air of uncontrollable disgust – as he sat eyeing the table with gloomy looks, whilst his sister good-humouredly apologized for the hardness of the fare.

'Shall I have the satisfaction of helping you to a little of this cow?' inquired he, balancing his knife and fork with his hand, and pointing with them to the condemned steak. 'I recommend you to try it, Elizabeth, and then you may, perhaps, remember another time, and make better provision for such unfortunate individuals as are compelled, through circumstances, to become your guests – you ought to be ashamed of yourself, Elizabeth –'

'Upon my word, Robert, I could not help it; I will try and give you a better dinner tomorrow; but it's not my fault entirely, that the steak is tough. I thought, perhaps, it would be; but it was the only thing we could dress – and I thought that you would like that better than nothing.'

'I cannot comprehend such bad management – why is not your

cook to dress a dinner for me? – what else had she to do of much importance? she can*not* be wanted by my father! For *me* – you will look very blank, I expect, when you come to live with me, if I set you down to such fare as this!'

Elizabeth had the sense and the forbearance to remain perfectly silent; and Robert, finding that all his indignation could not overcome impossibilities, or cook him a dinner where the materials were actually wanting, thought it best to make some attempts at eating; and proceeded, with an air of injured dignity, to devour the unfortunate subject of his wrath.

'I think Jane would be rather astonished if she knew what sort of dinner I have been compelled to make,' was his observation when he laid down his knife and fork. 'She would hardly expect to find me dining so contentedly off a tough old steak – ill-cooked, and no sauce. I always have observed in most houses, here especially, none are so badly provided for as the eldest sons. I suppose anything is good enough for them – it does not signify what I eat at all – I am only your brother, only the head of the house – only the man on whom you will be dependent when – but no matter, I hope you will fare better in my house, that's all!'

Mrs Hubback, 1850, on the basis of
Jane Austen's unfinished novel *Sanditon*

When a man was near death, word was sent to his wife's brothers, who immediately travelled to a place close to their sister. There they prepared a special knotted bark cloth and awaited final word. When they had heard of the death they came quickly to their sister's side and looked after her while the grave was dug and her husband's body placed within. The widow was given betel nut to chew, but no water or food while she sat by her husband's grave through the night until dawn. At dawn she was strangled; her brothers took the knotted bark cloth and while one sat on her lap holding her down, another placed the cloth so that one knot pressed against the windpipe while the others closed off the flow of blood to the brain.

Death was 'easy and quick'; the woman lost consciousness rapidly without struggle. The brothers then placed her body in the grave with her husband and closed the grave. (They were afterwards obliged to care for her orphans.)

C. Goodale, 'Siblings as Spouses: The Reproduction and Replacement of Kaulong Society', in *Siblingship in Oceania*, ed. Mac Marshall, 1983

A girl's first menstruation and the accompanying ceremonial take place in the husband's home. But her brothers must play a part in it and they are sent for [. . .] Her brothers build her a menstrual hut, which is stronger and better-constructed than are the menstrual huts of older married women; [. . .] for this first segregation a floor is built . . .

Margaret Mead, *Sex and Temperament in Three Primitive Societies*, 1935

I have always been a brother to my sisters. I have never punished them without reason, like if they didn't obey me, or because they talked back to my *papa*, or called me 'lousy black'. I am heartbroken at the thought of how many times I have beaten them. I want to ask their pardon, but when I see them I lose my courage. It makes me suffer because a man shouldn't beat a woman. But I only slapped them with my palm or the back of my hand. And when I slapped, it was only on the arm or the back of the head. And when I came home Consuelo would tell him that I had kicked her or hit her on the lung. *Ay!* my God! Those weren't caresses my father gave me because of those lies! On my word! I speak from my heart that I never hit her like that. She was a little liar then [. . .] when my sister accused me, [. . .] my *papa* thrashed me with that doubled electric cable that had copper wire inside and a knot on the end.

Oscar Lewis, *The Children of Sánchez*, 1962

From My Family and Other Animals

Leslie [. . .] decided to play the part of the outraged brother and kept appearing [. . .], brandishing a revolver and threatening to shoot Peter down like a dog if he dared to set foot in the house again. In the midst of all this Margo, tears trickling down her face, made tragic gestures and told us her life was blighted.

Gerald Durrell, 1959

From The Decameron

Know then that there were at Messina three young men, that were brothers and merchants, who were left very rich on the death of their father, who was of San Gimignano; and they had a sister, Lisabetta by name, a girl fair enough, and no less debonair, but whom, for some reason or another, they had not as yet bestowed in marriage. The three brothers had also in their shop a young Pisan, Lorenzo by name, who managed all their affairs, and who was so goodly of person and gallant, that Lisabetta bestowed many a glance upon him, and began to regard him with extraordinary favour; which Lorenzo marking from time to time, gave up all his other amours, and in like manner began to affect her, and so, their loves being equal, 'twas not long before they took heart of grace, and did that which each most desired. Wherein continuing to their no small mutual solace and delight, they neglected to order it with due secrecy, whereby one night as Lisabetta was going to Lorenzo's room, she [. . .] was observed by the eldest of the brothers, who, albeit much distressed by what he had learnt, yet, being a young man of discretion, was swayed by considerations more seemly, and, allowing no word to escape him, spent the night in turning the affair over in his mind in divers ways. On the morrow he told his brothers that which [. . .] he had observed in the night, which, that no shame might thence ensue either to them or to their sister, they after long consultation determined to pass over in silence [. . .] until such time as they in a safe and convenient manner might banish this disgrace from their sight [. . .]. Adhering to which purpose, they jested and laughed with Lorenzo as they had been wont; and after a while pretending that they were all three going forth of the city on pleasure, they took Lorenzo with them; and being come to a remote and very lonely spot [. . .] they took Lorenzo [. . .] and slew him, and buried him on such wise that none was ware of it. On their return to Messina they gave out that they had sent him away on business [. . .]. But as Lorenzo did not return, and Lisabetta questioned the brothers about him with great frequency and urgency [. . .] it so befell that one day [. . .] one of the brothers said: 'What means this? What hast thou to do with Lorenzo, that thou shouldst ask about him so often? Ask us no more, or we will give thee such answer as thou deservest.' So the girl, sick at heart and sorrowful, fearing she knew not what, asked no questions.

Boccaccio, translated by J. M. Rigg

From Isabella

Isabella/Lisabetta finds Lorenzo's head and takes it home . . .

Then in a silken scarf, – sweet with the dews
   Of precious flowers pluck'd in Araby,
And divine liquids come with odorous ooze
   Through the cold serpent-pipe refreshfully, –
She wrapp'd it up; and for its tomb did choose
   A garden-pot, wherein she laid it by,
And cover'd it with mould, and o'er it set
Sweet Basil, which her tears kept ever wet.

[. . .]

And furthermore, her brethren wonder'd much
   Why she sat drooping by the Basil green,
And why it flourish'd, as by magic touch;
   Greatly they wonder'd what the thing might mean:
They could not surely give belief, that such
   A very nothing would have power to wean
Her from her own fair youth, and pleasures gay,
And even remembrance of her love's delay.

Therefore they watch'd a time when they might sift
   This hidden whim; and long they watch'd in vain;
For seldom did she go to chapel-shrift,
   And seldom felt she any hunger-pain;
And when she left, she hurried back, as swift
   As bird on wing to breast its eggs again;
And, patient as a hen-bird, sat her there
Beside her Basil, weeping through her hair.

Yet they contriv'd to steal the Basil-pot,
   And to examine it in secret place;
The thing was vile with green and livid spot,
   And yet they knew it was Lorenzo's face:
The guerdon of their murder they had got,
   And so left Florence in a moment's space,
Never to turn again. – Away they went,
With blood upon their heads, to banishment.

O Melancholy, turn thine eyes away!
   O Music, Music, breathe despondingly!
O Echo, Echo, on some other day,
   From isles Lethean, sigh to us – O sigh!
Spirits of grief, sing not your 'Well-a-way!'
   For Isabel, sweet Isabel, will die;
Will die a death too lone and incomplete,
Now they have ta'en away her Basil sweet.

[. . .]

And so she pined, and so she died forlorn,
    Imploring for her Basil to the last.
No heart was there in Florence but did mourn
    In pity of her love, so overcast.
And a sad ditty of this story born
    From mouth to mouth through all the country pass'd:
Still is the burthen sung – 'O cruelty,
'To steal my Basil-pot away from me!'

John Keats, 1820

An Elopement

Zena, a young Pakistani woman, rejects the husband chosen for her by her family, and runs away with Jack, an Englishman.

'The first night we were away, I phoned Zena's family to tell them she was okay,' says Jack. 'Her brother came on and quite calmly told me that when we were found we would be in a few bin-liners. He said he had sold a car to get the money to find us. He told me that we were walking corpses. Then he said Zena's father had had a heart attack and was in hospital.' Jack immediately told Zena the news and they got together piles of 10p pieces and called every hospital in the area until they realized the story was untrue – a ploy to lure Zena home.

The B & B they stayed in those first few nights was the first of nineteen moves that the couple have made so far. A week after their departure, Jack phoned his mother to hear that four of Zena's brothers had come to her house after midnight one night, smashed the windows and hurled his mother (who they apparently knew was very sick) against the wall to 'introduce her to the man who was going to murder her son'.

'I felt so ashamed,' said Zena. 'We knew that they'd try to hunt us down, but both Jack's sister and mother had to be relocated after this. I was so angry with my family.'

Anna Blundy, *The Times*, Magazine, 14 January 1998

From Kinship and Marriage among the Ashanti

Brothers and sisters may joke with each other, tease each other, and even quarrel [. . .] without causing offence. This accent on informality is not found in any other kinship relation.

M. Fortes, 1950

Mozart and Nannerl

I hope you are well, my dear sister. When you receive this letter, my dear sister, that very evening the opera will have been performed, my dear sister. Think of me, my dear sister, and try as hard as you can to imagine that you, my dear sister, are hearing and seeing it too, my dear sister. That is hard, I admit, as it is already eleven o'clock. Otherwise I believe and do not doubt at all that during the day it is brighter than at Easter. We are lunching tomorrow, my dear sister, with Herr von Meyr, and why, do you think? Guess! Why because he has asked us. The rehearsal tomorrow is at the theatre, but Signor Castiglione, the impresario, has begged me not to tell anyone about it; otherwise a whole crowd of people will come running in and we do not want this. So, my child, I beg you not to mention it to anyone, my child, otherwise a whole crowd of people will come running in, and we do not want this. That reminds me. Have you heard what happened here? I will tell you. We left Count Firmian's today to go home and when we reached our street, we opened the hall door and what do you think we did? Why, we went in. Farewell, my little lung. I kiss you my liver, and remain as always, my stomach, your unworthy

frater ⎱
brother ⎰ Wolfgang

Mozart to his sister Maria Anne (Nannerl), 18 December 1772,
translated by Emily Anderson, 1966

I am delighted to hear that Mamma and Jack Pudding are cheerful and in good spirits. Alas, we poor orphans have to mope for boredom and fiddle away the time somehow or other. [...] I have no good news to send from home. So I kiss Mamma's hands and to you, you rascal! you villain! I give a juicy kiss and I remain Mamma's obedient daughter and your sister who is living in hopes – Marie Anne Mozart

Miss Pimpes too is living in hopes, for she stands or sits at the door whole half-hours on end and thinks every minute that you are going to come. All the same she is quite well, eats, drinks, sleeps, shits and pisses.

Nannerl to Mozart

Charles and Mary Lamb

... of afternoons we pick up primroses at Dalston, and Mary corrects me when I call 'em cowslips ...

Charles, mocking Mary's handwriting

The reason why my brother's so severe,
Vincentio is – my brother has no *ear* [. . .]
Of common tunes he knows not anything,
Nor 'Rule Britannia' from 'God save the King'.
He rail at Handel! He the gamut quiz!
I'd lay my life he knows not what it is.

Mary, teasing Charles on his lack of ear

From The Lake Poets

Mr J—, a fine towering figure, six feet high, massy and columnar in his proportions, happened to be walking, a little in advance, with Wordsworth; Miss Wordsworth and myself being in the rear; and from the nature of the conversation which then prevailed in our front rank, something or other about money, devises, buying and selling, we of the rearguard thought it requisite to preserve this arrangement for a space of three miles or more; during which time, at intervals, Miss Wordsworth would exclaim, in a tone of vexation, 'Is it possible, – can that be William! How very mean he looks!' And she did not conceal a mortification that seemed really painful, until I, for my part, could not forbear laughing outright at the serious interest which she carried into this trifle. She was, however, right, as regarded the mere visual judgement. Wordsworth's figure, with all its defects, was brought into powerful relief by one which had been cast in a more square and massy mould; and in such a case it impressed a spectator with a sense of absolute meanness, more especially when viewed from behind, and not counteracted by his countenance.

Thomas de Quincey, 1863

Intimacies: a Sister's Tale

Does being famous mean you can devalue those around you and rewrite history for even more personal gain? In the article written about my brother, Hanif Kureishi, in Weekend *Guardian*, he has sold his family down the line.

The article gives a false impression of our family life. We lived in a pleasant semi, down a quiet cul-de-sac in Bromley. My grandfather was not a 'cloth-cap working-class' person. He owned three shops locally and he was a kind, warm man.

My mother never worked in a shoe factory (there are no shoe factories in Bromley). She had several part-time jobs in the beginning, one of which was working for about three months in Russell and Bromley to help pay my school fees, as I went to a ballet school. My mother, after she left school, went to art college until the age of twenty-one: she is an intelligent, articulate and not uncultured person. I feel deeply saddened that it should come to this because I have felt so proud of Hanif and his achievements and have followed his success closely. I have felt and still do that, after our painful childhood where we both experienced a great deal of racism, Hanif deserved his success and I am thrilled that he has made it in a white world.

As regards my father and Hanif: to be kind to Hanif I won't tell you everything, but I will focus on the lies in this article. Obviously, your journalist has got the idea from Hanif that our father was a special kind of man, and he was that, but he certainly wasn't 'particularly devoted to him'. He loved us all equally.

Furthermore, my father was angry when *The Buddha of Suburbia* came out as he felt that Hanif had robbed him of his dignity and he didn't speak to Hanif for about a year. The description of my father at the end of his life as a 'bitter man' is grossly and cruelly exaggerated. My father led a full and active life. He had his grandson, whom he adored, he had me close by and we used to talk for hours in the garden about writing and life. He and my mother went on holidays, went out for meals and generally enjoyed themselves as best they could, despite my father's illnesses.

It is a shame that I have had to write this letter to you, but if our life has to become public knowledge at least get it right.

The memory of my father I hold very dear and I will do anything in my power to ensure that it is not fabricated for the entertainment of the public or for Hanif's profit, and that the feelings of my mother and I are not hurt more than they have been already.

And, by the way, my name is Yasmin, not 'Jasmine'.

Yasmin Kureishi
Kent

Letter to *Guardian*, 7 May 1998

From Tom Jones

'I hope, madam,' cries Sophia, with a little elevation of voice, I shall never do anything to dishonour my family; but as for Mr Blifil, whatever may be the consequence, I am resolved against him, and no force shall prevail in his favour.'

. Western, who had been within hearing during the greater part of the preceding dialogue, had now exhausted all his patience; he therefore entered the room in a violent passion, crying, 'D—n me then if *shatunt* ha' un, d—n me if *shatunt*, that's all – that's all – D—n me if *shatunt*.'

Mrs Western had collected a sufficient quantity of wrath for the use of Sophia; but she now transferred it all to the squire. 'Brother,' said she, 'it is astonishing that you will interfere in a matter which you had totally left to my negotiation. Regard to my family hath made me take upon myself to be the mediating power, in order to rectify those mistakes in policy which you have committed in your daughter's education. For, brother, it is you; it is your preposterous conduct which hath eradicated all the seeds that I had formerly sown in her tender mind. – It is you yourself who have taught her disobedience.' – 'Blood!' cries the squire, foaming at the mouth, 'you are enough to conquer the patience of the devil! Have I ever taught my daughter disobedience? – Here she stands; speak honestly, girl, did ever I bid you be disobedient to me? Have not I done everything to humour, and to gratify you, and to make you obedient to me? And very obedient to me she was when a little child, before you took her in hand and spoiled her, by filling her head with a pack of Court notions. – Why – why – why – did not I overhear you telling her she must behave like a princess? You have made a Whig of the girl; and how should her father, or anybody else, expect any obedience from her?' 'Brother,' answered Mrs Western, with an air of great disdain, 'I cannot express the contempt I have for your politics of all kinds; but I will appeal likewise to the young lady herself, whether I have ever taught her any principles of disobedience. On the contrary, niece, have I not endeavoured to inspire you with a true idea of the several relations in which a human creature stands in society? Have I not taken infinite pains to shew you, that the law of nature hath enjoined a duty on children to their parents? Have I not told you what Plato says on that subject? – A subject on which you was so notoriously ignorant when you came first under my care, that I verily believe you did not know the relation between a daughter and a father.' ' 'Tis a lie,' answered Western. 'The girl is no such fool, as to live to eleven years old without knowing she was her father's relation.' 'O more than Gothic ignorance,' answered the lady. – 'And as for your manners, brother, I must tell you, they deserve a cane.' 'Why then you may gi' it me, if you think you are able,' cries the squire! 'nay, I suppose your niece there will be ready to help you.' 'Brother,' said Mrs Western, 'tho' I despise you beyond expression, yet I shall endure your insolence no longer; so I desire my coach may be got ready immediately, for I am resolved to leave your house this very morning.' 'And a good riddance too,' answered he; 'I can bear your insolence no longer, an you come to that. Blood! it is almost enough of itself, to make my daughter undervalue my sense, when she hears you telling me every minute you despise me.' 'It is impossible, it is impossible,' cries the aunt, 'no one can undervalue such a boor.' 'Boar,' answered the squire, 'I am no boar; no, nor ass; no, nor rat neither, madam. Remember that – I am no rat. I am a true Englishman, and not of your Hanover breed, that have eat up the nation.' 'Thou art one of those wise men,' cries she, 'whose nonsensical principles have undone the nation; by weakening the hands of our Government at home, and by discouraging our friends, and encouraging our enemies abroad.' 'Ho! are you come back to your politics,' cries the squire, 'as for those I despise them as much as I do a f—t.' Which last word he accompanied and graced with the very action, which, of all others, was the most proper to it. And whether it was this word, or the contempt exprest for her politics, which most affected Mrs Western, I will not determine; but she flew into the most violent rage, uttered phrases improper to be here related, and instantly burst out of the house.

Henry Fielding, 1749

From Dibs in Search of Self

'Here I am again!' Dibs exclaimed when he came into the waiting room the following Thursday. 'There won't be many more times to come before we go away for the summer.'

'Yes. About three more times, counting today,' I said. 'Then we will both go away for a vacation.'

'We go way out on the island,' Dibs said. 'I expect to like my vacation this year. And Grandmother plans to spend the summer with us this year instead of her usual vacation time. I like that idea.'

He walked around the playroom. Then he picked up the doll. 'Well, here is sister,' he exclaimed, as though he had never seen the doll before. 'Isn't she a brat of a thing? I'm going to get rid of her. I'll get her to eat some nice rice pudding only I will have poison in it and I'll poison her and she'll go away to stay for ever and ever.'

'You want to get rid of the sister?' I remarked.

[. . .]

He went over to the easel and picked up a jar of paint and a glass. He poured some paint into the glass, added a little water, stirred it slowly and carefully. Then he added other colours to the mixture, stirring it well. 'This is poison for the sister,' he said. 'She'll think it is cereal and she'll eat it and then that will be the end of her.'

'So that is poison for the sister and after she eats it, then that will be the end of her?'

Dibs nodded. Then he looked at me. 'I won't give it to her just yet a while,' he said. 'I'll wait and think it over.'

Virginia Axline, 1966

From Children of the People

The relationship between brothers and sisters is perhaps the most curious and interesting of all the pairs. Feelings are undoubtedly polarized in two directions. At one pole there is much attraction, much genuine warmth and affection; at the other, periodic friction is the rule. The latter stems from Navaho social organization, which gives each the duty of interfering in the life of the other and causes each to be caught in an emotional crossfire. [. . .]

The strength of the taboos on physical contact between mature brothers and sisters and the gossip about incest suggest that, in the isolated conditions under which most Navaho children grow up, the incipient sexual attraction between brother and sister is strong and temptation must be sharply curtailed. It may be that the popular form of mating where a brother and sister from one family marry a sister and brother from another is an unconscious substitution for incestuous desires. Certainly the training in avoidance of physical contact begins early and is carried to what are, from the white point of view, extremes. One Navaho man in his thirties described the attitude and practice of his people as follows.

When girls are very small, we teach them to keep their skirts down. We say, 'If anyone sees up your legs they will go blind.' When we all grow up so we think about these things, we are told not to touch our sister. After she or her brother is married, if she asks for a shoe or a plate he can't hand it to her. He puts it on the ground first. Then she takes it. If she wants to change her skirt she has to go outside or wait till her brother is gone. They say a brother must never see her knees or her breasts. [If she has a baby does she nurse it if her brother is in the hogan?] Yes, but she covers it up.

Clyde Kluckhohn and Dorothea Leighton, 1947

From Moments of Being

There was a small looking-glass in the hall at Talland House. It had, I remember, a ledge with a brush on it. By standing on tiptoe I could see my face in the glass. When I was six or seven, perhaps, I got into the habit of looking at my face in the glass. But I only did this if I was sure that I was alone. I was ashamed of it. A strong feeling of guilt seemed naturally attached to it. [. . .] Another memory, also of the hall, may help to explain this. There was a slab outside the dining-room door for standing dishes upon. Once when I was very small Gerald Duckworth lifted me on to this, and as I sat there he began to explore my body. I can remember the feel of his hand going under my clothes; going firmly and steadily lower and lower. I remember how I hoped that he would stop; how I stiffened and wriggled as his hand approached my private parts. But it did not stop. His hand explored my private parts too. I remember resenting, disliking it – what is the word for so dumb and mixed a feeling? It must have been strong, since I still recall it. This seems to show that a feeling about certain parts of the body; how they must not be touched; how it is wrong to allow them to be touched; must be instinctive. It proves that Virginia Stephen was not born on 25 January 1882, but was born many thousands of years ago; and had from the very first to encounter instincts already acquired by thousands of ancestresses in the past.

Virginia Woolf, published in 1978

The Marvellous History of Major Weir and His Sister

Major Weir was burnt between Edinburgh and Leith at a place called the Gallow-Lee on Thursday 14 April 1670.

There was one minister in the city who could never be persuaded to speak with [Major Weir] in prison. But no sooner was he dead than he went to the tollbooth and called for his sister, who had some remorse. He told her, that her brother was burnt and how he died. She believed nothing of it; but after many attestations, she asked, where his staff was? For, it seems, she knew that his strength and life lay therein. He told her, it was burnt with him. Whereupon, notwithstanding of her age, she nimbly and in a furious rage fell on her knees, uttering words horrible to be remembered. And in rising up, as she was desired, her raging agony closed with these words; 'Oh sir, I know he is with the devils; for with them he lived.' She entreated that minister to assist her, and attend her to her death, which at her violent importunity, he yielded unto. She avouched that from her being sixteen years of age to her fiftieth year her brother had had the incestuous use of her, and then loathed her for her age. She was pretty old at this time, and he, when he died, was about seventy. He asked her if ever she was with child by him? She declared [. . .] he hindered that by means abominable, which she was beginning to relate, when the preacher stopped her [. . .]

In often and returned visits she was interrogated, if she had any hand in her brother's devilry? She declared but in a passive way, and gave this for an instance. A fiery chariot or coach [. . .] was coming to his door, at broad day, a stranger invited him and her to go to visit a friend in Dalkeith, a small town about four miles from Edinburgh. They both entered and went forward in their visit; at which time [. . .] one came and whispered something in his ear which affected him. They both returned after the same manner that they had gone out. And Weir going after to make some visits, told them he had strong apprehensions, that that day the King's forces were routed at Worcester, which within two or three days was confirmed by the post. She affirmed that none saw the coach but themselves. The devil hath wrought far greater ferlies in his time than this.

She knew much of the enchanted staff; for by it he was enabled to pray, to commit filthinesses not to be named, yea even to reconcile neighbours, man and wife, when at variance. She oft hid it from him, and because without it he could do nothing, he would threaten and vow to discover her incest, fearing which she would deliver it again.

[. . .]

In the morning before her execution, she told the minister she resolved to die with all the shame she could, to expiate under mercy her shameful life; this he understood to be an ingenuous confession of her sins, in opposition to her brother's despair and desperate silence, to which he did encourage her [. . .] Ascending up the ladder she spoke somewhat confusedly, of her sins, of her brother and his enchanting staff. And with a ghostly countenance, beholding a multitude of spectators all wondering and some weeping, she spake aloud. 'There are many here this day, wondering and greeting for me, but alas, few mourn for a broken —'; at which words many seemed angry; some called to her to mind higher concerns; and I have heard it said, that the preacher declared he had much ado to keep a composed countenance. The executioner falling about his duty, she prepared to die stark naked; then, and not before, were her words relating to shame understood; the hangman struggled with her to keep on her cloaths and she struggled with him to have them off; at last he was forced to throw over open-faced, which afterwards he covered with a cloth . . .

George Sinclair, 1685

343

From The Second Book of Samuel

So Amnon lay down, and made himself sick: and when the king was come to see him, Amnon said unto the king, 'I pray thee, let Tamar my sister come, and make me a couple of cakes in my sight, that I may eat at her hand.'

Then David sent home to Tamar, saying, 'Go now to thy brother Amnon's house, and dress him meat.'

So Tamar went to her brother Amnon's house; and he was laid down. And she took flour, and kneaded it, and made cakes in his sight, and did bake the cakes. And she took a pan, and poured them out before him; but he refused to eat. And Amnon said, 'Have out all men from me.' And they went out every man from him.

And Amnon said unto Tamar, 'Bring the meat into the chamber, that I may eat of thine hand.' And Tamar took the cakes which she had made, and brought them into the chamber to Amnon her brother. And when she had brought them unto him to eat, he took hold of her, and said unto her, 'Come lie with me, my sister.'

And she answered him, 'Nay, my brother, do not force me; for no such thing ought to be done in Israel: do not thou this folly. And I, whither shall I cause my shame to go? And as for thee, thou shalt be as one of the fools in Israel. Now therefore, I pray thee, speak unto the king; for he will not withhold me from thee.' Howbeit he would not hearken unto her voice: but, being stronger than she, forced her, and lay with her.

Then Amnon hated her exceedingly; so that the hatred wherewith he hated her was greater than the love wherewith he had loved her. And Amnon said unto her, 'Arise, be gone.'

And she said unto him, 'There is no cause: this evil in sending me away is greater than the other that thou didst unto me.'

But he would not hearken unto her. Then he called his servant that ministered unto him, and said, 'Put now this woman out from me, and bolt the door after her.' And she had a garment of divers colours upon her: for with such robes were the king's daughters

that were virgins apparelled. Then his servant brought her out, and
bolted the door after her.

The Bible, 1610 translation

Had you been a Nun – and I a Monk – that we might have talked
through a grate instead of across the sea – no matter – my voice
and my heart are ever thine –

Lord Byron to Augusta Leigh, 17 September 1816

From 'Tis Pity She's a Whore

GIOVANNI. Come, sister, lend your hand; let's walk together;
  I hope you need not blush to walk with me;
  Here's none but you and I.
ANNABELLA. How's this?
GIOVANNI. I' faith, I mean no harm.
ANNABELLA. Harm?
GIOVANNI. No, good faith.
  How is it with thee?
ANNABELLA. I trust he be not frantic (*aside*).
  I am very well, brother.
GIOVANNI. Trust me, but I am sick; I fear so sick,
  'Twill cost my life.
ANNABELLA. Mercy forbid it! 'tis not so, I hope.
GIOVANNI. I think you love me, sister.
ANNABELLA. Yes, you know I do.
GIOVANNI. I know it, indeed – you are very fair.
ANNABELLA. Nay, then I see you have a merry sickness.
GIOVANNI. That's as it proves. The poets feign, I read,
  That Juno for her forehead did exceed
  All other goddesses; but I durst swear
  Your forehead exceeds hers, as hers did theirs.

345

ANNABELLA. 'Troth, this is pretty.

GIOVANNI. Such a pair of stars
    As are thine eyes, would, like Promethean fire,
    If gently glanced, give life to senseless stones.

ANNABELLA. Fie upon you!

GIOVANNI. The lily and the rose, most sweetly strange,
    Upon your dimple cheeks do strive for change:
    Such lips would tempt a saint: such hands as those
    Would make an anchorite lascivious.

ANNABELLA. Do you mock me, or flatter me?

GIOVANNI. If you would see a beauty more exact
    Than art can counterfeit, or nature frame,
    Look in your glass, and there behold your own.

ANNABELLA. Oh, you are a trim youth!

GIOVANNI. Here! (*Offers his dagger to her.*)

ANNABELLA. What to do?

GIOVANNI. And here's my breast; strike home!
    Rip up my bosom, there thou shalt behold
    A heart, in which is writ the truth I speak –
    Why stand you?

ANNABELLA. Are you earnest?

GIOVANNI. Yes, most earnest.
    You cannot love?

ANNABELLA. Whom?

GIOVANNI. Me. My tortured soul
    Hath felt affliction in the heat of death.
    Oh, Annabella, I am quite undone!
    The love of thee, my sister, and the view
    Of thy immortal beauty, have untuned
    All harmony both of my rest and life.
    Why do you not strike?

ANNABELLA. Forbid it, my just fears!
    If this be true, 'twere fitter I were dead.

GIOVANNI. True! Annabella; 'tis no time to jest.
    I have too long suppressed my hidden flames,
    That almost have consum'd me; I have spent
    Many a silent night in sighs and groans;

Ran over all my thoughts, despised my fate,
Reason'd against the reasons of my love,
Done all that smooth-cheek'd virtue could advise,
But found all bootless: 'tis my destiny
That you must either love, or I must die.

ANNABELLA. Comes this in sadness from you?

GIOVANNI. Let some mischief
Befall me soon, if I dissemble aught.

ANNABELLA. You are my brother Giovanni.

GIOVANNI. You
My sister Annabella; I know this.
And could afford you instance why to love
So much the more for this; to which intent
Wise nature first in your creation meant
To make you mine; else't had been sin and foul
To share one beauty to a double soul.
Nearness in birth and blood, doth but persuade
A nearer nearness in affection.
I have ask'd counsel of the holy church,
Who tells me I may love you; and, 'tis just,
That, since I may, I should; and will, yes will:
Must I now live, or die?

ANNABELLA. Live; thou hast won
The field, and never fought: what thou hast urged,
My captive heart had long ago resolv'd.
I blush to tell thee, – but I'll tell thee now – [. . .]

John Ford, 1633

From The Coffey Sisters

For the first eleven years of her life, Janice Coffey's sole siblings were all brothers – a fraternal twin and three older boys. She was especially close to the brother who was fifteen years her senior – the one who bought her the most wonderful little outfits, read her stories, and played dolls with her. Then, when she was four years old, he suddenly vanished, like a drawing on her Magic Slate. For the next seven years, their only contact was a monthly telephone call.

[. . .]

One day, without warning, her mother revealed the family secret. 'We were in the kitchen,' Janice recalls. 'My father left the room, and, as tactfully as she could, Mother told us that our brother was no longer our brother; he was now our sister, Elizabeth. [. . .]'

The reunion was scheduled for a big party that Elizabeth was giving to celebrate her twenty-sixth birthday. Except for the new bumps on her chest, Janice didn't think that Elizabeth looked all that different.

'We rebonded instantly,' Janice says. 'To me the whole thing, honestly, was no more than a name change. I was so happy to have this person back in my life, it never really fazed me. Gender wasn't the issue; the person was the issue.'

[. . .]

'Quite frankly,' Elizabeth says, 'I think we always related as sisters. I came back into Janice's life at a time when I was able to enrich her and myself through our relationship. If Janice were not my sister, she'd be my friend. We have so much in common. Both of us care about music, painting, reading. And then there were all the sister things we shared.'

Carol Saline, 1994

8

Ageing and Death

On my mother's side of the family, over the generations I know about, the hereditary doom has prevented sisters heading for the sunset, hand in hand. It's put paid, already, to the chance of my twin and me doing it. And now even my youngest sister has had her brush with the said doom, it's reduced our chances, too. It's very sad.

Some sisters, of course, have no more desire for each other's company in old age than they ever had. My aunts Olive and Ruth to name but two. But for others, it's where sisterhood really kicks in; the more so for sisters brought up in the nineteenth century, whose friendships always were with their siblings rather than anyone outside. My grandmother saw her siblings frequently throughout their lives. Out of thirteen, only three produced children, and of those only her descendants have continued beyond my generation: a strange outcome for such an abundance of offspring. She, though the fifth out of six daughters, was very much the mother in her family. She found furniture and a housekeeper for one unmarried clerical brother, and entertained all of her ageing siblings as often as she could. Aunt Augusta came for tea every Sunday till she died. Aunt Janey, much the most fun, according to my father, visited from Maidenhead almost as often. I wish I'd known Aunt Janey. But since my grandmother was fifty when my father was born, this whole generation – although many of them achieved a full life span, unlike my mother's lot – was also way out of sight of his children.

God knows how many ailments they suffered; I only know about Aunt Augusta's rheumatism because it led to her falling under a bus. One of the lesser charms of ageing, as I'm beginning to be aware, is previously unseen signs of disintegration appearing in contemporaries; how much more distressing to watch them appearing in your siblings and also in yourself. Having watched my ex-mother-in-law and her brothers oversee each other's decline, it's an aspect of sisterly sharing and mutual support I'm not looking forward to.

Sometimes even inimical sisters bury their differences when ageing. Who else is there who understands the past, who can connect you to it? Making sense of the past gets more important the older you get. It's not the twenty-year-olds who start obsessively comparing memories, let alone chasing up family history. It's much older sisters who know that if they don't pick each other's brains now, if they don't remind each other lovingly of this or that or the other, it will soon be too late to complete the pattern. This is all about ordering, making sense of lifetimes, I think.

And then there's the matter of familiarity. The business of making new friends gets more wearing with age, or so I'm told. Sisters, on the other hand, can be shrugged on comfortably, like old sweaters. In the sociological literature, ageing sisters see far more of each other than brothers do, and far more than they see of their brothers, apart from bachelor brothers. Not all meetings are comfortable. Ancient tensions, old antipathies, can surface – Katherine Anne Porter's child observes with amazement her grandmother bickering with her great-aunt the way that she bickers with her own sister. And though younger sisters may still need care from their elder sisters, they may find, like the younger of Sylvia McCurdy's Victorian sisters, that having been dominated all their lives, power has now shifted in their favour. On the other hand, where two sisters have lived together since childhood, the relationship is much like a marriage. They finish each other's sentences, read each other's thoughts. If one dies the other does not know how to live without her. And even when they haven't lived together for years, a living sister can find herself missing a dead one at any moment, as Margaret Mead's mother, quoted in the section on sisterhood, misses hers.

My first literary agent lived most of her life with her youngest sister. They were a splendid pair. The younger, an ex-nightclub hostess, who spoke with a drawl, smoked cigarettes in long holders, and constantly telephoned her bookie, wrote sentimental books about Napoleon's sisters. She seemed the tougher of the two. This was not so. Her sister, the successful agent, was much less temperamental and fragile, altogether more worldly. Though a fervent Zionist, she did not, like her sister, go to synagogue, and certainly did not keep kosher – the meat that arrived in dripping parcels from a butcher in Eastbourne was for her sister. The younger sister died first, luckily; she would have been lost without the elder. For Joyce herself it was worse than widowhood. Even then I could see that the death of such a sister takes away still more than the death of a husband does. The spirit and humour with which Joyce confronted the loss not only of her adult life but also of her childhood could not keep her alive for long; she died less than seven months later. Similarly, it does not seem to me coincidental that my mother's sister, my Aunt Janet, had her bout of breast cancer not long after my mother died; or that she remained peculiar over the ten years or so she managed to survive it.

These long lives and short deaths of sisters who are as if 'married' to each other may be one thing. But the distress of the one at the other's death is only a more extreme version of the grief that affects most sisters on the death of a sibling. Such pain is not confined to adults, let alone ageing adults. The death of a sibling even in infancy, even before the birth of other children, can affect them and their elders in profound ways, not least because of the effect on their parents. My elder aunt's relationship with her mother was blighted by the death of her elder brother before she was born. Such children may find themselves resented, as she was; alternatively, they may be expected to take their dead sibling's place, no matter how unlike her. The way my twin and I were haunted in our different ways by the baby brother we never saw is not untypical, I suspect. Before the twentieth century, a much higher rate of child and infant mortality would have left many more children, if not most, confronting the loss of sisters and brothers of all ages, throughout childhood.

But grief for siblings at any age has always been underrated. My grief for my twin was not underrated – the word 'twin' arouses different levels of interest and sympathy – but it would have been different if I had lost a mere sister at the same age. The grief of children, especially, is vastly underestimated. Many are expected to comfort their parents, rather than being comforted themselves. No one addresses their pain – let alone what transpires very often, their sense of guilt. A family history says of my eight-year-old father, after the death of his two elder brothers in the First World War, that he was 'too young to realize fully the grief that it brought to his parents'. This is the same child who, being told of the likely loss of his favourite of the two, flung himself down on the path in Kensington Gardens and couldn't be shifted for more than ten minutes. And the same old man whose eyes fill with tears when he talks about the First World War. What his sisters felt about the deaths, the grief of which permeated my own childhood in one way or another, I don't know. They never referred to them. When the younger one died ten years ago, at well over ninety, the last of a family which, like so many in that generation – like Vera Brittain quoted here – had known so much premature loss, my father howled at her funeral.

Loss of brothers in war, of course, is an experience sisters have always had to face; though not to the extent that they did during the 1914–18 war. In more recent wars, civilians – sisters – have been among those lost. All discussion of our war-ridden century underrates, I think, the long-term effect of these myriad deaths on our collective psyche, and the effect of that traumatized psyche on events. The mortality of soldiers in Vietnam, as in another piece here, mortality has influenced American foreign policy ever since.

In the past, of course, illness was more likely to strike sisters down before their time – and often did; tuberculosis especially, as with the Brontës. Today, if less commonly, breast cancer is a more likely culprit. Though I am grateful for the fact that members of my family tend to get twenty more years before that beast devours us, Ruth Picardie's death reverberates with me for obvious reasons; I will let Justine Picardie's account of it stand for the experience of all of us. Such very early death is especially shocking, of course, not least because of the young children often left behind. For siblings, in particular, it means the premature loss of a shared childhood, before anyone has considered comparing notes. My sister and I never got round to comparing notes, for all our extra years. Even this week, an old schoolfriend phoned out of the blue, and before I could catch myself I thought, 'I must tell Judy . . .'; the sense of loss acute all over again. No one else, anywhere, knows the history that this phone call invoked.

A. AGEING SISTERS

From Family Life of Old People

A widow of sixty-five lived alone in a flat adjoining another occupied by her single sister. Once on one visit to the home the latter was seen. She had wild, staring eyes, a croaky voice, wiry grey hair sticking out from her head like a brush, and one yellow tooth in an otherwise toothless mouth. The widow said her sister was 'funny in the head' and she assumed the role of protector, getting the shopping, helping with the cleaning and keeping her company. 'She spends an evening with me. We talk about our home life when we were children and have a good laugh, remembering things.'

Peter Townsend, 1957

The Lennox Sisters

Nothing but a mother or a sister can inspire that sort of friendship that occupies the mind so much late in life.

Sarah Lennox

I spent three hours yesterday with my two dear sisters. All hearts opened to each other's griefs. Our sorrows and our comforts all passed before us in review for their early childhood. Oh what a heartfelt satisfaction to hear them say as they both held me in their arms that the precepts I had early instilled had been of much use to them and been the comfort and support of their lives, that they owed more to me than any human being . . . I found both these dear hearts in perfect unison with my own. Griefs have this effect!

Emily Lennox to her daughter Lucy, November 1804

From Buddenbrooks

But far more remarkable were two other extraordinary old creatures, twins, who went about hand in hand through the town doing good deeds, in shepherdess hats out of the eighteenth century and faded clothes out of the long, long ago. They were named Gerhardt, and asserted that they descended in a direct line from Paul Gerhardt. People said they were by no means poor; but they lived wretchedly and gave away all they had. 'My dears,' remarked the Frau Consul who was sometimes rather ashamed of them, 'God sees the heart, I know; but your clothes are really a little – one must take some thought for oneself.' But she could not prevent them kissing their elegant friend on the brow with the forbearing, yearning, pitying superiority of the poor in heart over the worldly great who seek salvation. They were not at all stupid. In their homely shrivelled heads – for all the world like ancient parrots – they had bright soft brown eyes and they looked out at the world with a wonderful expression of gentleness and understanding. Their hearts were full of amazing wisdom. They knew that in the last day all our beloved gone before us to God will come with song and salvation to fetch us home. They spoke the words 'the Lord' with the fluent authority of early Christians, as if they had heard out of the Master's own mouth the words. 'Yet a little while and ye shall see me.' They possessed the most remarkable theories concerning inner light and intuition and the transmission of thought. One of them, named Lea, was deaf, and yet she nearly always knew what was being talked about!

It was usually the deaf Gerhardt who read aloud at the Jerusalem evenings, and the ladies found that she read beautifully and very affectingly. She took out of her bag an old book of a very disproportionate shape, much taller than it was broad, with an inhumanly chubby presentment of her ancestor in the front. She held it in both hands and read in a tremendous voice, in order to catch a little herself of what she read. It sounded as if the wind were imprisoned in the chimney: ' "If Satan me would swallow." '

'Goodness!' thought Tony Grünlich, 'how could Satan want to swallow her?' But she said nothing and devoted herself to the pudding, wondering if she herself would ever become as ugly as the two Miss Gerhardts.

Thomas Mann, translated by H. T. Lowe Porter, 1924

From The Crommarty Sisters

'We never separated too much,' Margaret reckons. 'We's always been side by side. You know how it is when you got a younger sister and your father tells you to be together and love one another. In them days you did what you was told, so we never got too far apart. Never fought much either. What we gonna fight for? We was raised not to fight. Came up in the church and never knew much else.'

Once upon a time, these eighty-something sisters did everything and went everywhere together. Now they go nowhere and feel blessed simply to still be together. Their parents are long gone; of the eleven children in the family – Margaret was the eighth and Bernetta the youngest – their only remaining sibling is a ninety-five-year-old brother in a nursing home. Their husbands, divorced, are forgotten. 'If they weren't right, I didn't stay with them,' Bernetta declares. Neither has children. What they do have is a deep faith and an unconditional commitment to one other that makes it pointless to paraphrase the biblical question and ask, *Am I my sister's keeper?*

[. . .]

'I'm gonna tell you, Margaret does *everything* for me,' Bernetta says with a tired wave of her hand. 'I sit in this chair. I can't go get nothing. She gives me something to eat. Helps me wash myself. I don't know what to do but love her.'

Their daily routine rarely varies. Margaret rises each day around seven a.m., folds up the roll-away bed she sleeps on and wheels it into the front hall, where it remains until she pushes it back into the living-room every night so her sister won't be alone. Then she prepares their breakfast from food a nephew brings once or twice a week.

'Bernetta don't like cereal, so I make potatoes and eggs, or hash and eggs. Maybe toast. Before we eat, I bring her teeth and some water to wash her mouth. I has to give her all her medications – three pills before she eats, for her sugar and something else, and four more after she eats. I clean up from breakfast, dusts a little, makes her bed. Then Bernetta needs to be washed. I can't get her to the bathroom. I bring in a pan of water, wash her down, and put on a clean nightgown and robe. I wash up the same way. Can't get in the tub myself 'cause I can't get out. Besides, if I went upstairs to shower and fell, who would hear me? I is supposed to soak her foot every morning in warm water and she should be greased all over 'cause she's so dry but I can't do more than her foot. Comes the evening, I read my Bible and pray.'

'I'm always telling her sit down and rest. Seems there's nothing Margaret hates doing for me.'

'Sometimes I say I ain't gonna do so and so, but I get right up and does it anyway. If I weren't here, I don't know where she'd be or who'd look after her.'

Lately Bernetta's mind has begun to wander, making her dependent on Margaret not just for her medications but also for her memories.

'Did I used to sing in the choir, Margaret?'

'Yes, you surely did, honey.'

'What did we sing?'

'We sang "Jesus loves me."'

And in reedy, off-key voices, they hold hands and sing, 'Jesus loves me. Yes, Jesus loves me, for the Bible tells me so. Oh yes, God is real. He's real in my so-oo-ul.'

Though the memories are foggy, Margaret and Bernetta love to talk about the past and sometimes even about the present. But they rarely talk about the future.

'Lots of sisters don't look after each other like we do, Bernetta.'

'I didn't know that. Why not?'

'Because they wasn't raised like we was to stick together. We're blood.'

'Yes, that's true. But we is *old* blood. And you wouldn't leave me nohow 'cause we always been close. Very close.' Bernetta raises her index and middle fingers and squeezes them together. 'This close,' she says. And they both grin.

Carol Saline, 1994

From The Daughters of the Late Colonel

Father would never forgive them. That was what they felt more than ever when, two mornings later, they went into his room to go through his things. They had discussed it quite calmly. It was even down on Josephine's list of things to be done. *Go through father's things and settle about them.* But that was a very different matter from saying after breakfast:

'Well, are you ready, Con?'

'Yes, Jug – when you are.'

'Then I think we'd better get it over.'

It was dark in the hall. It had been a rule for years never to disturb father in the morning, whatever happened. And now they were going to open the door without knocking even . . . Constantia's eyes were enormous at the idea; Josephine felt weak in the knees.

'You – you go first,' she gasped, pushing Constantia.

But Constantia said, as she always had said on those occasions, 'No, Jug, that's not fair. You're eldest.'

Josephine was just going to say – what at other times she wouldn't have owned to for the world – what she kept for her very last weapon, 'But you're the tallest,' when they noticed that the kitchen door was open, and there stood Kate . . .

'Very stiff,' said Josephine, grasping the door handle and doing her best to turn it. As if anything ever deceived Kate!

It couldn't be helped. That girl was . . . Then the door was shut behind them, but – but they weren't in father's room at all. They might have suddenly walked through the wall by mistake into a different flat altogether. Was the door just behind them? They were too frightened to look. Josephine knew that if it was it was holding itself tight shut; Constantia felt that, like the doors in dreams, it hadn't any handle at all. It was the coldness which made it so awful. Or the whiteness – which? Everything was covered. The blinds were down, a cloth hung over the mirror, a sheet hid the bed; a huge fan of white paper filled the fireplace. Constantia timidly put out her hand; she almost expected a snowflake to fall. Josephine felt a queer tingling in her nose, as if her nose was freezing. Then a cab klop-klopped over the cobbles below, and the quiet seemed to shake into little pieces.

'I had better pull up a blind,' said Josephine bravely.

'Yes, it might be a good idea,' whispered Constantia.

They only gave the blind a touch, but it flew up and the cord flew after, rolling round the blind stick, and the little tassel tapped as if trying to get free. That was too much for Constantia.

'Don't you think – don't you think we might put it off for another day?' she whispered.

'Why?' snapped Josephine, feeling, as usual, much better now that she knew for certain that Constantia was terrified. 'It's got to be done. But I do wish you wouldn't whisper, Con.'

'I didn't know I was whispering,' whispered Constantia.

'And why do you keep on staring at the bed?' said Josephine, raising her voice almost defiantly. 'There's nothing *on* the bed.'

'Oh, Jug, don't say so!' said poor Connie. 'At any rate, not so loudly.'

Josephine felt herself that she had gone too far. She took a wide swerve over to the chest of drawers, put out her hand, but quickly drew it back again.

'Connie!' she gasped, and she wheeled round and leaned with her back against the chest of drawers.

'Oh, Jug – what?'

Josephine could only glare. She had the most extraordinary feeling that she had just escaped something simply awful. But how could she explain to Constantia that father was in the chest of drawers? He was in the top drawer with his handkerchiefs and neckties, or in the next with his shirts and pyjamas, or in the lowest of all with his suits. He was watching there, hidden away – just behind the door handle – ready to spring.

She pulled a funny old-fashioned face at Constantia, just as she used to in the old days when she was going to cry.

'I can't open,' she nearly wailed.

'No, don't, Jug,' whispered Constantia earnestly. 'It's much better not to. Don't let's open anything. At any rate, not for a long time.'

'But – but it seems so weak,' said Josephine, breaking down.

'But why not be weak for once, Jug?' argued Constantia, whispering quite fiercely. 'If it is weak.' And her pale stare flew from the locked writing table – so safe – to the huge glittering wardrobe, and she began to breathe in a queer, panting way. 'Why shouldn't we be weak for once in our lives, Jug? It's quite excusable. Let's be weak – be weak, Jug. It's much nicer to be weak than to be strong.'

And then she did one of those amazingly bold things that she'd done about twice before in their lives: she marched over to the wardrobe, turned the key, and took it out of the lock. Took it out of the lock and held it up to Josephine, showing Josephine by her extraordinary smile that she knew what she'd done – she'd risked deliberately father being in there among his overcoats.

If the huge wardrobe had lurched forward, had crashed down on Constantia, Josephine wouldn't have been surprised. On the contrary, she would have thought it the only suitable thing to happen. But nothing happened. Only the room seemed quieter than ever, and bigger flakes of cold air fell on Josephine's shoulders and knees. She began to shiver.

'Come, Jug,' said Constantia, still with that awful callous smile; and Josephine followed just as she had that last time when Constantia had pushed Benny into the round pond.

Katherine Mansfield, 1922

From The Supper at Elsinore

This moment at the end of their parties always went strangely to the sisters' hearts. They were happy to get rid of their guests; but a little silent, bitter minute accompanied the pleasure. For they could still make people fall in love with them. They had the radiance in them which could refract little rainbow effects in the atmosphere of Copenhagen existence. But who could make them feel in love? That glass of mental and sentimental alcohol which made for warmth and movement within the old phlebolitic veins of their guests – from where were they themselves to get it? From each other, they knew, and in general they were content with the fact. Still, at this moment, the *tristesse* of the eternal hostess stiffened them a little.

Not so tonight, for no sooner had they lowered the blind again than they were off to the kitchen, making haste to send their pretty maid to bed, as if they knew the real joy of life to be found solely amongst elderly women. They made Madam Baek and themselves a fresh cup of coffee, lifting down the old copper kettle from the wall. [. . .]

Had it been in the old days that the sisters and their servant met again after a long separation, the girls would have started at once to entertain the widow with accounts of their admirers. [. . .] But there was something in Madam Baek's face which caught their attention. It was heavy with fate; she brought news herself. Very soon they paused to let her speak.

Madame Baek allowed the pause to wax long.

'Master Morten,' she said at last, and at the sound of her own thoughts of these last long days and nights she herself grew very pale, 'is at Elsinore. He walks in the house.'

At this news a deadly silence filled the kitchen. The two sisters felt their hair stand on end. The terror of the moment lay, for them, in this: that it was Madam Baek who had recounted such news to them. They might have announced it to her, out of perversity and fancies, and it would not have meant much. But that Hanne, who was to them the principle of solidity and equilibrium for the whole world, should open her mouth to throw at them the end of all things – that made these seconds in their kitchen feel to the two younger women like the first seconds of a great earthquake.

Madam Baek herself felt the unnatural in the situation, and all which was passing through the heads of her ladies. It would have terrified her as well, had she still had it in her to be terrified. Now she felt only a great triumph.

'I have seen him,' she said, 'seven times.'

Here the sisters took to trembling so violently that they had to put down their coffee cups.

'The first time,' said Madam Baek, 'he stood in the red dining-room, looking at the big clock. But the clock had stopped. I had forgotten to wind it up.'

Suddenly a rain of tears sprang out of Fanny's eyes, and bathed her pale face. 'Oh, Hanne, Hanne,' she said.

'Then I met him once on the stair,' said Madam Baek. 'Three times he has come and sat with me. Once he picked up a ball of wool for me, which had rolled on to the floor, and threw it back in my lap.'

'How did he look to you?' asked Fanny, in a broken, cracked voice, evading the glance of her sister, who sat immovable.

'He looks older than when he went away,' said Madam Baek. 'He wears his hair longer than people do here; that will be the American fashion. His clothes are very old, too. But he smiled at me just as he always did. The third time that I saw him, before he went – for he goes in his own way, and just as you think he is there, he is gone – he blew me a kiss exactly as he used to do when he was a young man and I had scolded him a little.'

Eliza lifted her eyes, very slowly, and the eyes of the two sisters met. Never in all their lives had Madam Baek said anything to them which they had for a moment doubted.

'But,' said Madam Baek, 'this last time I found him standing before your two pictures for a long time. And I thought that he wanted to see you, so I have come to fetch you to Elsinore.

At these words the sisters rose up like two grenadiers at parade. Madam Baek herself, although terribly agitated, sat where she had sat, as ever the central figure of their gatherings.

'When was it that you saw him?' asked Fanny.

'The first time,' said Madam Baek, 'was three weeks ago today. The last time was on Saturday. Then I thought, "Now I must go and fetch the ladies."'

Fanny's face was suddenly all ablaze. She looked at Madam Baek with a great tenderness, the tenderness of their young days. She felt that this was a great sacrifice, which the old woman was bringing out of her devotion to them and her sense of duty. For these three weeks, during which she had been living with the ghost of the outcast son of the De Coninck house, all alone, must have been the great time of Madam Baek's life, and would remain so for her for ever. Now it was over.

It would have been difficult to say if, when she spoke, she came nearest to laughter or tears. 'Oh, we will go, Hanne,' she said, 'we will go to Elsinore.'

'Fanny, Fanny,' said Eliza, 'he is not there; it is not he.'

Fanny made a step forward towards the fire, so violently that the streamers of her cap fluttered. 'Why not, Lizzie?' she said. 'God means to do something for you and me after all. And do you not remember, when Morten was to go back to school after the holiday, and did not want to go, that he made us tell Papa that he was dead? We made a grave under the apple tree, and laid him down in it. Do you remember?' The two sisters at this moment saw, with the eyes of their minds, exactly the same picture of the little ruddy boy, with earth in his curls, who had been lifted out of his grave by their angry young father, and of themselves, with their small spades and soiled muslin frocks, following the procession home like disappointed mourners. Their brother might play a trick on them this time.

As they turned to each other their two faces had the same expression of youthful waggishness. Madam Baek, in her chair, felt at the sight like a happily delivered lady-in-the-straw. A weight and a fullness had been taken from her, and her importance had gone with it. That was ever the way of the gentry. They would lay their hands on everything you had, even to the ghosts.

Isak Dinesen, 1934

From The Old Wives' Tale

The express from London was late, so that Constance had three quarters of an hour of the stony calmness of Knype platform when it is waiting for a great train. At last the porters began to cry, 'Macclesfield, Stockport, and Manchester train'; the immense engine glided round the curve, dwarfing the carriages behind it, and Constance had a supreme tremor. The calmness of the platform was transformed into a mêlée. Little Constance found herself left on the fringe of a physically agitated crowd which was apparently trying to scale a precipice surmounted by windows and doors from whose apertures looked forth defenders of the train. Knype platform seemed as if it would never be reduced to order again. And Constance did not estimate highly the chances of picking out an unknown Sophia from that welter. She was very seriously perturbed. All the muscles of her face were drawn as her gaze wandered anxiously from end to end of the train.

Presently she saw a singular dog. Other people also saw it. It was the colour of chocolate; it had a head and shoulders richly covered with hair that hung down in thousands of tufts like the tufts of a modern mop such as is bought in shops. This hair stopped suddenly rather less than halfway along the length of the dog's body, the remainder of which was naked and as smooth as marble. The effect was to give to the inhabitants of the Five Towns the impression that the dog had forgotten an essential part of its attire and was outraging decency. The ball of hair which had been allowed to grow on the dog's tail, and the circles of hair which ornamented its ankles, only served to intensify the impression of indecency. A pink ribbon round its neck completed the outrage. The animal had absolutely the air of a decked trollop. A chain ran taut from the creature's neck into the middle of a small crowd of persons gesticulating over trunks, and Constance traced it to a tall and distinguished woman in a coat and skirt with a rather striking hat. A beautiful and aristocratic woman, Constance thought, at a distance! Then the strange idea came to her: 'That's Sophia!' She was sure . . . She was not sure . . . She was sure. The woman emerged from the crowd. Her eye fell on Constance. They both hesitated, and, as it were, wavered uncertainly towards each other.

'I should have known you anywhere,' said Sophia, with apparently careless tranquillity, as she stooped to kiss Constance, raising her veil.

Constance saw that this marvellous tranquillity must be imitated, and she imitated it very well. It was a 'Baines' tranquillity. But she noticed a twitching of her sister's lips. The twitching comforted Constance, proving to her that she was not alone in foolishness. There was also something queer about the permanent lines of Sophia's mouth. That must be due to the 'attack' about which Sophia had written.

'Did Cyril meet you?' asked Constance. It was all that she could think of to say.

'Oh, yes!' said Sophia, eagerly. 'And I went to his studio, and he saw me off at Euston. He is a *very* nice boy. I love him.'

She said 'I love him' with the intonation of Sophia aged fifteen. Her tone and imperious gesture sent Constance flying back to the sixties. 'She hasn't altered one bit,' Constance thought with joy. 'Nothing could change Sophia.' And at the back of that notion was a more general notion: 'Nothing could change a Baines.' It was true that Constance's Sophia had not changed. Powerful individualities remain undisfigured by no matter what vicissitudes. After this revelation of the original Sophia, arising as it did out of praise of Cyril, Constance felt easier, felt reassured.

'This is Fossette,' said Sophia, pulling at the chain.

Constance knew not what to reply. Surely Sophia could not be aware what she did in bringing such a dog to a place where people were so particular as they are in the Five Towns.

'Fossette!' She repeated the name in an endearing accent, half stooping towards the dog. After all, it was not the dog's fault. Sophia had certainly mentioned a dog in her letters, but she had not prepared Constance for the spectacle of Fossette.

All that happened in a moment. A porter appeared with two trunks belonging to Sophia. Constance observed that they were superlatively 'good' trunks; also that Sophia's clothes, though 'on the showy side', were superlatively 'good'. The getting of Sophia's ticket to Bursley occupied them next, and soon the first shock of meeting had worn off.

In a second-class compartment of the loop-line train, with Sophia and Fossette opposite to her, Constance had leisure to 'take in' Sophia. She came to the conclusion that, despite her slenderness and straightness and the general effect of the long oval of her face under the hat, Sophia looked her age. She saw that Sophia must have been through a great deal: her experiences were damagingly printed in the details of feature. Seen at a distance, she might have passed for a woman of thirty, even for a girl, but seen across a narrow railway carriage she was a woman whom suffering had aged. Yet obviously her spirit was unbroken. Hear her tell a doubtful porter that of course she would take Fosette with her into the carriage! See her shut the carriage door with the expressed intention of keeping other people out! She was accustomed to command. At the same time her face had an almost set smile, as though she had said to herself: 'I will die smiling.' Constance felt sorry for her. While recognizing in Sophia a superior in charm, in experience, in knowledge of the world, and in force of personality, she yet with a kind of undisturbed, fundamental superiority felt sorry for Sophia.

Arnold Bennett, 1908

From The Color Purple

Dear God. Dear stars, dear trees, dear sky, dear peoples. Dear Everything. Dear God.

Thank you for bringing my sister Nettie and our children home.

Wonder who was coming yonder? ast Albert, looking up the road. Us can see the dust just aflying.

Me and him and Shug sitting out on the porch after dinner. Talking. Not talking. Rocking and fanning flies. Shug mention she don't want to sing in public no more – well, maybe a night or two at Harpo's. Think maybe she retire. Albert say he want her to try on his new shirt. I talk bout Henrietta. Sofia. My garden and the store. How things doing generally. So much in the habit of sewing something I stitch up a bunch of scraps, try to see what I can make. The weather cool for the last of June, and sitting on the porch with Albert and Shug feel real pleasant. Next week be the fourth of July and us plan a big family reunion outdoors here at my house. Just hope the cool weather hold.

Could be the mailman, I say. Cept he driving a little fast.

Could be Sofia, say Shug. You know she drive like a maniac.

Could be Harpo, say Albert. But it not.

By now the car stop under the trees in the yard and all these peoples dress like old folks git out.

A big tall whitehaired man with a backward turn white collar, a little dumpty woman with her gray hair and plaits cross on top her head. A tall youngish man and two robust-looking youngish women. The white-haired man say something to the driver of the car and the car leave. They all stand down there at the edge of the drive surrounded by boxes and bags and all kinds of stuff.

By now my heart is in my mouth and I can't move.

It's Nettie, Albert say, gitting up.

All the people down by the drive look up at us. They look at the house. The yard. Shug and Albert's cars. They look round at the fields. Then they commence to walk real slow up the walk to the house.

I'm so scared I don't know what to do. Feel like my mind stuck. I try to speak, nothing come. Try to git up, almost fall. Shug reach down and give me a helping hand. Albert press me on the arm.

When Nettie's foot come down on the porch I almost die. I stand swaying, tween Albert and Shug. Nettie stand swaying tween Samuel and I reckon it must be Adam. Then us both start to moan and cry. Us totter toward one nother like us use to do when us was babies. Then us feel so weak when us touch, us knock each other down. But what us care? Us sit and lay there on the porch inside each other's arms.

After while, she say *Celie*.

I say *Nettie*.

Little bit more time pass. Us look round at a lot of peoples knees. Nettie never let go my waist. This my husband Samuel, she say, pointing up. These our children Olivia and Adam and this Adam's wife Tashi, she say.

I point up at my peoples. This Shug and Albert, I say.

Everybody say Pleased to Meetcha. Then Shug and Albert start to hug everybody one after the other.

Me and Nettie finally git up off the porch and I hug my children. And I hug Tashi. Then I hug Samuel.

Alice Walker, 1983

Sisters Reunited

It was a chance meeting at a seaside nursing home, but pensioner Lily Webster was in no doubt, the bright blue eyes staring at her across the room were those of the big sister she had last seen in a miserable convent-run orphanage almost three quarters of a century ago.

By a strange twist of fate the two women, born and brought up in Ireland, had been living within five hundred yards of each other after retiring to the Somerset resort of Weston-super-Mare in the 1980s.

Their chance reunion came recently as Lily paid her daily visit to the nursing home that has been caring for her husband.

'Even though she was only fifteen the last time I saw her, I knew it was Kate right away,' Lily said yesterday. 'It was her bright blue eyes. I have thought about her for years and I never really gave up hope, but it has been such a shock to find she was living just around the corner.'

The sisters – née Dillon – were born into a family of five girls and three boys in County Clare, Ireland, before the First World War.

Their mother died of a heart attack when Lily, the youngest in the family, was aged only three. Unable to cope, their father sent the three youngest girls to the local orphanage where they were trained for domestic service. It is a time Lily remembers with deep sadness. The orphanage regime was harsh, with canings for children who wet their beds, and meagre meals of bread and dripping.

Nuns would wake their charges throughout the night in an effort to prevent bedwetting and after being roused at 6 a.m., the children would be forced to scrub the unheated corridors with cold water. 'They were very cruel to us when we were very young,' Lily recalls.

The sisters were separated in 1924 when Kate, who was then fifteen, was sent out to work as a maid for a family in Kildare. Two years later Lily left Ireland to start a new life in London, where her sister Eileen, also from the convent, had become a housekeeper.

Lily and Kate – the only surviving members of their immediate family – lost all contact with one another after leaving the orphanage. Sadly, Kate Upton, now eighty-eight, suffers from senile dementia and did not recognise her sister when they met again after a gap of seventy-four years. But Lily is patiently beginning to piece together her story with the help of Carmel, one of Kate's seven children, who checked the women's birth certificates and confirmed they were sisters.

Geoffrey Gibbs, *Guardian*, 12 February 1998

From Wives and Daughters

. . . the carriage came round, and she had the long solitary drive back to the Miss Brownings'. It was dark out of doors, when she got there; but Miss Phoebe was standing on the stairs, with a lighted candle in her hand, peering into the darkness, to see Molly come in.

'Oh, Molly! I thought you'd never come back! Such a piece of news! Sister has gone to bed; she's had a headache – with the excitement, I think; but she says it's new bread. Come upstairs softly, my dear, and I'll tell you what it is! Who do you think has been here – drinking tea with us, too, in the most condescending manner?'

'Lady Harriet?' said Molly, suddenly enlightened by the word 'condescending'.

'Yes. Why, how did you guess it? But, after all, her call, at any rate in the first instance, was upon you. Oh dear, Molly! if you're not in a hurry to go to bed, let me sit down quietly and tell you all about it; for my heart jumps into my mouth still, when I think of how I was caught. She – that is, her ladyship – left the carriage at the George, and took to her feet to go shopping – just as you or I may have done many a time in our lives. And sister was taking her forty winks; and I was sitting with my gown up above my knees and my feet on the fender, pulling out my grandmother's lace, which I'd been washing. The worst has yet to be told. I'd taken off my cap, for I thought it was getting dusk and no one would come; and there was I in my black silk skullcap, when Nancy put her head in, and whispered, "There's a lady downstairs – a real grand one, by her talk"; and in there came my Lady Harriet, so sweet and pretty in her ways, it was some time before I forgot I had never a cap on. Sister never wakened; or never roused up, so to say. She says she thought it was Nancy bringing in the tea, when she heard someone moving; for her ladyship, as soon as she saw the state of the case, came and knelt down on the rug by me, and begged my pardon so prettily for having followed Nancy upstairs without waiting for permission; and was so taken by my old lace, and wanted to know how I washed it, and where you were, and when you'd be back, and when the happy couple would be back; till sister

369

wakened – she's always a little bit put out, you know, when she first wakens from her afternoon nap – and, without turning her head to see who it was, she said, quite sharp – "Buzz, buzz, buzz! When will you learn that whispering is more fidgeting than talking out loud? I've not been able to sleep at all, for the chatter you and Nancy have been keeping up all this time." You know that was a little fancy of sister's, for she'd been snoring away as naturally as could be. So I went to her, and leant over her, and said in a low voice –

'"Sister, it's her ladyship and me that has been conversing."

'"Ladyship here, ladyship there! have you lost your wits, Phoebe, that you talk such nonsense – and in your skullcap, too!"

'By this time she was sitting up – and, looking round her, she saw Lady Harriet, in her velvets and silks, sitting on our rug, smiling, her bonnet off, and her pretty hair all bright with the blaze of the fire. My word! sister was up on her feet directly; and she dropped her curtsey, and made her excuses for sleeping, as fast as might be, while I went off to put on my best cap; for sister might well say I was out of my wits, to go on chatting to an earl's daughter in an old black silk skullcap! Black silk, too! when, if I'd only known she was coming, I might have put on my new brown silk, lying idle in my top drawer. And, when I came back, sister was ordering tea for her ladyship – our tea, I mean. So I took my turn at talk, and sister slipped out to put on her Sunday silk. But I don't think we were quite so much at our ease with her ladyship as when I sat pulling out my lace in my skullcap. And she was quite struck with our tea, and asked where we got it, for she had never tasted any like it before; and I told her we gave only 3s. 4d. a pound for it, at Johnson's – (sister says I ought to have told her the price of our company tea, which is 5s. a pound, only that is not what we were drinking; for, as ill-luck would have it, we'd none of it in the house) – and she said she would send us some of hers, all the way from Russia or Prussia, or some out-of-the-way place, and we were to compare and see which we liked best; and if we liked hers best, she could get it for us at 3s. a pound. And she left her love for you; and, though she was going away, you were not to forget her. Sister thought such a message would set you up too much, and told me she would not be chargeable for the giving it you. "But," I said, "a message is a message, and it's on Molly's own shoulders if she's set up by it. Let us show her an example of humility, sister, though we have been sitting cheek-by-jowl in such company." So sister humphed, and said she'd a headache, and went to bed. And now you may tell me your news, my dear.'

So Molly told her small events; which, interesting as they might have been at other times to the gossip-loving and sympathetic Miss Phoebe, were rather pale in the stronger light reflected from the visit of an earl's daughter.

Mrs Gaskell, 1866

From The Fig Tree

Great-Aunt Eliza, halfway up a stepladder pitched against the flat-roofed chicken house, was telling Hinry just how to set up her telescope. 'For a fellow who never saw or heard of a telescope,' Great-Aunt Eliza said to Grandmother, who was really her sister Sophia Jane, 'he doesn't do so badly so long as I tell him.'

'I do wish you'd stop clambering up stepladders, Eliza,' said Grandmother, 'at your time of life.'

'You're nothing but a nervous wreck, Sophia, I declare. When did you ever know me to get hurt?'

'Even so,' said Grandmother tartly, 'there is such a thing as appropriate behaviour at your time of . . .'

Great-Aunt Eliza seized a fold of her heavy brown pleated skirt with one hand, with the other she grasped the ladder one rung higher and ascended another step. 'Now Hinry,' she called, 'just swing it around facing west and leave it level. I'll fix it the way I want when I'm ready. You can come on down now.' She came down then herself, and said to her sister: 'So long as you can go bouncing off on that horse of yours, Sophia Jane, I s'pose I can climb ladders. I'm three years younger than you, and *at your time of life* that makes all the difference!'

Grandmother turned pink as the inside of a seashell, the one on her sewing table that had the sound of the sea in it; Miranda knew that she had always been the pretty one, and she was pretty still, but Great-Aunt Eliza was not pretty now and never had been. Miranda, watching and listening – for everything in the world was strange to her and something she had to know about – saw two old women, who were proud of being grandmothers, who spoke to children always as if they knew best about everything and children knew nothing, and they told children all day long to come here, go there, do this, do not do that, and they were always right and children never were except when they did anything they were told right away without a word. And here they were bickering like two little girls at school, or even the way Miranda and her sister Maria bickered and nagged and picked on each other and said things on purpose to hurt each other's feelings. Miranda felt sad and strange and a little frightened. She began edging away.

Katherine Anne Porter, *Collected Stories*, 1964

From The Peace of Utrecht

I have been to visit Aunt Annie and Auntie Lou. This is the third time I have been there since I came home and each time they have been spending the afternoon making rugs out of dyed rags. They are very old now. They sit in a hot little porch that is shaded by bamboo blinds; the rags and the half-finished rugs make an encouraging, domestic sort of disorder around them. They do not go out any more, but they get up early in the mornings, wash and powder themselves and put on their shapeless print dresses trimmed with rickrack and white braid. They make coffee and porridge and then they clean the house, Aunt Annie working upstairs and Auntie Lou down. Their house is very clean, dark and varnished, and it smells of vinegar and apples. In the afternoon they lie down for an hour and then put on their afternoon dresses, with brooches at the neck, and sit down to do hand work.

They are the sort of women whose flesh melts or mysteriously falls away as they get older. Auntie Lou's hair is still black, but it looks stiff and dry in its net as the dead end of hair on a ripe ear of corn. She sits straight and moves her bone-thin arms in very fine, slow movements; she looks like an Egyptian, with her long neck and small sharp face and greatly wrinkled, greatly darkened skin. Aunt Annie, perhaps because of her gentler, even coquettish manner, seems more humanly fragile and worn. Her hair is nearly all gone, and she keeps on her head one of those pretty caps designed for young wives who wear curlers to bed. She calls my attention to this and asks if I do not think it is becoming. They are both adept at these little ironies, and take a mild delight in pointing out whatever is grotesque about themselves. Their company manners are exceedingly light-hearted and their conversation with each other falls into an accomplished pattern of teasing and protest. I have a fascinated glimpse of Maddy and myself, grown old, caught back in the web of sisterhood after everything else has disappeared, making tea for some young, loved, and essentially unimportant relative – and exhibiting just such a polished relationship; what will anyone ever know of us?

Alice Munro, 1984

From Victorian Sisters

It was not until after Beatrice had left her own house that Grace began to visit her sister frequently. In earlier days Grace had resented the elder-sisterly air of superiority that Beatrice had assumed towards her. That resentment had passed. She was glad to gratify her. The superiority of a blind and deaf nonagenarian who seldom left her room without glasses and could travel freely, unattended, was more a semblance than a reality, even though Beatrice was as conscious of it as ever.

[. . .]

After lunch the two old ladies, the only survivors of the four sisters, would sit on either side of the fire. Winter or summer the fire was alight, the two tall sash-windows were shut and sandbags in green baize covers smothered the join where otherwise a breath of dangerous outside air might penetrate. The elder sister sat upright in a low, high-backed chair, its cane seat barely softened by a horsehair cushion covered with canvas worked in cross-stitch of red and blue wool. Grace's chair was rather easier. Both its back and seat were thinly stuffed with horsehair and covered with woollen material of a dismal sage green. Neither chair had arms. Grace lolled against the small round dining table and rested her left arm on the maroon tablecloth trimmed with a tight narrow edging. Her conscience pricked her a little. She never would have dared to sit thus had her sister been able to see her. But she did so hate sitting upright. [. . .]

When Beatrice had been able to see and hear, Grace was always ready for an argument and enjoyed the battle of tongues, but it was different now. She no longer felt rebellious. In her youth it had been a fair game. Their wits and strength of will were evenly matched. Now Beatrice might snub and question her as much as she chose; Grace would remain meek. It was a bit of a tussle, though, to hold herself in hand when Beatrice bluntly accused her of distorting the truth or of answering like a fool. [. . .] There was one subject on which Grace had the hardest work to keep her temper. A wireless with headphones had been installed in Beatrice's room a few years before she died. Grace strongly disapproved. She did not think that people were meant to listen to things miles away that did not concern them. She called it eavesdropping. They would probably be punished as Eve was punished for eating of the Tree of Knowledge. Beatrice delighted in the contrivance for its modernity, though she was too deaf to hear anything but the very loudest music. She called Grace a fool for her pains and even went so far as to say that Adam and Eve were out of date.

Sylvia McCurdy, 1940

From Raspberry Jam

That night both the sisters began to drink heavily. Miss Dolly lay like some monstrous broken doll, her red hair streaming over her shoulders, her corsets unloosed and her fat body poking out of an old pink velvet ball dress – pink with red hair was always so audacious – through the most unexpected places in bulges of thick blue-white flesh. She sipped at glass after glass of gin, sometimes staring into the distance with bewilderment that she should find herself in such a condition, sometimes leering pruriently at some pictures of Johnny Weismuller in swimsuits that she had cut out of *Film Weekly*. [. . .]

So they continued for two or three days with wild spasms of drinking and horrible, sober periods of remorse. They cooked themselves odd scraps in the kitchen, littering the house with unwashed dishes and cups, but never speaking, always avoiding each other. [. . .] On the fourth day, the sisters were reconciled and sat in Miss Dolly's room. That night they slept, lying heavily against each other on Miss Dolly's bed, open-mouthed and snoring, Miss Marian's deep guttural rattle contrasting with Miss Dolly's high-pitched whistle. They awoke on Thursday morning, much sobered, to the realization that Johnnie was coming to tea that afternoon.

It was characteristic that neither spoke a word of the late debauch. Together they went out into the hot July sunshine to gather raspberries for Johnnie's tea. But the nets in the kitchen garden had been disarranged and the birds had got the fruit. The awful malignity of this chance event took some time to pierce through the fuddled brains of the two ladies, as they stood there grotesque and obscene in their staring pink and clashing red, with their heavy pouchy faces and bloodshot eyes showing up in the hard, clear light of the sun. But when the realization did get home it seemed to come as a confirmation of all the beliefs of persecution which had been growing throughout the drunken orgy. There is little doubt that they were both a good deal mad when they returned to the house.

Johnnie arrived punctually at four o'clock, for he was a small boy of exceptional politeness. Miss Marian opened the door to

him, and he was surprised at her appearance in her red bandana
and her scarlet waistcoat, and especially by her voice which, though
friendly and gruff as usual, sounded thick and flat. Miss Dolly, too,
looked more than usually odd with one eye closed in a kind of
perpetual wink, and with her pink dress falling off her shoulders.
She kept on laughing in a silly, high giggle. The shock of discovering
that the raspberries were gone had driven them back to the bottle
and they were both fairly drunk. They pressed upon the little boy,
who was thirsty after his walk, two small glasses in succession, one
of brandy, the other of gin, though in their sober mood the ladies
would have died rather than have seen their little friend take strong
liquor. The drink soon combined with the heat of the day and the
smell of vomit that hung around the room to make Johnnie feel
most strange. The walls of the room seemed to be closing in and
the floor to be moving up and down like sea waves. The ladies'
faces came up at him suddenly and then receded, now Miss Dolly's
with great blobs of blue and scarlet and her eyes winking and
leering, now Miss Marian's a huge white mass with her moustache
grown large and black. He was only conscious by fits and starts of
what they were doing or saying. [. . .]

For a while he must have slept, since he remembered that later
he could see and hear more clearly though his head ached terribly.
Miss Dolly was seated at the piano playing a little jig and bobbing
up and down like a mountainous pink blancmange, whilst Miss
Marian more than ever like a pirate was dancing some sort of a
hornpipe. Suddenly Miss Dolly stopped playing. 'Shall we show
him the prisoner?' she said solemnly. 'Head up, shoulders straight,'
said Miss Marian in a parody of her old manner, 'you're going to
be very honoured, me' lad. Promise you'll never betray that honour.
You shall see one of the enemy punished. Our father gave us close
instructions "Do good to all," he said, "but if you catch one of the
enemy, remember you are a soldier's daughter." We shall obey that
command.' Meanwhile Miss Dolly had returned from the kitchen,
carrying a little bird which was pecking and clawing at the net in
which it had been caught and shrilling incessantly – it was a little
bullfinch. 'You're a very beautiful little bird,' Miss Dolly whispered,
'with lovely soft pink feathers and pretty grey wings. But you're a

very naughty little bird too, *tanto cattivo*. You came and took the fruit from us which we'd kept for our darling Gabriele.' She began feverishly to pull the rose breast feathers from the bird, which piped more loudly and squirmed. Soon little trickles of red blood ran down among the feathers. 'Scarlet and pink a very daring combination,' Miss Dolly cried. Johnnie watched from his chair, his heart beating fast. Suddenly Miss Marian stepped forward and holding the bird's head she thrust a pin into its eyes. 'We don't like spies round here looking at what we are doing,' she said in her flat, gruff voice. 'When we find them we teach them a lesson so that they don't spy on us again.' Then she took out a little pocket knife and cut into the bird's breast; its wings were beating more feebly now and its claws only moved spasmodically, whilst its chirping was very faint. Little yellow and white strings of entrails began to peep out from where she had cut. 'Oh!' cried Miss Dolly, 'I like the lovely colours, I don't like these worms.' But Johnnie could bear it no longer, white and shaking he jumped from his chair and seizing the bird he threw it on the floor and then he stamped on it violently until it was nothing but a sodden crimson mass. 'Oh, Gabriele, what have you done? You've spoilt all the soft, pretty colours. Why it's nothing now, it just looks like a lump of raspberry jam. Why have you done it, Gabriele?' cried Miss Dolly. But little Johnnie gave no answer, he had run from the room.

Angus Wilson, *The Wrong Set*, 1949

From The Darkling Sisters

'Jack, who owned the house before us?'

'Two old maid sisters. Lived there for umpteen years.'

'What were they like?'

His glasses gleam in the light. 'Better not say. It's got dark history, that house.'

'Weren't they sweet old things, devoted?'

'Sweet old things!' he snorts. 'Barmy, the two of 'em, but she should have been reported. I would have done it meself but I was too young.'

'Reported for what?'

'The way she treated 'er, the young one, bit simple, a giggler, made on the men.' His voice grows softer. He weighs and wraps in a dream. 'But there was no cause to keep her locked up in her bedroom day and night. You could hear her crying from the lane. I stood on a fruit box once and looked through the window, saw her sitting there sobbing, her hair all over her face. She beckoned and called and showed 'er knickers but I ran away.' Portentous with secrets, he leans across the counter. 'That winter she was locked out in the shed, freezing cold with snow on the mountains, you could hear her coughing and wheezing. She died out there of pneumonia.'

'And the other one?'

'Oh, she lived on in the house, had it all to herself now, had what she wanted, didn't she? But her conscience was bad. She'd come out into the front yard with an old satin hat and a moth-eaten monkey hair coat on, trying to leave, trying to get away. She did look a guy. "They're coming for me, Jack," she'd say. They came all right, took her off to the loony bin where her brother had gone before her. Maybe she was lucky at that, the younger one, dying.'

'What were their names?'

'They were the Darkling sisters, Eleanor, Milly. Mother knew them when they were young. Sullen, never mixed, she said. There was a younger brother they had to take care of, finished up out at the funny farm. Have you got all you wanted?'

And here they come now, Eleanor and Milly. Brows fierce and sullen under their satin helmets, they are dragging a little boy by the hand. Dressed in an old-fashioned sailor suit, he whines and walks awkwardly, his fat knees rubbing together. He has pissed his pants.

Dorothy Hewett, 1993

B. DEATH AND MOURNING

Letter from a Father to His Daughter on the Death of Her Sister, 1805

Not to feel or to suppress the feelings of sorrow for a dear and beloved sister, is not what I wish you to do on my account. It would be neither respectful to the memory of the deceased, nor creditable to yourself. The tears which we shed are due to her ashes; and so far from closing the wound that was made in your heart, I wish you to keep it open as a constant monitor to direct you to the end of your life [. . .] You ask me what it is [. . .] what can ever heal a wound like this? – what can supply the loss of such a child and such a sister – what can fill up the blank which will ever present itself to your view, whichever way we turn, through all the remainder of our lives? – what can restore to those scenes which we enlivened by her presence, that cheerfulness which her good humour and spirits diffused around her upon all occasions? . . .

Letter from M. Lamb to Mrs Cowden Clarke Spring, 1820

The image of a little sister I once had comes as fresh into my mind as if I had seen her lately. A little cap, with white satin ribbon, grown yellow with long keeping and a lock of light hair, were the only relics left of her. The sight of them always brought her fair pretty face to my view, that to this day I seem to have a perfect recollection of her features.

From M'Lissa

The death of your sister – what was her name? – was your stupid mother Nafa's fault. It was not absolutely sure the chief would make us return to circumcision. After all, he was always grinning into the faces of the white missionaries and telling them he was a modern man. Not a barbarian, which he could have been, for they called the 'bath' barbaric. He was chief, they said, he could stop it. Or was he chief? So of course he stopped it, to prove to them he was chief. His decision had nothing to do with us. One heard his own wives screaming when their time came. Did he care? No. Every man's wife screamed at the appropriate time.

Her name, I say, was Dura. She was small, thin; there was a crescent-shaped scar just above her lip; when she smiled it seemed to slide into her cheek.

I could lie, says M'Lissa, and tell you I remember her. After all the years I did this work, faces are the last thing I remember. If she'd been hermaphroditic, then perhaps.

No, I say. I believe she was normal.

It is all normal, as far as that goes, says M'Lissa. *You* didn't make it, so who are you to judge?

I am nobody, I say. You made sure of that.

Stop feeling sorry for yourself! she says. You are like your mother. If Dura is not bathed, she said, no one will marry her. She never seemed to notice no one had ever married me, and that I lived anyway. This was even before the white missionaries left. Being bathed did not kill me, she said. And my husband has always been patient with me. Well, M'Lissa snorts, your father spread himself among six wives; he could afford patience.

As soon as she heard the new missionaries were black, she felt certain the village would be returned to all its former ways and that uncircumcised girls would be punished. She could not imagine a black person that was not Olinkan, and she thought all Olinkans demanded their daughters to be bathed. I told her to wait. But no. She was the kind of woman who jumps even before the man says boo. Your mother helped me hold your sister down.

Stop, I say. Even if she were lying, as I now knew she often did, I could not bear to hear it.

But she says, No, I will not stop. You are mad, but you are not mad enough. Don't you think your mother might have told you how Dura died? She didn't, did she? That she was that one in a hundred girls so constructed that the slightest scratch made her bleed like a stuck cow. She had noticed this herself, from trying to stop the bleeding of the scratches your sister got while playing. When I bathed you, this was something of which I thought.

And yet you said nothing, I say, though you might have killed me just as you killed Dura.

You'd come so far, and were so foolish, says M'Lissa. Besides, by then I did not care.

Alice Walker, *Possessing the Secret of Joy*, 1992

From Melanie Klein

The debt Melanie felt she owed her other sister deserves reflection. Sidonie died of scrofula in 1886, when she was eight and Melanie four. This was the first of a long series of deaths that punctuated Klein's life, each reactivating the original fear, grief, and bewilderment. It is not clear how long Sidonie was ill before her death, but since the disease was a form of tuberculosis it is probable that it was at least a year or two. At that time tuberculosis was highly infectious (and there was also a belief that it was hereditary), so Melanie is clearly repressing a deep fear of illness that was implanted in her from early childhood. Her memories of Sidonie date from her sister's return from hospital. 'She was, I have no doubt, the best-looking of us,' Klein says; 'I don't believe it was just idealization when, after her death, my mother maintained that. I remember her violet-blue eyes, her black curls, and her angelic face.' No wonder Melanie was 'absolutely never shy'. She had to assert herself in view of the fact that her mother told her that she had been unwanted, Sidonie was the best-looking in the family, her father openly

expressed his preference for Emilie, and Emanuel was considered
something of a genius. Sidonie must have been the centre of family
attention as she lay in bed wasting away; yet what Melanie remem-
bers is her sister's kindness to her. Emilie and Emanuel took great
pleasure in teasing little Melanie, coming up with difficult geogra-
phical names like Popocateptl, while the bewildered child had no
idea whether they were genuine or not. The ailing girl took pity on
her sister and taught her the fundamentals of arithmetic and reading.
'It is quite possible that I idealize her a little,' Melanie reflects, 'but
my feeling is that, had she lived, we would have been the greatest
friends and I still have a feeling of gratitude to her for satisfying
my mental needs, all the greater because I think she was very ill at
the time.' She continues: 'I have a feeling that I never entirely got
over the feeling of grief for her death. I also suffered under the grief
my mother showed, whereas my father was more controlled. I
remember that I felt that my mother needed me all the more now
that Sidonie was gone, and it is probable that some of the spoiling
was due to my having to replace that child.'

Phyllis Grosskurth, 1986

From To the Is-land

The school year began. The schools were not to reopen. We were
to have lessons by correspondence. My school tunic arrived from
Aunty Polly. It fitted closely, with two instead of three pleats, but
I was satisfied enough to let Dad take my photo to send to Aunty
Polly.

As if school holidays and summer had been destined to go hand
in hand, yet another summer came, with hot winds, nor'westers
burning from the Canterbury Plains, copper sulphate, or 'blue-
stone' skies, and no place for comfort except the water, the sea, or
the baths, with us going back and forth from both. And on the last
Friday before the book lists and the first school lessons were
to arrive, Myrtle suggested we go swimming first and then go

downtown to look at the boys, but I refused, interested now in my lessons, how to get my new books without too much pleading and argument, wondering whether I'd like senior high, thinking, too, of the notebooks I would fill with poetry. Myrtle and I quarrelled about my refusal to go with her; only the quarrel was really about me as 'Dad's pet' because I'd been Dux, and I was now going to senior high, to be a teacher like Dad's Cousin Peg, who immigrated to Canada; I was entering the world that Myrtle had once shared with Joan of Arc and the Prince of Sleep, with the promise of many more wonderful characters lost; besides, Dad was cruellest to Myrtle, who was rebellious, daring, openly disobedient, always under the threat of being sent to the industrial school at Caversham, whereas I who wanted only to be 'good' and approved of, was timidly obedient except where I could deceive with a certainty of not being caught.

As a result of that afternoon quarrel, Myrtle went with Marguerite and Isabel to the baths while I stayed home, dutifully preparing myself for the new school year. It was late afternoon when someone knocked at the door, and Mother, thinking it was a salesman, opened the door, said quickly, 'Nothing today, thank you,' and was about to shut the door in the man's face when he, like the stereotype of a salesman, wedged his foot in and forced his way into the kitchen, while Mother, who had told us tales of such actions, prepared herself to, in her usual phrase, 'floor him'. I was standing by the door into the dining-room. The man glanced at me and said sharply, 'Send that child away.' I stayed and listened. 'I'm a doctor,' the man said. 'I've come to tell you about your daughter Myrtle. She's been drowned. They've taken her body to the morgue.'

I stared, able only to absorb the news, 'They've taken her body to the morgue.' We children had always fancied we knew which building was the morgue, a small, moss-covered stone hut down by the Post Office, near where the Oamaru creek rolled green and slimy over an artificial waterfall. We used to frighten one another by referring to the morgue as we passed it on our short cut through Takaro Park toward Tyne Street and the beach, and sometimes we tried to look through the small barred window ('for air, so the bodies don't smell') to see within. The place was so small, sealed, inaccessible that we knew it must be the morgue, and when we spoke of it at home, Mother had always shown fear, which encouraged us, after the many examples from our teasing father, to repeat the word.

'Morgue, morgue.'

'Don't say that word, kiddies.'

Now, when the doctor had delivered his news and gone, Mum herself spoke the word, for it had convinced her, too, that Myrtle had really died. 'They've taken her to the morgue,' she said.

This sudden intrusion of the word *morgue* into our lives, where before it had been a forbidden word, with us now saying it openly, made me feel grown-up, accomplished, and alone. Myrtle was dead, drowned. At first I was glad, thinking there'd be no more quarrels, crying, thrashings, with Dad trying to control her and angry with her and us listening frightened, pitying, and crying, too. Then the sad fact came home to me that there might be a prospect of peace, but the cost was the entire removal of Myrtle, not just for a holiday or next door or downtown or anywhere in the world, but off the face of the earth and out of the world, a complete disappearance and not even a trial, just to see how it worked. And where would be the fun-loving, optimistic, confiding, teasing Myrtle with the scar on her knee and the high instep ('it proves I'm cut out to be a dancer') and her grown-up monthlies, and the ambition to go to Hollywood to be a film star, to tap-dance with Fred Astaire, singing and dancing her way to fame and fortune? Where would be the Joan of Arc with her painted silver armour and helmet, the wireless performer who recited 'over the air':

> I met at eve the Prince of Sleep,
> His was a still and lovely face.

Myrtle's entire removal was stressed when she didn't come home that night to do the things she ordinarily did, to finish what she had begun in the morning, bring in the shoes cleaned with white cleaner and left to dry on the wash-house window-sill in the sun. Dad came home early and put his arms around Mum and cried, and we'd never seen him cry before. And everyone seemed to forget about Isabel, and it was quite late, almost dark, when Isabel came in, her fair hair still wet and bedraggled from swimming in the baths, her small, scared face telling everyone where she had been and what she had seen.

That night we cuddled in bed together, and as the next day passed and the next, with the grown-ups talking about inquests and coroners and undertakers and Mother naming each with a sharpness of tone that allowed them to take a share of the 'blame' and the talk of the funeral and the mechanics of burial, I gradually acquired a new knowledge that hadn't reached me through the other deaths in the family; but this was Myrtle, her death by drowning, her funeral notice, her funeral, her flowers, her coffin, her grave; she had never had so many possessions all at once.

After the inquest, when they brought her home in her coffin into the Sturmer-smelling front room and Mum asked, 'Do you want to see Myrtle?' I said no. 'We'll see her on Resurrection Day,' Mum said, conjuring once again in my mind the turmoil of Resurrection Day, the crowds, the wild scanning of faces, the panic as centuries of people confront each other and only a miracle provides room for all.

Myrtle was buried, her grave covered with wreaths from many people in Oamaru, including the swimming club where she had been a member, and some of the boys that we'd watched showing off with their muscles and their togs. And soon the rain rained on the flowers, and the ink on the cards was smudged, and the coloured ribbons frayed and rotted, and the grave itself sank until it was level with the earth. 'It always sinks, you know,' they said.

And one afternoon, when I was putting fresh flowers on Myrtle's grave and crumbling Aspros into the water in the jam jar because 'they' had said Aspros made the flowers last, I saw Miss Lindsay nearby visiting her mother's grave, Miss Lindsay of the 'jewelled sword Excalibur and the arm clothed in white samite, mystic, wonderful'.

'Is Myrtle there?' Miss Lindsay asked.

I nodded.

'What are you putting in the water?'

'Aspros,' I said. Miss Lindsay's suddenly gentle tone and her ooze of understanding infuriated me.

'They won't bring her back,' she said gently.

'I know,' I said coldly, explaining the reason for the Aspros.

I had lately learned many techniques of making flowers and other things 'last', for there had suddenly been much discussion at home and amongst people who came to the house to offer their sympathy in our 'sad loss'. They were obsessed with means of preventing the decay of their 'floral tributes', of preserving the cards and ribbons. They spoke of Myrtle, too, of keeping her memory 'green'.

'And you'll have photos of her, too, Lottie,' they said to Mother (as they sat patting and arranging their 'permanent' waves). And that was so, for when we finally realized that Myrtle had really collapsed in the water and been drowned, that she was never coming home again to wear her clothes and sleep in the bed and just be there, everyone searched for recent photos and found only the 'ghost' photo taken at Rakaia and one other, with us all in our bathing suits, I with a beginning titty showing where my shoulder strap had slipped; but it was Myrtle's photo that was needed. The photographer downtown was able to extract Myrtle entirely from that family group, although he was forced to leave behind one of Myrtle's arms that had been around Marguerite. Undaunted, the photographer fashioned for Myrtle a new photographic arm and at last presented us with a complete, enlarged photo of Myrtle. Everyone said how lucky we were to have a recent photo, and only those who knew could discern the grafted arm.

Janet Frame, 1983

Lady Jane Grey

A letter written by the Lady Jane [aged fifteen], in the end of the New Testament, in Greek, the which she sent unto her sister, Lady Catherine, the night before she suffered

I have here sent you (good sister Catherine), a book, which, though it be not outwardly trimmed with gold, yet inwardly is worth more than precious stones. It is the book (dear sister) of the law of the

Lord: it is his last testament and last will, which he bequeathed unto us wretches, which shall lead you to path of eternal joy: and if you with a good mind read it, and with an earnest mind do purpose to follow it, it shall bring you to an immortal and everlasting life: it shall teach you to live, and learn you to die: it shall win you more than you should have gained by the possessions of your woeful father's lands. For as if God had prospered him, you should have inherited his lands; so if you apply diligently this book, seeking to direct your life after it, you shall be an inheritor of such riches, as neither the covetous shall withdraw from you, neither thief shall steal, neither yet the moths corrupt.

Desire with David, good sister, to understand the law of the Lord God. Live still to die, that you (by death) may purchase eternal life. And trust not that the tenderness of your age shall lengthen your life; for as soon (if God call) goeth the young as the old; and labour always to learn to die. Defy the world, deny the devil, and despise the flesh, and delight yourself only in the Lord. Be penitent for your sins, and yet despair not; be strong in faith, and yet presume not; and desire with St Paul to be dissolved, and to be with Christ, with whom, even in death, there is life. Be like the good servant, and even at midnight be waking, lest, when death cometh, and stealeth upon you like a thief in the night, you be with the evil servant found sleeping, and lest, for lack of oil, you be found like the five foolish women, and like him that had not on the wedding garment, and then ye be cast out from the marriage.

Rejoice in Christ, as I do. Follow the steps of your Master Christ, and take up your cross, lay your sins on his back, and always embrace him. And as touching my death, rejoice as I do (good sister), that I shall be delivered of this corruption, and put on incorruption. For I am assured, that I shall for losing of a mortal life win an immortal life, the which I pray God grant you, and send you of his grace to live in his fear, and die in the true Christian faith, from the which (in God's name) I exhort you that you never swerve, neither for hope of life, nor for fear of death: for if you will deny his truth for to lengthen your life, God will deny you, and yet shorten your days. And if you will cleave unto him, he will prolong your days to your comfort and his glory, to the which glory God bring me now, and you hereafter, when it pleaseth him to call you. Fare you well, good sister, and put your only trust in God, who only must help you.

From Amrita

My mother cried her eyes red for the next several days, but oddly enough I couldn't bring myself to grieve. Only once did I shed tears over my sister. It happened two or three days after Nipper arrived in the mail. My brother and Mikiko had gone to the video store and picked up the animated *My Neighbor the Totoro*. Then they stopped by my room to invite me to watch it with them. As I walked down the hallway, I realized their actions were innocent, there were no bad intentions. No one could have known what would happen. After casually putting a small tray of cookies together and boiling a hot pot of tea, I moved into the living-room and sat down around the coffee table with the others.

Five minutes into the video I knew it was not going to be fun.

The movie was about two sisters. The images were familiar, and memories from my past came tumbling in, one after another, like waves rolling up on a beach. The two were together throughout their childhood, but that youthfulness was short-lived. The colour and the blissfulness, the light, the wind – everything was imprinted on my mind.

Actually, I wasn't trying to think about my own sister.

When we were kids we would often go with our mother to the mountain highlands, just the three of us. Mayu and I would snuggle up inside the mosquito tents and fall asleep telling ghost stories. Her thin, brown hair; her babylike smell. I didn't want to recall any of those things while watching the video, but the memories hit me anyway, striking me with a tremendous blow. It was as though the world had suddenly turned to darkness.

[. . .]

When the film was over I got up and headed for the bathroom. The shock that had come over me in watching the movie was already gone, and I opened the door, saying to myself, like I normally would, 'What a pleasant movie.' Now that I think about it, I realize the first thing I saw was Nipper. There hadn't been room for him upstairs, so I'd given him a home in the bathroom downstairs.

Sitting down, I turned to look at the statue. He seemed to be leaning forward in a painful way, his quiet head cocked to one side. All at once I felt like crying, and before I could see them coming, the tears just started to flow. Altogether the experience lasted only about five minutes, but in that time I'd managed to let go, inasmuch as the world was spinning around me, and I'd lost track of who was who, and what was what. It was the same kind of nauseating feeling you get when you're about to throw up. I held my breath as the tears continued to fall. I wasn't crying for my sister. I wasn't crying for Mayu, painted in thick make-up, so drunk and drugged that in the last days of her life she'd lost the ability to feel joy or anger. I cried for time lost – time lost between sisters everywhere.

Banana Yoshimoto, translated by Russell W. Wasden, 1997

Ruth Picardie

Ruth, who was diagnosed with breast cancer last October at the age of thirty-two, has already described the rapid spread of the disease: to her lymph, her bones, her liver, her lungs and, finally, her brain. She had predicted, wryly, that she would 'turn the colour of a bruised lemon and go bonkers'; and in fact a few weeks ago, the brain tumours did make her quite mad. She raged in a hospital bed, while the doctors looked embarrassed at their failure to save her, and was then moved to a hospice. But slowly, after an unwilling stint among the dying, Ruth seemed to claw her way back to life: in time to return home and celebrate her twins' second birthday at the end of August with chocolate cake and champagne; in time to have her own brief Indian summer.

True, she was by now confined to a wheelchair, and very weak; but still she seized hold of the big things she loved in life: her children, her family, her friends; and also the small things that make people happy yet are too often forgotten: the colour of a bright lipstick, the scent of late-flowering sweet peas, the pleasure of a newly planted pot of lavender.

Less than a fortnight before she died, she made an expedition into the centre of London: to buy some fabulous face-cream and to have her eyebrows shaped. A few days later, she came to a picnic in the park for my son's eighth birthday. She ate birthday cake and prawn sandwiches and the children rode gaily in the wheelchair with her. We talked about her plans for a weekend away in Ireland, about next year's summer holidays, about her children's third birthday, about her writing a book.

Instead, last Sunday, Ruth became very, very ill: unable to breathe without oxygen, choked by the obscene tumours that had invaded every part of her brave body. She was racked with pain, and returned in an ambulance to the hospice that had nursed her in previous crises. She had pulled through before, inexorable in her determination to go on living, and I expected her to recover again: to open her eyes and ask for a cup of cocoa or a chocolate biscuit; to demand to be taken home or out to lunch or to a party: somewhere, anywhere, more interesting.

But somehow, Ruth slipped away to a different place, a place where I could not go with her. It seems impossible: impossible to comprehend; impossible to find the words to describe the loss. After she died, I sat with her body, stroking her face, holding her hand. She was cold, and my hand could not warm her hand, but I could not believe that she had stopped breathing: even at the end, she had still been so full of life.

Her face looked peaceful; though her eyebrows were raised in a slightly quizzical manner: as if to say, how can this be?

Justine Picardie, *Observer*, 28 September 1997

From Life of Charlotte Brontë

. . . Emily was growing rapidly worse. I remember Miss Brontë's shiver at recalling the pang she felt when, after having searched in the little hollows and sheltered crevices of the moors for a lingering spray of heather – just one spray, however withered – to take in to Emily, she saw that the flower was not recognized by the dim and indifferent eyes. Yet, to the last, Emily adhered tenaciously to her habits of independence. She would suffer no one to assist her. Any effort to do so roused the old stern spirit. One Tuesday morning, in December, she arose and dressed herself as usual, making many a pause, but doing everything for herself, and even endeavouring to take up her employment of sewing: the servants looked on, and knew what the catching, rattling breath, and the glazing of the eye too surely foretold; but she kept at her work; and Charlotte and Anne, though full of unspeakable dread, had still the faintest spark of hope. [. . .]

The morning drew on to noon. Emily was worse: she could only whisper in gasps. Now, when it was too late, she said to Charlotte, 'If you will send for a doctor, I will see him now.' About two o'clock she died.

21 December 1848

Emily suffers no more from pain or weakness now. She never will suffer more in this world. She is gone, after a hard, short conflict. She died on *Tuesday*, the very day I [Charlotte] wrote to you. I thought it very possible she might be with us still for weeks; and a few hours afterwards, she was in eternity. Yes; there is no Emily in time or on earth now. Yesterday we put her poor, wasted, mortal frame quietly under the church pavement. We are very calm at present. Why should we be otherwise? The anguish of seeing her suffer is over; the spectacle of the pains of death is gone by; the funeral day is past. We feel she is at peace. No need now to tremble for the hard frost and the keen wind. Emily does not feel them. She died in a time of promise. We saw her taken from life in its prime. But it is God's will, and the place where she is gone is better than that she has left.

Mrs Gaskell, 1857

Cassandra Austen on the
Death of Jane

I have lost such a sister, such a friend as can never have been
surpassed . . . I had not a thought concealed from her and it is as
if I had lost part of myself.

Mary Callas

'Your sister,' the man said, pushing open the heavy door to the
darkened room. He half-bowed so that I would have to pass in
front of him.

He had told me his name but in the rush of images – the grandeur
of the entrance with its arched portico and heavy brass lantern,
the *fer-forgé* lift and the polished double doors – I had instantly
forgotten it. I had been told that he was something between a butler
and a chauffeur and, being unused to such grand servants, I kept
my eyes on his respectful expression as I squeezed past him. It was
only when he repeated the words that I turned and saw her.

'Your sister,' he said again in a hushed, reverential tone. I instinc-
tively thanked him and, with the same force of habit, raised the index
and second finger of my right hand to my forehead to commence the
triple genuflexion of the Orthodox faith. Only when I had made
this sign did I turn to look at her. My mind echoed the words 'your
sister' as if to reassure myself that the figure laid on the bed really
had some connection with me. How beautiful she looked, too
beautiful to be part of my memories – death plays such tricks. Some
age or look pained but in death she had lost all sign of suffering.
She was the sister who had never been; the face and the body were
self-created, were never like that in youth. Now they had become
young, she was the Mary Callas she had always wanted to be.

[. . .]

I looked at her again. [. . .] Even after all the photographs, even after our last meeting in Athens, it still seemed impossible that that slim figure, that beautiful angular face could really be Mary Callas, dumpy Mary Callas, spotty Mary Callas stuffing her face with food before hurrying off to high school in Washington Heights. Now her hair was beautiful, her hands so long and fine – they were crossed, palms uppermost, the same gesture she used when receiving applause and I wondered if they had fallen naturally into that position or whether the person who had arranged her body had done it intentionally. Oh yes, she was very beautiful. She had had everything in the end. I had been the beautiful one, I was the sister who would marry. Mary, dumpy, fat-legged Mary, would sing. Now there I was, sixty and unmarried and there was Mary, one of the most famous women in the world, married, divorced, the victim of one of the most famous affairs of all time. It was unfair. Then I told myself I was being ridiculous, how could I feel like that? Had she been happy? What did it mean, this apartment with its high windows looking out on to the Avenue, the heavy drapes, the antique furniture? I knew what it meant: she told me whenever she telephoned it was a gilded prison. No, I was right: Maria Callas was not Mary Callas. Mary Callas had died years before. What I was looking at was *La Traviata* – she looked like the dead Violetta, that same ethereal, consumptive beauty. *La Traviata*, the first opera we ever saw. [. . .] They had put on her make-up, her hair was spread out, there was no crucifix, no flowers or candles, nothing to distract from her performance. She was Violetta, she was *playing* dead. Even dead she performed the role better than anyone could. I lowered my head and said a prayer for her soul. I asked God to forgive what she had done to me.

Jackie Callas, in *Sisters*, ed., 1989

The Death of Virginia Woolf

Charleston
24 April [1941]

My dear dear Janie,

I am sending this by Lydia who is going with M[aynard] to America via Lisbon and will post it there for me and so I hope it may get to you quicker than usual. Your telegram to Quentin came. We had to answer it brutally, but it seemed better to leave no possible doubt, the worst of all things. I had been so afraid you would hear in some such way, but did not see how to prevent it. Perhaps Pippa or Marjorie may by now have told you all there is to tell. But I am writing because I know how terribly one wants details at a distance, even I think painful ones. Somehow one has to hear the truth or one may imagine even worse things. Things *could* have been worse – for us – for at least there was no suspense. For her, one knows so little. Leonard had been worried, but I, though she seemed even thinner than usual, had no idea till a week before that anything was the matter at all. Then she talked to me, and so did L., and I saw that she was in a state when rest and food were essential – as of course had often been the case before. But I had absolutely no fear of this. It simply didn't occur to me. L. had been afraid, but wasn't so at the end. He took her to see a doctor, a sensible woman whom they knew quite well, and she also thought there was no danger. So at the end it was very sudden. She simply went for a walk, leaving letters to me and L. which he found later and which made it so clear that we neither of us had any doubt what she meant. He found her stick by the river and her footsteps. I happened to go to Rodmell just afterwards. So we both knew from the beginning and had no terrible days of waiting. I think if she could have been guarded for a time she would have recovered, but there had to be these times of danger – any suspicion of being watched would simply have hastened disaster. L. himself, I am thankful to say, realizes he couldn't have done otherwise. Nothing was found at first, but now it has been. I think people have been as kind and considerate as possible. Leonard is amazing – calm, sensible. I could do nothing to help him, but I think he preferred to do all himself.

Dear Janie, these are the facts. I seem incapable of writing of anything but bare facts. It seems unnecessary for us to speak of feelings to each other, and by you I mean your mother and father too. One knows it all without saying it. We are all well here, leading our usual lives. You can imagine what Quentin and Angelica have been to me. Leonard is going the same at Rodmell, and working I think even harder than usual. It is difficult to see much of him – petrol scarcity, etc. But I go when I can and he has been here several times. I feel very useless as far as he is concerned. He could not exist I think anywhere but there and yet one wishes he need not be there alone.

I know that I have told you very little of what you probably most long to know, the state of mind which led her to it. But it is still to me mysterious, for she had seemed nowhere near the state in which she had been several times before when I had dreaded this. I think she had gradually starved herself more and more, partly as always from overwork, for besides the life of Roger she had written a novel and begun other things, and partly from the difficulty of getting the usual kind of food. L. said he simply could not get her to rest. But to me she seemed perfectly normal and herself, only of course I didn't see her often enough really to judge. But I think she must have got very much worse rather suddenly at the end. She said in her letter to me that she felt she was going mad and couldn't stand it. But only the day before I had rung her up and said I was coming to tea and she had seemed pleased.

I will write again my dear when perhaps I may be able to write less matter of factly. Don't worry about any of us. We shall get on somehow. I wish last night you could have heard Angelica singing and seen her and Q. teasing and laughing at each other. The garden is a mass of fruit blossom and things coming up. How much love I send you all.

Vanessa

From *The Selected Letters of Vanessa Bell*, 1993

From We the Tikopia

My sister, my nourisher, you have leapt into the ocean
And you did not turn your head to shore

You formed your idea, your foolish thought
You went away that you might die.

I stood here in the Tikopia channel
Thinking of my sister
Not lost to my mind.

I wail away.
Wail for me then my sister
That our eyes may meet again

Dwell still then my sister
I am going first to gaze upon
Our father in the district of the West.

Raymond Firth, 1936

Logs on the Hearth.
A Memory of a Sister

The fire advances along the log
    Of the tree we felled,
Which bloomed and bore striped apples by the peck
Till its last hour of bearing knelled

The fork that first my hand would reach
    And then my foot
In climbings upward inch by inch, lies now
Sawn, sapless, darkening with soot.

Where the bark chairs is where, one year,
    It was pruned, and bled –
Then outgrew the wound. But now, at last,
Its growings all have stagnated.

My fellow-climber rises dim
    From her chilly grave –
Just as she was, her foot near mine on the bending limb,
Laughing, her young brown hand awave.

Thomas Hardy, December 1915

From Only My Brother

I was twenty when my seventeen-year-old brother died in a car accident. He was killed in the early evening of an ordinary Sunday, and the familiar rhythm of my life stuttered and then stopped as the world tipped and tilted and set itself down in entirely the wrong place.

I shall never forget the sight of my parents' small country pub when I arrived there. It lay in total darkness at a time when bright lights should have been shining out into the lane, and there was silence where there should have been laughter and noise. It was a terrible anomaly, an incongruity which jarred so badly that I felt that never again would I be able to trust the safety of the mundane.

My brother and I had just become friends. Like many siblings, we had spent much of our lives locked in conflict over the sort of pettinesses that acquire their true perspective only with the dawning of adulthood. When he died, we were both aware that we stood on the threshold of a new relationship in which we would be partners, not opponents.

There was no chance to grieve. Almost immediately I was surrounded by my parents' friends telling me that my parents had experienced the most terrible loss. Part of me wanted to cry out that I, too, had suffered a devastating loss, but I was only twenty and the prospect of my parents falling apart was terrifying. Besides, these older, surely wiser, people seemed not to acknowledge that I might be affected.

I did what was required of me. I was strong for my parents, and buried my own grief in some remote, inaccessible place. I emerged strangely unscathed. Or so I thought.

A sudden devastating, disabling panic attack on the Underground one day ended with me being hospitalized, then reassured. I'd lost a brother recently, they said, so this was reaction, nothing to worry about. The panic attacks continued, but it was 'only stress'. The notion of suppressed grief was not proposed. No one suggested bereavement counselling. The loss of a brother, it appeared, did not occupy a noteworthy place in the hierarchy of tragedy.

Inside me, something was growing like a fungus. Part of my life had disappeared and nobody would acknowledge it. I had moved to a different part of the country where my brother had had no place, no connection, and therefore no existence. I kept wanting to return to the village where we had been brought up, where I could tap into the memories of our history and somehow take hold of him again, and of the past we had shared.

Throughout the next twenty or so years, my brother was rarely mentioned. My parents had banished all reminders of him: photographs were put away, his possessions had been disposed of, his name was not spoken. I did not know how to answer the standard question: 'Have you any brothers or sisters?' Sometimes, perhaps to avoid the pain I had not touched, I said I was an only child; sometimes I told the truth. 'How dreadful,' came the sympathetic response. 'How terrible for your parents.'

Shelley Bovey, *Independent*, 13 November 1996

From Testament of Youth

By the following Saturday we had still heard nothing of Edward.
The interval usually allowed for news of casualties after a battle
was seldom so long as this, and I began, with an artificial sense of
lightness unaccompanied by real conviction, to think that there was
perhaps, after all, no news to come. I had just announced to my
father, as we sat over tea in the dining-room, that I really must do
up Edward's papers and take them to the post office before it closed
for the weekend, when there came the sudden loud clattering at the
front-door knocker that always meant a telegram.

For a moment I thought that my legs would not carry me, but
they behaved quite normally as I got up and went to the door. I
knew what was in the telegram – I had known for a week – but
because the persistent hopefulness of the human heart refuses to
allow intuitive certainty to persuade the reason of that which it
knows, I opened and read it in a tearing anguish of suspense.

'Regret to inform you Captain E. H Brittain MC killed in action
Italy June 15th.'

'No answer,' I told the boy mechanically, and handed the telegram
to my father, who had followed me into the hall. As we went back
into the dining-room I saw, as though I had never seen them before,
the bowl of blue delphiniums on the table; their intense colour,
vivid, ethereal, seemed too radiant for earthly flowers.

Then I remembered that we should have to go down to Purley
and tell the news to my mother.

Late that evening, my uncle brought us all back to an empty flat.
Edward's death and our sudden departure had offered the maid –
at that time the amateur prostitute – an agreeable opportunity
for a few hours' freedom of which she had taken immediate ad-
vantage. She had not even finished the household handkerchiefs,
which I had washed that morning and intended to iron after tea;
when I went into the kitchen I found them still hanging, stiff as
boards, over the clothes-horse near the fire where I had left them
to dry.

Long after the family had gone to bed and the world had grown silent, I crept into the dining-room to be alone with Edward's portrait. Carefully closing the door, I turned on the light and looked at the pale, pictured face, so dignified, so steadfast, so tragically mature. He had been through so much – far, far more than those beloved friends who had died at an earlier stage of the interminable war, leaving him alone to mourn their loss. Fate might have allowed him the little, sorry compensation of survival, the chance to make his lovely music in honour of their memory. It seemed indeed the last irony that he should have been killed by the countrymen of Fritz Kreisler, the violinist whom of all others he had most greatly admired.

And suddenly, as I remembered all the dear afternoons and evenings when I had followed him on the piano as he played his violin, the sad, searching eyes of the portrait were more than I could bear, and falling on my knees before it I began to cry 'Edward! Oh, Edward!' in dazed repetition, as though my persistent crying and calling would somehow bring him back.

Vera Brittain, 1933

From A Yellow Raft in Blue Water

After the Requiem Mass, the mourners filed in a long line past the coffin, each man and woman pausing at the left end to say his or her farewell. When it was my turn, second to last since I was the sister, Pauline took Rayona from my arms and I went to the exact same spot. I thought how embarrassing it was to be lying down when everyone else was standing. I closed my eyes and pictured Lee lifelike and done-up, just on the other side of those boards. He smiled like he did when he saw me off on the bus to Seattle, sad to see me go but no way was he going to show it. Afraid. Then he stood on those golden stairs, extending his hand.

Aunt Ida was breathing down my neck, so I moved along, and in less than a minute we were standing side by side at the centre of a group in the cemetery behind church. A lot of people had cried, last night and this morning, but they weren't the ones who knew Lee best. [. . .]

The sky had cleared to a thin blue, and the far horizon blurred to a line between earth and air. The scene before me was flat as a child's drawing, the few scattered houses and trees close against the land behind them, everything white and still. It was an island, it was the roof of the tallest building. In jungles, like where Lee was sent, they say you have to cut paths with long knives through plants that grow right back, through vines and palm trees and razor-sharp grasses. Sunlight doesn't reach the ground because the trees are too thick. You can't see five feet in front of you. Everywhere it smells of rot.

The men walked by with the box and slid it on the school cafeteria table placed above where the grave would be dug. This late in February the ground was frozen too hard for even a pickaxe, and all the winter dead had to wait in the root cellar attached to the church basement until the first deep thaw. But we pretended. One of the altar boys brought around a plastic bag of potting soil, the kind they sell at every supermarket, and each mourner scooped out a handful. It wasn't real dirt at all, just black and dry tailings, dust that I squeezed in my fist while Father Hurlburt read from his book. It oozed through my fingers as I pressed it tighter and tighter, etching on to its core the print of my hand.

Finally it was time. The words stopped, and above our heads the bell from Holy Martyrs began to clang as a nun pulled the rope to turn it back and forth against the clapper. Now was when the box should be lowered into a pocket of ground, but it fell to us. In the noon light we formed a circle as if for a dance, a ring within the ring of the world, and raised our hands.

'*Requiescat in pace*.' Father Hurlburt spoke, and threw his clump of soil against the casket.

Others followed, some calling 'Lee!' others simply yelling, screaming, howling animal sounds that pounded together in my ears with the thuds of dirt on wood. My arm was cocked, ready, but unmoving as the bough of a tree.

When the thunder stopped, when only the crying remained, Aunt

Ida, singing in a voice so high that I couldn't make out its meaning, stripped the red scarf from her head and used it to sweep and clean every trace of dirt from the coffin. She shook cedar on the lid in a six-point pattern, blessing each direction, then rummaged in the pocket of her long black coat and placed Lee's champion buckle in the centre. Only then, when she was done, did she let Father Hurlburt lead her away with the rest of the crowd.

And still I stood there, poised and stuck, the centre of nobody's interest. I searched my memory for Lee's face, but it was gone. I inhaled deeply and slowly, resolving not to breathe again until I had some image to take with me.

A hand closed on my wrist, broke the spell by bending my arm back an inch further.

'Bury him, Christine,' Dayton said, and when he opened his grip, my arm sprang free.

Michael Dorris, 1988

The Death of Gertrude Stein

About Baby's last words. She said upon waking from a sleep – What is the question. And didn't answer thinking she was not completely awakened. Then she said again – What is the question and before I could speak she went on – If there is no question then there is no answer. And she turned and went to sleep again. Were they not a summing up of her life and perhaps a vision of the future – often they meant that to me and then they are a comfort . . .

Alice B. Toklas to Carl Van Vechton, 24 April 1953

9

Symbolic Sisters

INTRODUCTION

There sits on the desk beside me a stout white mug, on which is written in a neat blue italic script: *The Florence Nightingale School of Nursing. St Thomas' Hospital, London.* I did not formally inherit it from my mother's elder sister, my dead aunt, so God knows how it found its way here. But I'm glad it did. It reminds me not only of her life but of her two other, symbolic sisterhoods: first as a nurse in one of those ridiculous goffered St Thomas's caps, and, briefly, till the system did its best to kill her by failing to notice or treat her TB, as a nun. The latter was not very sisterly behaviour. But symbolic sisterhood is as fallible as the genetic kind, and anyway based on a misapprehension, that sisterhood both as concept and as reality wipes out disharmony and dissent – or ill-treatment, in my aunt's case. All those wretched children abused in homes run by nuns in Ireland or elsewhere know that this is not so (sisterhood in their homes applied only between sisters, and not to their charges). The generations of probationers bullied by so-called sisters on the wards of hospitals till recently also know it – the theory was, no doubt, that if they couldn't take it they'd get out and good riddance. Such an attitude led, in the sixties, to my eighteen-year-old younger sister being required to lay out a dead child as her very first task, on her very first day in training at Great Ormond Street Children's Hospital.

To go back to nuns for a moment; in the Middle Ages at least, and across Catholic Europe, sisterhood was often imposed rather than chosen, to get unwanted or politically inconvenient sisters, or daughters, out of the way. Women incarcerated so unwillingly could find their own way into the world, especially as the system

grew more corrupt – Eileen Power, the historian of medieval nun-
neries, quotes a report of one 'who [. . .] did pass night with Austin
friars at N'hampton and did dance and play lute with them in same
place till midnight . . .', an example of a sister who clearly preferred
brothers. But even where the veil was taken voluntarily, as by my
aunt – judging by the snapshot I have, she looked beautiful in *her*
habit – seventy women cannot live together without 'some sparks
being struck', or so observed Dame Laurentia McLachlan of Stan-
brook Abbey. In the light of hints given by an ex-nun friend of
mine who spent twelve years in the same institution thirty years
later, this was almost certainly an understatement.

Though the earliest recorded use of the term 'sister' to describe
nurses was in 1552, it did not seem that common before Florence
Nightingale professionalized what had been a corrupt and ill-trained
freelance occupation – in the manner of Dickens's Mrs Gamp, from
whose sisterhood God keep us. Florence Nightingale's assumption
of the word was ironic really, given her own poor relationship with
her sister, Parthenope, though they did get closer in later life. Yet
she made nursing one of the first respectable careers for idealistic
middle-class women, in particular for the nurses who went through
her school. Hence my aunt receiving her training there; hence my
drinking coffee out of a Florence Nightingale School of Nursing mug.

Neither nurses nor nuns, I dare say, would care to share the
term sisterhood with witches, let alone prostitutes. But these are
sisterhoods for all that. The witch Isobel Gowdie's confession might
be largely madness and delusion, but for mad, outcast and often
old women what was there but an assumption of power – and each
other's sisterhood? So their persecutors thought, at least. While as
for those other kinds of social outcasts, prostitutes, sisterhood may
be all that protects them from some of their clients. Economically
speaking, of course, they are competitors when they walk the streets.
But the Poor-Whores Petition shows seventeenth-century whores
as no less willing to unite than members of the London prostitutes
collective PUSSY have shown themselves today. I doubt if such
sisters idealize their relationship. That has to be left to the mythol-
ogists: the image of the happy, golden-hearted tart or – where
they work alongside each other in brothels – tarts, whom de

Maupassant's story both sends up and celebrates, could only have come from the head of a man. The reality can never have been so cosy. Even up-market whores are prey to disease, to abuse, to old age.

But sisterhoods remain; more potent, or at least more necessary than brotherhoods, because the repressed can only achieve their ends by collective action. That is why women united, as suffragettes, as women's liberationists, as feminists; why, shades of Lysistrata, they camped *en masse* at Greenham Common in the 1980s. Even well-heeled, successful sisters like Virginia Woolf saw the need for women to make common cause. In her youth, women were not merely barred from voting or becoming lawyers or taking degrees; they could not even join the London Library. Nor is it an accident that, years later, the first truly successful foray into women's publishing was by an all-female collective.

In other societies, of course, across the world, cousins, sisters-in-law, close neighbours, even temporary visitors, like anthropologists, are designated 'sister', thereby bestowing on the recipient of the title all the honour and privilege due to a genetic sister, and making out of otherwise heterogeneous relationships a social accord. The same would apply in worlds where women are not allowed to mix with men other than the closest of relatives, where they may be largely confined to the home, as in 'Inside the Haveli' here. The assumption of sisterhood between daughters and sisters-in-law, within and between households, defines society for such women most of the time and, as Gita, the resentful heroine, comes reluctantly to appreciate, may make their restricted community tolerable or even sweet. But dissension arises in this world as in all others. It arises, too, between those other kinds of devoted sisters, lesbians, despite the touching affection between the possibly celibate Ladies of Llangollen, and the equally touching devotion of the far-from-celibate Alice B. Toklas and Gertrude Stein. Mysteriously, Ernest Hemingway fled, never to return, after overhearing Alice speak vilely to her lover, in sexual role-play maybe. But how could such sisters not fight, any less than real ones? Especially given the added complication of sex, its potential for betrayal.

No sisterhood is utterly secure; in relation to each other, all sisters have to change and grow. And if I end with the collapse of one sisterhood, the publishing collective, a fictional version of the real thing, I do not do so pessimistically. Informal, voluntary sisterhoods are always the most at risk; it is only the myth that denies such sisters the right to discard or outgrow each other. Symbolic sisters are lucky here. A real sister, in psychic terms, has no such choice. Even sisters who've never met, and so don't share psychic baggage, have a genetic history in common; they cannot escape the blows it chooses to inflict. Whether we like it or not, dear sisters, *our* sisterhood is written in the body.

From The Life of George Crabbe by His Son

From this town we proceeded to a sweet little villa called Normanston, another of the early resorts of my mother and her lover, in the days of their anxious affection. Here four or five spinsters of independent fortune had formed a sort of Protestant nunnery, the abbess being Miss Blacknell, who afterwards deserted it to become the wife of the late Admiral Sir Thomas Graves, a lady of distinguished elegance in her tastes and manners. Another of the sisterhood was Miss Waldron, late of Tamworth – dear, good-humoured, hearty, masculine Miss Waldron, who could sing a jovial song like a fox-hunter, and like him, I had almost said, toss a glass; and yet was there such an air of high *ton*, and such intellect mingled with these manners, that the perfect lady was not veiled for a moment – no, not when, with a face rosy red, and an eye beaming with mirth, she would seize a cup and sing 'Toby Fillpot', glorying as it were in her own jollity. When we took our morning rides, she generally drove my father in her phaeton, and interested him exceedingly by her strong understanding and conversational powers.

George Crabbe, first published 1948

The Ladies of Llangollen

By Cafaill Sarah in the Cambrian tongue,
In ours the Vale of Friendship, let this spot
Be harm'd where faithful to a low-roofed cot
On Deva's banks, ye have abode so long,
Sisters in love, a love allowed to climb
Even on this century above the reach of time.

From a sonnet by William Wordsworth, 1827

I kept my bed all day with one of My dreadful Headaches. My Sally. My Tender, My Sweet Love lay beside me holding and supporting My Head till one o'clock when I by Much entreaty prevailed with her to rise and get my breakfast. She never left me for half a Moment the entire day Except at Two o'clock when she perceived Mr Whalley and little Richard coming down the Field. She ran out to Prevent his rapping at the door and to borrow the 1st Volume of Tab de Suisse which she knew I was pining for. [. . .] My beloved Sat by My Bed side reading it to me for near Two Hours – I wou'd not permit her to continue – lest it should impair her precious health . . . [. . .] My Sally How can I acknowledge the grateful Sense My Heart labours under of Your Tenderness, anxiety and incessant attention to your B.

Elizabeth Butler, *Journal*, 2–6 December 1785

From Dear Sammy

I looked up the street leading to the station, and there they were – Gertrude and Alice, large and small.
     [. . .] Gertrude was wearing one of her best pink silk brocaded

vests with a pale yellow crêpe de Chine shirt, a kind of monk's cloth or burlap skirt, and flat-heeled walking shoes. Alice was almost all in black, save for the wild fruits and flowers on her yellow hat and purple beads that swung in a triple loop down to her waist. I found it difficult to take my eyes away from her faint moustache, which held me almost as intently as did Gertrude's grey hair, cut short and circling into a fascinating whorl at the back of her head. She looked like a Roman senator about to break into voluble Latin.

We climbed into their Matford and set off, with Gertrude driving and Alice sitting in the back seat, filing her nails.

'What with all this waiting and looking, it's the dogs I'm worried about,' Gertrude said. 'We'll have to stop at the butcher and get them some scraps. It's far beyond their feeding time.'

'They can wait, lovey,' Alice said.

'Not on your life, Pussy,' Gertrude said. 'We can wait, but dogs can't.' And so we stopped at a butcher's shop in Culoz to get some meat for them, while the butcher's wife made up some raspberry syrup with a little wine mixed in . . .

Suddenly [Gertrude] grabbed my knee. 'Sammy,' she said, 'do you think that Alice and I are Lesbians?'

[. . .]

'I don't see that it's anybody's business one way or another,' I said.

'Do you care whether we are?' she asked.

'Not in the least,' I said. I was suddenly dripping wet. [. . .]

'It bothers a lot of people,' Gertrude said. 'But like you said, it's nobody's business.'

Samuel M. Steward, 1977

From Inside the Haveli

The noise and confusion were getting worse; the air was stifling around Bhabha's bed, as one woman after another came to her offering their congratulations and placing money in the tiny clenched fists of Vijay. The amount they gave was according to the status of each haveli and its relationship to Sangram Singhji. The family accountant with his steel-rimmed glasses sat with his head bent, noting down the name of the haveli and the amount, as it was called out by Pari.

It was nearly twelve o'clock by the time the last woman had greeted Bhabha Sa and blessed her little great-granddaughter. The priests had left with gifts of fruit, grain and cloth. The maids had spread thick white strips of cloth along the veranda surrounding the courtyard and on the edge of the cloth they placed large green banana leaves for plates and cups made of dry leaves pinned together with thin twigs. Steaming rice, dhal, vegetables and different kinds of curries were in buckets, ready to be served. The sweets were in large thalis. The aroma of spices, mixed with incense, made the air heavy.

Once everything was ready, Bhagwat Singhji's wife, with great formality, invited the women to sit down to eat, as if they were guests who had come to the house for the first time. Tantalized by the smell of food, the children were getting restless. They jostled and scrambled to get what places remained or squeezed themselves next to their mothers or grandmothers. The chatter of voices was soon replaced by the smacking of lips. The close relatives served the guests. As soon as the serving buckets were empty, full ones were brought.

Bhagwat Singhji's wife with her elder relatives went around coaxing the guests, 'Have some more rice', 'One more puree', 'At least a ladoo'. There were protests, but finally they were persuaded to take something more. Having eaten with relish they belched with satisfaction and got up, washed their hands and crossed into the adjoining courtyard where there was room for them to stretch their legs and relax.

The first group of women having finished, the maids quickly picked up the leaves and cups and threw them outside the courtyard wall. The stray dogs and cows were ready to lick them. The maids moved rapidly; through years of experience they had become experts at feeding a large number of people without getting flustered. The relay of feeding and clearing went on till all the guests had been served. Bhagwat Singhji's wife was on her feet till the last row of women had been served.

[. . .]

Late in the afternoon the household seemed to be astir again. The professional singing group had arrived and started to serenade the ancient house of Sangram Singhji. The families of these women had served the havelis for several generations, singing and dancing on festive occasions. As the singing gathered momentum, an elderly lady got up and came to where the young married girls sat huddled together and said, shaking one of them by the shoulders: 'You have had enough time to digest your food. Get up and dance. This is an auspicious day, you have also talked enough.'

The girls coyly demurred and dipped their hands deeper into their laps. 'Come on! Don't act as if you have fresh henna on your feet, as if you are a bride,' said Kanta, the widowed niece of Bhagwat Singhji. 'In my days I didn't wait to be persuaded; in fact I had to be forcibly taken off the floor. Ask Parijiji if you do not believe me.'

One of the girls reluctantly got up, pulled her sari well over her face and shyly went to the centre of the courtyard. At first she made graceful gestures with her hands but her body refused to tilt or bend to the beat of the drum. She tried for a while and then fled in embarrassment. The singers did not conceal their disappointment.

After nudging and nagging a tall slim girl got up and went hurriedly to the centre. At first she too faltered and hesitated, but then her limbs became supple. Her body turned and twisted with grace, her skirt swirled and her hands were cupped in the shape of a lotus and the arms turned into floating fishes. The singers raised the pitch of their voice and the drummers quickened the beat. The courtyard echoed with rhythm and song. The girl paused for a moment to pull the sari over her face and then she started again.

'She is graceful, she is talented,' the women said with admiration as they came up with their rupee notes, carefully taken out from inside the blouse. Solemnly they encircled the girl's head with the money and then threw it into the lap of the singers. Thus the evil spirit was bribed from casting its envious eyes on the youthful dancer.

'Come on, you are next,' said Kanta to a plump girl who sat bundled up, her head between her knees. She shook her head vehemently but Kanta took her by the hand and led her to the middle of the courtyard.

The girl stood awkwardly for a second and giggled and then she looked through her sari at the drummers. They took the hint that they had to go a little slow; the singers cleared their throats and struck the tune that was romantic but languid.

'Oh! She can dance,' said the women surprised as the girl swirled effortlessly around the courtyard.

'Who could have said that with a heavy body like that she could be so graceful.'

'She was slim once; it is after her fourth child that she became fat,' put in another woman.

The girl's tight face relaxed and she smiled, then her lips parted and she began to sing with the women. Her body contours kept the romantic mood and her gestures portrayed the sentiments of love.

'One more dance. No you cannot now sit down,' the women shouted as the girl stopped to wipe the perspiration from her face. Geeta was relieved when the girl did not leave the courtyard. She was terrified lest anyone asked her to perform. She did not know that there was no danger of her being asked as she was not considered strong enough after childbirth.

The senior women got up as before, encircled the rupee notes over the head of the dancer and then gave them to the smiling drummers. The singers glanced at the ever-growing pile of notes and continued with their singing with renewed force. The ladies of the havelis for once were not going to stint. This was a special occasion. Even the older women shed their reserve and danced to the slow familiar rhythm they had heard a thousand times before.

Amidst the singing and dancing the women didn't notice that the sun had gone down and that the evening light was turning dark; the lights were switched on unnoticed, but the ladies were in no hurry to leave. The singers had cast a spell that kept them longer than usual.

Rama Mehta, 1977

The Poor-Whores Petition

To the most splendid, illustrious, serene and eminent lady of pleasure, the Countess of Castlemayne, &c.

The Humble Petition of the Undone Company of poor distressed Whores, Bawds, Pimps, and Panders, etc.

Humbly sheweth, –
That Your Petitioners having been for a long time connived at, and countenanced in the practice of our Venereal pleasures (a Trade wherein your Ladyship hath great Experience, and for your diligence therein, have arrived to high and Eminent Advancement for these late years), But now, We, through the Rage and Malice of a Company of *London-Apprentices*, and other malicious and very bad persons, being mechanick, rude and ill-bred Boys, have sustained the loss of our Habitations, Trades, and Employments; And many of us, that have had foul play in the Court and Sports of *Venus*, being full of Ulcers, but were in a hopeful way of Recovery, have our Cures retarded through this Barbarous and un-*Venus*-like Usage, and all of us exposed to very hard shifts, being made uncapable of giving that Entertainment, as the Honour and Dignity of such persons as frequented our Houses doth call for, as your Ladyship by your own practice hath experimented the knowledge of.

We therefore being moved by the imminent danger now impending, and the great sense of our present suffering, do implore your Honour to improve your Interest, which (all know) is great, That some speedy Relief may be afforded us, to prevent Our Utter Ruine and Undoing. And that such a sure Course may be taken with the Ringleaders and Abetters of these evil-disposed persons, that a stop may be put unto them before they come to your Honours Pallace, and bring contempt upon your worshipping of *Venus*, the great Goddess whom we all adore.

[. . .]

Signed by Us, *Madam Cresswell* and *Damaris Page*, in the behalf of our Sisters and Fellow-Sufferers (in this day of our Calamity) in *Dog and Bitch Yard, Lukeners Lane, Saffron-Hill, Moor fields, Chiswell-street, Rosemary-Lane, Nightingale-Lane, Ratcliffe-High-way, Well-close Church-Lane, East-Smithfield* etc., this present 25th day of March 1668.

From Madame Tellier's Establishment

The new communicants were now leaving their homes and making their way to the village hall, which housed the two schools and the mayor's office: it stood at one end of the village, while the House of God occupied the other. Their relations, in their Sunday best, looking uncomfortable and moving awkwardly as a result of their life of back-breaking toil, followed their children. The little girls were lost in a cloud of snowy tulle like whipped cream, while the little boys, like miniature waiters, their hair plastered down with grease, walked with their feet far apart so as not to dirty their black trousers.

The reputation of a family was enhanced when a large number of relations from a distance surrounded a child; so the carpenter's triumph was assured. Constance was followed by the Tellier contingent, headed by Madame; the father had his sister on his arm, the mother walked with Raphaële, Flora with Rosie, and the two Beer Pumps brought up the rear. The troop deployed with the dignity of staff officers in full dress. The effect on the village was electric.

At the school the girls fell in under the coif of the kindly Sister of Mercy, the boys under the top-hat of the schoolmaster, a handsome man of commanding presence; then they moved off, chanting a psalm.

The boys, leading the procession, advanced in two long files between the two lines of unharnessed vehicles, the girls following in the same formation; and as the local people respectfully gave pride of place to the ladies from the town, they came immediately behind the little girls, thus continuing the double line of the procession, three on the left and three on the right, their frocks blazing like a firework display.

Their entry into the church dumbfounded the natives, who jostled each other, turned round and pushed to get a good view. Pious women almost forgot to lower their voices, amazed at the sight of ladies more lace-bedizened than the cantors' cottas. The mayor offered his pew – the top pew on the right near the choir – and Madame Tellier took her seat in it with her sister-in-law, while Fernande and Raphaële, Rowdy Rosie and the two Beer Pumps occupied the second pew with the carpenter.

The choir was packed with kneeling children, girls on one side and boys on the other, the long wax candles in their hands looking like lances tilted at every angle.

In front of the lectern stood three men, singing in deep bass voices. They held the sonorous Latin syllables interminably, with an exaggerated lengthening of the A-a of the Amens, supported by the long-drawn note of the serpent, bellowing from its brazen throat. A boy's shrill treble gave the responses. And from time to time a priest, seated in a stall with a square biretta on his head, got up, mumbled something and resumed his seat; whereupon the three cantors started off again, with their eyes fixed on the great plainsong book open in front of them and supported by the outspread wings of a wooden eagle mounted on a revolving base.

Suddenly there was silence. The whole congregation knelt as one man as the celebrant appeared, a venerable, white-haired old man, bending over the chalice in his left hand. In front of him walked two servers in red cassocks, and behind came a crowd of cantors in clumping shoes, who took their places in two lines on each side of the choir.

A little bell tinkled in the dead silence and the holy office began. The celebrant moved slowly before the gilded tabernacle, genuflected and, in a cracked voice quavering with age, intoned the introductory prayers. As soon as he had finished, all the cantors and the serpent came in together, the men in the body of the church joining in less loudly and more humbly, as it is fitting that a congregation should sing.

Suddenly the Kyrie Eleison burst forth, uplifted to Heaven from every breast and heart. Particles of dust and even splinters of worm-eaten wood fell from the ancient vaulted ceiling, dislodged by the impact of the voices. The sun, striking on the slate roof, heated the little church like an oven. A wave of emotion and eager expectation, as the moment of the ineffable mystery drew near, swept over the children's hearts and the mothers felt a tightening of the throat.

The priest, who had been sitting down for some time, went up the steps to the altar, and, his head bare save for his silvery locks, with tremulous gestures approached the miracle of the Mass.

He turned towards the congregation, and, stretching out his hands, he intoned: 'Orate, Fratres; Brethren, let us pray.' Everyone knelt. The old priest now murmured the words of the supreme mystery; the bell tinkled three times; the congregation, bending low, invoked the name of God; the children were faint with anxious anticipation.

At that moment Rosie, her face in her hands, suddenly remembered her own mother, the village church, her own First Communion. Memories of the day flooded back; she was a tiny girl again, lost in her white dress, and she began to cry. At first she wept silently, the tears welling slowly from her closed eyes; then with the memories of the past her emotion overcame her, and with bursting throat and heaving breasts she sobbed aloud. She had taken out her handkerchief and was wiping her eyes and dabbing at her nose and mouth to stop her tears. But it was no use. A hoarse cry tore her throat, answered by two other deep, heart-rending sighs, for her two neighbours, Louise and Flora, completely overcome by similar recollections of the past, were also in floods of noisy tears.

Tears being infectious, Madame in her turn soon felt her own eyelids moist, and, turning towards her sister-in-law, saw that the whole of her pew was weeping.

The priest was transforming the elements into the body and blood

415

of Christ. The children were beyond thinking, bowed down to the stone floor in an ecstasy of awe and devotion; and here and there in the church a woman, a mother or sister, caught by the mysterious sympathy of violent emotion and upset by the sight of the smart ladies, whose shoulders were shaking and heaving with sobs as they knelt, was soaking her check calico handkerchief, pressing her left hand against her violently beating heart.

Like a spark which sets fire to a whole ripe cornfield, the tears of Rosie and her friends swept the whole congregation in a flash. Men and women, old men and boys in their smart blouses were all sobbing in a moment; and above them there seemed to hover the supernatural presence of an all-pervading spirit, the miraculous breath of an invisible almighty power.

Guy de Maupassant, 1883, translated by N.P. Sloman, 1946

From No Money, No Honey

Prostitutes in Djakarta

Jealousies and rivalries between prostitutes seem to be inevitable when there is good money to be made, opportunities to visit expatriate palaces with air-conditioning, videos, pools, and so on, with always the dream of marriage or at least being financially supported with their children in their own house. Most of the women say they grow tired of the insecurity of their lives. Greater contact with materialist culture leads to blatant materialist aspirations which are only beginning to emerge in Manggarai.

However, there are also strong links between the Bintang girls. The daytime is occupied with shopping and getting made up at home, and the women frequently visit one another, share houses and go to the Bintang together. If one of them has a severe problem or illness, even their worst enemies will contribute to cover the cost, for example, Rp 200,000 was raised for an intestinal operational for Tina, who lived in Blok P with Veryati. This group reliance is important for women who have chosen the 'bad path', where crime and danger are a part of life, but the Bintang girls also have a strong sense of their own individuality. They wear a range of outfits from casual jeans to elaborate dresses which defy description. Girls, especially new girls, who arrive in particularly unflattering clothes (calf-length flares, socks and sandals, etc.), are generally put down by the others as cheap, common, or the ultimate insult, too '*kampung*'. Most of them drink and take pills, some have morphine scars, tattoos, or acid burns where tattoos used to be, although these are usually covered up. They believe in various kinds of 'black magic' depending on which region they come from and use lucky talismans, heirlooms, and found objects to bring good luck or to sabotage others. One night a girl brought a snake into the Paradise to work a spell but it was discovered and chopped in half by one of the security men.

Alison J. Murray, 1991

From The Prostitution Papers

Prostitutes in New Jersey

My first experience with prostitution was in a whorehouse, and you're in a cage no matter which way you look at it. That was a real dragged-out horror; I'll never forget that as long as I live. I was taken there by some old woman who was a prostitute, who was teaching me to be a prostitute. She'd been a prostitute since she was about thirteen years old; her name was Djuna Mae. So she was going to teach me to be a prostitute. She went through the whole thing of taking me to her room, showing me how to give head and all that. So she finally took me to this whorehouse in Trenton, New Jersey. This place was too much to believe. The police, the detectives used to come every day for their payoff. They used to talk to the madam of the house; they'd pick up their money and leave. Only white men came into this place. Right in the middle of Trenton.

The girls were all black, with a few exceptions. Not entirely all black. There were a few exceptions. Variety. Very important – variety in a whorehouse. And you'd just sit there. A guy would come in; he'd look everybody over and he'd pick you and you'd go off to the room. You could never see your money. The madam would demand the money, and when you got ready to leave she would give you your half. I decided after three days it wasn't for me. I didn't like it, and I wanted to leave. And she didn't have my money. She'd gambled it away.

Kate Millett, 1975

From Sister Aileen Survives the Novitiate

Audrey was novice mistress. I've forgotten a lot about who else taught us. Isn't that strange? Well, anyway, you ask what happened in a day. We got up at five every morning. On Monday the whole day was washing day. You had to get the boilers going. I used to get up at five with one of the South Australians. We were the boiler ladies. We had these great big coppers and the steam would be dripping from the ceiling, and the perspiration – well, imagine, we were in these habits! This was our spiritual formation. The first-year novices had to wash. We'd be washing for 120 novices. It was all done by hand. None of this fancy washing-machine business or tumble dryers. Imagine the ironing! And there were the gimps and the coifs and the veils. Dreadful, you know. We're talking big time, Anne.

I can remember I used to get mad. And I used to look at it all and the perspiration was running everywhere and I used to say, 'It's wonderful to be doing this for Jesus.' What a lot of nonsense. Now I can laugh. I mean, it was just part of the routine. And there would be others in the kitchen, other first-years. Monday was work day for the first-years.

In second year we studied all the time, we had spiritual formation. A priest came for lectures on Saturday afternoon. But on Saturday morning it was clean-up. Everything was done on your knees – all those long corridors on your knees. One year we all had blown-up knees. They had to get the doctors.

[. . .]

Getting used to wearing all that stuff was funny. At first the older novices helped. For a few days the bands and everything were all saggy and you'd feel it was all going to fall off. But after a time I could whip it on in a minute. You'd put your chin up so it would be firm and then relax when the pins were in place. The piece that went under your throat was rectangular, like a small square inserted, and you had to put it in the right spot or it would hurt your throat. Then you had a coif that was starched. I couldn't wear a starched one because I perspired so much and it would be all soggy. So I had to have celluloid inside a cloth. I just pulled out the celluloid and washed the cloth. Others had the same. It was worked out years before. You had a string on the bottom and the top. You tied the top string and that held it. Some of the novices would put foam rubber inside to push it out. I didn't like it sticking out. There were different ways of looking more attractive; some had their veils really tight, others would have them sitting in flat.

And you asked about hair, Anne. Well, if you didn't have it really short it pulled. Some had it long but a lot of us found it was easier shaved. But I hated it. The first time I felt as if my womanliness had been shaved off. And it was presumed that you'd shave it. At first the older novices would do it for you. We laugh at the photos now.

When I started teaching I was at Nhill, back in Victoria. I went across the road for afternoon tea with a family there. The four-year-old sat at my feet and he suddenly started yelling, 'Mummy, Sister's got legs!' And I thought, what do they think of me?

Anne Henderson, *Mary MacKillop's Sisters*, 1997

From The Best of Friends

Stanbrook Abbey, Worcester
24 April 1907

Dear Mr Cockerell,

[. . .] I could not help smiling at your regrets on Stonehenge. You do not think of us, I hope, as caged birds (or lions); we do not answer a bit to that description. The only place where there is any impression of cutting-off is in the parlour, and we look on the grate as a barrier not to keep us in but to keep you out. We are not debarred either from enjoying nature, though we have not the variety that you so-called free people can procure. Inside the walls of our own Paradise we have a lovely little bit of God's world, and enough living creatures to satisfy even St Francis. I say nothing of the beauty of the country itself. Besides these human and natural joys there are, as you suspect, others, better far. It might be difficult for you to understand the intense and ever-growing joy that a monk or nun finds in the Choir – *Domus Dei et porta coeli*. You won't be sorry for me again, will you?

[. . .]

Believe me, Yours very sincerely,
Sister Laurentia McLauchlan, OSB

November 1922

Dear Mr Cockerell,

Many thanks for your letter of the 4th, which quite satisfies me.
[. . .]

You do not think – do you? – that in religious life one avoids thorns and thistles. To begin with, seventy people cannot live together without occasional sparks being struck out. Then the ordeals of an earnest spiritual life are very searching. Besides that, Communities often have severe trials of one sort or another. I don't wish to make you believe that we are the most deeply afflicted people on earth! – only to remark that one does not get out of troubles by leaving the world. For my own part I think it would be immoral if we did, for why should we have such a blessed life for nothing?

Had I the choice again as a young girl, I should most certainly repeat my life. I sometimes marvel at my wisdom in making the choice, for I was young and fairly foolish and terribly fond of pleasure. Perhaps my youth had something to do with the wisdom [. . .]

Yours always
Sister Laurentia

From Laundry

She drained the last of her calvados from her tiny earthenware cup, and yawned.

– The cellaress told me, she remarked: that the poor young monk who brings the laundry over to the convent got attacked in the forest yesterday. A wild boar, he said it was.

– Really? asked Austreberthe.

– Apparently, went on her mother: he saw something leaping in the long grass, with a bristly brown back. Then it charged him, so he had to run away. The donkey carrying the dirty washing bolted, and the panniers fell off, and everything ended up wet and muddy in the stream. The young man was so upset that the nuns had to feed him slices of honeybread to cheer him up. Of course it wasn't his fault. No one would dream of punishing him. But just fancy! A wild boar in that part of the forest, so near to our home!

– How fortunate, remarked Austreberthe: that it was the dirty washing that fell into the stream and not the clean!

She entered the convent a week later, taking gifts for the nuns of eggs, butter and more mushrooms. The cellaress received her kindly, kissing her on both cheeks and setting a plate of the famous spiced honeybread in front of her, and with her own hands dressing Austreberthe in her new habit, cutting off her hair with a large pair of shears, and showing her how to pin the white linen veil over her close-fitting coif.

– Try not to get your clothes too dirty, warned the cellaress: even with all the rough work you have to do you can't be having clean aprons and habits all the time. That would lead to the sin of vanity. And please remember that *we*, unlike our dear brothers in Christ at Jumièges, bathe only twice a year, at Christmas and at Easter, lest we fall into the sin of impurity, in thought at least if not in deed!

Austreberthe nodded. With the hair she disliked cut off, and the sticking-out ears that so distressed her concealed, she felt cheerful. She was ready for business. She set to immediately in the wash-house, sorting out the great heap of wet and muddy laundry that had arrived a week ago from Jumièges, after its dousing in the stream, and had not yet been dealt with.

There were, it seemed to her, a hundred pairs at least of long underpants in heavy unbleached wool. These, clearly, belonged to the monks. The Abbot's drawers, however, were of the finest white linen, with tiny tucks and pleats, and Austreberthe admired them very much. She stoked up the fire under the copper in the back scullery, then soaked and washed and scrubbed and scoured and rinsed and wrung until her body streamed with sweat and ached with exhaustion. But Austreberthe did not complain. She carried the washing outside and hung it to dry in the orchard, looping it from branch to branch of the apple trees and spreading it on the hedges behind. Next day she pressed it with a heated flat-iron, and then packed it, interleaved with sprigs of lavender and rosemary, into panniers ready for collection. Then, having first made sure the other nuns were not around, she stripped off her habit and veil and washed herself all over under the pump in the back yard.

Since her own drawers were still damp with sweat from her labours on the day before, and she wouldn't be allowed a clean pair till Christmas, she tossed them aside. Then she dressed herself again, very carefully, in her habit and veil.

Clip-clop. Clip-clop.

The donkey's hooves rang on the cobbles of the convent yard. The young monk came into a damp, steamy wash-house, his blue eyes modestly cast down and the corners of his plump red lips turned up, his graceful arms hidden in his sleeves. He inclined his head to the young lay sister, who nodded back.

– Bring in the washing, then, she directed him: I'm ready for you.

Her voice, as befitted the inhabitant of such a holy place as a convent, was pitched very low. Its contralto note sounded tuneful and sweet as the whistle of a bird. The young monk raised his eyes shyly to Austreberthe's smiling face, so becomingly framed in her white coif.

– We're grateful to you, dear sister, he stammered: for the service that you do us.

He picked up the two baskets of clean washing and carried them outside. Then he brought in the baskets of dirty washing and set them on the stone floor.

– A slice of honeybread before you go? suggested Austreberthe: a tot of calvados? You've a long journey ahead of you through the forest. You must keep up your strength. And while you refresh yourself I'll just finish ironing the Abbot's drawers for you to take back with you.

She guided the young monk into the back scullery where the flat-irons were set at the edge of the stove, and shut the door behind them. In here it was quite dark. The room was warm. It smelt of lavender soap and sun-dried linen, as sweet as grass.

Austreberthe gave a cry and pointed.

– Over there. In the corner. A wild boar!

She clutched at the young monk and fell over backwards with him on to a heap of nuns' nightdresses and wimples.

– A wild boar? shouted the monk: in here? Don't be ridiculous!

Austreberthe flung back the skirts of her habit.

– Look, she cried: all brown and bristly.

She held tightly to the young monk so that he could not run away. Her skin seemed scented with the tang of wild mushrooms. Her mouth, close to his, tasted of honey and apples.

– Though some, she murmured: would not say bristly but silky soft. Brown and curly. Wouldn't you?

[. . .]

As for Sister Austreberthe, such was her piety, wit and intelligence that she was quickly promoted to the position of Bursar and thence to that of Mistress of Novices. For her humility in insisting on continuing to do the monks' laundry, even after her elevation, in later years, to the lofty rank of Prioress, she was revered as the holiest of nuns. After her death she was canonized, and made patroness of the forest of Jumièges. Many stories are told about Saint Austreberthe, though not this one, you may be sure.

Michèle Roberts, *During Mother's Absence*, 1994

From Hospital Training

However, not long after, we stopped, and I saw a great gateway, over which was in large letters, 'St Thomas's Hospital', so a bell was rung, and I said 'Nightingale nurse'; the gate opened and we drove on a little way and then saw a long half-covered way leading to a large well-lighted room. Up to this I walked; saw porter No. 2, and was admitted into a large warm hall, well panelled and partitioned, as all the house is, with well-planed deal, varnished its own colour, which looks so clean and light. I had a long wait while the cabman brought in the luggage, and then was conducted past the doors of some wards, in which I saw a few patients in bed and two nurses seated most comfortably at work at a table in the middle of the room; then we crossed a large space with trees, giving, as did all I saw, the idea and feeling of being far from any town; and though I have not yet been out, there is the perfect stillness of the country. But to go on and introduce you as I was. The porter led me into a kind of small hall, and instantly two nice-looking, almost deaconess-looking, nurses came forward and received me most kindly, saying Mrs W. (the lady-superintendent) had been in several times during the afternoon and evening, and had just left, having given me up for that day. However, nothing could exceed the kindness of these nurses; their dress a kind of grey stuff, very neat, white aprons and caps, rather too round and coquettish I thought for sisters, but a neat pretty style of dress, which will, I am sure, be most becoming to Nurse Agnes. [. . .] There are fourteen Nightingale nurses, besides sisters, and about 280 patients, when the house is full, which it is not yet, as this place was only opened a few days ago. I went to bed soon after tea, and was up for breakfast this morning at 6.30. Everything is so quiet that you more feel than know that others are moving around you. My nurse friend summoned me to breakfast where I had tea last night, and I found the whole party assembled; a nice respectable-looking set; all amiable-looking, some pretty; the sister sat at the head of the table.

Agnes Elizabeth Jones, 1871

Notes on Nurses Sent to Florence Nightingale

Nurse Q: prim little body;
Nurse W: poor creature;
Nurse G: makings of a nice nurse, no pretensions, most willing, good in ward;
Nurse M: good influence, quiet and religious;
Nurse B: Lydia Languish;
Nurse N: hoyden, vulgar, slangy, so ill-brought up;
Nurse W: useful little body; rather bright and perky;
Nurse S: green young saint.

Miss Crossland, Nightingale Home Sister, 1875–1895, quoted Lucy Seymer, *Florence Nightingale's Nurses*, 1960

Memorandum of Instructions by Matron to Ward Sisters on Duties to Probationers

(by Mrs Wardroper)

1. Every new Probationer to be shown, once or twice at least, by 'Ward Sister' or Staff Nurse, how to do her work to the Ward Sister's satisfaction: to be shown not only what things are to be done, and how they are to be done; but guarded against how they are not to be done, as well as against what is not to be done – the Sister kindly remembering that the Probationer cannot be made responsible for doing well what she did not know how to do.

2. Every new Probationer to have pointed out to her the various cupboards where Lint, Tow, Bandages, Ointments, etc., are kept;

Also, any Instruments or Utensils not in sight, that may be required;

Also, what her Ward work is (independently of that immediately about the patients), e.g. how to dust the Ward; the Screens with their inside ledges; the Chairs, etc.

3. Every Probationer to be shown the Lavatories and what she is to do in the Lavatory, and in washing up, washing Swing Basins and ledges underneath; Bath, etc.; cleansing Urinals and inside gratings, etc.

To be shown what the respective Towels are for in Lavatory, and the 'Ticket' under which each Towel is to be hung; what the respective Mops are for, and Brushes; how to use Soap in washing Patients; disinfectants; Bed-pans and all such utensils to be explained to her; and how to empty Bed-pan, and how to use disinfectants in it.

4. (*a*) Every new Probationer to be shown how to wash and cleanse helpless Patients, especially men, without exposure; that is to say, by washing them between blankets.

How to wash *daily* the axilla, flexures of thighs, etc., of Patients – between Towels or Blankets.

[. . .]

From Treason

'Early in the day,' I says to the wounded men. 'Your fighting is over mighty early when the enemy is creeping about only fifteen versts away from the town and when the *Red Trooper* says about our international position that it's real terrible, and that the horizon is full of clouds.' But my words bounced off the heroic infantry like sheep dung off the regimental drum, and all that came of our talk was the sisters led us to the beds and began yarning about laying down arms as if we was already conquered! They upset Kustov proper, I can tell you, and he began tearing at his wound on his left shoulder above his loyal soldier's and proletarian heart. When they saw him taking on so, the nurses shut up, but only for a minute. Then they carried on again with their jeering, the jeering of the partyless masses, and began to urge everyone that did not mind to come and pull the clothes off us as we dozed, or make us play theatre-parts in women's clothes for educational purposes, which is not decent.

Regular sisters of mercilessness, they was. They tried giving us sleeping-powders more than once to get our clothes away, so we had to rest in turn with one eye open, and used to go to the lavatory in full uniform with revolvers, even – if you'll pardon the expression – to pee. And when we had been through all this a week and a day, we began to get wild and have visions, and in the end, when we woke up on the accursed morning of 4 August, we noticed a change in us, for we was lying in bathrobes with numbers on like convicts, without arms or the clothes that our mothers, feeble old women in the Kuban, had wove. And the sun, we saw, was shining grand, and the trench infantry among which three Red Cavalrymen had been through so much was going on making fun of us, and the sisters of mercilessness also, as had bunged us up with sleeping-draughts the night before, was now wobbling their young breasts bringing us cocoa on plates with milk enough to drown in!

Isaac Babel, 1920, translated by Walter Morison, 1957

From The Confession of Isobel Gowdie

The second confession, made at Aulderne, on 3 May 1662, is not less remarkable than the foregoing:

'. . . After that time there would meet but sometimes a Covin [*i.e.*, thirteen], sometimes more, sometimes less; but a Grand Meeting would be about the end of each Quarter. There is thirteen persons in each Covin; and each of us has one Sprite to wait upon us, when we please to call upon him. [. . .]

'When we raise the wind, we take a rag of cloth, and wet it in water; and we take a beetle and knock the rag on a stone, and we say thrice over:

> "I knock this rag upon this stane,
>   To raise the wind, in the Devil's name;
>   It shall not lie until I please again!"

When we would lay the wind, we dry the rag, and say (thrice over):

> "We lay the wind in the Devil's name,
>   [It shall not] rise while we [or I] like to raise it again!"

We have no power of rain, but we will raise the wind when we please. He made us believe [. . .] that there was no God beside him.'

[. . .] 'When we go in the shape of a hare, we say thrice over:

> "I shall go into a hare,
>   With sorrow, and such, and mickle care;
>   And I shall go in the Devil's name,
>   Ay, until I come home [again!]"

And instantly we start in a hare. And when we would be out of that shape, we will say:

> "Hare! hare! God send thee care!
> I am in a hare's likeness just now,
> But I shall be in a woman's likeness even [now]."

When we would go in the likeness of a cat, we say thrice over:

> "I shall go [intill ane cat],
> [With sorrow, and such, and a black] shot!
> And I shall go in the Devil's name,
> Ay, until I come home again!"

And if we [would go in a crow, then] we say thrice over:

> "I shall go intill a crow,
> With sorrow, and such, and a black [thraw!
> And I shall go in the Devil's name,]
> Ay, until I come home again!"

If we go in the shape of a cat, a crow, a hare, or any other likeness, etc., to any of our neighbours' houses, being witches, we will say: "[I (or we) conjure] thee go with us [or me]!" And presently they become as we are, either cats, hares, crows, etc., and go [with us whither we would. When] we would ride, we take windle-straws, or been-stakes, and put them betwixt our feet, and say thrice:

> "Horse and Hattock, horse and go,
> Horse and pellatris, ho! ho!"

And immediately we fly away wherever we would; and lest our husbands should miss us out of our beds, we put in a besom, or a three-legged stool, beside them, and say thrice over:

> "I lay down this besom [or stool] in the Devil's name,
> Let it not stir till I come home again!"

And immediately it seems a woman, by the side of our husband.'

Davenport Adams, 1889

From Lysistrata

(*The attendant begins to pour the wine into the cup.*)

CALONICE. What lovely red blood! And how well it flows!

LAMPITO. And how sweet it smells forby, by Castor!

MYRRHINE (*pushing to the front*): Let me take the oath first!

CALONICE. Not unless you draw the first lot, you don't!

LYSISTRATA. Lampito and all of you, take hold of the cup. One of you repeat the oath after me, and everybody else signify assent. (*All put their hands on the cup.* CALONICE *comes forward; and as she repeats each line of the following oath, all the others bow their heads.*)

LYSISTRATA. I will not allow either boyfriend or husband –

CALONICE. I will not allow either boyfriend or husband –

LYSISTRATA. – to approach me in an erect condition. Go on!

CALONICE. – to approach me in an – erect – condition – help, Lysistrata, my knees are giving way! (*She nearly faints, but recovers herself.*)

LYSISTRATA. And I will live at home without any sexual activity –

CALONICE. And I will live at home without any sexual activity –

LYSISTRATA. – wearing my best make-up and my most seductive dresses –

CALONICE. – wearing my best make-up and my most seductive dresses –

LYSISTRATA. – to inflame my husband's ardour.

CALONICE. – to inflame my husband's ardour.

LYSISTRATA. But I will never willingly yield to his desires.

CALONICE. But I will never willingly yield to his desires.

LYSISTRATA. And should he force me against my will –

CALONICE. And should he force me against my will –

LYSISTRATA. I will be wholly passive and unresponsive.

CALONICE. I will be wholly passive and unresponsive.

LYSISTRATA. I will not raise my legs towards the ceiling.

CALONICE. I will not raise my legs towards the ceiling.

LYSISTRATA. I will not take up the lion-on-a-cheese-grater position.

CALONICE. I will not take up the lion-on-a-cheese-grater position.

LYSISTRATA. As I drink from this cup, so will I abide by this oath.

CALONICE. As I drink from this cup, so will I abide by this oath.

LYSISTRATA. And if I do not abide by it, may the cup prove to be filled with water.

CALONICE. And if I do not abide by it, may the cup prove to be filled with water.

LYSISTRATA (*to the others*). Do you all join in this oath?

ALL. We do.

(CALONICE *drinks from the cup*.)

LYSISTRATA (*taking the cup*): I'll dispose of the sacred remains.

MYRRHINE. Not all of them, my friend – let's share them, as friends should.

(LYSISTRATA *drinks part of the remaining wine and, with some reluctance, hands the rest to* MYRRHINE. *As she is drinking it off a shout of triumph is heard backstage.*)

Aristophanes, c.411 BC

From On the Perimeter

No one seemed to know why anyone had come to the camps. It was just accepted that they had arrived. Women came from all over the world. A lot of Australians and Americans would suddenly turn up. A bus load of women would appear from Spain. Benders had to be made for them. They were always given the best food that was available. I was astonished by the way that the Greenham women managed their very severe problems as hostesses. I knew I could never be so calm if 150 strangers from Sweden turned up without warning at my house and I had to feed them. But the Greenham women somehow managed. They never appeared to be ruffled by any of the impromptu arrivals. Because of the floating in and out nature of the camps it was impossible to gauge how many women were actually protesting at the base at any given moment. There was one solid coterie of permanent Greenham residents, then there were the semi-residents who only camped part-time and also had part-time jobs. Then there were the campers from abroad who came only for a short time in order to make a gesture of support.

Women often hardly knew each other's names on the camps. Sometimes one got to know their first names, but with such a constant influx of women their surnames were impossible to remember. Names hardly seemed to matter on the camps, and neither did the women's ordinary occupations. They were just 'women' and they shared a terror of 'nukes' and that was all they had to unify them.

I was told that there was hardly a profession that was not represented on the camps. 'We have two psychoanalysts living on the base,' a Scottish girl told me. 'We also have a forester. Isn't it funny to think of a forester meeting a psychoanalyst. I'm sure they would never have normally met in their entire lives.'

This was very probably true.

A woman from Yorkshire suddenly joined the group at Green Gate and she kept saying how wonderful it was to be out in the cold. No one who was sitting around agreed with her at all. But she then explained she'd spent the whole morning in the Newbury courthouse, where it had been so hot it had been suffocating. I wondered why the Newbury courthouse was like an inferno, but she never really explained. I still got a powerful image of a magistrate sweltering as he tried case after case of Greenham women.

The new arrival said she'd spent the morning in court giving support to a woman who was accused of cutting the perimeter fence. A soldier had identified her and he had given a lot of long-drawn out evidence, all of which proved her to be the culprit. The woman had let him give his testimony without making any objection. He was asked which hand he'd seen her use to cut the fence and he swore he'd seen her use her right hand.

When he'd finished, the woman on trial had held up her right hand to the magistrate and showed him that she'd lost her thumb and several fingers in an accident. The magistrate had been discomfited for he'd been just on the point of sentencing her. After seeing her hand, he'd had no choice but to release her.

All the little dramas that took place in the Newbury courtroom were valuable to the peace women because they provided entertainment, something that was desperately lacking in the camps.

Many of the symbolic activities in which the women engaged themselves were employed, ironically, as 'deterrents'. They protected the peace campers from the danger that their will and their determination to remain protesting at the missile might be sapped by insidious boredom.

With brightly coloured wools the women would endlessly darn the steel looped wire of the perimeter fence. All this darning ostensibly represented the humble tasks of womenfolk. Symbolically, the Greenham women seemed only to ask to be allowed life so that they could carry on their useful little modest contribution to humanity's welfare. In symbol, they begged that they be spared from nuclear destruction so that they could still patch up the holes the men had made, and continue to make the male foot rest more comfortably in his shoe.

The peace women's darning of the perimeter was both a black joke and, paradoxically, a light one. Never have I seen such beautiful, meticulous darning. Since the beginning of time, no man has probably ever had his socks and woollens darned with such loving and perfectionist dedication as the Greenham women devoted to darning the perimeter. Huge areas of the hideous fence soon started to look like beautiful tapestries. There were no congested woolly lumps. It all turned into one lovely smooth surface, for they sewed it with such ingenuity and care. But then the military would spot what the women had done and it was the look of rage and horror on their faces that made all this exquisite darning so effective as a boredom 'deterrent'.

The women despised the workings and attitudes of the military mind and they managed to needle it with this ridiculous darning. The soldiers would rush at the patches of darned perimeter like monkeys when they go berserk in their cage. Nothing seemed to anger them like the sight of even the smallest sock-sized darn on the fence that defended the missile.

When the soldiers had finished ripping and tearing off the wool with various sharp instruments, the poor perimeter looked truly terrible. The paratroopers couldn't be bothered to make a really diligent job of removing every strand of wool. That was quite understandable. But the little bits of brightly coloured ruined darns that clung tenaciously to the fence had a sleazy pathos and they looked extremely messy and unpleasant. Why couldn't the military leave things as they were when they were nice? That was the peace women's simple, but also serious symbolic message.

Caroline Blackwood, 1984

Mrs Pankhurst at Bow Street

I was brought up by a father who taught his children [. . .] to realize they had a duty towards their country. I married a man whose wife I was but also his comrade in his public life. [. . .] I was for many years a Guardian of the Poor and a Member of the School Board, and, when that was abolished, of the Education Committee. This experience brought me into contact with many of my own sex who found themselves in a deplorable position because of the state of the English law as it affects women. You must have seen women come into this Court who would never have come here if married women were afforded by law that better claim to maintenance which should in justice be theirs when they give up their economic dependence on marriage and are unable to earn a subsistence for themselves. You know how unjust the marriage and divorce laws are, and that the married woman has no right of guardianship over her own children. Great suffering is endured by women because of the state of the law. I have seen that men are encouraged by law to take advantage of the helplessness of women. Many women have thought as I have, and for many years we have tried, by that influence of which we have so often been reminded, to alter those laws, but we find that influence counts for nothing. When we went to the House of Commons we used to be told, when we were persistent, that Members of Parliament were not responsible to women, they were responsible only to voters, and that their time was too fully occupied to reform those laws, although they agreed that they needed reforming. We have tried constitutional methods. We women have presented larger petitions in support of our enfranchisement than were ever presented for any other reform; we have succeeded in holding greater public meetings than were ever held for any reform, in the spite of the difficulty women have in throwing off their natural diffidence, that desire to escape publicity which we have inherited from generations of our foremothers. We have broken through that. We have faced hostile mobs at street corners, because we were told that we could not have that representation for our taxes that men have won unless we converted the whole of the country to our sides. Because we have done this we have been misrepresented, we have been ridiculed, we have had contempt poured upon us and the ignorant mob has been incited to offer us violence, which we have faced unarmed and unprotected by the safeguards which Cabinet Ministers enjoy. We have been driven to do this; we are determined to go on with this agitation because we feel in honour bound. Just as it was the duty of your forefathers, it is our duty to make the world a better place for women than it is today.

Lastly, I want to call attention to the self-restraint which was shown by our followers on the night of the thirteenth, after we had been arrested. Our rule has always been to be patient, exercise self-restraint, show our so-called superiors that we are not hysterical; to use no violence, but rather to offer ourselves to the violence of others. That is all I have to say to you, Sir. We are here, not because we are law breakers, but because we want to become law-makers.

Mrs Emmeline Pankhurst, Bow Street, 14 October 1908

Quoted in My Own Story, *1914. Also quoted in a somewhat different version by Christabel Pankhurst in* Unshackled, *1959. I have amalgamated these two accounts; but finding the mother's own words more eloquent than the daughter's have taken more from her.*

From Professions for Women

These then were two very genuine experiences of my own. These were two of the adventures of my professional life. The first – killing the Angel in the House – I think I solved. She died. But the second, telling the truth about my own experiences as a body, I do not think I solved. I doubt that any woman has solved it yet. The obstacles against her are still immensely powerful – and yet they are very difficult to define. Outwardly, what is simpler than to write books? Outwardly, what obstacles are there for a woman rather than for a man? Inwardly, I think, the case is very different; she has still many ghosts to fight, many prejudices to overcome. Indeed it will be a long time still, I think, before a woman can sit down to write a book without finding a phantom to be slain, a rock to be dashed against. And if this is so in literature, the freest of all professions for women, how is it in the new professions which you are now for the first time entering?

Those are the questions that I should like, had I time, to ask you. And indeed, if I have laid stress upon these professional experiences of mine, it is because I believe that they are, though in different forms, yours also. Even when the path is nominally open – when there is nothing to prevent a woman from being a doctor, a lawyer, a civil servant – there are many phantoms and obstacles, as I believe, looming in her way. To discuss and define them is I think of great value and importance; for thus only can the labour be shared, the difficulties be solved. But besides this, it is necessary also to discuss the ends and the aims for which we are fighting, for which we are doing battle with these formidable obstacles. Those aims cannot be taken for granted; they must be perpetually questioned and examined. The whole position, as I see it – here in this hall surrounded by women practising for the first time in history I know not how many different professions – is one of extraordinary interest and importance. You have won rooms of your own in the house hitherto exclusively owned by men. You are able, though not without great labour and effort, to pay the rent. You are earning your five hundred pounds a year. But this freedom is only a beginning; the room is your own, but it is still bare. It has to be furnished; it has to be decorated; it has to be shared. How are you going to furnish it, how are you going to decorate it? With whom are you going to share it, and upon what terms? These, I think are questions of the utmost importance and interest. For the first time in history you are able to ask them; for the first time you are able to decide for yourselves what the answers should be.

Virginia Woolf, published in 1942

From Big Women

They were all there at the Board Meeting on the Monday morning. The Furies, as some called them: Layla, Stephanie, Nancy, Alice. And Saffron, of course, who parked her car in a Director's parking space without so much as a by your leave. Rosaline and Wendy were there, and everyone else who ever spoke up, and women whose names no one could ever remember, all of whose lives had been changed, one way or another, by the pursuit of feminism. They made a lively, intelligent, attractive, undisappointed lot. Age had been kind to them. They had lived by mind and principle, not by their looks, and it showed. You could imagine that the best of their lives was in front of them, not behind them.

They had got things wrong, personally and politically, but who ever got everything right? They had wept, screamed, shouted, protested, loved and laughed more than most. If the separatists had won over the socialists and the radicals, if young women everywhere assumed men were an optional extra, a decoration not a necessity, not essential to their well-being, or survival, that too in time would shift and change, and become more merciful. Men are people too. Gender, like the state in Marxist aspiration, might in the end wither away, and be relevant only in bed and the approach to it, and the aftermath. There is no harm in living in hope.

[. . .]

'People don't get forgiven for telling the truth,' observed Saffron, 'but on the other hand they often get what they want.' Hostile faces turned to look at her.

'Without Stephanie, Alice and Nancy,' Layla went on, 'who is there? No one. Small publishing houses live and breathe by the vision, passion and commitment of a driving force. We found it in feminism; feminism found it in us. We were swept along with the tidal wave of a great cause, on the crest of anger. The wave did its work, receded, passed on elsewhere, and has left us floundering in the shallows. Stephanie, Nancy and Alice, all three of you, you need to bow out of Medusa now. Resign, along with me. New brooms sweep cleaner if the old rubbish is gone. Alice, will you resign?'

'No,' said Alice.

'Nancy?' inquired Layla.

'No,' said Nancy.

'Stephanie?' asked Layla.

'You're out of your fucking mind,' said Stephanie.

'This being the case,' said Layla, 'I have no choice but to ask the meeting to vote on the following proposal; that Medusa allows itself to be bought. We have two offers. Marcus Liebling is an interested party. ComArt is diversifying into the world of books.'

'Liebling!' shrieked Rosalie. 'Medusa sell out to the gutter press! Never –'

'Or there's Chapter Books,' said Layla, 'one of the few small publishing houses left, with a good list and capacity for growth. I understand they're prepared to make us an offer. Not such a good one. Mingy in fact. And honestly, the future of publishing is not with the small presses, however much emotional attachment we have to them. Medusa is dreary enough already. So dreary and full of self-pity the magazines won't even accept our ads.'

'You mean Zoe's daughter Saffron wouldn't take them,' interceded Wendy. 'Everyone knows she has a grudge.'

'You'll need Saffron's votes to swing it, Layla,' said Nancy, who'd been doing sums.

'I will,' said Layla. 'And I don't know which way she'll jump.'

'You'll need more than that, Layla,' said Stephanie. 'You are the only person in this room who wants to sell, and it's who's in the room that counts.'

And in triumph Stephanie produced the printed booklet which had been on everyone's chair when they came in, and demanded those assembled turn to page three, section four.

'You will see here,' she said, 'that under Rule 16A of our constitution proxy votes are disallowed on a majority vote of a quorate meeting.'

'What have we come to!' lamented Layla. 'Stephanie appealing to an agenda technicality! How very male. I told you this was the age of lawyers, and Stephanie's living with one. As it happens, Stephanie, I'm not using proxies. Saffron now owns the votes I used to hold by proxy. She was sold them by our mystery backer, only yesterday. Saffron is now a thirty-two per cent shareholder, counting the two from Johnny. Shall we take a vote? That we sell Medusa? For the proposition?'

No hands rose other than Layla's and Saffron's.

'I win,' said Layla.

Fay Weldon, 1997

Bibliography

Adams, Davenport W. H., 'Confessions of Isabel Gowdie', in *Witches, Warlocks and Magicians*, Chatto & Windus, 1889.

Adcock, Fleur, 'Bluebell Seasons', in *Cherries on a Plate*, ed. M. Duckworth, Random House, New Zealand, 1996

Aeschylus, *The Libation Bearers*, in *The Oresteia* (458 BC, trs. Robert Fagles, Penguin Books, 1979

Alcott, Louisa M., *Little Women*, 1868–9

Andersen, Hans, 'The Wild Swans', *Fairy Tales*, Adam Black, 1912

Anderson, Emily, ed. *Letters of Mozart*, Macmillan, 1966

Anon., The Poor-Whores Petition, London, 1668

Anon., Letter of consolation and advice from a father to his daughter on the death of her sister, London, 1805

Anon., *The Sister's Gift or The Bad Boy Reformed. Published for the Advantage of the Rising Generation*, York, 1826

Anon., Lady Ann Foley, 1782

Anon., A Ballad, Dublin, 1726

Anon., Reasons against marriage with a wife's sister, Plymouth, 1855

Arenus, Reinaldo, 'Goodbye Mother', trs. Jo Labanyi, in *Faber Book of Contemporary Latin American Short Stories*, ed. Nick Caistor, Faber & Faber, 1989

Aristophanes, *Lysistrata* (411 BC) trs. Alan Sommerstein, Penguin Books, 1973

Atkinson, Kate, *Behind the Scenes at the Museum*. Doubleday, 1995

Austen, Caroline, *My Aunt Jane Austen*, Jane Austen Society, 1952

Austen, Jane, *Pride and Prejudice*, 1813

Austen, Jane, *Sense and Sensibility*, 1811

Austen-Leigh, James Edward, *A Memoir of Jane Austen*, 4th edn, London, 1879

Axline, Virginia M. *Dibs in Search of Self*, Gollancz, 1966

Babel, Isaac, 'Treason', in *Red Cavalry: Collected Stories of Isaac Babel*, revised Walter Morison, Penguin Books, 1961

Balzac, Honoré, de, *Père Goriot* (1834), tr. M. A. Crawford, Penguin Books, 1951

Barnard, Marjorie, 'Habit', in *The Persimmon Tree*, 1945; in *Such Devoted Sisters*, ed. Shena Mackay, Virago

Bartas, Du, *La Semaine*, trs. Sylvester, 1578

Beauvoir, Simone de, *Memoirs of a Dutiful Daughter*, trs. James Kirkup, André Deutsch, 1957

Bell, Vanessa, *Selected Letters*, ed. Regina Miller, Bloomsbury, 1993

Bennett, Arnold, *The Old Wives' Tale*, 1908

Bennett, Lynne, *Dangerous Wives and Sacred Sisters*, Columbia UP, 1983

Bible, The 1610 Authorized Version

Blackwood, Caroline, *On the Perimeter*, Heinemann, 1984

Blundy, Anna, 'Life Stories – Jack and Zena', in *The Times*, Magazine, 14.1.98

Boccacio, Giovanni, *The Decameron*, trs. J. M. Rigg, J. M. Dent, 1930

Bovey, Shelley, 'Only My Brother', in *Independent*, 13.11.96

Bowen, Elizabeth, 'A Queer Heart', in *Collected Stories*, Jonathan Cape, 1980

Bowles, Jane, 'Camp Cataract', in *Collected Works*, Peter Owen, 1984

Brittain, Vera, *Testament of Youth*, Gollancz, 1933

Brontë, Charlotte, Preface to the new edition of *Wuthering Heights*, 1850

Brontë, Emily, in *The Brontes: Interviews and Recollections*, ed. H. Orel, Macmillan, 1997

Brown, A. Radcliffe-, and Forde, C. Daryll, *African Systems of Kinship and Marriage*, ed. Brown, A. Radcliffe- and Forde, C. Daryll, OUP, 1950

Browning, Elizabeth Barrett, *Letters to Her Sisters*, ed. L. Huxley, John Murray, 1929

Burney, Fanny, *Early Diary of Fanny Burney*, ed. Annie Raine Ellis, London, 1889

Burns, Edward, ed. *Letters of Alice B. Toklas*, Angus & Robertson, 1973

Butler, Elizabeth, Elizabeth Butler's Journal (Ormonde MS)

Byatt, A. S., *The Game*, Chatto & Windus, 1968

Byron, Lord, Letter to his sister Augusta, quoted Phyllis Grosskurth, *Byron, The Flawed Angel*, London, Hodder & Stoughton, 1997

Callas, Jackie, *Sisters*, Macmillan, 1989

Carrington, Leonora, 'The Seventh Horse', in *The Sisters*, Virago, 1989

Cather, Willa, *The Professor's House*, Knopf, 1925; Virago, 1981

Chadwick, Douglas H., *The Fate of the Elephant*, Viking, 1992

Chekhov, Anton, *Three Sisters*, in *Plays*, trs. Elisavela Fen, Penguin Books, 1951

Clark, Brian, *The Sibling Constellation*, Penguin Books, 1999

Cockerell, Sydney, *The Best of Friends*, Hart Davis, 1956

Cocteau, Jean, *Les Enfants Terribles*, 1929

Cook, Emma, 'Ruth Ellis', *Independent*, 15.8.98

Coppard, A. E., *A Broadsheet Ballad. Adam and Eve and Pinch Me*, Golden Cockerell Press, Waltham St Lawrence, 1921

Cornwall, Barry, *Charles Lamb, A Memoir*, London, 1876

Crabbe, George, *The Life of George Crabbe by His Son*, The Cresset Press, 1948

Craig, Amanda, 'Drabble and Byatt', *Good Housekeeping*, Aug. 1998

Crompton, Richmal, 'William the Matchmaker', from *Still William*, George Newnes, 1924

Dalal, Nergis, *The Sisters*, Hind Pocket Books, Delhi, 1973

Dalyell, Tam, Obituary of Marjorie Wilson, in *Independent*, 11.3.98

Dawkins, Richard, *The Selfish Gene*, Penguin Books, 1978

De Quincey, Thomas, *Recollections of the Lakeland Poets*, 1863

Dillner, Luisa, 'Whose Life is It Anyway', in *Guardian*, 29.4.97

Dinesen, Isak, 'The Supper at Elsinore', *Seven Gothic Tales*, Putnam, 1934

Dinesen, Isak, *Letters from Africa*, trs. Anne Born, Picador, 1983

Dorris, Michael, *A Yellow Raft in Blue Water*, Hamish Hamilton 1988

Drabble, Margaret, *A Summer Birdcage*, Weidenfeld & Nicolson, 1962

Du Pre, Hilary and Piers, *A Genius in the Family. An Intimate Memoir Of Jacqueline Du Pré*, Chatto & Windus, 1997

Duckworth, Marilyn, 'A Game of Pretend', in *Such Devoted Sisters*, ed. Shena Mackay, Virago, 1993

Dunmore, Helen, *Talking to the Dead*, Viking, 1996

Dunn, Jane, *A Very Close Conspiracy*, Cape, 1990

Dunn, Judy, *The Beginnings of Social Understanding*, Blackwell, 1988

Durrell, Gerald, *My Family and Other Animals*, Penguin Books, 1959

Edward VI, in Frank Murphy, *The Girlhood of Queen Elizabeth*, Constable, 1909

Eliot, George, *Middlemarch* 1872

Eliot, George, *The Mill on the Floss*, 1860

Elizabeth I, in Frank Murphy, *The Girlhood of Queen Elizabeth*, Constable, 1909

Ferrier, Susan, *Marriage*, Edinburgh, 1818

Fielding, Henry, *Tom Jones*, 1749

Firth, Raymond, *We The Tikopia*, George Allen & Unwin, 1936

Fitzgerald, F. Scott, 'More than Just a House', in *The Price was High. Last Uncollected Stories*, Vol. I, Pan, 1989

Fontaine, Joan, *No Bed of Roses*, W. H. Allen, 1978

Ford, John, *T'is Pity She's a Whore*, 1633

Forde, C. Daryll, 'Kinship among the Swazi', in *African Systems of Kinship and Marriage*, ed. Brown, A. Radcliffe-, and Forde, C. Daryll, OUP, 1950

Forster, E. M., *Howards Ends*, 1910

Fortes, M., 'Kinship and Marriage among the Ashanti', in *African Systems of Kinship and Marriage*, ed. Brown, A. Radcliffe-, and Forde, C. Daryll, OUP, 1950

Fossey, Dian, *Gorillas in the Mist*, Hodder & Stoughton, 1983

Frame, Janet, *The the Is-land*, The Women's Press, 1983

Frisch, Karl von, *Bees, Their Vision, Chemical Senses and Language*, NY, Cornell UP, 1950

Gallimore, Ronald, Boggs, Joan W., and Jordan, Cathie, *Culture, Behavior and Education, A Study of Hawaiian-Americans*, Vol. II, Beverly Hills and London, Sage Publications (Sage Library of Social Research), 1974

Garcia, Cristina, *The Agüero Sisters*, Picador, 1997

Gaskell, Mrs, *Life of Charlotte Brontë*, (1857), London, 1882

Gaskell, Mrs, *Wives and Daughters*, 1866

Gellisen, Rena Kornreich, and MacAdam, Heather Dune, *Sisters in Auschwitz*, Weidenfeld & Nicolson, 1997

Gerrard, Nicci, 'The Soul of My Sister', in *Observer*, Review, 8.12.96

Gibbs, Geoffrey, 'Sisters Reunited', in *Guardian*, 12.2.98

Goodale, C., 'Siblings as Spouses. The Reproduction and Replacement of Kaulong Society', in Mac Marshall, ed., *Siblingship in Oceania*, London University Press of America, 1983

Goodall, Jane, *Through a Window*, Weidenfeld & Nicolson, 1990

Goodall, Jane, *In the Shadow of Man*, Collins, 1971

Gosley, Margaret, Letter in *Independent*, 21.9.98

Goyen, William, *Savata, My Fair Sister*, Peter Owen, 1963

Grimm Brothers, 'Cinderella', in *Fairy Tales*, 1812

Grosskurth, Phyllis, *Melanie Klein, Her Life and Work*, Hodder & Stoughton, 1986

Hamermesh, Mira, Unpublished autobiography

Hannah, Barbara, *Jung, His Life and Works*, Michael Joseph, 1977

Hardy, Thomas, 'Logs on the Hearth', in *Collected Poems*, Macmillan, 1920.

Hartley, L. P., 'The Shrimp and the Anemone', in *Eustace and Hilda*, Putnam, 1958

Hazlitt, W. C., *Charles and Mary Lamb: Poems, Letters and Remains*, London, 1874

Head, Bessie, 'The Collector Of Treasures', in *Looking for the Rain God*, Heinemann (African Writers Series), 1977

Henderson, Anne, *Mrs Mackillop's Sisters*, Angus & Robertson, Australia, 1997

Herschel, Caroline Lucretia, *Memoir and Correspondence*, ed. Mrs John Herschel, 1876

Hewett, Dorothy, 'The Darkling Sisters', in *Sisters*, ed. Drusilla Modjeska, Angus & Robertson, Australia, 1993

Hofland, Mrs, *The Sisters: A Domestic Tale*, London, 1828

Hubback, Mrs, *The Younger Sister*, London, 1850

Hulme, Keri, 'I Aim Carefully', in *Cherries on a Plate*, ed M. Duckworth, Random House, New Zealand, 1996

Hunt, Diana Holman, *My Grandfather: His Life and Loves*, Hamish Hamilton, 1969

Jacobs, Joseph, 'Binnorie' and 'Cap o'Rushes', in *English Fairy Tales*, G. Putnam & Sons and David Nutt, 1898

Jacobs, Joseph, 'Rushen Coatie', in *More English Fairy Tales*, G. Putnam & Sons and David Nutt, 1898

Jolley, Elizabeth, 'My Sister Dancing', in *Sisters*, ed. Drusilla Modjeska, Angus & Robertson, Australia, 1996

Jones, Agnes Elizabeth: *Memorials of Agnes Elizabeth Jones by her Sister*, London, 1871

Keats, John, 'Isabella and the Pot of Basil', in *Poetical Works*, Oxford, 1934

Kingsley, Charles, *The Heroes*, Cambridge, 1856

Kluckhohn, Clyde, and Leighton, Dorothea, *Children of the People*, Cambridge Mass., Harvard University Press, 1947

Kovalevsky, Sonya, *The Sisters Rajevsky*, London, 1885

Kureishi, Yasmin, in *Guardian*, 7.5.98

Lamb, Mary, in Hazlitt, W. C., *Charles and Mary Lamb: Poems, Letters and Remains*, London, 1874

Lamb, Charles, *Collected Poems*, and in Hazlitt, W. C., *Charles and Mary Lamb: Poems, Letters and Remains*, London, 1874

Lavin, Mary, 'A Visit to the Cemetery', in *The Stories of Mary Lavin*, Constable, 1964

Lawrence, D. H., *Women in Love*, Martin Secker, 1921

Lee, Hermione, *Virginia Woolf*, Chatto & Windus, 1996

Lee, Phyllis, 'Influence of Sibling on Infant's Relationship with Mother and Others', in *Primate Social Relationships*, ed. R. A. Hinde, Blackwell Scientific Publications, 1983

Lefroy, Anna, 'Original memories of Jane Austen', in *The Review of English Studies*, NS vol. XXIX, no. 155, Aug. 1988

Lewis, Oscar, *The Children of Sánchez*, Secker & Warburg, 1962

Lijembe, Joseph A., 'Little Boy Nurse', in *East African Childhood*, ed. Fox, OUP, 1967

Litvinoff, Sarah, 'An Accident of Birth', in *Independent on Sunday*, 2.11.97

Longrigg, Clare, *Mafia Women*, Chatto & Windus, 1997

McCarthy, Mary, *A Nineteenth-Century Childhood*, Heinemann, 1924

McCullers, Carson, 'Like That', in *The Mortgaged Heart*, Barrie & Jenkins, 1972

McCurdy, Sylvia, *Victorian Sisters*, Hurst & Blackett, 1940

McKenney, Ruth, *My Sister Eileen*, Chatto & Windus, 1938

McLauchlan, Dame Laurentia, in Cockerell, Sydney, *The Best of Friends*, Hart Davis, 1956

Mahy, Margaret, 'Stories, Songs and Sisters', in *Cherries on a Plate*, ed. M. Duckworth, Random House, New Zealand, 1996

Mann, Thomas, *Buddenbrooks*, trs. H. T. Lowe-Porter, Knopf, 1924

Mansfield, Katherine, 'At the Bay', and 'The Daughters of the Late Colonel', in *The Garden Party*, Constable, 1922

Marshall, Elizabeth Thomas, *The Tribe of Tiger*, Weidenfeld & Nicolson, 1994

Martineau, Harriet, *Autobiography*, vol. I, London, 1877

Maupassant, Guy de, 'Mme Tellier's Establishment', trs. H. N. P. Sloman, in *Boule de Suif*, Penguin Books, 1947

Mead, Margaret, *Blackberry Winter*, Angus & Robertson, 1973

Mead, Margaret, 'Sex and Temperament', in *Three Primitive Societies*, 1935

Mead, Margaret, 'Manus Kinship', in *Anthropological Papers of the American Museum of Natural History*, vol. XXXIV

Menta, Rama, *Inside the Haveli*, New Delhi, Arnold-Heinemann, 1977

Middleton, Joseph, *Love versus Law. Or Marriage with a Deceased Wife's Sister*, London, 1855

Miller, Regina, ed., *Letters of Virginia Bell*, Bloomsbury, 1993

Millett, Kate, *The Prostitute Papers*, Paladin, 1975

Mills, D. E., 'About the Great Strength of Younger Sister', in *A Collection of Tales from Uji*, CUP, 1970

Mitford, Jessica, *Hons and Rebels*, Gollancz, 1960

Modjeska, Drusilla, ed., *Sisters*, Angus & Robertson, Australia, 1996

Moggach, Deborah, Interview in *Radio Times*, June 1998

Moore, Susanna, *The Whiteness of Bones*, Chatto & Windus, 1989

Moravia, Alberto, 'Home is a Sacred Place', in *The Wayward Wife*, Secker & Warburg, 1960

Moss, Cynthia, *Elephant Memories*, Elm Tree Books, 1988

Mrabat, Mohammed, 'The Lute', trs. Paul Bowles, in *Five Eyes*, ed. and trs. Paul Bowles, Santa Barbara, Black Sparrow, 1979

Munro, Alice, 'The Peace of Utrecht', in *Dance of the Happy Shades*, Penguin Books, 1984

Murphy, Frank, *The Girlhood of Queen Elizabeth*, Constable, 1909

Murray, Alison, J., *No Money, No Honey*, Singapore and Oxford, OUP, 1991

Nash, Elizabeth, 'Superwoman Sisters', *Independent on Sunday*, 15.1.98

Njau, Rebeka, *Ripples in the Pool*, Heinemann (African Writers Series), 1975

Nuckolls, Charles W., 'An Introduction to the Cross-cultural Study of Sibling Relationships', in *Siblings in South Asia*, ed. Charles W. Nuckolls, London and NY, The Guilford Press, 1993

Padel, Ruth, 'Sisters' (poem), in *Rembrandt Would Have Loved You*, Chatto & Windus, 1998

Pankhurst, Christabel, *Unshackled*, Hutchinson, 1959

Pankhurst, Mrs Emmeline, *My Own Story*, Everleigh Nash, 1914

Paul, Caroline, 'My Life as a Twin', in *Fighting Fire*, Bloomsbury, 1998

Pathak, Saroj, 'The Trump Card', in *Gujerati Short Stories*, ed. S. J. Mohan, Vikas Publishing House, PVT Ltd, 1982

Perrault, Charles, *Fairy Tales*, 1967

Phillips, Jayne Anne, *Shelter*, Faber & Faber, 1996 (published in the US 1995)

Picardie, Justine, 'The Death of Ruth Picardie', in *Observer*, 28.9.97

Pollack, Barbara, *The Collectors*, Bobbs Merrill, 1962

Porter, Katherine Anne, 'The Fig Tree', in *Collected Stories*, Cape, 1964

Pritchett, V. S., 'The Cage Birds', in *Collected Stories*, Chatto & Windus, 1982

Pym, Barbsra, *Some Tame Gazelle*, Jonathan Cape, 1950

Roberts, Michèle, 'Laundry', in *During Mother's Absence*, Virago, 1994

Robinson, Marilyn, *Housekeeping*, Farrar Straus & Giroux, 1981

Rossetti, Christina, 'Goblin Market' and 'Sister Maude', in *A Choice of Christina Rossetti's Verse*, selected and ed. Elizabeth Jennings, Faber & Faber, 1970

Saline, Carol, *Sisters*, Philadelphia, Running Press, 1994

Schapera, I., 'Kinship and Marriage among the Tswana,' in *African Systems of Kinship and Marriage*, ed. Brown, A. Radcliffe-, and Forde, C. Daryll, OUP, 1950

Seeber, Claire, in *Independent on Sunday*, 26.4.98

Seymer, Lucy, *Florence Nightingales's Nurses*, London, Pitman Medical, 1960

Seymour, Susan, 'Sociocultural Contexts: Examining Sibling Roles in South Asia', in *Siblings in South Asia*, ed. Charles W. Nuckolls, London and NY, The Guilford Press, 1993

Shakespeare, William, *King Lear* and *Macbeth*

Sherwood, Mrs, *History of The Fairchild Family*, London, 1807

Simpson, Helen, 'Christmas Jezebels', in *Four Bare Legs in a Bed*, Heinemann, 1990

Sinclair, George, 'Major Weir and His Sister', in *Satan's Invisible World Disclos'd*, Edinburgh, 1686

Singer, I. B., 'A Tale of Two Sisters', in *Passions and Other Tales*, Cape, 1976

Smiley, Jane, *A Thousand Acres*, Flamingo, 1992

Small, Hugh, *Florence Nightingale*, Constable/Avenging Angel, 1998

Sophocles, Antigone, trs. Sir George Young, Everyman, 1906

Spalding, Frances, *Vanessa Bell*, London, 1983

Spinage, C. A., *Elephants*, London, T. & A.D. Poyser Ltd, 1994

Steward, Samuel M. (ed., with a Memoir), *Dear Sammy: Letters from Gertrude Stein and Alice B. Toklas*, Houghton Mifflin, 1977

Tan, Amy, *The Hundred Secret Senses*, HarperCollins, 1996

Tanizaki, Janichiro, *The Makioka Sisters*, trs. Edward G. Seidensticker, Secker & Warburg, 1957

Taylor, Elizabeth, 'Sisters', in *The Devastating Boys*, Chatto & Windus, 1975

Tennyson, Alfred Lord, 'The Sisters', in *Poetical Works*, Macmillan, 1890

Thompson, Laura, 'Isn't That You Know Who? Not Quite', *Guardian*, 11.4.98

Thorn, Ismay, *Quite Unexpected*, London, 1889

Thurman, Judith, *Isak Dinesen*, Penguin 1982

Tillyard, Stella, *Aristocrats*, Chatto & Windus, 1982

The Times, Magazine 28.1.98, 'The Korean Sisters'

Toklas, Alice B, *Letters*, ed. Edward Burns, Angus & Robertson, 1973

Toklas, Alice B., *What is Remembered*, Michael Joseph, 1963

Townsend, Peter, *Family Life of Old People*, Routledge, 1957

Wagner, Richard, *Das Rheingold*, trs. William Mann, Friends of Covent Garden, 1964

Walker, Alice, *The Color Purple*, The Women's Press, 1983

Walker, Alice, *Possessing the Secret of Joy*, Cape 1992

Walsh, John, 'The Golden Girls: The Beverley Sisters', in *Independent*, 26.10.96

Wasserstein, Wendy, *The Sisters Rosensweig*, Samuel French, 1996

Weldon, Fay, *Big Women*, Flamingo, 1997

West, Rebecca, *The Fountain Overflows*, Macmillan, 1957

Wharton, Edith, 'The Bunner Sisters' (1916), in *Madame de Treymes*, Virago, 1984

Wilson, Monica, 'Nyakusa Kinship', in *African Systems of Kinship and Marriage*, ed. Brown, A. Radcliffe-, and Forde, C. Daryll, OUP, 1950

Wilson, Angus, 'Raspberry Jam' (short story), in *The Wrong Set*, Secker & Warburg, 1949

Woolf, Leonard, *Beginning Again* (autobiography), Hogarth Press, 1964

Woolf, Leonard, *The Wise Virgins*, Edward Arnold, 1914

Woolf, Virginia, 'Professions for Women', in *The Death of the Moth and Other Essays*, Hogarth Press, 1942

Woolf, Virginia, *The Flight of the Mind: Letters 1882–1941*, vol. 1, Hogarth Press, 1975

Woolf, Virginia, 'Reminiscences', in *Moments of Being* ed. Jeanne Schulkind, Hogarth Press, 1978

Wordsworth, Dorothy, *Grasmere Journals*, OUP, 1958

Wordsworth, William, 'A Sonnet on the Ladies of Llangollen', from *The Prelude*, in *Collected Poems*, OUP, 1904

Yapp, Beth, 'Houses, Sisters, Cities', in *Sisters*, ed. Drusilla Modjeska, Angus & Robertson, Australia, 1993

Yoshimoto, Banan, *Amrita*, trs. Russell W. Wasden, Faber & Faber, 1997

Yü, Li, 'Marital Frustrations', in *Twelve Towers, Stories retold by Nathan Mao*, Hong Kong Chinese Press, 1979

Index of Authors